Contents

Part 3: Parsing Hebrew Verbs

A
WORKBOOK
FOR
INTERMEDIATE
HEBREW

Grammar, Exegesis, and Commentary
on Jonah and Ruth

ROBERT B. CHISHOLM JR.

Kregel
Academic & Professional

A Workbook for Intermediate Hebrew: Grammar, Exegesis, and Commentary on Jonah and Ruth

© 2006 by Robert B. Chisholm Jr.

Published by Kregel Publications, a division of Kregel, Inc., P.O. Box 2607, Grand Rapids, MI 49501.

Library of Congress Cataloging-in-Publication Data
Chisholm, Robert B.
  A workbook for intermediate Hebrew: grammar, exegesis, and commentary on Jonah and Ruth / By Robert B. Chisholm Jr.
    p.   cm.
    Includes the texts of the books of Jonah and Ruth.
1. Hebrew language—Grammar—Problems, exercises, etc.
2. Bible. O.T. Jonah—Language, style. 3. Bible. O.T. Ruth—Language, style. 4. Hebrew language—Verb—Charts, diagrams, etc. I. Bible. O.T. Jonah. Hebrew. 2006. II. Bible. O.T. Ruth. Hebrew. 2006. III. Title.
PJ4567.3C53   2006
492.4'56—dc22   2006008677

ISBN 978-0-8254-2390-1

Printed in the United States of America

07 08 09 10 11 / 6 5 4 3 2

*To Prof. Donald R. Glenn,
my mentor, colleague, and friend,
in appreciation for his many years of faithful service
to Dallas Theological Seminary.*

Introduction

Purpose

This book builds a bridge between elementary biblical Hebrew, which typically emphasizes morphology and basic vocabulary acquisition, and intermediate biblical Hebrew, which typically introduces syntax. It is not a reference grammar, but a workbook, utilizing an inductive approach to the books of Jonah and Ruth. The format is interactive and the style repetitive. This approach encourages the student to engage the text and reinforces patterns and principles. The primary purpose of the book, then, is twofold: reviewing Hebrew morphology and introducing the student to syntactical analysis of the Hebrew text.

As we work through the biblical text, we will review the basic patterns of Hebrew morphology, especially the verb system. To facilitate such review I have provided links to various first-year grammars. Links with Fuller and Choi (Ful.) and with Pratico and Van Pelt (PVP) are included in the text itself; other grammars are referenced in footnotes accompanying the PVP links. These include Futato (Fut.), Garrett (Gar.), Kelley (Kel.), Ross (Ross), and Seow (Seow):

Fuller, Russell, and Kyoungwon Choi. *Invitation to Biblical Hebrew*. Grand Rapids: Kregel, 2006. (Ful.)

Futato, Mark D. *Beginning Biblical Hebrew*. Winona Lake, Ind.: Eisenbrauns, 2003. (Fut.)

Garrett, Duane A. *A Modern Grammar for Classical Hebrew*. Nashville: Broadman & Holman, 2002. (Gar.)

Kelley, Page. *Biblical Hebrew*. Grand Rapids: Eerdmans, 1992. (Kel.)

Pratico, Gary D. and Miles V. Van Pelt. *Basics of Biblical Hebrew Grammar*. Grand Rapids: Zondervan, 2001. (PVP)

Ross, Allen P. *Introducing Biblical Hebrew*. Grand Rapids: Baker, 2001. (Ross)

Seow, C. L. *A Grammar for Biblical Hebrew*. Rev. ed. Nashville: Abingdon, 1995. (Seow)

Learning how to parse Hebrew verbs can be a daunting task; some simply give up and resort to a parsing guide. However, if one becomes familiar with verbal patterns through repetition and practice, parsing is not as difficult as one may think. In this volume I employ a systematic approach to parsing verbs that highlights and reinforces verbal patterns. This method uses eleven charts to enable students to parse most verbal forms. The charts are included in part 3 of the book, along with instructions for how to use them. By using this system, a student will be able to explain why a form is parsed the way it is and will gain confidence in understanding the language. Some may object that such a system is a crutch. My response is that the system is more like training wheels on a bicycle; it is designed to help the learner through the difficult and awkward stages of acquiring the skill of parsing. The more the system is used, the more patterns become reinforced. Eventually students should be able to parse accurately and confidently with little, if any, need for the charts.

The book also introduces the student to syntactical analysis of the Hebrew text. Since our approach is inductive, this book is best used in conjunction with a more formal introduction to syntax. I have provided links to various syntactical tools, including the standard advanced grammars, as well as more abbreviated outlines and surveys. The following sources (with abbreviations) are used:

Arnold, Bill T., and John H. Choi. *A Guide to Biblical Hebrew Syntax*. Cambridge: Cambridge University Press, 2003. (AC)

Chisholm, Robert B., Jr. *From Exegesis to Exposition*. Grand Rapids: Baker, 1998. (EE)

Joüon, Paul. *A Grammar of Biblical Hebrew*. Corrected 1st ed. Translated and revised by T. Muraoka. 2 vols. Rome: Pontifical Biblical Institute, 1993. (Joüon)

Kautzsch, E., ed. *Gesenius' Hebrew Grammar*. 2nd English ed. Translated and revised by A. E. Cowley. Oxford: Clarendon Press, 1910. (GKC)

van der Merwe, Christo H. J., Jackie A. Naudé, and Jan H. Kroeze, *A Biblical Hebrew Reference Grammar*. Sheffield: Sheffield Academic Press, 1999. (BHRG)

Waltke, Bruce K., and Michael O'Connor. *An Introduction to Biblical Hebrew Syntax*. Winona Lake, Ind.: Eisenbrauns, 1990. (W-OC)

Williams, Ronald J. *Hebrew Syntax: An Outline*. 2nd ed. Toronto: University of Toronto Press, 1976. (WHS)

Features

When working closely in the biblical text it is easy to lose sight of the whole. To prevent this I have included interpretive observations and commentary throughout the volume to remind students that the overall goal of analysis is interpretation.

Even in relatively easy-to-read books like Jonah and Ruth, it is inevitable that students will encounter difficult morphological and syntactical phenomena not covered in an elementary or even intermediate course. To help them over these potential obstacles and bumps in the road, I have included technical notes on problematic and/or relatively rare forms and constructions. I also provide links to advanced grammars (GKC, Joüon, W-OC) and critical commentaries so the student may read about the phenomena in more detail and begin to gain familiarity with and appreciation for these helpful tools.

Jonah is an ideal book to read when making the transition from elementary to intermediate Hebrew. It is short, has few technical difficulties, and can be covered easily in a semester or portion of a semester. However, the second chapter of Jonah contains a prayer in poetic form (vv. 3–10). Since poetry is more difficult than prose, some teachers choose to skip over this portion of the text, but actually it is an ideal opportunity to give students brief exposure to Hebrew poetry in preparation for more thorough study. To facilitate the reading of Jonah's prayer, I have included below a brief introduction to Hebrew poetic form and style. This introduction should be read carefully before the student attempts to work through Jonah 2:3–10. Since this is the only poetic text appearing in either Jonah or Ruth, this brief foray into the world of Hebrew poetry will have to suffice for now. However, I am planning to publish a companion volume to this one that will cover samples of poetic texts from various literary genres, including hymnic, proverbial, and prophetic literature.

The focus of this book is morphology and syntax, but since semantic analysis is an important part of interpretation as well, I have included semantic observations throughout the volume, usually dealing with nonroutine phenomena. It will be easier for students to do the assignments if they have access to the standard dictionaries and have been instructed in their use. I have included many links to the standard dictionaries BDB and *HALOT*. I have also included glossaries for both Jonah and Ruth to speed up the reading and translation process. These glossaries are keyed to BDB and *HALOT* in case the student wants to access a more thorough discussion of any given word. The glossaries do not include conjunctions, negative particles, common prepositions, or pronouns.

Each section of the book follows a four-step procedure for interacting with the text:

1. *Initial Viewing of the Text:* The student reads through the text, identifies verb forms, and notes any words or constructions he/she does not recognize.
2. *Analysis:* The student reads the comments and answers the questions in the section titled "Analyzing the Text." At this stage, it is often helpful and wise to consult various translations to see how they have attempted to reflect the meaning of the text. One who has worked in the Hebrew text can also discern what interpretive decisions underlie any given translation. To facilitate this kind of analysis, the workbook interacts with several English translations, including the KJV, NIV, NASB, NRSV, NLT, and NET.
3. *Translation:* Taking into consideration observations made during analysis, the student translates the text in a paraphrastic style that reflects interpretive decisions.
4. *Structural Outline:* Finally the student outlines the narratival (or discourse) structure of the passage.

Some may want to use the questions in the analysis section as course assignments. I have included below a set of sample questions and answers on Joshua 5:13–14 so that both instructors and students will have an idea of what I expect from my own students. Following the sample questions and answers is a sample outline of the narrative structure of Joshua 5:13–14 (for a detailed discussion on outlining narrative structure, see EE, 119–42).

In addition to this brief sample, I have also included a "Teacher's Guide" for both Jonah and Ruth following part 3 of the book. These guides contain suggested answers to the questions in the analysis sections of the assignments. They are designed (a) to assist instructors, (b) to give students immediate feedback as they do the assignments, and (c) to facilitate learning for those using the workbook outside of a classroom setting.

Of course, teachers will debate the value of making the answers to the assignments accessible to students. In conducting an informal survey, I have found that some lament the inclusion of an "answer key," while others applaud it! I suggest that teachers use the workbook in a classroom setting in one of the following ways:

1. Use a grading system to evaluate the assignments. In this case, students sign a statement agreeing they will not change their answers once they have consulted the answer key. To encourage proper use of the answer keys, the teacher may want to give periodic quizzes and a final exam.
2. Such an honor system may seem naïve and overly idealistic to some teachers. In this case I suggest that grades not be assigned for the assignments. Instead they can be required as homework designed to prepare the student for an exam. This is the way that many teachers of first-year Hebrew use the exercises in an elementary grammar. In this system graded evaluation comes in the form of quizzes and exams. I suggest that teachers give a quiz after each chapter of Jonah/Ruth and an exam after each book is completed.

Hebrew Narrative Structure

A Hebrew narrative is typically initiated with a wayyiqtol form, often וַיְהִי (cf. Ruth 1:1; Jonah 1:1). A succession of wayyiqtol verb forms constructs the framework or main line of the narrative. These verbal forms typically indicate sequence, but they exhibit other functions as well. See the appendix (cf. EE, 120–23). Quotations and dialogues are frequently embedded within the narrative framework (EE, 133–35). Various types of offline constructions also appear within the narrative. These include the following three kinds of clauses:

1. *Disjunctive clauses* typically place the subject or some other nonverbal element after the initial *waw*. They often describe circumstances surrounding the main action or provide supplemental information that is important to the story, but they have a variety of discourse functions. See the appendix (cf. EE, 124–28).

2. *Negated verbal clauses* typically have the structure *waw* + negative particle (לֹא) + perfect verbal form. They often indicate a consequence or unrealized intention, but can have other functions as well, including providing a complementary angle that can emphasize, qualify, or summarize what precedes.

3. *Nonconsecutive weqatal clauses* have a perfect verbal form immediately after the *waw* where one expects to see a wayyiqtol. Like disjunctive clauses, these clauses have a variety of functions (EE, 128–33), frequently describing action that is complementary to the preceding action. Because of their nonstandard form, they can also be used to highlight certain statements.

Hebrew Poetry: An Overview

Structure

The structure of Hebrew poetry differs significantly from prose. The backbone of Hebrew narrative is the succession of wayyiqtol (imperfect/preterite with *waw* consecutive) verbal forms. The dominant structure in poetry is parallelism. In the simplest form of parallelism, two conceptually related statements are juxtaposed. For example, consider 2 Samuel 22:5:

> The waves of death engulfed me;
> the currents of chaos overwhelmed me.

The conceptual relationship between poetic lines can vary. The most common types of parallelism are the following:

1. *Synonymous parallelism:* As illustrated by 2 Samuel 22:5, the second statement often reiterates the first, using synonymous terms.

2. *Progressive or consequential parallelism:* Sometimes the second line describes an action that chronologically and/or logically follows what precedes.

> I called to the LORD, who is worthy of praise,
> and I was delivered from my enemies.
> —2 Samuel 22:4

3. *Specifying parallelism:* The second line may specify how a preceding general statement is realized.

> The one true God completely vindicates me;
> he makes nations submit to me.
> —2 Samuel 22:48

4. *Complementary parallelism:* The second line can provide a perspective that is complementary to the preceding statement. The parallel lines often reflect two different, but related perspectives—two sides of the same coin, as it were.

> For I have obeyed the LORD's commands;
> I have not rebelled against my God.
> —2 Samuel 22:22

5. *Contrastive (Antithetical) parallelism:* The second line sometimes provides a contrast with the preceding statement.

> You deliver oppressed people,
> but you watch the proud and bring them down.
> —2 Samuel 22:28

Parallelism can be more complex than the basic two-line structures illustrated above. Sometimes a third line is added to a couplet, creating a triplet:

> He rescued me from my strong enemy,
> from those who hate me,
> for they were too strong for me.
> —2 Samuel 22:18

In this example the first two lines are synonymous, while the third line gives an explanation for why God rescued the psalmist.

> The one true God acts in a faithful manner;
> the LORD's promise is reliable;
> he is a shield to all who take shelter in him.
> —2 Samuel 22:31

Here the first two lines are synonymous or perhaps complementary (if one focuses on the distinction between divine acts and words), while the third line specifies how God proves to be faithful to his people (he protects them).

Often a poetic unit will be comprised of four lines (sometimes called a quatrain):

> The depths of the sea were exposed;
> the inner regions of the world were uncovered
> by the LORD's battle cry,
> by the powerful breath from his nose.
> —2 Samuel 22:16

Lines one and two correspond (synonymous parallelism), as do lines three and four (synonymous or complementary, if one distinguishes between the battle cry per se and the physical phenomena that accompany it). The second couplet (lines three and four) is grammatically connected to the first (lines one and two) by the prepositions (indicating instrumentality) at the beginning of each line.

Style

Hebrew poetic style differs from prose in several respects:

1. In addition to the usual forms, poetry uses longer, alternative forms of certain prepositions and pronominal suffixes.

2. The parallel structure of poetry invites variety of expression. Consequently poetry contains many relatively rare synonyms of more common terms. For example, Jonah 2:6 (Eng. v. 5) uses the verb אָפַף, "engulf," in parallelism with the more common סָבַב, "surround." אָפַף occurs only five times in the Hebrew Bible, exclusively in poetic texts (2 Sam. 22:5 = Ps. 18:5; see also Pss. 40:13; 116:3).

3. It is common for words to appear with a metaphorical sense in poetry. For example the noun שַׁחַת, "pit, trap," is used in Jonah 2:7 (Eng. v. 6) as an epithet for the grave (Sheol, cf. v. 3). See *HALOT,* 1473.

4. In poetry some words retain archaic meanings that are not as common in prose. For example, in Jonah 2:7 (Eng. v. 6) the noun אֶרֶץ, normally referring to the earth or land, is used in its relatively rare sense of "underworld, grave" (see *HALOT,* 91), a meaning it exhibits in the cognate languages Akkadian and Ugaritic. In Jonah 2:6 (Eng. v. 5) the noun נֶפֶשׁ, normally referring to the breath, life, or soul, is used of the throat or neck (see *HALOT,* 712), a relatively rare use that occurs almost exclusively in poetry and is attested in Akkadian and Ugaritic.

5. Poetry is characterized by an economy of language. It does not employ the article, relative pronoun, and accusative sign with the regularity seen in prose.

6. Within the parallel structure of poetic lines, ellipsis of certain elements is common. Consider, for example, 2 Samuel 22:15:

> He shot arrows and scattered them;
> lightning and routed them.

The second line corresponds to the first (arrows // lightning; scattered them // and routed them), except that the verb (he shot) is omitted. It must be understood by ellipsis in the second line as well.

7. Within narratival poetry, one may encounter the wayyiqtol verbal pattern, but its use is subordinate to the dominating parallelistic structure. The use of the wayyiqtol is not as sustained as in prose and chronological overlapping occurs more frequently.

For example, the wayyiqtol at the beginning of Jonah 2:4 (Eng. v. 3) (וַתַּשְׁלִיכֵנִי, "You cast me") flashes back to a time before the events described in verse 3 (Eng. v. 2). Verses 4–7 (Eng. vv. 3–6) then unfold in chronological sequence, but there is repetition within the parallel structure (vv. 4b, 6a), subjects appear before their verbs in instances where the wayyiqtol could have been employed (vv. 4, 6), and the wayyiqtol is not utilized again until verse 7b (וַתַּעַל, "you brought me up").

Within the parallel, repetitive structure of poetry, the reiterative use of the wayyiqtol construction is more common than in prose. See, for example, 2 Samuel 22:8:

> The earth heaved and shook [wayyiqtol];
> the foundations of the sky trembled.
> They heaved [wayyiqtol] because he was angry.

8. Because word order is more flexible in poetry and the subject appears before its verb more often, the Hebrew prefixed verbal form, though appearing to be an imperfect, is sometimes better understood as a preterite. This can be confusing to a beginning student who is accustomed to seeing the preterite with the *waw* consecutive. Jonah 2:4 (Eng. v. 3) provides a clear example of this:

You cast me [wayyiqtol] into the deep waters,
into the middle of the sea;
the ocean current engulfed me [yiqtol form];
all the mighty waves you sent swept [qatal/perfect form] over me.

The parallelism makes it clear that the yiqtol form (יְסֹבְבֵנִי), though apparently an imperfect, is actually a preterite. Note the wayyiqtol form prior to this and the perfect after it. Similarly in verse 6 (Eng. v. 5) a perfect verbal form (אֲפָפוּנִי, "engulfed me") is parallel to יְסֹבְבֵנִי.

Sample Questions and Answers (Joshua 5:13–14)

5:13

וַיְהִי בִּהְיוֹת יְהוֹשֻׁעַ בִּירִיחוֹ וַיִּשָּׂא עֵינָיו וַיַּרְא וְהִנֵּה־אִישׁ עֹמֵד לְנֶגְדּוֹ וְחַרְבּוֹ שְׁלוּפָה בְּיָדוֹ וַיֵּלֶךְ יְהוֹשֻׁעַ אֵלָיו וַיֹּאמֶר לוֹ הֲלָנוּ אַתָּה אִם־לְצָרֵינוּ:

1. Parse בִּהְיוֹת. How do you determine the root? How is the preposition functioning? What is the time frame of the verb here?

   Qal infinitive construct from הָיָה with prepositional prefix. This verb form is found in chart 8 (for forms with וֹת- ending). Since the form has no prefix, we use section 1 of chart 8. The form has a *shewa* under the first root letter *(he),* only two root letters visible, and an וֹת- ending, so it is a Qal infinitive construct from a III-*he* root. The וֹת- ending is characteristic of the III-*he* infinitive construct in all stems. See PVP, 237 (20.4); Ful., 268 (37.4). When prefixed to an infinitive construct, the preposition -בְּ typically has a temporal nuance. See PVP, 244–46 (20.12). This makes good sense here, "When (Joshua) was." The preceding וַיְהִי, literally, "and it was," indicates a past time frame. See PVP, 245; Ful., 120 (20.4).

2. Parse וַיַּרְא. How do you determine the *(a)* stem, *(b)* root, and *(c)* P-G-N?

   Qal wayyiqtol 3ms, from רָאָה. Since the verb has the prefixed *yod* characteristic of the imperfect/wayyiqtol, we use chart 10. Only two root letters are visible and the prefix vowel is *pathaq,* followed by a *shewa*. Normally the form would be a III-*he* Hiphil, but as footnote 1 of the chart explains, the Qal and Hiphil overlap in form if the first root letter is a guttural (or, in the case of *resh,* a quasi-guttural). Since the form in Joshua 5:13 has no object, the Qal meaning ("he looked/saw") is preferable here, for the causative Hiphil must have an object ("he showed"). The final *he* has apocopated (see PVP, 198 [17.4]); Ful., 266 [37.4]); the absence of an ending indicates the form is 3ms.

3. What type of clause is . . . וְהִנֵּה? How do you know this from the form? How is the clause functioning here?

   The clause is a nonstandard disjunctive type that interrupts the wayyiqtol sequence of the narrative. The *waw* is followed by the interjection, a subject, and finally the verb, which is a participle. In this case, the clause has a dramatic function, inviting the readers to view the scene through Joshua's eyes. See the appendix (cf. EE, 123–27, especially p. 126, category 6).

4. How is the participle עֹמֵד functioning here? What is the time frame?

The participle (which is a verbal adjective) is the predicate in the clause. In this narratival context it has a past durative sense, "was standing." See PVP, 262 (22.5); Ful., 116 (19.2); EE, 67.

5. The form לְנֶגְדּוֹ consists of what elements? Identify the antecedent of the pronominal suffix.

The form consists of the preposition -לְ, the preposition נֶגֶד, and a 3ms suffix that refers back to Joshua.

6. What type of clause is . . . וְחַרְבּוֹ? How do you know this from the form? How is the clause functioning here?

The clause is disjunctive, as the *waw* + subject + predicate pattern indicates. The clause is circumstantial, describing what this unidentified "man" was doing at the time Joshua saw him. See the appendix (cf. EE, 125–26).

7. Parse שְׁלוּפָה. How do you determine each element in the parsing? How is the form functioning in the clause?

Qal passive participle feminine singular from שָׁלַף. Since the form has an ה ָ - ending, we use chart 2. There is no prefix and a *shewa* under the first root letter, so the form is a passive participle (note the distinctive *shureq* theme vowel). The ה ָ - ending indicates the gender and number (fs). See PVP, 263–64 (22.7); Ful., 116 (19.3). The participle is the predicate in the sentence, "and his sword was drawn in his hand." See PVP, 265 (22.9); Ful., 117 (19.3).

8. What is the function of the prefixed *he* on הֲלָנוּ?

This is an interrogative marker. See PVP, 75–76 (8.10); Ful., 42 (9.3).

9. The form לְצָרֵינוּ consists of what elements? How can you tell the noun is plural?

The form consists of the preposition -לְ, a masculine plural form of the noun צַר, and a 1cp suffix. The noun is plural because of the *yod* that is part of the suffix. See PVP, 81–83 (9.2–9.4); Ful., 71 (12.2).

5:14

וַיֹּאמֶר לֹא כִּי אֲנִי שַׂר־צְבָא־יְהוָה עַתָּה בָאתִי
וַיִּפֹּל יְהוֹשֻׁעַ אֶל־פָּנָיו אַרְצָה וַיִּשְׁתָּחוּ וַיֹּאמֶר לוֹ מָה אֲדֹנִי מְדַבֵּר אֶל־עַבְדּוֹ:

1. Parse וַיִּפֹּל. How do you determine the *(a)* stem, and *(b)* root?

Qal wayyiqtol 3ms from נָפַל. Since the verb has the prefixed *yod* characteristic of the imperfect/wayyiqtol, we use chart 10. Only two root letters are visible and the prefix vowel is *hireq*. The letter following the prefix is doubled and accompanied by a *holem*, so the verb is either a Qal I-*nun* or geminate. A verb פָּלַל is attested, but not in the Qal or Niphal. So the root must be a Qal form from a I-*nun* root with the doubling indicating assimilation of the *nun*.

2. What is the signficance of the הָ- on אַרְצָה?

   This is the directive ending, indicating movement toward the object, "to/toward the ground." See PVP, 64–65 (7.6); Ful., 56–57 (10.11).

3. Parse מְדַבֵּר. How can you tell the form is a participle? How do you determine the stem? What is the time frame of the participle?

   Piel participle masculine singular from דָּבַר. The prefixed *mem* is characteristic of participial forms in verbal stems other than Qal and Niphal. The form has no ending, so we use chart 9, prefixed *mem* section. There is a shewa beneath the *mem* followed by a *pathaq* so the stem is Piel. The participle is used in a present sense here; Joshua wants to know why, at the very moment of the dialogue, the captain of the Lord's army is speaking to him.

Translation and Outline of Narrative Structure of Joshua 5:13–14

The translation that follows is an adaptation of NET that reflects in a more literal manner the clause structure of the Hebrew text. In the outline each independent clause in the narrative framework of the Hebrew text is indicated by a letter (e.g., a, b, c). Disjunctive clauses are in bold. Quotations are placed in a block (indented) and italicized.

    a. When Joshua was near Jericho (introductory)
    b. he looked up (initiatory)
    c. and saw (sequential)
    d. **and there was a man standing in front of him (dramatic)**
    e. **with his sword drawn. (circumstantial)**
    f. Joshua approached him (sequential)
    g. and asked him (sequential)
        "Are you on our side or allied with our enemies?"

                                            —verse 13

    a. He answered (sequential)
        "Truly I am the commander of the LORD's army. Now I have arrived!"
    b. Joshua bowed low with his face to the ground (consequential)
    c. and knelt (sequential)
    d. and asked (sequential)
        "What does my master want to say to his servant?"

                                            —verse 14

Abbreviations

Bible Versions

KJV	King James Version
NASB	New American Standard Bible
NET	New English Translation
NLT	New Living Translation
NIV	New International Version
NRSV	New Revised Standard Version

Bibliographic

AC	Arnold, Bill T., and John H. Choi. *A Guide to Biblical Hebrew Syntax.* Cambridge: Cambridge University Press, 2003.
BDB	Brown, Francis, S. R. Driver, and Charles A. Briggs. *A Hebrew-English Lexicon of the Old Testament.* Oxford: Oxford University Press, 1907.
BHRG	van der Merwe, Christo H. J., Jackie A. Naudé, and Jan H. Kroeze, *A Biblical Hebrew Reference Grammar.* Sheffield: Sheffield Academic Press, 1999.
BSac	*Bibliotheca Sacra*
EE	Chisholm, Robert B., Jr. *From Exegesis to Exposition: A Practical Guide to Using Biblical Hebrew.* Grand Rapids: Baker, 1998.
Ful.	Fuller, Russell, and Kyoungwon Choi. *Invitation to Biblical Hebrew.* Grand Rapids: Kregel, 2006.
Fut.	Futato, Mark D. *Beginning Biblical Hebrew.* Winona Lake, Ind.: Eisenbrauns, 2003.
Gar.	Garrett, Duane A. *A Modern Grammar for Classical Hebrew.* Nashville: Broadman & Holman, 2002.
GKC	Kautzsch, E., ed. *Gesenius' Hebrew Grammar.* 2d. English ed. Translated and revised by A. E. Cowley. Oxford: Oxford University Press, 1910.
HALOT	Koehler, L., W. Baumgartner, and J. J. Stamm. *A Hebrew-Aramaic Lexicon of the Old Testament.* Translated and edited under the supervision of M. E. J. Richardson. 5 vols. Leiden: Brill, 1994–2000.
Joüon	Joüon, Paul. *A Grammar of Biblical Hebrew.* Corrected 1st ed. Translated and revised by T. Muraoka. 2 vols. Rome: Pontifical Biblical Institute, 1993.
JPSBC	Jewish Publication Society Bible Commentary
Kel.	Kelley, Page. *Biblical Hebrew.* Grand Rapids: Eerdmans, 1992.
NAC	New American Commentary
NICOT	New International Commentary on the Old Testament
NIDOTTE	Van Gemeren, Willem A., ed. *New International Dictionary of Old Testament Theology and Exegesis.* 5 vols. Grand Rapids: Zondervan, 1997.
PVP	Pratico, Gary D., and Miles V. Van Pelt. *Basics of Biblical Hebrew Grammar.* Grand Rapids: Zondervan, 2001.
Ross	Ross, Allen P. *Introducing Biblical Hebrew.* Grand Rapids: Baker, 2001.
Seow	Seow, C. L. *A Grammar for Biblical Hebrew.* Rev. ed. Nashville: Abingdon, 1995.
WBC	Word Biblical Commentary
WHS	Williams, Ronald J. *Hebrew Syntax: An Outline.* 2nd ed. Toronto: University of Toronto Press, 1976.

W-OC   Waltke, Bruce K., and Michael O'Connor. *An Introduction to Biblical Hebrew Syntax*. Winona Lake, Ind.: Eisenbrauns, 1990.

Parsing

1cp	first person common plural
1cs	first person common singular
2fp	second person feminine plural
2fs	second person feminine singular
2mp	second person masculine plural
2ms	second person masculine singular
3cp	third person common plural
3fp	third person feminine plural
3fs	third person feminine singular
3mp	third person masculine plural
3ms	third person masculine singular
fp	feminine plural
fs	feminine singular
coh.	cohortative
inf. abs.	infinitive absolute
inf. const.	infinitive construct
impf.	simple imperfect (without *waw*)
impv.	imperative
juss.	jussive
mp	masculine plural
ms	masculine singular
part.	participle
P-G-N	person, gender, and number
pf.	simple perfect (without *waw*)
act. part.	active participle
pass. part.	passive participle
wc-y	*waw* consecutive with the yiqtol, usually identified as a preterite or imperfect
wc-q	*waw* consecutive with the qatal, that is, perfect

Part I

ANALYSIS OF THE
BOOK OF JONAH

Looking at the Whole

The book exhibits a symmetrical structure in which act 1 (chaps. 1–2) stands parallel to act 2 (chaps. 3–4).[1] Several elements in the first act have corresponding elements in the second act:

Act 1: Jonah 1–2
> A: Jonah *rejects* the Lord's commission (1:1–3).
> B: The sailors *submit* to the Lord and *avert* disaster (1:4–16).
> C: The Lord *prepares* a fish *to teach* Jonah a lesson (2:1).
> D: Jonah *prays,* thanking the Lord for saving his life (2:2–11).

Act 2: Jonah 3–4
> A´: Jonah *accepts* the Lord's commission (3:1–4).
> B´: The Ninevites *submit* to the Lord and *avert* disaster (3:5–10).
> D´: Jonah *prays,* complaining that the Lord has saved Nineveh (4:1–5).
> C´: The Lord *prepares* a plant, a worm, and a wind *to teach* Jonah a lesson (4:6–11).

The symmetry between chapters 1 and 3 is obvious. Each chapter begins with Jonah's response to his commission and then focuses on the reaction of foreigners to God's self-revelation. The structural parallelism between chapters 2 and 4 is not as tight. Each chapter presents a prayer of Jonah and focuses on the prophet's reaction to the Lord's intervention. In chapter 2 the Lord's preparations precede the prayer; in chapter 4 they follow the prayer. There is a sharp contrast between Jonah's prayer of thanksgiving for his own deliverance, and his complaint that God has delivered Nineveh.

Note Regarding the Hebrew Text

The Hebrew text is presented without its cantillation marks/accents, with the exception of *soph pasuq* (meaning "end of verse") at the end of each verse and *athnaq* (meaning "rest"), which, in most cases, marks the major break in thought within a verse.

---

1. See Phyllis Trible, *Rhetorical Criticism: Context, Method, and the Book of Jonah* (Philadelphia: Fortress, 1994), 109–17; Terence E. Fretheim, *The Message of Jonah* (Minneapolis: Augsburg, 1977), 55; and Uriel Simon, *Jonah*, JPSBC, trans. J. L. Schramm (Philadelphia: Jewish Publication Society, 1999), xxiv–xxv.

Act I
Jonah 1–2

Scene 1: Jonah 1:1–3: Jonah Runs from God

Assignment

Step 1: Initial View

Read Jonah 1:1–3 in the Hebrew text, using an interlinear if you desire.[1] Underline any words or forms you do not recognize. Try to identify verbal forms and label them as follows:

- wayyiqtol verbal forms: wc-y (the so-called *waw* consecutive with the yiqtol, usually identified as a preterite or imperfect)
- weqatal forms: wc-q (the so-called *waw* consecutive with the qatal, that is, perfect)
- simple perfects (without *waw*): pf.
- simple imperfects (without *waw*): impf.
- imperatives: impv.
- jussives: juss.
- cohortatives: coh.
- infinitives construct: inf. const.
- infinitives absolute: inf. abs.
- participles: part.

Step 2: Analyzing the Text

1:1

וַיְהִי דְּבַר־יְהוָה אֶל־יוֹנָה בֶן־אֲמִתַּי לֵאמֹר׃

1. וַיְהִי—The narrative begins with a wayyiqtol form (from the verb הָיָה). See PVP, 196; Ful., 122 (20.3).[2] The expression "the word . . . was to [proper name]" indicates that the object of the preposition was the recipient of a message from God. See BDB, 225–26; *HALOT,* 243. Most translations (see KJV, NIV, NASB, NRSV) have "the word of the LORD came to," but NET's "The LORD said to Jonah" is more idiomatic. NLT's "The LORD gave this message to" strives to be idiomatic, but is wordy.
2. דְּבַר—This noun is the subject of the verb (and therefore nominative case). Though Hebrew nouns do not have case endings, they do have case function. Basically, nouns functioning as subjects are nominative, nouns modifying other nouns (in the construct relationship) are genitive, and nouns

---

1. The following outline of the book's scenes and episodes follows Trible, *Rhetorical Criticism*, 237–44.
2. See also AC, 84, note 107.

completing or modifying verbs are accusative. See EE, 60–65; as well as AC, 4–5; and W-OC, 126. Note that the form is construct. How does the construct form differ from the absolute form? Explain these vowel changes. See PVP, 102–3 (10.5); Ful., 62 (11.3).[3]

_____

_____

3. יְהוָה—Since the divine name follows the construct form, it is genitive. How is it functioning here? (What is the relationship between Yahweh and his word? NIV and NLT are helpful here.) For categories of the genitive see EE, 62–64; W-OC, 143–54.[4]

_____

_____

4. לֵאמֹר—The form is a Qal infinitive construct from אָמַר with a prepositional prefix. This form typically introduces direct quotations where no dialogue is involved. For a helpful discussion of לֵאמֹר see BHRG, 155–56.

1:2

קוּם לֵךְ אֶל־נִינְוֵה הָעִיר הַגְּדוֹלָה וּקְרָא עָלֶיהָ כִּי־עָלְתָה רָעָתָם לְפָנָי:

1. קוּם—This form is a Qal imperative. See chart 9: no prefix, two root letters, and a *shureq* = Qal imperative or infinitive construct from a hollow *u*-class. Here the imperative is a better choice—note the following imperatival form לֵךְ, from the root הָלַךְ. Normally the pattern of no prefix, two root letters, and a *tsere* indicates a I-*yod* verb (see chart 9), but הָלַךְ fits this pattern as well (see PVP, 213 [18.11]; Ful., 241 [35.5]).[5]

How are these imperatives functioning? Review the discussion of the imperative in EE, 105–6; W-OC, 571–73.[6]

_____

_____

The juxtaposition of these two imperatives without an intervening *waw* occurs in eleven other passages. There is sometimes a tone of excitement or urgency. (See Gen. 28:2; Deut. 10:11; 1 Sam. 9:3; 2 Sam. 13:15; 1 Kings 17:9; Song 2:13.) This may well be the case here, where the Lord commissions his prophet to go and confront Nineveh's sin. Some translations attempt to convey this sense of urgency: "Go at once" (NRSV); "Go immediately" (NET).

---

3. Fut., 70 (12.6); Gar., 96 (17.E.2); Kel., 61–62 (26.4); Ross, 101 (12.4); Seow, 118 (2.b, 2.d).
4. See also AC, 8–13; BHRG, 197–200; GKC, 416–19; Joüon, 465–73; WHS, 36–49.
5. Fut., 109 (18.3); Gar., 229 (40.A); Kel., 167 (48.2); Ross, 254 (35.4); Seow, 239 (3.e).
6. See also AC, 63–65; BHRG, 150–51; GKC, 324–25; Joüon, 378–79; WHS, 188–91.

2. הָעִיר—The noun is appositional to "Nineveh."[7] It classifies Nineveh as being a city. How is the definite article functioning? See the discussion of the article in EE, 72–73; W-OC, 242–50.[8]

_____

_____

3. הַגְּדוֹלָה—What part of speech is this form? How is it functioning? See PVP, 61–66 (7.1–7.7); Ful., 54–55 (10.8).[9] It is not clear if the term refers to the city's size or to its importance. The two concepts would, of course, be related. The expression also occurs in Jonah 3:3 (where the qualifying phrase "a journey of three days" suggests the city's size is in view) and 4:11. For the phrase "great city/cities" outside of Jonah, see Genesis 10:12; Numbers 13:28; Deuteronomy 1:28; 6:10; 9:1; Joshua 10:2; 14:12; 1 Kings 4:13; Jeremiah 22:8.

_____

_____

4. וּקְרָא—The form is a Qal imperative with *waw* prefixed (chart 9: no verbal prefix, three root letters with *shewa* under the first). In this context the collocation קְרָא + עַל probably means "cry out against." See Deuteronomy 15:9; 24:15; 1 Kings 13:2; Jeremiah 49:29. NIV interprets this as "preach against," while NLT (cf. NET) has "announce judgment against."

5. עָלֶיהָ—This form consists of what elements? See PVP, 87–88 (9.10–9.11); Ful., 85 (14.4).[10] What is the antecedent of the suffix? To determine this, you must first analyze the gender and number of the suffix. Now you must find a noun in the preceding context that agrees with the pronoun in gender and number and makes suitable sense as an antecedent.

_____

_____

_____

6. כִּי—The particle introduces a dependent (subordinate) clause. What type of clause is this? For a list of dependent clauses see EE, 113–17; W-OC, 632–46.[11] On uses of כִּי see BHRG, 300–303.[12]

_____

_____

_____

7. עָלְתָה—The form is a Qal perfect 3fs from עָלָה. Note that the form has an ה‎ָ- ending (see chart 2). Since there is no prefix, the stem must be Qal, Piel, or Pual. The *qamets* under the first root letter indicates

_____

7. On the syntax of apposition see AC, 21–24; BHRG, 229–30; Joüon, 477–81; W-OC, 226–34.
8. See also AC, 28–32; BHRG, 189–91; GKC, 404–10; Joüon, 505–13; WHS, 82–93.
9. Fut., 57–58 (10.7–10.10); Gar., 62–64 (11); Kel., 45–46 (21.1); Ross, 81–82 (9.1–9.2); Seow, 72 (3).
10. Fut., 136 (22.1); Gar., 91 (16.F); Ross, 123 (15.8); Seow, 97 (2.b).
11. See also AC, 171–86; WHS, 482–569.
12. See also WHS, 444–52.

Qal. Since the form has two root letters with a *taw* before the ending, it is a perfect 3fs from a III-*he* root. See PVP, 154 (14.7); Ful., 265 (37.4).[13] How is the perfect verbal form עָלְתָה functioning? For a list of functions for the perfect see EE, 86–89; W-OC, 486–95.[14]

_____

_____

_____

8. רָעָתָם—The form consists of the noun רָעָה, "evil," and a 3mp pronominal suffix. Pronominal suffixes on nouns are classified as genitives. So the suffix on רָעָתָם, "their evil," is genitival in function and probably indicates the possessor or doer (subject) of the evil.[15] The antecedent of the plural suffix is implied, but not stated. The pronoun obviously refers to the inhabitants of the aforementioned city. Note the same phenomenon in verse 3, where we are told that Jonah "went down into it [the boat] in order to go with them [the sailors]." The sailors have not been directly mentioned at this point, but their presence is implied by the reference to the boat.[16] In the same way in verse 2 the presence of the inhabitants is implied in the reference to the city.

רָעָה, "evil," is a key thematic word in Jonah. The term can refer to moral/ethical behavior ("evil"), as it does here (see also the use of the adjective רָעָה in 3:8, 10a). However, it need not have this moral/ethical connotation. Elsewhere in the book it refers to a calamity sent by God (1:7–8, viz., the storm), the destructive judgment threatened by God (3:10b; see 4:2 as well), Jonah's displeasure over God's merciful treatment of Nineveh (4:1), and Jonah's physical discomfort (4:6). However, in this last instance the word appears to have a double meaning. For further discussion of how this term functions thematically, see the comments below on each of these verses.

9. לְפָנָי—The form consists of לִפְנֵי (PVP, 59 [6.11])[17] and a 1cs suffix (pausal form, see PVP, 406 [36.3]; Ful., 85 [14.4]).[18] The phrase here carries the idea "in full (mental) view of." See BDB, 817, 4.a.(*c*). NET tries to reflect this: "has come to my attention."

1:3

וַיָּקָם יוֹנָה לִבְרֹחַ תַּרְשִׁישָׁה מִלִּפְנֵי יְהוָה

וַיֵּרֶד יָפוֹ וַיִּמְצָא אָנִיָּה בָּאָה תַרְשִׁישׁ וַיִּתֵּן שְׂכָרָהּ וַיֵּרֶד בָּהּ לָבוֹא עִמָּהֶם תַּרְשִׁישָׁה מִלִּפְנֵי יְהוָה:

1. וַיָּקָם—Parse the verb. How do you determine the person, gender, and number (P-G-N)? (If you need help with the stem and root, see parsing chart 10, which covers imperfect and wayyiqtol forms. The form has only two root letters and the vowel pattern is *qamets* + *qamets hatuph*, so the verb must be a Qal form from either a hollow or geminate verb. There is no verb קָמַם; so the root must be hollow קוּם, "arise," the meaning of which fits well here.) The wayyiqtol clause continues the narrative framework

_____

13. Fut., 89–90 (15.6); Gar., 165 (27.E); Kel., 288 (72.3); Ross, 260 (36.2); Seow, 161 (3.a).
14. See also AC, 54–56; BHRG, 144–46; GKC, 309–13; Joüon, 359–65; WHS, 161–66.
15. See GKC, 439, §135m.
16. See GKC, 441, §135p.
17. Fut., 136 (22.1); Gar., 70 (12.C); Kel., 70 (27.1); Ross, 129 (16.5).
18. Gar., 159 (26.D); Ross, 158 (21.4); Seow, 97 (2.b).

and is sequential to verse 1 (see EE, 120–21). (Verse 2 contains a quotation embedded within the narrative main line.) The verb itself can be classified as simple (narratival) past. See EE, 94–97.

_____

_____

_____

2. לִבְרֹחַ—Parse the form. (See parsing chart 9. The form has no verbal prefix and there is a *shewa* under the first root letter, so it must be a Qal imperative masculine singular or infinitive construct. The preposition makes it an infinitive construct. Also since the verb is III-guttural, the imperatival form is בְּרַח. See PVP, 210 [18.8]; Ful., 216 [32.4-32.5] and Gen. 27:43.) How is the form functioning in relation to the main verb? Review the discussion of the usage of the infinitive construct with the preposition -לְ in PVP, 241–47 (20.10–20.13)[19] and then read W-OC, 605–10.[20]

_____

_____

_____

3. תַּרְשִׁישָׁה —Explain the ָה- ending on the proper name תַּרְשִׁישָׁה. See PVP, 64–65 (7.6); Ful., 55–56 (10.11).[21] Nouns with the directive ending are classified as accusatives. How is the accusative functioning here? For categories of the accusative see EE, 64–65; W-OC, 162–77 (especially 169–73).[22]

_____

_____

The precise location of Tarshish is uncertain; it was located west of Israel somewhere on the coast of the Mediterranean Sea. Most translations use the proper name, but some try to bring out the connotation of the reference: NET has "a distant seaport," while NLT reads "in the opposite direction."

4. מִלִּפְנֵי—The form is a compound preposition, comprised of מִן and לִפְנֵי. See PVP, 59 (6.11).[23]

5. וַיֵּרֶד—Parse the form. How do you determine the P-G-N? (For help with the stem and root see parsing chart 10. The form has only two root letters visible and the vowel pattern is *tsere + seghol,* so it is a Qal from a I-*yod* root.) This wayyiqtol clause continues the sequence of action described by the narrative main line. The verb is narratival/simple past. See EE, 94–97.

_____

_____

_____

19. Fut., 122 (20.8); Gar., 212 (36.B.2); Kel., 182 (56.2); Ross, 164 (22.4); Seow, 57 (4.a).
20. See also AC, 71–73; BHRG, 154–55; GKC, 348–51; Joüon, 436–38; WHS, 192–200.
21. Gar., 158 (26.B); Kel., 146–47 (44); Ross, 133 (17.4); Seow, 152–53 (6).
22. See also AC, 13–21; Joüon, 440–63; WHS, 50–60.
23. Gar., 70 (12.C); Ross, 418 (54.4); Seow, 60.

6. יָפוֹ—What is the case and case function of יָפוֹ? (Hint: Note that you have to supply a preposition in translation, though there is no preposition in the Hebrew text.) See EE, 64–65; W-OC, 169–73.[24]

_____

_____

7. וַיִּמְצָא—The verb is a Qal (a *hireq* prefix vowel followed by *shewa;* see chart 10) wayyiqtol, carrying on the sequence of action. The verb is simple past in function.

8. אֳנִיָּה—This noun is the object of the verb. Why is there no accusative sign before it? See PVP, 54–56 (6.7); Ful., 33 (7.7).[25]

_____

_____

In 1999 archaeologists discovered two Phoenician ships that were wrecked at sea sometime between 750–700 B.C. Each was transporting over twelve tons of wine at the time it sank. The ships were approximately sixteen meters (52.5 feet) long and six meters (19.7 feet) wide. Reliefs from Sennacherib's palace depict such ships leaving the harbor at Tyre. For a discussion of the archaeological evidence and the biblical references pertaining to ancient seafaring and to the "ships of Tarshish," see Philip J. King and Lawrence E. Stager, *Life in Biblical Israel* (Louisville: Westminster John Knox, 2001), 178–85.

9. בָּאָה—Parse the form. Look at chart 2 (for verbs with a ה ָ - ending). With no prefix, *qamets* under the first letter, only two root letters, and the accent on the last syllable, the form is a hollow feminine singular participle (there is no III-*he* verb באה). The participle can be distinguished from the 3fs perfect of בּוֹא by the placement of the accent. See PVP, 261 (22.4); Ful., 255 (36.5).[26] How do you determine the gender and number? How is the form functioning in relation to the preceding noun אֳנִיָּה. See PVP, 262 (22.5); 115–16 (19.2); Ful., 115–16 (19.2).[27]

_____

_____

_____

_____

10. תַּרְשִׁישׁ—Note that תַּרְשִׁישׁ does not have the directional ending here, as it does earlier and later in the verse. There is no preposition before it, yet one must supply one in English. This means that the proper noun is functioning here as an adverbial accusative, indicating the direction in which the ship was going (EE, 64; W-OC, 169–71).

11. וַיִּתֵּן—Parse the verb. How do you determine the *(a)* stem, *(b)* root, and *(c)* P-G-N? (See chart 10.) Once more the wayyiqtol clause is sequential in the narrative, with the verb being simple past. The verb

---

24. See also AC, 18–21; Joüon, 440–63; WHS, 50–60.
25. Fut., 36–37 (7.6); Gar., 47 (8.A); Kel., 12 (5); Ross, 90–91 (10.6); Seow, 98 (3.a).
26. Gar., 202–3 (34.B.5); Kel., 318 (74.3); Ross, 276 (38.2.2); Seow, 163 (4).
27. Fut., 130 (21.7); Gar., 63–65 (11.B–C); Kel., 199 (60); Ross, 127–28 (16.3); Seow, 81–84 (4).

נָתַן is typically translated "give," but it can also mean "put, place, set" (see BDB, 680; *HALOT*, 734). It occasionally refers to placing a purchase price or wage into another's hand and can be translated "pay" (see Gen. 23:13, as well as BDB, 679).

---

12. שְׂכָרָהּ—This form consists of the noun שָׂכָר, "wage, fare," which is the object of the verb, and a 3fs pronominal suffix. What is the antecedent of the suffix?

---

13. וַיֵּרֶד—This verb appears again (see note 5 above). It continues the narratival sequence.
14. בָּהּ—The form consists of what elements? See PVP, 96 (9.19); Ful., 83 (14.2).[28]

---

15. לָבוֹא—Parse the form. See chart 9. (Note that the prepositional prefix rules out the possibility of this form being an imperative or an infinitive absolute.) How is the form functioning in relation to the main verb? Review the discussion of the usage of the infinitive construct with the preposition -לְ in PVP, 241–47 (20.10–20.13)[29] and then read W-OC, 605–10.[30]

---

16. עִמָּהֶם—The form consists of the preposition עִם and a 3mp pronominal suffix, referring to the sailors. The antecedent of the pronoun is implied. See comments on רָעָתָם in verse 2, note 8.

Step 3: Interpretive Translation

In light of the decisions you have made in your analysis, provide an interpretive, paraphrastic translation of Jonah 1:1–3.

---

28. Fut., 135–36 (22.1); Gar., 82 (15.A.2); Kel., 68 (27.1); Ross, 108 (13.1); Seow, 94 (2.a).
29. Fut., 122 (20.8); Gar., 212 (36.B.2); Kel., 182 (56.2); Ross, 164 (22.4); Seow, 258–59 (3).
30. See also AC, 71–73; BHRG, 154–55; GKC, 348–51; Joüon, 436–38; WHS, 192–200.

_____

_____

_____

_____

_____

_____

Step 4: Structural Outline

Outline the narrative structure of Jonah 1:1–3. Carefully delineate the narrative mainline (initiated and extended by wayyiqtol forms), offline (nonstandard) constructions, and quotations. Using the categories listed in the appendix (cf. EE, 120–27), classify all wayyiqtol and disjunctive clauses that are in the narrative framework. You need not classify clauses within quotations.

_____

_____

_____

_____

_____

_____

_____

_____

_____

_____

> Jonah is portrayed as an anti-prophet here. One expects verse 3 to mirror the Lord's command (see v. 2) and read, "Jonah arose and went and cried out" (cf. 3:1–4; as well as Num. 22:20–21; 1 Kings 17:9–10; 19:7–8; Ezek. 3:22–23), but instead we read, "Jonah arose _to flee._" To draw attention to Jonah's disobedience, the narrator uses repetition. Twice he describes Jonah as moving "from before the Lord" and three times he identifies Jonah's destination as Tarshish. The author does not tell us Jonah's reason for running away; he lets Jonah himself reveal his motive later in the story (see 4:2).

Scene 2: Jonah 1:4–6: God Gets Jonah's Attention

Assignment

Step 1: Initial View

Read Jonah 1:4–6 in the Hebrew text, using an interlinear if you desire. Underline any words or forms you do not recognize. Try to identify verbal forms and label them as follows:

- wayyiqtol verbal forms: wc-y (the so-called *waw* consecutive with the yiqtol, usually identified as a preterite or imperfect)
- weqatal forms: wc-q (the so-called *waw* consecutive with the qatal, that is, perfect)
- simple perfects (without *waw*): pf.
- simple imperfects (without *waw*): impf.
- imperatives: impv.
- jussives: juss.
- cohortatives: coh.
- infinitives construct: inf. const.
- infinitives absolute: inf. abs.
- participles: part.

Step 2: Analyzing the Text

1:4

וַיהוָה הֵטִיל רוּחַ־גְּדוֹלָה אֶל־הַיָּם וַיְהִי סַעַר־גָּדוֹל בַּיָּם וְהָאֳנִיָּה חִשְּׁבָה לְהִשָּׁבֵר׃

1. Note the disjunctive structure (*waw* + subject + verb) at the beginning of the verse. How is this offline construction functioning here? See the appendix (cf. EE, 124–27), for a list of the categories of usage for disjunctive clauses.[31] Note that KJV, NRSV, NLT, and NET attempt to interpret and reflect the clause function, while NIV ("Then the LORD") and NASB ("And the LORD") do not.

   _____

   _____

   _____

   _____

2. הֵטִיל—Parse the form. How do you determine the *(a)* stem, *(b)* root? (Why is the verb hollow, not geminate?), and *(c)* P-G-N? See chart 9 (prefixed *he* section). How is the perfect functioning here? See EE, 86–89; W-OC, 486–95.[32] Apart from one passage, this verb appears in the causative stem (Hiphil/

---

31. In this clause the subject is placed first (or "fronted"). For a helpful discussion of fronting, see BHRG, 344–50. See also W-OC, 650–52.
32. See also AC, 54–56; BHRG, 144–46; GKC, 309–13; Joüon, 359–65; WHS, 161–66.

Hophal) with the meaning "throw, hurl, fling" (cf. BDB, 376; *HALOT,* 373; and see 1 Sam. 18:11; Ezek. 32:4). Most translations reflect this (cf. NASB, NRSV, NLT, NET); KJV ("sent out") and NIV ("sent") do not adequately reflect the force or exact nature of the action.

_____

_____

_____

_____

3. רוּחַ—How is the noun functioning in relation to the preceding verb? (Why does it not have אֵת before it?) The term רוּחַ is frequently understood as "spirit," but it can also refer to the breath of the nostrils/ mouth or, as here, to wind.

_____

_____

4. גְּדוֹלָה—How is the form functioning in relation to רוּחַ? (Remember that רוּחַ, despite its lack of a feminine ending, is nevertheless feminine.) See PVP, 62–64 (7.4); Ful., 54–55 (10.8).[33]

_____

_____

5. וַיְהִי—The verb (on the form see 1:1, note 1) here introduces a clause that is consequential to the preceding clause; it describes the result of God's throwing a powerful wind into the sea. One could translate, "So there was a . . ." NLT reflects this well, "causing a violent storm."

6. סַעַר—How is the noun functioning in the sentence? What is the relationship of גָּדוֹל to סַעַר? The adjective "great," indicates magnitude; in translation it can be given a nuance that fits the noun it modifies. See, for example, "mighty tempest" (KJV), "violent storm" (NIV, NLT), as opposed to NASB's "great storm."

_____

_____

_____

7. בַּיָּם—The form consists of what elements? Why is there a *dagesh* in the *yod?* See PVP, 52; Ful., 37 (8.2).[34]

_____

_____

_____

---

33. Fut., 57–58 (10.7–10.10); Gar., 62–64 (11); Kel., 45–46 (21.1); Ross, 81–82 (9.1–9.2); Seow, 72 (3).
34. Fut., 50 (9.11); Gar., 68 (12.A.1); Kel., 29 (15.1); Ross, 59 (5.6); Seow, 55–56 (2).

8. Note the disjunctive structure (*waw* + subject + verb) in the second half of the verse (after the *athnaq*). How is this offline construction functioning here? See the appendix (cf. EE, 124–27).[35] Translations treat the clause as indicating result (cf. "so that" [KJV, NASB], "that" [NIV, NRSV, NET]), but this is not a typical category for disjunctive clauses and there are other ways to indicate result in Hebrew. It is more likely that the disjunctive structure is used to highlight the statement and add to the dramatic tension of the story. To reflect this it might be better to translate, "Even the ship . . ."

    _____

    _____

9. חִשְּׁבָה—Parse the verb. How do you determine the *(a)* stem, and *(b)* P-G-N? (See chart 2 for forms with an הָ - ending.) How is the perfect functioning? The Hebrew verb means "think, plan." With this verb the Piel stem is probably frequentative (cf. W-OC's discussion of this use, pp. 414–16).[36] If the Qal means "think," then the Piel may in this case be rendered "expected to be, was convinced it would be." One expects an animate subject with this verb; the narrator personifies the ship for rhetorical effect. If illustrated, the ship would have eyes reflecting the panicked look that characterizes someone convinced that doom is close and sure. Most translations shy away from reflecting the personification: "was about to" (NASB), "threatened to" (NIV, NRSV, NET). NLT resorts to "that threatened to send them to the bottom of the sea." Such a radical paraphrase fails to capture the literary dimension of the story or the dramatic effect the narrator intended.

    _____

    _____

    _____

    _____

10. לְהִשָּׁבֵר—Parse the form. How do you determine the stem? How can you tell this is an infinitive construct? (See chart 9, prefixed *he* section.) Some translations treat the Niphal as middle in function ("to break up," cf. NIV, NASB, NRSV, NET), but the context definitely suggests the presence of an outside agent. A passive nuance seems better (cf. KJV, "to be broken"). In this case, the infinitive with -לְ is a verbal complement, introducing the object of the preceding verb. See W-OC, 606.[37] It tells us *what* the personified ship was thinking.

    _____

    _____

    _____

    _____

---

35. See also BHRG, 344–50; W-OC, 650–52.
36. See also Joüon, 155.
37. See also BHRG, 154; Joüon, 437; WHS, 193.

1:5

וַיִּירְאוּ הַמַּלָּחִים וַיִּזְעֲקוּ אִישׁ אֶל־אֱלֹהָיו וַיָּטִלוּ אֶת־הַכֵּלִים אֲשֶׁר בָּאֳנִיָּה אֶל־הַיָּם לְהָקֵל מֵעֲלֵיהֶם וְיוֹנָה יָרַד אֶל־יַרְכְּתֵי הַסְּפִינָה וַיִּשְׁכַּב וַיֵּרָדַם:

1. וַיִּירְאוּ—The verb is a Qal wayyiqtol from יָרֵא, "be afraid" (see chart 10, two root letters section). How do you determine the P-G-N? The clause describes a consequence of the storm (v. 4a). The verb is simple past in function.

2. הַמַּלָּחִים—The form consists of the article and the plural form of מַלָּח, "sailor." This noun pattern with a doubled middle root letter often signifies an occupation or profession in which an action is typically repeated. See W-OC, 89 (5.4).

3. וַיִּזְעֲקוּ—The verb is a Qal wayyiqtol that describes a consequence of the preceding action; their fear prompted them to pray.

4. אִישׁ—The noun is used here in a distributive sense, "each one" (see BDB, 36; *HALOT*, 44).

5. אֱלֹהָיו—The form consists of what elements? The form may be translated "his gods," if we assume the sailors were polytheists (cf. NLT), or "his god," if we understand each one's patron deity to be in view (cf. KJV, NIV, NASB, NRSV, NET).[38] In the latter case the plural is one of respect; the suffixed form of אֱלֹהִים can be used as a plural of respect for foreign gods (see Judg. 9:27; 11:24; 1 Sam. 5:7; 1 Kings 18:24).

6. וַיָּטִלוּ—Parse the verb. How do you determine the *(a)* stem, *(b)* root, and *(c)* P-G-N? (See chart 10, two root letters section. Note that the *hireq* is a defectively written *hireq yod* here.) In this case the wayyiqtol clause, rather than being purely sequential, may be complementary.[39] This action may have happened concurrently with their praying. This is the same verb used in verse 4 of God hurling the wind into the sea. The repetition is ironic—the sailors' action mirrors that of God. He threw a wind into the sea and now they throw their cargo into the sea. By verse 15 the irony will reach humorous dimensions as the sailors throw Jonah, the one whose disobedience precipitated God's action, into the sea!

---

38. See Aaron Jed Brody, *"Each Man Cried Out to His God": The Specialized Religion of Canaanite and Phoenician Seafarers* (Atlanta: Scholars Press, 1998), 82.

39. This relatively rare category is not included in EE, 120–23. See BHRG, 167–68.

7. הַכֵּלִים—Why is the direct object הַכֵּלִים preceded by אֶת־? See PVP, 54–56 (6.7); Ful., 33 (7.7).[40] Most translations render the form "cargo," even though the Hebrew noun is plural. כְּלִי refers in a general way to an item or piece of equipment (see BDB, 479; *HALOT*, 478). The plural would refer in this context to the various items (i.e., the cargo) being transported by the ship.

_____

_____

8. בָּאֳנִיָּה—The form consists of what elements? Explain the vowel pointing under the *beth*. See PVP, 41 (5.4); Ful., 31 (7.2).[41]

_____

_____

_____

9. לְהָקֵל—Parse the form. How do you determine the (a) stem, and (b) root? (See chart 9, prefixed *he* section.) The *lamed* prefix is a tip-off that this is an infinitive construct. How is it functioning in relation to the main verb? See PVP, 241–47;[42] W-OC, 605–10.[43] How is the Hiphil stem functioning here? (The basic meaning of the verb קָלַל in the Qal stem is "be light.") Review the categories of usage for the Hiphil (see EE, 82–83; W-OC, 433–46)[44] and, if need be, survey the discussion of the verb in one of the standard dictionaries (BDB, 886; *HALOT*, 1103–4).

_____

_____

_____

_____

10. מֵעֲלֵיהֶם—The form consists of מִן + עַל + 3mp suffix. See PVP, 60 (6.11), 88; Ful., 85 (14.4).[45]
11. Note the disjunctive structure (*waw* + subject + verb) in the second half of the verse (after the *athnaq*). How is this offline construction functioning here? See the appendix (cf. EE, 124–27).[46]

_____

_____

---

40. Fut., 36–37 (7.6); Gar., 47 (8.A); Kel., 12 (5); Ross, 90–91 (10.6); Seow, 98 (3.a).
41. Fut., 25–26 (5.9); Gar., 43 (7.A); Kel., 29 (15.1); Ross, 64–65 (6.3); Seow, 54–56 (1–2).
42. Fut., 122 (20.8); Gar., 212 (36.B.2); Kel., 182 (56.2); Ross, 164 (22.4); Seow, 258–59 (3).
43. See also AC, 71–73; BHRG, 154–55; GKC, 348–51; Joüon, 436–38; WHS, 192–200.
44. See also AC, 48–52; Joüon, 162–64.
45. Fut., 136 (22.1); Gar., 70 (12.C.1), 91 (16.F); Ross, 418 (54.4), 123 (15.8); Seow, 97 (2.b).
46. See also BHRG, 344–50; W-OC, 650–52.

12. יָרַד—How is the perfect verbal form יָרַד functioning here? For a list of functions for the perfect see EE, 86–89; W-OC, 486–95.[47] There are two main options here.[48] What are they? (The translation "had gone below/down" [NIV, NASB, NRSV, NET] reflects one of the options.) One option for understanding the disjunctive clause with the perfect is illustrated in Genesis 31:19; the other is illustrated in Genesis 4:4 (cf. v. 3).

_____

_____

_____

_____

13. יַרְכְּתֵי—This form is derived from the feminine noun יְרֵכָה, "far part" (see HALOT, 439; BDB, 438). It is a dual construct form: יַרְכָתַיִם > יַרְכְּתֵי. On the feminine dual absolute form, see PVP 29 (4.3); Ful., 54 (10.6). How can you tell that יַרְכְּתֵי is a construct form? See PVP, 103 (10.5); Ful., 65 (11.7).[49] (Though PVP deals specifically with masculine dual forms, feminine dual forms have the same construct ending.) Following the construct, הַסְּפִינָה is a genitive, indicating here the larger entity (the ship) of which the preceding word is part. This is a different term for the ship than the one used previously. Derived from the root סָפַן, "to cover, panel" (BDB, 706; HALOT, 764–65), it pictures the ship as having a covered hold, where Jonah found a suitable place to rest.[50]

_____

_____

14. וַיִּשְׁכַּב—The verb is a Qal wayyiqtol (see chart 10). Intransitive verbs (those that take no direct object) sometimes take a pathaq theme vowel in the imperfect/wayyiqtol (rather than the usual holem). See PVP, 168–69 (15.6); Ful., 128–29 (21.4).[51] The wayyiqtol is sequential to the preceding action.

15. וַיֵּרָדַם—Parse the verb. How do you determine the stem? (See chart 10.) (Why is the prefix vowel tsere, rather than hireq? See PVP, 299–300 [25.6–25.7]; Ful., 190 [29.4].)[52] This verb occurs exclusively in the Niphal stem. For this reason it is difficult to know for sure how the stem is functioning, but a stative-ingressive use ("became asleep," i.e., "went to sleep") seems likely in this case.[53]

_____

_____

_____

47. See also AC, 54–56; BHRG, 144–46; GKC, 309–13; Joüon, 359–65; WHS, 161–66.
48. See Uriel Simon, Jonah, JPSBC, trans. J. L. Schramm (Philadelphia: Jewish Publication Society, 1999), 9, for a helpful discussion of the issue.
49. Fut., 75 (13.1); Gar., 97 (17.E.2); Kel., 59 (26); Ross, 100–101 (12.3); Seow, 118 (2.c).
50. Simon, Jonah, 9.
51. Fut., 63 (11.4); Gar., 240 (42.A); Kel., 129 (39.6); Ross, 144–45 (19.4); Seow, 205–6 (2).
52. Fut., 232; Gar., 245 (43.D.1); Kel., 224 (66.3); Ross, 232–33 (33.1.1); Seow, 292 (4.b).
53. On this function of the Niphal stem, see W-OC, 386.

1:6

וַיִּקְרַב אֵלָיו רַב הַחֹבֵל וַיֹּאמֶר לוֹ מַה־לְּךָ נִרְדָּם
קוּם קְרָא אֶל־אֱלֹהֶיךָ אוּלַי יִתְעַשֵּׁת הָאֱלֹהִים לָנוּ וְלֹא נֹאבֵד:

1. וַיִּקְרַב—Parse the verb. (See chart 10.) On the *pathaq* theme vowel, see note 14 under 1:5.

2. אֵלָיו—The form consists of what elements? See PVP, 96 (9.19); Ful., 85 (14.4).[54]

3. רַב—The form is the subject of the verb "drew near." It is either a noun ("chief," so BDB, 913) or substantival adjective (lit. "great one"). It is in construct with הַחֹבֵל, "the crew." After the construct, the latter is a genitive, indicating either the whole entity of which the captain is a part or the entity owned by the captain. חֹבֵל is derived from a root meaning "to tie, bind." A derived noun, חֶבֶל, refers to a rope and then by extension to a length of rope used as a unit of measure and to a plot of land that is measured in such terms (see *HALOT*, 285–86). חֹבֵל is a collective noun (participial form) that refers to the sailors as "ropers," those skilled in the use of ropes used in the rigging of ancient ships.[55]

4. מַה־לְּךָ—The expression (lit., "what to you?") is an idiom. See *HALOT*, 551. Combined with the following נִרְדָּם it can be translated, "What are you doing sleeping?" (cf. NET, NRSV), or "How can you sleep?" (NIV, NLT), or "What right have you to sleep?"

5. נִרְדָּם—Parse the form. (See chart 9, prefixed *nun* section.) How do you determine the stem? How can you tell the form is a participle, not a perfect? See PVP, 291 (24.14).[56] The participle is used here as an accusative of state (see EE, 65),[57] giving an attribute of the pronoun. See Joüon, 459–60, §127a; 611–12, §161i.

6. קוּם קְרָא—On these imperatival forms see 1:2, notes 1, 4.

---

54. Fut., 136 (22.1); Gar., 91 (16.F); Kel., 70 (27.1); Ross, 123 (15.8); Seow, 97 (2.c).
55. Simon, *Jonah*, 9.
56. Fut., 226–27 (36.1, 36.5); Gar., 249–50 (44.C); Kel., 113 (37), 195 (59.3); Ross, 188 (26.2); Seow, 294–95 (7.a).
57. See AC, 20; Joüon, 459–60; W-OC, 171–72.

7. אֱלֹהֶיךָ—The form consists of what elements? Should we translate the noun as singular or plural? See the following sentence, as well as 1:5, note 5.

_____

_____

8. יִתְעַשֵּׁת—Parse the verb. How do you determine the stem? (See chart 10.) How is the imperfect functioning here? (Note the preceding אוּלַי.) For categories of usage of the imperfect see EE, 89–94; W-OC, 504–13.[58] The verb עָשַׁת occurs only here in biblical Hebrew; the Aramaic cognate appears in Daniel 6:4 (Eng. v. 3) with the meaning "consider, intend." Here in Jonah 1:6 it appears to have the nuance, "consider, take notice of."

_____

_____

_____

9. הָאֱלֹהִים—How is the article on the form functioning? Review the discussion of the article in EE, 73; W-OC, 242–50.[59]

_____

_____

10. לָנוּ—The form consists of what elements? See PVP, 88; Ful., 83 (14.2).[60] After the Hithpael verb, the preposition probably indicates interest or advantage. See W-OC, 207–8. For comparable examples of Hithpael verb forms collocated with a -לְ of interest, see Genesis 24:41; 27:42; Exodus 1:10; 1 Samuel 2:25; 2 Kings 5:7.

_____

_____

11. נֹאבֵד—The verb is a Qal imperfect. (See chart 10.) Recall that some I-*aleph* verbs have a *holem* prefix vowel. See PVP, 178–79 (16.10–16.11); Ful., 201 (30.2).[61] How do you determine the P-G-N? The negated imperfect indicates consequence in relation to the preceding verb: "Perhaps God will take notice of us so that we do not perish." See NASB, NRSV, NET.

_____

_____

---

58. See also AC, 56–60; BHRG, 146–49; GKC, 313–19; Joüon, 365–72; WHS, 167–75.
59. See also AC, 28–32; BHRG, 189–91; GKC, 404–10; Joüon, 505–13; WHS, 82–93.
60. Fut., 135 (22.1); Gar., 82 (15.A.1); Kel., 68 (27.1); Ross, 108 (13.1); Seow, 94 (2.a).
61. Fut., 109–10 (18.4); Gar., 192 (32.C); Kel., 237–38 (67.2–67.4); Ross, 228–29 (32.3.1); Seow, 214 (1.c).

Step 3: Interpretive Translation

In light of the decisions you have made in your analysis, provide an interpretive, paraphrastic translation of Jonah 1:4–6.

_____

_____

_____

_____

_____

_____

_____

_____

_____

Step 4: Structural Outline

Outline the narrative structure of Jonah 1:4–6. Carefully delineate the narrative mainline (initiated and extended by wayyiqtol forms), offline (nonstandard) constructions, and quotations. Using the categories listed in the appendix (cf. EE, 120–27), classify all wayyiqtol and disjunctive clauses that are in the narrative framework. You need not classify clauses within quotations.

_____

_____

_____

_____

_____

_____

_____

_____

> The Lord refused to let Jonah run away. He "threw" a powerful wind into the sea and stirred up a raging storm. To emphasize the storm's severity, the narrator pictures the ship as actually thinking it would be destroyed. NIV translates the last clause in verse 4 as "the ship threatened to break up," but the Hebrew text literally says, "the ship thought (it) would be broken." Everything and everyone responds to the Lord's intervention, except sleeping Jonah. The captain roused him and told him to "arise and cry out" to his God. The captain's words echo the Lord's command to Jonah (see v. 2).

Scene 3: Jonah 1:7–16: Prophet Overboard!

Assignment

Step 1: Initial View

Read Jonah 1:7–16 in the Hebrew text, using an interlinear if you desire. Underline any words or forms you do not recognize. Try to identify verbal forms and label them as follows:

- wayyiqtol verbal forms: wc-y (the so-called *waw* consecutive with the yiqtol, usually identified as a preterite or imperfect)
- weqatal forms: wc-q (the so-called *waw* consecutive with the qatal, that is, perfect)
- simple perfects (without *waw*): pf.
- simple imperfects (without *waw*): impf.
- imperatives: impv.
- jussives: juss.
- cohortatives: coh.
- infinitives construct: inf. const.
- infinitives absolute: inf. abs.
- participles: part.

Step 2: Analyzing the Text

1:7

וַיֹּאמְרוּ אִישׁ אֶל־רֵעֵהוּ לְכוּ וְנַפִּילָה גוֹרָלוֹת וְנֵדְעָה בְּשֶׁלְּמִי הָרָעָה הַזֹּאת לָנוּ
וַיַּפִּלוּ גּוֹרָלוֹת וַיִּפֹּל הַגּוֹרָל עַל־יוֹנָה:

1. וַיֹּאמְרוּ—Parse the verb. (See chart 10.) How do you determine the P-G-N? Recall that אָמַר is one of the I-*aleph* verbs that has a *holem* prefix vowel in the imperfect/wayyiqtol. See PVP, 178–79 (16.10–16.11); Ful., 201 (30.2).[62]

_____

_____

2. אִישׁ אֶל־רֵעֵהוּ—The expression (lit. "a man to his neighbor") is idiomatic, meaning "one to another." See BDB, 945–46, II.3; *HALOT,* 44. אִישׁ is used in a distributive sense, "each one" (see 1:5, note 4). The 3ms suffix הוּ- is an alternate form of the more common וֹ-. See PVP, 93; Ful., 86 (14.5).[63] For other examples of the idiom "a man (i.e., each one) to his neighbor" after a plural verb, see Genesis 11:3; Judges 6:29; 2 Kings 7:3, 9; Jeremiah 22:8; 36:16.

---

62. Fut., 109–10 (18.4); Gar., 192 (32.C); Kel., 238–39 (67.5); Ross, 228–29 (32.3.1); Seow, 214 (1.c).
63. Ross, 113 (14.2); Seow, 97.

3. לְכוּ—The verb is a Qal imperative, 2mp from הָלַךְ. (See chart 5, no prefix section.) Normally this pattern (no prefix, two root letters, and a *shewa*) means the verb is III-*he*, I-*nun*, or I-*yod*, but הָלַךְ follows I-*yod* patterns in some forms (PVP, 213; Ful., 241).[64] How do you determine the P-G-N?

_____

_____

4. וְנַפִּילָה—Parse the verb. How do you determine the *(a)* stem, *(b)* root, and *(c)* P-G-N? Note the *nun* prefix and the *he* ending. See PVP, 214–15 (18.13); Ful., 110–11 (18.4).[65] This is a cohortative (analogous to the imperfect), so use chart 10. How is the Hiphil stem functioning here? See AC, 48–52; EE, 82–83; W-OC, 433–46; as well as a lexicon (BDB, 656–58; *HALOT,* 709–11).

_____

_____

_____

_____

5. וְנֵדְעָה—Parse the verb. How do you determine the *(a)* stem, and *(b)* root? (Use chart 10 since this is a cohortative form analogous to an imperfect. Note the *nun* prefix and the הָ- ending.) The form is connected by *waw* to the preceding cohortative. How is this second cohortative in this sequence functioning in relation to the preceding one? For a discussion of volitional forms in sequence see EE, 108–12. The translations provide a helpful hint here; note "so that" (NRSV, NET; cf. NASB). NLT does not translate the sailors' words as a dialogue, but renders the first part of the verse as if it were narrival!

_____

_____

_____

_____

6. בְּשֶׁלְמִי—The form is composed of the preposition -בְּ + the relative pronoun שֶׁל + the preposition -לְ + the interrogative מִי. The combination בְּשֶׁל means "on account of" (BDB, 980; *HALOT,* 1366), while לְמִי means "to whom?" NASB and NRSV ("on whose account") translate in a fairly literal manner; NIV ("who is responsible for") and NET ("whose fault it is") are more interpretive.

7. הַזֹּאת—The form consists of what elements? How is the form functioning in relation to the preceding הָרָעָה? See PVP, 71–74 (8.5–8.7); Ful., 55–56 (10.9).[66]

_____

_____

64. Fut., 150 (24.6); Gar., 229 (40.A); Kel., 340 (75.2); Ross, 254 (35.4); Seow, 239 (3.e).
65. Fut., 148 (24.3); Gar., 226 (39.A); Kel., 132 (41.2); Ross, 151 (20.4); Seow, 208 (4.a).
66. Fut., 102–3 (17.4); Gar., 77 (14.B.1); Kel., 53 (24.3); Ross, 94–95 (11.2–11.3); Seow, 104–5 (1.b).

8. לָנוּ—The preposition -לְ probably indicates disadvantage here, "upon, against." See W-OC, 207–8.

9. וַיַּפִּלוּ—Parse the verb. How do you determine the *(a)* stem, *(b)* root, and *(c)* P-G-N? (See chart 10.)

_____

_____

_____

10. גּוֹרָלוֹת—How is the form functioning in relation to the preceding verb? Why is there no אֵת before this form?

_____

_____

11. וַיִּפֹּל—Parse the verb. How do you determine the *(a)* stem, *(b)* root, and *(c)* P-G-N? (See chart 10.)

_____

_____

_____

_____

12. הַגּוֹרָל—How is the form functioning in relation to the preceding verb?

_____

_____

1:8

וַיֹּאמְרוּ אֵלָיו הַגִּידָה־נָּא לָנוּ בַּאֲשֶׁר לְמִי־הָרָעָה הַזֹּאת לָנוּ
מַה־מְּלַאכְתְּךָ וּמֵאַיִן תָּבוֹא מָה אַרְצֶךָ וְאֵי־מִזֶּה עַם אָתָּה:

1. הַגִּידָה—Parse the verb. (See the introduction to chart 2 and then consult chart 9.) How do you determine the *(a)* stem, and *(b)* root? Explain the ending on the form, as well as the particle נָּא. See PVP, 207–8 (18.4–18.6); Ful., 111 (18.4).[67] This verb occurs exclusively in the Hiphil/Hophal with the meaning "declare, tell." The verb may be related to the preposition נֶגֶד, "in front of," and carry the basic idea "to act in front of."[68]

_____

_____

_____

---

67. Gar., 109 (19.B.2); Kel., 172–73 (53–54); Ross, 150 (20.2); Seow, 241 (4) and 210 (6).
68. See W-OC, 444.

2. בַּאֲשֶׁר לְמִי—The expression is equivalent to בְּשֶׁלְּמִי in verse 7, with the more common relative pronoun אֲשֶׁר replacing שֶׁל. See 1:7, note 6.

3. מְלַאכְתְּךָ—The form is comprised of the noun מְלָאכָה, "occupation, work," and a pronominal suffix. The feminine ending ה ָ - appears as *taw* before the suffix. See PVP, 85 (9.7); Ful., 77–78 (13.2).[69] How does the noun function in relation to the preceding interrogative pronoun מָה?

_____

_____

4. מֵאַיִן תָּבוֹא—The expression means "From where?" (BDB, 32; *HALOT*, 42). For other examples of this construction collocated with תָּבוֹא(וּ), see Joshua 9:8; Judges 17:9; 19:17; Job 1:7.

Parse תָּבוֹא. (See chart 10.) How do you determine the *(a)* stem, *(b)* root, and *(c)* P-G-N? How is the imperfect functioning here? For categories of usage of the imperfect see EE, 89–94; W-OC, 504–13.[70]

_____

_____

_____

_____

5. אַרְצֶךָ—The form consists of what elements? The pronominal suffix on the noun is genitival; it probably indicates relationship here. See W-OC, 145. How does the noun relate to the preceding interrogative pronoun מָה?

_____

_____

_____

6. אֵי־מִזֶּה—This construction is comprised of the interrogative אֵי + מִן + demonstrative זֶה. In combination with the following noun it means, "From where (with regard to a people/nation are you)?" For a similar construction see 2 Samuel 15:2.

1:9

וַיֹּאמֶר אֲלֵיהֶם עִבְרִי אָנֹכִי וְאֶת־יְהוָה אֱלֹהֵי הַשָּׁמַיִם אֲנִי יָרֵא אֲשֶׁר־עָשָׂה אֶת־הַיָּם וְאֶת־הַיַּבָּשָׁה:

1. אֲלֵיהֶם—The form consists of what elements? See PVP, 96 (9.19); Ful., 85 (14.4).[71]

_____

_____

---

69. Fut., 96 (16.3); Gar., 89 (16.C); Kel., 72 (28.1); Ross, 114 (14.3); Seow, 133 (1.b).
70. See also AC, 56–60; BHRG, 146–49; GKC, 313–19; Joüon, 365–72; WHS, 167–75.
71. Fut., 136 (22.1); Gar., 91 (16.F); Kel., 70 (27.1); Ross, 123 (15.8); Seow, 97 (2.b).

2. עִבְרִי—This form is a so-called gentilic noun, functioning here as a predicate nominative. The *hireq yod* ending is a gentilic marker, indicating ethnicity. See W-OC, 92–93, 115.

3. יָרֵא—Parse the verb. The form is a participle here, not a perfect. Note the pronominal subject אָנֹכִי is first person. If יָרֵא were a perfect verbal form, it would have to be third masculine singular (it has no personal ending), but this does not agree with the first person subject. How is the participle functioning? See PVP, 61–66 (7.1–7.7); Ful., 115–16 (19.2).[72] Some translations understand the verb in its metonymic sense of "reverence, honor" (cf. BDB, 431), translating it as "worship" (cf. NIV, NRSV, NLT, NET).

---

4. אֲשֶׁר—The relative pronoun, despite the intervening words, modifies "the LORD God."

5. Note the compound object after עָשָׂה; each definite object is introduced by the accusative sign. See W-OC, 179.

1:10

וַיִּירְאוּ הָאֲנָשִׁים יִרְאָה גְדוֹלָה וַיֹּאמְרוּ אֵלָיו מַה־זֹּאת עָשִׂיתָ
כִּי־יָדְעוּ הָאֲנָשִׁים כִּי־מִלִּפְנֵי יְהוָה הוּא בֹרֵחַ כִּי הִגִּיד לָהֶם:

1. וַיִּירְאוּ—Parse the verb. (See chart 10.) How do you determine the *(a)* root, and *(b)* P-G-N? How is הָאֲנָשִׁים functioning in relation to the verb?

---

2. יִרְאָה—Note that this noun, meaning "fear," is from the same root as the verb וַיִּירְאוּ, "and they feared." When a verb and its accusative have a common derivation, grammarians call the latter a "cognate accusative."[73] However, cognate accusatives actually function as direct objects or in an adverbial manner. In this passage יִרְאָה, "fear," is adverbial (lit., "they feared with fear") and emphatic; it can be translated "were terrified" (NLT), "were exceedingly afraid" (KJV), or "became extremely frightened" (NASB).

3. גְדוֹלָה—What part of speech is this form? How is it functioning in relation to the preceding noun?

---

72. Fut., 130 (21.7); Gar., 62–64 (11); Kel., 200–201 (60.2); Ross, 127–28 (16.3); Seow, 81–84 (4).
73. See GKC, 366–67; W-OC, 167.

4. עָשִׂיתָ—Parse this verb. (See chart 1.) How do you recognize the *(a)* root, and *(b)* P-G-N? How is the perfect functioning here?

_____

_____

_____

_____

5. כִּי יָדְעוּ הָאֲנָשִׁים—What type of dependent clause is כִּי יָדְעוּ הָאֲנָשִׁים? (How does it relate to the main verb, "and they said"?) For a list of dependent clauses see EE, 113–17; W-OC, 632–46.[74]

_____

_____

6. כִּי מִלִּפְנֵי יהוה הוּא בֹרֵחַ—What type of dependent clause is כִּי מִלִּפְנֵי יהוה הוּא בֹרֵחַ? (How does כִּי relate to the preceding verb יָדְעוּ?)

_____

_____

7. בֹרֵחַ—How is the participle בֹרֵחַ functioning within this subordinate clause? What temporal nuance does it have here? See EE, 67; W-OC, 623–28.[75]

_____

_____

8. כִּי הִגִּיד לָהֶם—What type of dependent clause is כִּי הִגִּיד לָהֶם? (How does it relate to the verb "they knew"?)

_____

_____

9. הִגִּיד—Parse the verb. (Use chart 9.) How do you determine the *(a)* stem, and *(b)* root? How is the perfect functioning here? (Note how the NIV translates: "he had already told them.")

_____

_____

_____

_____

---

74. See also AC, 171–86; WHS, 72–73, 80–96. On the uses of כִּי see BHRG, 300–303.
75. See also AC, 79–82; BHRG, 162; GKC, 359–60; Joüon, 409–12; WHS, 213–14.

10. לָהֶם—The form consists of what elements? The preposition here introduces the object of the verb. See W-OC, 210–11.

> The order of events seems to have been: (1) The sailors asked Jonah about his background (v. 8). (2) Jonah identified himself (v. 9) and informed the sailors he was running from God (v. 10b). (3) The sailors responded with fear and shock (v. 10a). But the narrator does not choose to present the events in this order.[76] The narrator could have included a reference to Jonah's running away in the quotation (v. 9), since he later tells us that Jonah mentioned this in his response to the sailors (cf. v. 10b). Instead he omits this from the quotation, jumps ahead to their response, and waits until the end of the sequence to tell us that Jonah informed them that he was running away from God. Simon argues that the narrator chooses to present the material in this order because of a concentric pattern he wishes to maintain.[77]

1:11

וַיֹּאמְרוּ אֵלָיו מַה־נַּעֲשֶׂה לָּךְ וְיִשְׁתֹּק הַיָּם מֵעָלֵינוּ כִּי הַיָּם הוֹלֵךְ וְסֹעֵר׃

1. נַּעֲשֶׂה—Parse this verb. (See chart 10 and pay attention to footnote 1.) How do you determine the P-G-N? The form could be Qal or Hiphil, but in this case the Qal meaning fits ("What should we do?"); a causative nuance does not. Furthermore a look at the dictionary will show that this verb does not occur in the Hiphil (BDB, 793–95; *HALOT*, 889–92). If this is a Qal form, why is the prefix vowel *pathaq*? See PVP, 177–78 (16.8–16.9) and 186 (16.21); Ful., 191–92 (29.6).[78] How is the imperfect functioning? (Note that the verb is used here in a question.) The accompanying prepositional phrase (לָּךְ, a pausal 2ms form; see GKC, 97, §29n) indicates interest/advantage here, "What should we do to/for you?"

---

76. Note how the NLT departs from the Hebrew clause order and presents the material as it actually happened chronologically.
77. See Simon, *Jonah,* 13 (cf. p. xxviii for the proposed concentric structure).
78. Gar., 178 (30.A); Kel., 224–25 (66.3); Ross, 227 (32.2.1); Seow, 214 (1).

2. וְיִשְׁתֹּק—The form is an imperfect (or jussive) prefixed with nonconsecutive *waw*. After a question this construction can indicate purpose/result, which seems to be the case here.[79] How does הַיָּם relate to the verb? The verb שָׁתַק is rare, occurring only in this passage (cf. v. 12 as well) and in Psalm 107:30 and Proverbs 26:20. Apparently it means "be quiet, still."

3. מֵעָלֵינוּ—The form consists of what elements? See 1:5, note 10.

4. כִּי—What type of dependent clause does כִּי introduce? If it is part of the quotation, then it must be understood in relation to נַעֲשֶׂה, but if it is a comment by the narrator (as in v. 13) it must be understood in relation to "they said." (See the translations, some of which reverse the Hebrew word order [cf. NIV, NLT, NET].)

5. הוֹלֵךְ וְסֹעֵר—The final clause contains two Qal active participles. How can you tell they are participles from their form? What is the temporal nuance of the participles? (Your decision will hinge on whether or not this is part of the quotation. See note 4 above.) See EE, 67; W-OC, 623–28.[80] The first participle is used adverbially;[81] it indicates that the action described by the following verb was occurring continuously. Note how the translations try to reflect this: "was getting rougher and rougher" (NIV), "was becoming increasingly stormy" (NASB), "was growing more and more tempestuous" (NRSV), "was getting worse all the time" (NLT), and "was growing worse and worse" (NET).

1:12

וַיֹּאמֶר אֲלֵיהֶם שָׂאוּנִי וַהֲטִילֻנִי אֶל־הַיָּם וְיִשְׁתֹּק הַיָּם מֵעֲלֵיכֶם
כִּי יוֹדֵעַ אָנִי כִּי בְשֶׁלִּי הַסַּעַר הַגָּדוֹל הַזֶּה עֲלֵיכֶם׃

1. שָׂאוּנִי—The verb is a Qal imperative masculine plural with 1cs suffix from נָשָׂא. This doubly weak verb (I-*nun* and III-*aleph*) is not covered in the parsing charts. In many I-*nun* imperatives, the *nun* drops

79. See BHRG, 171–72; GKC, 322, §109f; Joüon, 383–84, §116e.
80. See also AC, 79–82; BHRG, 162; GKC, 359–60; Joüon, 409–12; WHS, 213–14.
81. On the idiomatic use of הוֹלֵךְ here, see BDB, 233, 4.d; *HALOT*, 246–47.

(PVP, 211; Ful., 232 [34.4]).[82] One expects the 2mp imperative of this verb to be שְׂאוּ, but with the suffix attached the vowel *qamets* appears under the *sin*. How do you determine the P-G-N? How is the pronominal suffix functioning in relation to the verb?

_____

_____

_____

2. וַהֲטִילֻנִי—Parse this verb. Note *(a)* that the prefix vowel *qamets* has reduced to a composite *shewa* due to an accent shift in conjunction with the addition of the pronominal suffix, and *(b)* that the *qibbuts* ending is a defectively written *shureq*. How do you determine the *(a)* stem, *(b)* root, and *(c)* P-G-N? How is the pronominal suffix functioning in relation to the verb?

_____

_____

_____

_____

3. וְיִשְׁתֹּק—Following the imperative וַהֲטִילֻנִי, how is the form וְיִשְׁתֹּק (which is either imperfect or jussive) functioning? See EE, 110. Note NET, "to make the sea quiet down."

_____

_____

4. כִּי יוֹדֵעַ אָנִי—What type of dependent clause is כִּי יוֹדֵעַ אָנִי? (How does it relate to the earlier imperatives "pick me up and throw me"?) What is the time frame of the participle יוֹדֵעַ?

_____

_____

5. כִּי בְשֶׁלִּי . . . עֲלֵיכֶם—What type of dependent clause is כִּי בְשֶׁלִּי . . . עֲלֵיכֶם? (How does כִּי relate to the preceding verb יוֹדֵעַ?)

_____

_____

6. הַסַּעַר הַגָּדוֹל הַזֶּה —Explain each element in this sequence. See PVP, 72–74; Ful., 51–56.

_____

_____

_____

82. Gar., 217 (37.B.3); Kel., 304 (73.2); Ross, 244 (34.2.2); Seow, 239–40 (3.f).

7. עֲלֵיכֶם—This form consists of what elements?

_____

_____

> Jonah's proposal sounds quite noble, but this is actually another ploy to circumvent his commission. Having been thwarted in his attempt to flee via the sea, he now tries to escape from God via death. Why did Jonah tell the men to throw him into the sea? Simon suggests that assisted suicide was not viewed as being as reprehensible as directly taking one's own life (cf. Judg. 9:54; 1 Sam. 31:4).[83] However, perhaps the rocking of the ship in the turbulent waters made it impossible for Jonah to throw himself into the sea without assistance from the sailors.

1:13

וַיַּחְתְּרוּ הָאֲנָשִׁים לְהָשִׁיב אֶל־הַיַּבָּשָׁה וְלֹא יָכֹלוּ כִּי הַיָּם הוֹלֵךְ וְסֹעֵר עֲלֵיהֶם:

1. וַיַּחְתְּרוּ—Parse this verb. (See chart 10.) How do you determine the *(a)* stem, and *(b)* P-G-N? Why is the prefix vowel *pathaq*, rather than *hireq*? See PVP, 178 (16.9); Ful., 191–92 (29.6).[84] The verb חָתַר means "to dig" (cf. Job 24:16; Ezek. 8:8; 12:5, 7, 12; Amos 9:2). It is used here to describe how the men were digging their oars into the water as they attempted to row to land.

_____

_____

_____

_____

2. לְהָשִׁיב—Parse this form. (See chart 9.) How do you determine the *(a)* stem, and *(b)* root? How is the infinitive construct functioning in relation to the main verb וַיַּחְתְּרוּ? One expects the causative Hiphil to have an object; we should probably understand the ship to be the implied object. See KJV ("to bring it"), NRSV ("to bring the ship back"), and NLT ("to row the boat").

_____

_____

_____

_____

---

83. See Simon, *Judges,* 13.
84. Fut., 82 (14.6); Gar., 178 (30.A); Kel., 225 (66.3); Ross, 227 (32.2.1); Seow, 214 (1).

3. וְלֹא יָכֹלוּ—In a narratival structure the wayyiqtol is used to carry along the sequence of action, but when a verb is negated in the series, a perfect is used. See PVP, 197.[85] וְלֹא יָכֹלוּ illustrates this; in this case the negated construction states a consequence contrary to the intention of the participants (cf. "they rowed to return").

4. כִּי הַיָּם . . . עֲלֵיהֶם—What type of dependent clause is כִּי הַיָּם . . . עֲלֵיהֶם? (How does כִּי relate to the preceding verb יָכֹלוּ?)

_____

_____

5. הוֹלֵךְ וְסֹעֵר—What is the temporal nuance of the participles in this clause? See EE, 67; W-OC, 623–28.[86]

_____

_____

1:14

וַיִּקְרְאוּ אֶל־יְהוָה וַיֹּאמְרוּ אָנָּה יְהוָה אַל־נָא נֹאבְדָה בְּנֶפֶשׁ הָאִישׁ הַזֶּה וְאַל־תִּתֵּן עָלֵינוּ דָּם נָקִיא
כִּי־אַתָּה יְהוָה כַּאֲשֶׁר חָפַצְתָּ עָשִׂיתָ׃

1. אָנָּה—This word is an interjection (BDB, 58; HALOT, 69–70) before the vocative יְהוָה.

2. נֹאבְדָה—Parse this verb. What does the ending (in a form with a nun prefix) indicate about the form? How do you determine the P-G-N? How is the form functioning? See EE, 107.[87] On the preceding אַל־נָא, which combines the negative אַל and the particle נָא, see BDB, 609. On the holem prefix vowel, see PVP, 178–79; Ful., 201 (30.2).[88]

_____

_____

_____

_____

3. בְּנֶפֶשׁ—How is the preposition -בְּ functioning with בְּנֶפֶשׁ? For a list of uses for this preposition see AC, 102–6; W-OC, 196–99; BDB, 88–91; HALOT, 104–5. (NASB, NRSV, and NET are particularly helpful here.)

_____

_____

---

85. Ross, 137 (18.2).
86. See also AC, 79–82; BHRG, 162; GKC, 359–60; Joüon, 409–12; WHS, 213–14. On the idiomatic use of הוֹלֵךְ here, see BDB, 233, 4.d; HALOT, 246–47.
87. See also AC, 65–66; BHRG, 151–52; GKC, 319–20; Joüon, 374–76; W-OC, 573–75.
88. Fut., 109–10 (18.4); Gar., 192 (32.C); Kel., 238 (67.4); Ross, 228 (32.3.1); Seow, 214 (1.c).

4. תְּתֵן—Parse this verb. How do you determine the root? The prefixed negative אַל indicates this is a jussive. How is it functioning here? See EE, 103–5.[89] The verb נָתַן has the nuance "place, set" here. KJV ("lay not upon us") and NASB ("do not put . . . on us") render the expression quite literally, while others attempt to bring out the meaning of the idiom: "Do not hold us accountable" (NIV), "Do not make us guilty" (NRSV), "don't hold us responsible" (NLT), "Don't hold us guilty" (NET).

_____

_____

_____

_____

5. דָּם נָקִיא—How does דָּם relate to the verb? How does נָקִיא relate to דָּם?

_____

_____

6. כִּי אַתָּה . . . עָשִׂיתָ—What type of clause is כִּי אַתָּה . . . עָשִׂיתָ? How does it relate to the preceding request?

_____

_____

7. חָפַצְתָּ עָשִׂיתָ—How are the perfect verbal forms חָפַצְתָּ and עָשִׂיתָ functioning? Are they referring to this specific event or are they generalizing, as in Psalms 115:3 and 135:6?

_____

_____

_____

1:15

וַיִּשְׂאוּ אֶת־יוֹנָה וַיְטִלֻהוּ אֶל־הַיָּם וַיַּעֲמֹד הַיָּם מִזַּעְפּוֹ׃

1. וַיִּשְׂאוּ—Parse this verb. How do you determine the P-G-N? The root is difficult to spot here because the *dagesh*, indicating *nun* assimilation, does not appear in the letter *sin*. Why not? See PVP, 186 (16.21).[90]

_____

_____

_____

---

89. See also AC, 61–63; BHRG, 152–53; GKC, 321–23; Joüon, 376–78; W-OC, 568–70.
90. Ross, 243 (34.2.1); Seow, note on p. 217.

2. וַיְטִלֻהוּ—Parse this verb. The stem is Hiphil and the root hollow.[91] In determining the P-G-N, note that the *qibbuts* is a defectively written *shureq*. How is the pronominal suffix functioning in relation to the verb? (The form הוּ- is an alternate form of the 3ms suffix. See PVP, 223 [19.2].)[92] On the irony involved here, see 1:5, note 6.

_____

_____

_____

_____

3. וַיַּעֲמֹד—Parse this verb. How do you determine the stem? (Why is the prefix vowel *pathaq*, not *hireq*?)

_____

_____

_____

_____

4. מִזַּעְפּוֹ—This form consists of the preposition מִן (with assimilated *nun*), the noun זַעַף, "raging," and a pronominal suffix. What is the antecedent of the suffix? Pronominal suffixes on nouns are genitival. What is the genitival function of the suffix here? (Note that the noun has an implied verbal idea.)

_____

_____

1:16

וַיִּירְאוּ הָאֲנָשִׁים יִרְאָה גְדוֹלָה אֶת־יְהוָה וַיִּזְבְּחוּ־זֶבַח לַיהוָה וַיִּדְּרוּ נְדָרִים׃

1. The verb "feared" takes a double accusative here—the cognate, adverbial accusative יִרְאָה (see v. 10) and the direct object accusative יְהוָה, which is preceded by the sign of the accusative. For a discussion of double accusatives see W-OC, 173–77.[93]
2. Note the use of two more cognate accusatives in the second half of the sentence (after the *athnaq*). In this case both of them (זֶבַח and נְדָרִים) function as direct objects.

---

91. For a hollow verb the Hiphil form would normally be יָטִילוּ, with the accent on the middle syllable. See PVP, 361 (31.14); Gar., 278 (48.B.6); Ross, 280 (38.7); Seow, 278–79 (1.j). However, the addition of the suffix causes an accent shift to the personal ending, leaving the *qamets* in an open propretonic syllable. The *qamets* reduces to *shewa* under these conditions.
92. Gar., 157 (26.A); Kel., 157 (47.1); Ross, 175–77 (24.5–24.6); Seow, 248 (1.c).
93. See also AC, 17–18; Joüon, 451–54 (especially §125u, note 1).

3. וַיִּדְרוּ—Parse this verb. How do you determine the *(a)* stem, *(b)* root, and *(c)* P-G-N?

_____

_____

_____

_____

Step 3: Interpretive Translation

In light of the decisions you have made in your analysis, provide an interpretive, paraphrastic translation of Jonah 1:7–16.

_____

_____

_____

_____

_____

_____

_____

_____

_____

_____

_____

_____

_____

Step 4: Structural Outline

Outline the narrative structure of Jonah 1:7–16. Carefully delineate the narrative mainline (initiated and extended by wayyiqtol forms), offline (nonstandard) constructions, and quotations. Using the categories listed in the appendix (cf. EE, 120–27), classify all wayyiqtol and disjunctive clauses that are in the narrative framework. You need not classify clauses within quotations.

_____

_____

_____

_____

_____

Jonah was sent to Nineveh to confront foreigners with their "evil" (v. 2, רָעָה). When he disobeyed, he brought "calamity" down upon himself and the foreign sailors (v. 7, רָעָה). Hebrew רָעָה is used in verse 2 in its moral sense for Nineveh's sin and in verse 7 in its nonmoral sense for the punishment that results from sin. Ironically the one sent to eliminate sin (and impending divine judgment) was now, due to his disobedience, the catalyst for an outpouring of divine judgment.

In his response to the sailors Jonah sounds quite orthodox. He claims to fear "the LORD, the God of heaven, who made the sea and the dry land" (v. 9). But if this was the case, why did he try to run away from God via the sea? His actions give his words a hollow ring.

In contrast to Jonah, who preached but did not pray, the sailors did cry out to God. Unlike Jonah, who said he feared God but acted contrary to his claim, the sailors, who had just met Jonah's God under less than ideal circumstances, responded to him with genuine fear.

Scene 4: Jonah 2:1–11: Praising God in Odd Places

Assignment

Step 1: Initial View

Read Jonah 2:1–11 in the Hebrew text, using an interlinear if you desire. Underline any words or forms you do not recognize. Try to identify verbal forms and label them as follows:

- wayyiqtol verbal forms: wc-y (the so-called *waw* consecutive with the yiqtol, usually identified as a preterite or imperfect)
- weqatal forms: wc-q (the so-called *waw* consecutive with the qatal, that is, perfect)
- simple perfects (without *waw*): pf.
- simple imperfects (without *waw*): impf.
- imperatives: impv.
- jussives: juss.
- cohortatives: coh.

- infinitives construct: inf. const.
- infinitives absolute: inf. abs.
- participles: part.

Note: Jonah's prayer (vv. 3–10) is in poetic form and differs significantly in its syntax from the rest of the book. Before attempting to answer the questions below, you should read the introduction to poetic structure and syntax in the introduction to the workbook.

Step 2: Analyzing the Text

2:1 (= 1:17 in English)

וַיְמַן יְהוָה דָּג גָּדוֹל לִבְלֹעַ אֶת־יוֹנָה וַיְהִי יוֹנָה בִּמְעֵי הַדָּג שְׁלֹשָׁה יָמִים וּשְׁלֹשָׁה לֵילוֹת:

1. וַיְמַן—Parse this verb. How do you determine the stem? Note that the third root letter *he* has dropped from the form (apocope). In the Piel stem the verb means "send, appoint" (BDB, 584; *HALOT*, 599).

_____

_____

2. לִבְלֹעַ—Parse this form. How is the form functioning in relation to the main verb וַיְמַן?

_____

_____

3. בִּמְעֵי הַדָּג—How can you tell that מְעֵי is construct? See PVP, 103 (10.5); Ful., 62–63 (11.4).[94] Following the construct, הַדָּג is a genitive, indicating here the larger entity (the fish) of which the preceding word is part.

_____

_____

4. שְׁלֹשָׁה יָמִים וּשְׁלֹשָׁה לֵילוֹת—In the phrase שְׁלֹשָׁה יָמִים, "three days," the cardinal number precedes the plural noun. שְׁלֹשָׁה is in the absolute form and functions as a temporal adverbial accusative in relation to the verb וַיְהִי. יָמִים is in apposition to the number, specifying what is being numbered (see GKC, 432, §134b).[95] As is usual with numbers three through ten, the number appears in a singular form and does not agree in gender with the object measured (see PVP, 112).[96] The same is true of the accompanying phrase שְׁלֹשָׁה לֵילוֹת, "three nights." Despite its apparent feminine ending, לַיְלָה (plural לֵילוֹת) is understood as masculine (see GKC, 250, §90f.).[97]

---

94. Fut., 75 (13.1); Gar., 97 (17.E.2); Kel., 59 (26.4); Ross, 100–101 (12.3); Seow, 118 (2.c).
95. See also AC, 23; Joüon, 479, §131g.
96. Fut., 188–89 (30.1); Gar., 152 (25.D); Kel., 97 (35.1); Ross, 180–81 (25.1); Seow, 269 (6.a.i).
97. See also Joüon, 280, §93g.

2:2 (= 2:1 in English)

וַיִּתְפַּלֵּל יוֹנָה אֶל־יְהוָה אֱלֹהָיו מִמְּעֵי הַדָּגָה:

1. וַיִּתְפַּלֵּל—Parse this verb. How do you determine the stem? This verb occurs in the Piel stem with the meaning "mediate, judge." In the Hithpael stem it is reflexive ("mediate on one's own behalf"), though the usual English translation ("pray") does not reflect this.[98]

   _____

   _____

2. הַדָּגָה—Note the ending on הַדָּגָה and contrast the form with הַדָּג in verse 1. Apart from this chapter (see v. 11 as well), the masculine singular form occurs only in Nehemiah 13:16, where it is collective. The feminine singular form is collective everywhere else (fourteen occurrences in twelve other passages) but here. The significance of the variation is not apparent.

The poem in verses 3–10 is a thanksgiving song in which Jonah recalls his experience. Verses 3–8 form a narrative of sorts, but it does not proceed in an "a to z" sequential manner. Verse 3a gives a summary of what happened: "I cried out . . . and he answered me." The parallel couplet in verse 3b essentially repeats this: "I called out . . . you heard." Verses 4–7 give a more detailed account of the event, describing what precipitated the crisis and how exactly God answered his prayer. God "threw" Jonah into the sea and he was overwhelmed by its waves (v. 4). Jonah records his thoughts at the time (v. 5) and then describes again how the water overpowered him (v. 6). He sank beneath the water and was trapped (v. 7a). But then God pulled him up to safety (v. 7b). Verse 8 returns to the time of crisis and reiterates verse 3. When Jonah was almost dead, he remembered the Lord (i.e., he prayed, see v. 3) and his prayer was heard (v. 8).

2:3 (= 2:2 in English)

וַיֹּאמֶר
קָרָאתִי מִצָּרָה לִי אֶל־יְהוָה וַיַּעֲנֵנִי
מִבֶּטֶן שְׁאוֹל שִׁוַּעְתִּי שָׁמַעְתָּ קוֹלִי:

1. קָרָאתִי—Parse this verb. How do you determine the P-G-N? How is the perfect functioning here? (Notice the wayyiqtol verbal form later in v. 3a.)

   _____

   _____

   _____

---

98. See W-OC, 428. According to Joüon (159, §53g), the stem has the nuance "to ask for (justice)" with this verb.

2. מִצָּרָה לִי—This phrase means literally, "from (the) distress to me." One might expect the form to be מִצָּרָתִי (cf. the suffixed form of the noun in Pss. 77:3; 86:7; 142:3 and the use of מִן with a suffixed form [3ms] of the noun in Isa. 46:7). This alternate form of indicating possession occurs only here and in Psalm 120:1 (note בַּצָּרָתָה לִי, "in distress to me" = "in my distress"). Elsewhere the preposition מִן, when used with the verb קָרָא, "call, summon," indicates the location from which the call is issued (2 Sam. 20:16; Isa. 21:11) or the place from which one is summoned (Judg. 16:25; Ps. 50:1; Isa. 46:11; 49:1). Here the preposition is followed by an abstract noun ("distress"), making a causal nuance possible. Note KJV ("I cried by reason of mine affliction"). However, the preposition may simply indicate the condition or situation from which his cry originated. Note NASB ("I called out of my distress"; cf. NRSV) and NET ("I called out . . . from my distress"). In this case the causal connection is implicit, not formal.

3. וַיַּעֲנֵנִי—Parse this verb. Since the prefix vowel is "a" the form could be Qal or Hiphil, but the sense requires the Qal ("he answered me") rather than a causative nuance. For help identifying the suffix, see PVP, 222–29 (19.1–19.7); Ful., 177–79 (28.2). The wayyiqtol is sequential to the preceding verb, "I cried out." When used in the context of prayer, the verb עָנָה, "to answer," has the connotation "respond favorably" (see BDB, 772).

4. מִבֶּטֶן—The noun בֶּטֶן, "belly," is in construct with the following genitive Sheol and involves a personification of death. Death is portrayed in both the Hebrew Bible (Prov. 1:12; Isa. 5:14; Hab. 2:5) and West Semitic myths as swallowing its victims. In the myths we read of Death having "a lip to the earth, a lip to the heavens . . . and a tongue to the stars."[99] Deified Death describes his own appetite as follows: "But my appetite is the appetite of lions in the waste. . . . If it is in very truth my desire to consume 'clay' [a reference to his human victims], then in truth by the handfuls I must eat it, whether my seven portions [indicating fullness and completeness] are already in the bowl or whether Nahar [the god of the river responsible for ferrying victims from the land of the living to the land of the dead] has to mix the cup."[100]

5. שְׁאוֹל—This is the name given to the dwelling place of the dead, viewed in ancient Israelite cosmology as being a subterranean region. Some translations treat it as a proper name (cf. NASB, NRSV, NET), while others are more interpretive. NIV has "grave," while NLT has "the world of the dead." KJV's "hell" is archaic and misleading, for the Hebrew term does not correspond to the concept of hell as articulated in Christian theology.

6. שִׁוַּעְתִּי—Parse this verb. How do you determine the (a) stem, and (b) P-G-N? How is the perfect functioning? In the synonymous poetic parallelism, this verb corresponds to קָרָאתִי. This poetic word pair is also used in Psalm 18:7 (Eng. v. 6) and Isaiah 58:9. The verb שָׁוַע occurs exclusively in the Piel stem with the meaning "cry for help." The stem function is not clear.

---

99. J. C. L. Gibson, *Canaanite Myths and Legends,* 2nd ed. (Edinburgh: T & T Clark, 1978), 69.
100. Ibid., 68–69.

7. שְׁמַעְתָּ—Parse this verb. How do you determine the P-G-N? The shift to direct address gives the prayer a more personal touch. In the poetic parallelism שְׁמַעְתָּ corresponds to וַיַּעֲנֵנִי. In the context of prayer the verb שָׁמַע, "hear," has the connotation "accept, respond favorably."

_____

_____

_____

2:4 (= 2:3 in English)

וַתַּשְׁלִיכֵנִי מְצוּלָה בִּלְבַב יַמִּים וְנָהָר יְסֹבְבֵנִי
כָּל־מִשְׁבָּרֶיךָ וְגַלֶּיךָ עָלַי עָבָרוּ׃

1. וַתַּשְׁלִיכֵנִי—Parse this verb. How do you determine the (a) stem, and (b) P-G-N? (Note that the direct address continues.) How is the pronominal suffix functioning in relation to the verb? The verb שָׁלַךְ occurs exclusively in the Hiphil/Hophal with the meaning "throw." The stem function is not clear.

_____

_____

_____

_____

Jonah claims that God threw him into the sea, but that is not exactly correct. The sailors actually threw Jonah into the sea, at the prophet's request. Based on God's subsequent deliverance and recommissioning of Jonah, God wanted the prophet to turn around and go to Nineveh. But in a last ditch attempt to dodge his commission, stubborn Jonah opted for assisted suicide and told the sailors to throw him into the sea. God certainly pursued Jonah, but he was not trying to kill him. However, from Jonah's warped perspective, God's refusal to let him run away was interpreted as an attack on his life.

2. מְצוּלָה—This noun is an adverbial accusative. (Note that one must supply a preposition in translation.) How is the accusative functioning here? For categories of the accusative see EE, 64–65; and W-OC, 162–77 (especially 169–73).[101]

_____

_____

3. בִּלְבַב יַמִּים—This phrase, "into the heart of the seas," is appositional to the preceding adverbial accusative מְצוּלָה. "Heart" is used here to indicate the midst (cf. KJV) or middle (cf. NET) of the sea, the point being that he was far from land and safety. The plural form "seas" is a so-called plural of extension, indicating the surface of the sea as something vast (cf. English "waters," used of vast quantities of water, as in "the waters of the Atlantic"). See W-OC, 120, as well as GKC, 397, §124b.

---

101. See also AC, 18–21; Joüon, 440–63; WHS, 50–60.

4. וְנָהָר—The noun נָהָר usually refers to a river or stream, but here the current of the sea is in view (cf. Ps. 24:2; Isa. 44:27). See NIV, "the currents"; NASB, "the current"; and NET, "the ocean-current." In West Semitic myth Nahar is a name or title for Yam, the god of the sea. However, the mythological undertones would be stronger if the singular יָם, rather than the plural form, had been used in the prior line. It is also noteworthy that the following line views the waves of the sea as belonging to the Lord.

5. יְסֹבְבֵנִי—This verb looks like an imperfect, but in this context where Jonah is reporting what happened, the form is better understood as a preterite, functioning as a definite past. Note the perfects and wayyiqtols in the immediate context and read EE, 95–96.[102] See verse 6 as well, where the prefixed form is parallel to a perfect. The stem is Poel, which is functionally equivalent to the Piel (see GKC, 178, §67l).[103] The verb is used in the Qal with the meaning "surround." The Poel may be functioning in a frequentative sense, picturing the water swirling around him like a whirlpool.[104]

6. מִשְׁבָּרֶיךָ וְגַלֶּיךָ—Jonah views the "breakers" and "waves" as being sent by the Lord (note the 2ms suffix on מִשְׁבָּרֶיךָ and גַלֶּיךָ). מִשְׁבָּר, derived from the root שָׁבַר, "break," apparently pictures the waves as surging and breaking into foam (cf. our English term "breaker"). See NASB.

7. עָלַי—This form consists of what elements?

_____

_____

8. עָבְרוּ—Parse this verb. How do you determine the P-G-N? What is the subject?

_____

_____

_____

2:5 (= 2:4 in English)

וַאֲנִי אָמַרְתִּי נִגְרַשְׁתִּי מִנֶּגֶד עֵינֶיךָ
אַךְ אוֹסִיף לְהַבִּיט אֶל־הֵיכַל קָדְשֶׁךָ:

1. וַאֲנִי—The placement of the pronoun אֲנִי first in the sentence signals a shift in focus. The preceding statements focused on God's activity; now Jonah relates what he was thinking.

2. אָמַרְתִּי—When the first person perfect אָמַרְתִּי follows the first person pronoun, it can mean "say to oneself" or "think" (cf. NET). See Ruth 4:4; Isaiah 49:4; Jeremiah 5:4; 10:19.

3. נִגְרַשְׁתִּי—Parse this verb. How do you determine the (a) stem, and (b) P-G-N? How is the stem functioning (see EE, 79).[105] How is the perfect functioning here?

_____

_____

_____

---

102. See also AC, 60; Joüon, 368–69, §113h; WHS, 176–77.
103. See also Joüon, 168, §59a.
104. On the frequentative function of the Piel stem see W-OC, 414–16, as well as Joüon, 155.
105. See also AC, 38–41; BHRG, 78; GKC, 137–38; Joüon, 150–51; WHS, 135–39; W-OC, 381–91.

Text critical note: The MT reads אַךְ, "yet, surely," at the beginning of the line. In this case the statement expresses Jonah's confidence that he will again visit God's temple (see v. 10), despite his difficult circumstances. However, an expression of confidence seems premature at this point in the song. For this reason some prefer to follow the lead of Theodotian's Greek recension and read אֵיךְ, "how?" In this case the statement is a rhetorical question expressing Jonah's despair prior to his being swallowed by the fish: "How will I again look upon your holy temple?" See NRSV, NLT, and NET (especially the text critical note).

4. אוֹסִיף—Parse this verb. How do you determine the stem? The verb יָסַף is collocated with the following infinitive to indicate repetition of action. See BDB, 415; *HALOT,* 418. In translation יָסַף may be treated as an adverb and the following infinitive as the main verb (cf. NIV, "look again").

5. לְהַבִּיט—Parse this form. How do you determine the *(a)* stem, and *(b)* root? With one exception, this verb is used exclusively in the Hiphil stem with the meaning "look, gaze." The stem function is not certain.

6. קָדְשֶׁךָ—After the construct הֵיכַל, "temple of," the noun קֹדֶשׁ, "holiness" is genitival. The form קָדְשֶׁךָ has a 2ms suffix; short *o* (a *qamets hatuph* derived from an original short *u*) appears under the *qoph*. (See GKC, 89, §27d.) How is the genitive functioning here? "Holy temple" may be a metonymy here for the Lord himself (cf. v. 8).

2:6 (= 2:5 in English)

אֲפָפוּנִי מַיִם עַד־נֶפֶשׁ תְּהוֹם יְסֹבְבֵנִי
סוּף חָבוּשׁ לְרֹאשִׁי:

1. אֲפָפוּנִי—Parse this verb. How do you determine the P-G-N? What is the subject? How is the pronominal suffix functioning in relation to the verb? The rare verb אָפַף means "encompass" (see BDB, 67; *HALOT,*

79). It corresponds in the parallelism to the more common סָבַב.

_____

_____

_____

_____

2. נֶפֶשׁ—This word is typically understood as referring to the soul (see KJV) or life (cf. NASB, "point of death"). But here, where the waters are described as encircling Jonah, it probably refers to the throat or neck. See *HALOT*, 712, as well as NET.

3. תְּהוֹם—This term is used of the primeval ocean in Genesis 1:2, but here it refers to the waters of the Mediterranean Sea (cf. Ezek. 26:19). On the accompanying verb יְסֹבְבֵנִי see 2:4, note 5.

4. חָבוּשׁ—Parse this form. How can you tell from the form that this is a passive participle? How is the participle functioning here? For options see PVP, 265–66 (22.9); Ful., 116–17 (19.3).[106] How is סוּף, "seaweed," functioning in relation to the participle?

_____

_____

_____

_____

5. לְרֹאשִׁי—This form consists of what elements?

_____

_____

2:7 (= 2:6 in English)

לְקִצְבֵי הָרִים יָרַדְתִּי הָאָרֶץ בְּרִחֶיהָ בַעֲדִי לְעוֹלָם

וַתַּעַל מִשַּׁחַת חַיַּי יְהוָה אֱלֹהָי:

> According to the traditional verse division, the first two words of verse 7 ("to the roots of the mountains") go with the following verb ("I went down"). In the biblical text, note the disjunctive accent above יָרַדְתִּי. In this case הָאָרֶץ, "the earth," begins the next line. However, the *BHS* editor arranges the lines differently. He suggests that לְקִצְבֵי הָרִים, "to the roots of the mountains," belongs with what precedes (v. 6b) and that יָרַדְתִּי goes with הָאָרֶץ. In this case the latter

---

106. Fut., 237 (38.2); Gar., 63–64 (11.B); Kel., 198–202 (60); Ross, 157–58 (21.3); Seow, 85 (5.c).

would be an adverbial accusative of direction. Following this arrangement verses 6b–7a would read as follows: "Seaweed was wrapped around my head at the roots of the mountains; I went down to the earth; its bars were around me forever." (See NRSV.) If one follows the poetic arrangement suggested by the traditional Hebrew text, הָאָרֶץ is a nominative absolute resumed by the third feminine singular suffix on the following noun (see EE, 61). In this case the line would read literally, "As for the earth—its bars were around me forever." Usage elsewhere is not determinative. יָרַד is collocated with -לְ, used in a directive sense (as proposed by *BHS*), in Judges 1:34; 5:11; 2 Samuel 11:8; Song of Songs 6:2; Ezekiel 26:11 (with preposition first, as in Jonah 2:7); Micah 1:12, but it can also be construed with an adverbial accusative of direction (as assumed in the traditional punctuation) (see Josh. 15:10; 18:16–17; 24:4; Prov. 18:8; Jer. 18:2; Ezek. 32:27).

1. הָאָרֶץ—This noun, normally meaning "the earth," refers here to the subterranean regions of the earth, where the mountains are rooted. More specifically the underworld land of the dead is in view. See *HALOT*, 91 (no. 5), as well as NLT and NET. The reference to the earth's "bars" reflects the ancient concept of the underworld as a place from which one cannot escape (see 2 Sam. 12:23). In a Mesopotamian text describing Ishtar's descent into this "land of no return," the goddess passes through seven gates, all of which would presumably be secured with bars. See James Pritchard, *Ancient Near Eastern Texts Relating to the Old Testament* (Princeton: Princeton University, 1969), 106–9. If this imagery forms the background for the description in verse 7, then בַעֲדִי should be translated "behind me" (*HALOT*, 141), not "about me" (KJV) or "around me" (NASB).

2. בְּרִחֶיהָ—This form consists of what elements? How can you tell the noun is plural?

3. וַתַּעַל—Parse this verb. How do you determine the P-G-N? The form can be either Qal or Hiphil, but the context requires the causative here ("you brought up"), rather than the Qal ("you went up"). Note the object חַיַּי, "my life."

4. מִשַּׁחַת—A שַׁחַת is a pit dug into the ground, but here it is used metaphorically of the grave or netherworld. See *HALOT*, 1473. Even though a definite region is in view, notice that the form is indefinite. (How would the form מִשַּׁחַת differ if it were definite?) Omission of the article is typical of Hebrew poetry. Another option is that the term is used here as a title or name. Note NRSV and NET, which translate "Pit." KJV's "corruption" assumes a derivation from שָׁחַת, "be ruined," but the term is probably a primary noun

(*HALOT*, 1472) or a derivative from שׁוּחַ, "sink down" (BDB, 1001).

_____

_____

5. יְהוָה אֱלֹהָי—How does יְהוָה אֱלֹהָי function in relation to what precedes? (Recall the P-G-N of the verb at the beginning of the line.)

_____

_____

2:8 (= 2:7 in English)

בְּהִתְעַטֵּף עָלַי נַפְשִׁי אֶת־יְהוָה זָכָרְתִּי
וַתָּבוֹא אֵלֶיךָ תְּפִלָּתִי אֶל־הֵיכַל קָדְשֶׁךָ׃

1. בְּהִתְעַטֵּף—Parse this form. How do you determine the stem? How is the preposition -בְּ functioning here? See PVP, 241–47 (20.10–20.13).[107] When used in the Hithpael stem, the verb עָטַף has the basic sense "feel weak" (*HALOT*, 815). It is used of fainting from starvation (Ps. 107:5; Lam. 2:12), of loss of strength due to discouragement and depression (Pss. 77:4; 142:4 [Eng. v. 3]), and of fatigue resulting from being hunted down by enemies (Ps. 143:4). The Qal meaning is "be weak"; the Hithpael probably has a frequentative or iterative function.[108]

_____

_____

_____

2. נַפְשִׁי—This term probably refers here to Jonah's "life" (for this meaning of the term, see *HALOT*, 713, no. 7, though our text is not listed).

3. זָכָרְתִּי—The verb זָכַר here carries the idea "to remember and turn to (in prayer)." Note "my prayer" in the second half of the verse. The accusative ("the LORD") is placed before the verb for emphasis.

4. וַתָּבוֹא—Parse this verb. How do you determine the *(a)* stem, *(b)* root, and *(c)* P-G-N?

_____

_____

_____

5. תְּפִלָּתִי—This form is comprised of the feminine noun תְּפִלָּה, "prayer," and a 1cs pronominal suffix. On the *taw* before the suffix, see PVP, 85 (9.7); Ful., 77–78 (13.2).[109] The *lamed* has a *dagesh forte* because

_____

107. Fut., 122 (20.9); Gar., 212 (36.B.2); Kel., 182 (56.2); Ross, 163 (22.4); Seow, 259 (3.e).
108. W-OC, 428.
109. Fut., 96 (16.3); Gar., 89 (16.C); Kel., 72 (28.1); Ross, 114 (14.3); Seow, 133 (1.b).

the noun is derived from the geminate verb פָּלַל, "pray." The nominal prefix *taw* often indicates a verbal idea within the noun. See W-OC, 90.[110] How is the noun functioning in relation to the preceding verb וַתָּבוֹא (a 3fs form; note the prefixed *taw*)?

_____

_____

2:9 (= 2:8 in English)

מְשַׁמְּרִים הַבְלֵי־שָׁוְא חַסְדָּם יַעֲזֹבוּ׃

1. מְשַׁמְּרִים—Parse this form. What does the prefixed *mem* indicate about the form? How do you determine the stem? How is the participle functioning here? (See AC, 77–83; EE, 66–67.) The stem seems to indicate repetitive action here, "watch intently." This in turn may be a metonymy for allegiance (cf. NIV, "cling to") or worship (cf. NRSV, NLT, NET).

_____

_____

_____

_____

2. הַבְלֵי—This is a construct plural form of הֶבֶל, "breath, vanity." (How can you tell the form is construct?) The noun refers in its most basic sense to that which lacks substance. In this case it probably refers to idols (cf. NIV, NASB, NRSV, NET) or false gods (NLT).

_____

_____

3. שָׁוְא—What case is this noun? How do you know this? (Note the preceding form הַבְלֵי.) How is the case functioning here? See EE, 62–64, as well as W-OC, 267.[111]

_____

_____

_____

4. חַסְדָּם—This form is comprised of the noun חֶסֶד, "loyalty, allegiance, devotion, faithfulness," functioning here as the object of the verb "abandon," and a 3mp pronominal suffix. The suffix is genitival. It is not certain if it is subjective (see NRSV, "their true loyalty"; NASB, "their faithfulness") or objective (see NIV, "the grace that could be theirs"; NET, "the mercy that could be theirs"; NLT, "all God's mercies"). In the

---

110. See also Joüon, 260, §88Lo.
111. See also AC, 8–13; BHRG, 197–200; GKC, 416–19; Joüon, 465–73, 525, §141m; WHS, 36–49.

only other passages where the verb עָזַב is collocated with a suffixed form of חֶסֶד as its object, the suffix is subjective. See Genesis 24:27 and Ruth 2:20. For a helpful discussion of the issue, see the NET note.

5. יַעֲזֹבוּ—Parse this verb. How do you determine the stem? (Why does the verb have a *pathaq* prefix vowel?) How do you determine the P-G-N? How is the imperfect functioning here?

2:10 (= 2:9 in English)

וַאֲנִי בְּקוֹל תּוֹדָה אֶזְבְּחָה־לָּךְ
אֲשֶׁר נָדַרְתִּי אֲשַׁלֵּמָה יְשׁוּעָתָה לַיהוָה׃

1. אֲנִי—The initial וַאֲנִי marks a shift in focus from the idolaters (v. 9) to Jonah and highlights the contrast Jonah seeks to emphasize.
2. בְּקוֹל תּוֹדָה—The preposition -בְּ in the phrase בְּקוֹל תּוֹדָה indicates accompaniment, "along with," or manner, "with." How is the genitive תּוֹדָה functioning here?

3. אֶזְבְּחָה—Parse this verb. How do you determine the P-G-N? What does the ◌ָה- indicate about the form (note the prefixed *aleph*)? How is the form functioning? See EE, 107.[112]

4. אֲשֶׁר נָדַרְתִּי—How is the relative pronoun אֲשֶׁר functioning in relation to נָדַרְתִּי? See W-OC, 333. How does the relative clause function in relation to the following אֲשַׁלֵּמָה. See W-OC, 644–46.[113]

---

112. See also AC, 65–66; BHRG, 151–52; GKC, 319–20; Joüon, 374–76; W-OC, 573–75.
113. See also Joüon, 597–98.

5. אֲשַׁלֵּמָה—Parse this verb. How do you determine the stem? How is the stem functioning? (See EE, 80–81.)[114] How is the cohortative functioning? (See EE, 107.)[115]

_____

_____

_____

_____

6. יְשׁוּעָתָה לַיהוָה—This statement means "deliverance (belongs) to Yahweh," in the sense that it originates with him.

2:11 (= 2:10 in English)

וַיֹּאמֶר יְהוָה לַדָּג וַיָּקֵא אֶת־יוֹנָה אֶל־הַיַּבָּשָׁה׃

1. וַיָּקֵא—Parse this verb. Theoretically, what are the two options for the (a) stem,[116] and (b) root?

_____

_____

_____

Step 3: Interpretive Translation

In light of the decisions you have made in your analysis, provide an interpretive, paraphrastic translation of Jonah 2:1–11.

_____

_____

_____

_____

_____

_____

_____

_____

_____

_____

114. See also Joüon, 154–56; W-OC, 400–416.
115. See also BHRG, 151–52; GKC, 319–20; Joüon, 374–76; W-OC, 573–75.
116. Joüon (164, §55f; 223, §81c) suggests this form is a pseudo-Hiphil.

Step 4: Structural Outline

Outline the narrative structure of Jonah 2:1–11. Carefully delineate the narrative mainline (initiated and extended by wayyiqtol forms), offline (nonstandard) constructions, and quotations. Using the categories listed in the appendix (cf. EE, 120–27), classify all wayyiqtol and disjunctive clauses that are in the narrative framework. You need not classify clauses within quotations. Treat verses 3–10 as one lengthy quotation.

The Lord foiled Jonah's attempt to avoid his prophetic commission. He prepared a great fish, which swallowed Jonah and carried him in its belly for three days and three nights (1:17) before disgorging him on to dry land (2:10). While in the fish Jonah prayed to the Lord (2:1). Oddly enough the prayer takes the form of a thanksgiving song, rather than a confession of sin. No mention is made of his disobedience; Jonah celebrated his deliverance, boasted of his superiority to foreigners, and made vows to the Lord. Jonah presumed he had been saved and, despite his apparent preference for death over obedience, he was overjoyed to be alive. Having come so close to death, he was thankful for God's mercy. One might think this near-death experience would instill in him some sympathy for the Ninevites and a greater appreciation for his prophetic mission. However, the disdain he showed for foreigners in his prayer foreshadows the attitude he displays in the final scene.

Act 2

Jonah 3–4

Scene 1: Jonah 3:1–4: On to Nineveh!

Assignment

Step 1: Initial View

Read Jonah 3:1–4 in the Hebrew text, using an interlinear if you desire. Underline any words or forms you do not recognize. Try to identify verbal forms and label them as follows:

- wayyiqtol verbal forms: wc-y (the so-called *waw* consecutive with the yiqtol, usually identified as a preterite or imperfect)
- weqatal forms: wc-q (the so-called *waw* consecutive with the qatal, that is, perfect)
- simple perfects (without *waw*): pf.
- simple imperfects (without *waw*): impf.
- imperatives: impv.
- jussives: juss.
- cohortatives: coh.
- infinitives construct: inf. const.
- infinitives absolute: inf. abs.
- participles: part.

Step 2: Analyzing the Text

3:1–2

וַיְהִי דְבַר־יְהוָה אֶל־יוֹנָה שֵׁנִית לֵאמֹר׃

קוּם לֵךְ אֶל־נִינְוֵה הָעִיר הַגְּדוֹלָה וּקְרָא אֵלֶיהָ אֶת־הַקְּרִיאָה אֲשֶׁר אָנֹכִי דֹּבֵר אֵלֶיךָ׃

1. שֵׁנִית—The ordinal number is used adverbially, "a second time."
2. The wording of the first part of this commission is similar to that of the earlier one (cf. v. 2a with 1:2), but the latter part differs. Instead of עָלֶיהָ, "against her," 3:2b has אֵלֶיהָ, "to her," followed by a cognate accusative (אֶת־הַקְּרִיאָה) of the verb קָרָא. The construction may be translated: "Proclaim to it (lit., her) the message." The verb קָרָא is collocated with the preposition אֶל and a following אֵת + accusative only here and in Jeremiah 36:18.
3. דֹּבֵר—What is the temporal function of the participle דֹּבֵר? See EE, 67 and W-OC, 623–28.[1] Discuss

---

1. See also AC, 79–81; BHRG, 162; GKC, 359–60; Joüon, 409–12; WHS, 213–14.

three options. NASB ("I am going to tell you") reflects one option, and NLT ("I have given you") a second. What would the third be?

_____

_____

_____

_____

3:3

וַיָּקָם יוֹנָה וַיֵּלֶךְ אֶל־נִינְוֵה כִּדְבַר יְהוָה וְנִינְוֵה הָיְתָה עִיר־גְּדוֹלָה לֵאלֹהִים מַהֲלַךְ שְׁלֹשֶׁת יָמִים:

1. In contrast to the book's first scene, Jonah carries out his commission. The wayyiqtol forms וַיֵּלֶךְ . . . וַיָּקָם, "and (Jonah) arose and went," mirror the imperatives in verse 2a. The phrase כִּדְבַר יְהוָה, "according to the word of Yahweh," reinforces the point (cf. 1 Kings 17:5).

2. וְנִינְוֵה—What type of clause does וְנִינְוֵה introduce? How can you tell this from the structure of the clause? How is the clause functioning? (See EE, 124–27.)

_____

_____

_____

3. הָיְתָה—Parse this verb. How do you determine the (a) stem, (b) root, and (c) P-G-N? On the ending תָה-, see PVP, 154 (14.7); Ful., 265 (37.4).[2]

_____

_____

_____

4. לֵאלֹהִים—The significance of לֵאלֹהִים, "to God," is not entirely clear. It could indicate that Nineveh belonged to God, but the divine name may be used here in an idiomatic sense to indicate the superlative degree ("a very great city"), perhaps conveying the notion "in God's estimation." See W-OC, 268.[3] Note the translations: "exceeding great city" (KJV; cf. NASB), "very important city" (NIV), "exceedingly large city" (NRSV), "enormous city" (NET).

5. מַהֲלַךְ—This noun is in apposition to "city." The construction מַהֲלַךְ שְׁלֹשֶׁת יָמִים, "a journey of three days," describes the size or importance of Nineveh. Unless hyperbole is being utilized, it is unlikely that it describes how long it took to walk across the city (cf. NRSV), for archaeology has revealed that Nineveh was not nearly this large. It is more likely that the expression envisions how long it would take one to travel throughout the city on a mission such as Jonah's, proclaiming God's message to the city's population (cf. NIV, NLT, NET, as well as Simon, *Jonah*, 28).

---

2. Fut., 89–90 (15.6); Gar., 165 (27.E); Kel., 288 (72.3); Ross, 260 (36.2); Seow, 161 (3.a).
3. See also WHS, 81.

3:4

וַיָּחֶל יוֹנָה לָבוֹא בָעִיר מַהֲלַךְ יוֹם אֶחָד וַיִּקְרָא וַיֹּאמַר עוֹד אַרְבָּעִים יוֹם וְנִינְוֵה נֶהְפָּכֶת׃

1. וַיָּחֶל—This verb is a Hiphil (see chart 10) wayyiqtol 3ms from the geminate verb חָלַל, which in the Hiphil means "begin." Like hollow verbs, geminates have a *qamets* prefix vowel in the Hiphil imperfect/wayyiqtol. In the imperfect the theme vowels differ; cf. יָקִים (from קוּם) as opposed to יָסֵב (from סָבַב). In the wayyiqtol the patterns overlap; cf. קוּם < וַיָּקֶם and סָבַב < וַיָּסֶב. In this context the geminate verb fits semantically.

2. לָבוֹא—Parse this form. In this case, the infinitive with -לְ is a verbal complement of the main verb וַיָּחֶל ("and he began to enter"). See W-OC, 606.[4]

_____

3. מַהֲלַךְ—This noun is an adverbial accusative in relation to the preceding infinitive. It informs us how far Jonah went into the city before proclaiming his message.

4. עוֹד אַרְבָּעִים יוֹם—The construction probably means "at the end of forty days," or "in forty more days." Elsewhere when עוֹד precedes a numeral followed by "day(s)," it has the idea "more, until/at the end of" (see Gen. 8:10, 12; 1 Kings 12:5 = 2 Chron. 10:5). On the use of the numeral, see W-OC, 280, and PVP, 113–14 (11.3–11.4).[5] The number "forty" is formed by pluralizing four (אַרְבַּע). When used as a measure of days, the numeral is followed by the singular form יוֹם.

5. נֶהְפָּכֶת—Parse this form. (See chart 7.) How do you determine the *(a)* gender, *(b)* number, and *(c)* stem? How is the stem functioning here? See EE, 79; BDB, 245–46; *HALOT,* 253.[6] How is the participle functioning? See EE, 67, and W-OC, 623–28.[7] The verb is used here of divine judgment.

_____

Step 3: Interpretive Translation

In light of the decisions you have made in your analysis, provide an interpretive, paraphrastic translation of Jonah 3:1–4.

_____

4. See also BHRG, 154; Joüon, 437; WHS, 193.
5. Fut., 189 (30.3); Gar., 153 (25.E); Kel., 99 (35.3); Ross, 183 (25.4); Seow, 270 (6.a.3).
6. See also BHRG, 78; GKC, 137–38; Joüon, 150–51; WHS, 135–39; W-OC, 381–91.
7. See also BHRG, 162; GKC, 359–60; Joüon, 409–12; WHS, 213–14.

_____

_____

_____

_____

_____

Step 4: Structural Outline

Outline the narrative structure of Jonah 3:1–4. Carefully delineate the narrative mainline (initiated and extended by wayyiqtol forms), offline (nonstandard) constructions, and quotations. Using the categories listed in the appendix (cf. EE, 120–27), classify all wayyiqtol and disjunctive clauses that are in the narrative framework. You need not classify clauses within quotations.

_____

_____

_____

_____

_____

_____

_____

_____

_____

_____

The second time around Jonah obeyed the Lord's command. Jonah's message was brief and to the point—in forty more days Nineveh would be destroyed by divine judgment (v. 4). Though the message sounds unconditional, the reference to "forty days" hints there may be a window of opportunity for Nineveh to repent and be spared.

Scene 2: Jonah 3:5–10: Mass Repentance!

Assignment

Step 1: Initial View

Read Jonah 3:5–10 in the Hebrew text, using an interlinear if you desire. Underline any words or forms you do not recognize. Try to identify verbal forms and label them as follows:

- wayyiqtol verbal forms: wc-y (the so-called *waw* consecutive with the yiqtol, usually identified as a preterite or imperfect)
- weqatal forms: wc-q (the so-called *waw* consecutive with the qatal, that is, perfect)
- simple perfects (without *waw*): pf.
- simple imperfects (without *waw*): impf.
- imperatives: impv.
- jussives: juss.
- cohortatives: coh.
- infinitives construct: inf. const.
- infinitives absolute: inf. abs.
- participles: part.

Step 2: Analyzing the Text

3:5

וַיַּאֲמִינוּ אַנְשֵׁי נִינְוֵה בֵּאלֹהִים וַיִּקְרְאוּ־צוֹם וַיִּלְבְּשׁוּ שַׂקִּים מִגְּדוֹלָם וְעַד־קְטַנָּם:

1. וַיַּאֲמִינוּ—Parse this verb. How do you determine the *(a)* stem, and *(b)* P-G-N? With this verb the Hiphil stem may have a delocutive (or declarative) sense, which is an extension of the causative use.[8] The subject esteems or declares the object to be in a state. In this case the Ninevites esteemed God to be reliable. The verb is collocated with בֵּאלֹהִים only here and in Psalm 78:22, where it is negated and used of the Israelites' refusal to trust in God's ability to provide for their needs. In Jonah 3:5 the expression refers to the Ninevites' belief in the trustworthiness of God's word, in this case, his threat to destroy the city (cf. Gen. 15:6, where the verb is collocated with בַּיהוָה and refers to Abraham's belief in the trustworthiness of the Lord's promise).

___

2. שַׂקִּים —The plural שַׂקִּים, "sackcloth," is used here because a group, comprised of many people, is involved (note the preceding plural verb). Compare 2 Kings 19:1, which tells how Hezekiah put on

---

8. On this function of the Hiphil stem see Joüon, 163; W-OC, 438–39.

sackcloth (singular) with 2 Kings 19:2, where the king's servants and the priests are described as clothed in sackcloth (plural).

3. מִגְּדוֹלָם וְעַד־קְטַנָּם—This construction, meaning "from the greatest of them even to the least of them," designates all without exception. The precise form used here (with suffixes) does not appear elsewhere, though see Jeremiah 6:13 and 31:34, where the suffixed adjectives are in reverse order. On the superlative use of the adjectives, see W-OC, 270.[9]

3:6

וַיִּגַּע הַדָּבָר אֶל־מֶלֶךְ נִינְוֵה וַיָּקָם מִכִּסְאוֹ וַיַּעֲבֵר אַדַּרְתּוֹ מֵעָלָיו וַיְכַס שַׂק וַיֵּשֶׁב עַל־הָאֵפֶר:

1. וַיִּגַּע—Parse this verb. How do you determine the *(a)* root, and *(b)* stem? (Why is the form not a Niphal, despite its *i + dagesh + a* pattern?)

_____

_____

_____

_____

2. מִכִּסְאוֹ—This form consists of what elements?

_____

_____

3. וַיַּעֲבֵר—Parse this verb. How do you determine the stem? The suffixed object (אַדַּרְתּוֹ, "his robe") is definite, but the accusative sign does not consistently appear before suffixed objects after the Hiphil of עָבַר (contrast 2 Kings 17:17 with 2 Sam. 12:13).

_____

_____

4. וַיְכַס—Parse this verb. How do you determine the stem? Note that the third root letter *he* has dropped off (apocopated). The stem is used in a rare reflexive manner here (see *HALOT*, 488, and cf. Gen. 38:14; Deut. 22:12) with שַׂק functioning as an adverbial accusative. One expects the Hithpael stem (see v. 8).

_____

_____

5. וַיֵּשֶׁב—Parse this verb. How do you determine the root?

_____

_____

---

9. See also AC, 28; GKC, 431, §133g; Joüon, 524, §141j.

3:7

וַיַּזְעֵק וַיֹּאמֶר בְּנִינְוֵה מִטַּעַם הַמֶּלֶךְ וּגְדֹלָיו לֵאמֹר
הָאָדָם וְהַבְּהֵמָה הַבָּקָר וְהַצֹּאן אַל־יִטְעֲמוּ מְאוּמָה אַל־יִרְעוּ וּמַיִם אַל־יִשְׁתּוּ:

1. וַיַּזְעֵק—Parse this verb. How do you determine the stem? Elsewhere the verb, when used in this stem, means "to summon" (Judg. 4:10, 13), "to call out to" (Zech. 6:8), or "utter a plaintive cry" (Job 35:9), but here it seems to have an implied causative nuance, "cause a proclamation to be made" (cf. KJV, NRSV).

_____

_____

_____

2. בְּנִינְוֵה—The accentuation in the Hebrew text suggests that בְּנִינְוֵה goes with "and he said," and is not part of the quotation. (The accent above the form is a disjunctive, *zaqeph parvum*.) Nevertheless, some translations reject this tradition and prefer to understand "in Nineveh" as part of the decree. See NASB and NET.

3. מִטַּעַם—The noun טַעַם has a primary meaning "taste" (see the related verb later in the verse), but it can also carry a figurative nuance, "feeling, discernment, sense." The meaning here, "order, decree," is a further extension of this figurative sense that is well attested in biblical Aramaic (see BDB, 381; *HALOT*, 377). The preposition מִן has the sense "at, by, in accordance with" (BDB, 580, 2.g; *HALOT*, 598, no. 6).

4. How is the article functioning on the four nouns after the *athnaq*? (Note the sequence הָאָדָם . . . וְהַצֹּאן.) See EE, 73 and W-OC, 242–50.[10] Explain the use of the singular here.

_____

_____

5. How are the three jussives in the second half of the verse (note prefixed אַל in each case) functioning here? See EE, 103–4.[11]

_____

_____

6. The verbs יִרְעוּ and יִשְׁתּוּ come from what type of root? Explain what has happened to the third root letter in these forms.

_____

_____

---

10. See also AC, 28–32; BHRG, 189–91; GKC, 404–10; Joüon, 505–13; WHS, 82–93.
11. See also AC, 61–63; BHRG, 152–53; GKC, 321–23; Joüon, 376–78; W-OC, 568–70.

3:8

וְיִתְכַּסּוּ שַׂקִּים הָאָדָם וְהַבְּהֵמָה וְיִקְרְאוּ אֶל־אֱלֹהִים בְּחָזְקָה
וְיָשֻׁבוּ אִישׁ מִדַּרְכּוֹ הָרָעָה וּמִן־הֶחָמָס אֲשֶׁר בְּכַפֵּיהֶם:

1. וְיִתְכַּסּוּ—Parse this verb. Because this is a continuation of the king's decree, it is best to take the prefixed verbal form as a jussive, rather than an imperfect. How do you determine the stem? What has happened to the third root letter? How is the stem functioning here? See EE, 82; BDB, 491–92; *HALOT,* 488.[12] (Contrast NET's "put on" with NIV's "be covered.")

_____

_____

_____

_____

2. בְּחָזְקָה—The preposition in the form בְּחָזְקָה indicates manner, "with strength," that is, loudly, as a sign of their earnestness (see NASB, NET).

3. וְיָשֻׁבוּ—Parse this verb. Again the form is best understood as jussive. How do you determine the *(a)* stem, *(b)* root, and *(c)* P-G-N?

_____

_____

_____

_____

4. אִישׁ—After the plural verb אִישׁ has a distributive sense, "each one." See BDB, 36; *HALOT,* 44.

5. מִדַּרְכּוֹ—This form consists of what elements? The noun, which literally means "way, road," is used here in a figurative manner of one's lifestyle and behavior. Note NET, "way of living."

_____

_____

6. הָרָעָה—What part of speech is הָרָעָה? How is it functioning here? See PVP, 61–66 (7.1–7.7); Ful., 54–55 (10.8).[13] Remember that the preceding form, though it does not have a prefixed article, is definite because of its pronominal suffix.

_____

_____

---

12. See also AC, 47–48; GKC, 149–51; Joüon, 159–60; WHS, 152–55; W-OC, 429–32.
13. Fut., 57–58 (10.8–10.10); Gar., 62–64 (11); Kel., 45–46 (21.1); Ross, 81–82 (9.1–9.2); Seow, 72 (3).

7. בְּכַפֵּיהֶם—This form consists of what elements?

_____

_____

3:9

מִי־יוֹדֵעַ יָשׁוּב וְנִחַם הָאֱלֹהִים וְשָׁב מֵחֲרוֹן אַפּוֹ וְלֹא נֹאבֵד:

1. יוֹדֵעַ—Parse this verb. When used without an object, the question מִי יוֹדֵעַ is rhetorical and expresses the speaker's belief that God may still extend mercy in the midst of (threatened) judgment (see 2 Sam. 12:22; Joel 2:14).

_____

_____

2. יָשׁוּב—How is this imperfect verbal form functioning here? See EE, 89–94; W-OC, 504–13.[14] Note that the question preceding this ("Who knows?") suggests an element of contingency.

_____

_____

3. וְנִחַם—This form consists of *waw* + perfect verbal form (Niphal 3ms from נָחַם, see BDB, 636–37). Following the imperfect, the *waw* is regarded as consecutive (though it has no special vowel pointing to indicate this) and the perfect carries the same aspectual nuance as the preceding imperfect. Review EE, 99–101.[15] On the meaning of נָחַם in the Niphal stem see 3:10, note 4.

4. הָאֱלֹהִים—How is the article functioning here? (Hint: Note the reference to אֱלֹהִים in v. 8.)

_____

_____

5. וְשָׁב—Parse this verb. How do you determine the root? Again this is a *waw* consecutive + the perfect with the verb functioning like an imperfect in the imperfect-initiated verbal sequence. Note the wordplay with יָשֻׁבוּ in verse 8. If the Ninevites turn back from their evil lifestyle, God may turn back from his anger at their sin and relent from sending judgment.

_____

_____

_____

---

14. See also AC, 56–60; BHRG, 146–49; GKC, 313–19; Joüon, 365–72; WHS, 167–75.
15. See also AC, 87–91; BHRG, 168–71; GKC, 330–39; Joüon, 396–406; W-OC, 519–39.

6. מֵחֲרוֹן אַפּוֹ—In this phrase synonyms are combined in a construct relationship. This is done to emphasize the degree of anger involved. See EE, 64; W-OC, 267–68. Note "fierce anger" in most of the translations.

7. נֹאבֵד—Parse this verb. How do you determine the P-G-N? When the verbal sequence is interrupted by negation of the verb (see וְלֹא), the verb reverts to the imperfect (see נֹאבֵד). In this case the negated verb expresses a desired consequence of what precedes.

3:10

וַיַּרְא הָאֱלֹהִים אֶת־מַעֲשֵׂיהֶם כִּי־שָׁבוּ מִדַּרְכָּם הָרָעָה
וַיִּנָּחֶם הָאֱלֹהִים עַל־הָרָעָה אֲשֶׁר־דִּבֶּר לַעֲשׂוֹת־לָהֶם וְלֹא עָשָׂה:

1. וַיַּרְא—This verb form could be either Qal ("he saw") or Hiphil ("he caused to see, showed"). Context indicates the former is correct here: God sees their repentance, he does not show anyone anything here. The *pathaq* prefix vowel is generated by the quasi-guttural *resh* and the third *he* of the verbal root has apocopated.

2. אֶת־... כִּי—This particle introduces the direct object ("their deeds") of the verb "saw," while כִּי introduces a noun clause that is appositional to the object and gives a more detailed, specific description of what he saw ("that they turned from their evil way"). On noun clauses see AC, 171–73; EE, 113–14; Joüon, 589–91, §157.[16]

3. שָׁבוּ—Parse this verb. How do you determine the (a) root (note the placement of the accent), and (b) P-G-N?

4. וַיִּנָּחֶם—Parse this verb. How do you determine the stem? The Niphal of נָחַם, when collocated with עַל־הָרָעָה, carries the sense "change one's mind, relent." It refers to changing one's mind with respect to one's own evil deeds (Jer. 8:6), one's past sufferings (Ezek. 14:22), or, in the case of God, judgment that has been threatened (Exod. 32:12; 1 Chron. 21:15; Jer. 18:8; Joel 2:13). The term רָעָה refers here to the calamity/disaster that God threatened to send upon Nineveh because of its moral evil (רָעָה, see vv. 8, 10a). Note NRSV, "changed his mind about," and NASB (cf. NET), "relented concerning." NIV ("had compassion") and NLT ("had mercy on") do not adequately reflect the meaning of the construction, while KJV ("repented of the evil") is archaic and misleading.

---

16. For other examples of this appositional construction after the verb "to see," cf. Genesis 1:4; 12:14; 46:30; Exodus 2:2; 32:25; 34:35; 1 Kings 11:28; 2 Kings 13:4.

_____

_____

5. דִּבֶּר—How is this perfect verbal form functioning here? See EE, 86–89; W-OC, 486–95.[17] (Note that the speaking took place before the relenting occurred.)

_____

_____

6. לַעֲשׂוֹת—Parse this form. How do you determine the root?

_____

_____

7. וְלֹא עָשָׂה—The negated perfect interrupts the sequence of wayyiqtols in the narrative structure (see 1:13 as well). In this case the construction describes a consequence of the previous action.

Step 3: Interpretive Translation

In light of the decisions you have made in your analysis, provide an interpretive, paraphrastic translation of Jonah 3:5–10.

_____

_____

_____

_____

_____

_____

_____

Step 4: Structural Outline

Outline the narrative structure of Jonah 3:5–10. Carefully delineate the narrative mainline (initiated and extended by wayyiqtol forms), offline (nonstandard) constructions, and quotations. Using the categories listed in the appendix (cf. EE, 120–27), classify all wayyiqtol and disjunctive clauses that are in the narrative framework. You need not classify clauses within quotations.

_____

_____

_____

17. See also AC, 54–56; BHRG, 144–46; GKC, 309–13; Joüon, 359–65; WHS, 161–66.

_____

_____

_____

_____

_____

_____

_____

_____

The Ninevite king was unsure if the announcement of judgment was unconditional or not, but he reasoned, correctly as it turned out, that God might show the city mercy and relent from destroying Nineveh. When God saw Nineveh's sincere response, he showed compassion and relented from sending the announced judgment.

Scene 3: Jonah 4:1–5: A Pouting Prophet

Assignment

Step 1: Initial View

Read Jonah 4:1–5 in the Hebrew text, using an interlinear if you desire. Underline any words or forms you do not recognize. Try to identify verbal forms and label them as follows:

- wayyiqtol verbal forms: wc-y (the so-called *waw* consecutive with the yiqtol, usually identified as a preterite or imperfect)
- weqatal forms: wc-q (the so-called *waw* consecutive with the qatal, that is, perfect)
- simple perfects (without *waw*): pf.
- simple imperfects (without *waw*): impf.
- imperatives: impv.
- jussives: juss.
- cohortatives: coh.
- infinitives construct: inf. const.
- infinitives absolute: inf. abs.
- participles: part.

Step 2: Analyzing the Text

4:1

וַיֵּרַע אֶל־יוֹנָה רָעָה גְדוֹלָה וַיִּחַר לֽוֹ׃

1. וַיֵּרַע—This verb is a Qal wayyiqtol from the root רָעַע, "be displeased, evil." The prefix vowel *tsere* normally signals a I-*yod/waw* verb, but geminate verbs can also follow this pattern if the verb is stative. See PVP, 180 (16.12); Ful., 280 (38.5); and parsing chart 10.[18] Used here in the sense of "displeasure," רָעָה is a cognate adverbial accusative used to emphasize how upset Jonah was over God's merciful treatment of Nineveh. The presence of "to Jonah" indicates the verb has an impersonal subject, "there was anger." One may smooth this out in translation, "Jonah was displeased." Apparently God revealed to Jonah his decision to relent from sending judgment upon Nineveh.
2. וַיִּחַר—Parse this verb. Explain what happened to the third root letter. See PVP, 198 (17.4); Ful., 266–67 (37.4). The presence of לוֹ, "to him," indicates that the verb has an impersonal subject, "there was anger." One may smooth this out in translation, "He was angry."

4:2

וַיִּתְפַּלֵּל אֶל־יְהוָה וַיֹּאמַר אָנָּה יְהוָה הֲלוֹא־זֶה דְבָרִי עַד־הֱיוֹתִי עַל־אַדְמָתִי עַל־כֵּן קִדַּמְתִּי לִבְרֹחַ
תַּרְשִׁישָׁה כִּי יָדַעְתִּי כִּי אַתָּה אֵל־חַנּוּן וְרַחוּם אֶרֶךְ אַפַּיִם וְרַב־חֶסֶד וְנִחָם עַל־הָרָעָֽה׃

1. אָנָּה יְהוָה—Jonah begins his prayer with the same construction used earlier by the sailors (cf. 1:14).
2. הֲלוֹא—Identify the function of the *he* in the construction הֲלוֹא. See PVP, 75–76 (8.10); Ful., 42 (9.3).[19]

3. הֱיוֹתִי—Parse this form. How do you determine the root? How is the pronominal suffix functioning in relation to the verb? The preceding preposition עַד has a temporal function here, "when I was."

---

18. Fut., 250; Gar., 187 (31.D.2); Kel., 359–60 (76.2); Ross, 286 (39.2.2); Seow, 309–10 (1.b), 312 (1.e).
19. Fut., 171 (27.5); Gar., 158–59 (26.C); Kel., 94 (34.1); Ross, 146 (19.5); Seow, 109 (6.b).

4. אַדְמָתִי—This form consists of what elements? Explain the *taw* before the suffix. See PVP, 85 (9.7); Ful., 77–78 (13.2).

5. קִדַּמְתִּי—Parse this verb. How do you determine the *(a)* stem, and *(b)* P-G-N? The verb is denominative here, being derived from קֶדֶם, "front, east." It carries the basic idea of "be in front, meet." Used here with the following infinitive, it has an adverbial force, "I fled before" (cf. KJV).

6. כִּי יָדַעְתִּי—What type of dependent clause is this?

7. כִּי אַתָּה . . .—What type of dependent clause is . . . כִּי אַתָּה?

8. אֵל חַנּוּן וְרַחוּם—What part of speech are the forms חַנּוּן וְרַחוּם? How are they functioning in relation to אֵל, "a god"? See PVP, 61–66 (7.1–7.7); Ful., 54–55 (10.8).[20]

9. אֶרֶךְ אַפַּיִם—The expression אֶרֶךְ אַפַּיִם, literally, "long with respect to nostrils," is a well-attested idiom meaning "slow to anger." See BDB, 74; *HALOT*, 88. (Recall that אַף, "nose," can also have an extended meaning "anger.") אֶרֶךְ is one of a series of adjectives modifying אֵל, while אַפַּיִם is a genitive of specification (see EE, 63).

10. וְרַב־חֶסֶד—After the adjective רַב, "great," what type of genitive is חֶסֶד? See EE, 62–64; W-OC, 143–54.[21]

---

20. Fut., 57–58 (10.7–10.10); Gar., 62–64 (11); Kel., 45–46 (21.1); Ross, 81–82 (9.1–9.2); Seow, 72 (3).
21. See also AC, 8–13; BHRG, 197–200; GKC, 416–19; Joüon, 465–73; WHS, 36–49.

11. נִחָם—Parse this form. How can you tell the form is a participle, not a perfect? This word is the last in the series of adjectives modifying אֵל. (Recall that participles are verbal adjectives.)

_____

_____

_____

> The appearance of the participle in this list of divine characteristics suggests that God's capacity to change his mind with respect to sending calamity (note עַל־רָעָה) is typical of his nature, like the other attributes listed before this. In this regard see Jeremiah 18:7–8. God's immutability (the doctrine that he is unchanging in his very essence or nature) logically demands that he be flexible in his relationships with humans. In other words, because he is immutably compassionate and predisposed to be merciful, he is willing to relent from sending calamity when human beings respond properly to his warnings. God makes plans and announces his intentions, but human response can and often does impact God's decision as to what will actually take place. As the Westminster Confession (V.2) affirms, God often works providentially through secondary causes, which can operate freely and/or contingently.[22] In doing so God's omniscience (defined in the classical sense), sovereignty, and immutability are not compromised. God fully knows what will transpire because he has decreed the future. But this decree, by God's sovereign decision, accommodates the choices and actions of creatures to whom God imparts a degree of freedom. It also makes room for God to respond to these choices and actions. As noted above, this relational flexibility is a corollary of his immutability, which encompasses both his justice and compassion.

4:3

וְעַתָּה יְהוָה קַח־נָא אֶת־נַפְשִׁי מִמֶּנִּי כִּי טוֹב מוֹתִי מֵחַיָּי:

1. קַח—Parse this verb. What does the particle נָא suggest about the form? See PVP, 208 (18.6).[23] Normally the pattern of no prefix, two root letters, and a short _a (pathaq)_ indicates a I-_nun_ or I-_yod_ verb, but לְקַח follows a I-_nun_ pattern (see PVP, 213; Ful., 233 [34.5]).[24] How is the imperative functioning?

_____

---

22. For a helpful analysis of contingency in prophecy as it relates to God's decree and providence, see the study by Reformed theologian Richard L. Pratt Jr., "Historical Contingencies and Biblical Predictions," in _The Way of Wisdom: Essays in Honor of Bruce K. Waltke_, ed. J. I. Packer and Sven K. Soderlund (Grand Rapids: Zondervan, 2000), 180–203.

23. Gar., 110 (19.B.4); Kel., 173 (54); Ross, 151 (20.5); Seow, 213 (6).

24. Gar., 230 (40.B); Kel., 307 (73.2); Ross, 247 (34.6); Seow, 240 (3.f).

2. מִמֶּנִּי—The form consists of what elements? See PVP, 89 (9.12–9.13); Ful., 86 (14.6).[25]

3. כִּי—What type of dependent clause does כִּי introduce here?

4. מֵחַיָּי—After the predicate adjective טוֹב, how is the preposition מִן functioning on מֵחַיָּי? See PVP, 53–54 (6.6); Ful., 165 (26.4).[26]

4:4

וַיֹּאמֶר יְהוָה הַהֵיטֵב חָרָה לָךְ׃

1. הַהֵיטֵב—What is the function of the prefixed *he* on הַהֵיטֵב? See PVP, 75–76 (8.10); Ful., 42 (9.3).[27]

2. הַהֵיטֵב—Parse this form. How do you determine the *(a)* stem, and *(b)* root? How can you tell the form is an infinitive absolute, rather than an infinitive construct? On the adverbial function of the infinitive here, see BDB, 406; *HALOT*, 408. Combined with the following finite verb, the construction reads literally, "Doing well is there anger to you?" This probably means, "Is it right for you to be angry?" (cf. NRSV, NLT) Another option is that the infinitive expresses intensity, "Are you really so very angry?" (cf. NET) According to Joüon (609–10, §161b), the construction has an exclamatory force here, "You are really angry!"

---

25. Fut., 136–37 (22.2); Gar., 84 (15.A.6); Kel., 70 (27.1); Ross, 159 (21.5); Seow, 96 (2.b).
26. Gar., 70 (12.B.2); Kel., 30 (15.3); Ross, 82–83 (9.3); Seow, 73 (5.a).
27. Fut., 171 (27.5); Gar., 158–59 (26.C); Kel., 94 (34.1); Ross, 146 (19.5); Seow, 109 (6.b).

4:5

וַיֵּצֵא יוֹנָה מִן־הָעִיר וַיֵּשֶׁב מִקֶּדֶם לָעִיר
וַיַּעַשׂ לוֹ שָׁם סֻכָּה וַיֵּשֶׁב תַּחְתֶּיהָ בַּצֵּל עַד אֲשֶׁר יִרְאֶה מַה־יִּהְיֶה בָּעִיר:

1. וַיֵּצֵא . . . וַיֵּשֶׁב—The verbs וַיֵּשֶׁב and וַיֵּצֵא are derived from what type of verbal root? How can you tell this? Since Jonah seems uncertain about the city's fate in verse 5, some understand verses 5–11 as a flashback that fits chronologically between 3:4–5. However, it is much less complicated to read the story as being in chronological succession. Apparently God revealed to Jonah his decision to spare the city (cf. 3:10), prompting Jonah's anger (4:1–4). Jonah, not willing to accept God's decision as final, waited outside the city to see if God might destroy the city after all. Perhaps he was even so arrogant to think his anger might prompt such a reversal in God's thinking. On the chronological issue involved, see Simon, *Jonah,* 39.

   _____

   _____

   _____

2. מִקֶּדֶם—In this phrase the preposition has the force of "off, on" (see BDB, 578, 1.c.), so the phrase means "eastward" (BDB, 869; *HALOT,* 597). On this use of מִן see W-OC, 212.[28]

3. וַיַּעַשׂ—Parse this verb. How do you determine the root? The form can be either Qal (prefix vowel *a* due to I-guttural) or Hiphil, but the sense requires the basic Qal meaning ("he made"), rather than a causative. The prepositional phrase לוֹ is reflexive, "for himself."

   _____

   _____

   _____

4. תַּחְתֶּיהָ—What is the antecedent of the suffix on תַּחְתֶּיהָ? You will first need to identify its gender and number.

   _____

   _____

5. עַד אֲשֶׁר . . . יִרְאֶה—How is the imperfect יִרְאֶה functioning? The preceding עַד אֲשֶׁר means "until (that)" (see BDB, 724–25). The action described by the verb, while past from the narrator's perspective, is subsequent to the action of the main verb ("he sat down"). See EE, 90–91.[29]

   _____

   _____

---

28. See also WHS, 323.
29. See also BHRG, 147; GKC, 316, §107k; Joüon, 370, §113k; WHS, 167; W-OC, 513.

6. מַה—This form is often interrogative ("what?"), but here it is used in an indefinite sense (cf. W-OC, 325) and functions as the object of the verb "see."

7. יִהְיֶה—The situation described by the imperfect יִהְיֶה, which we will label "B," and the action described by the preceding verb ("until he should see"), which we will label "A," were future in relation to the main verb ("he sat down"). Since developments in the city (B) would occur before Jonah's seeing them (A), we should label יִהְיֶה an anterior future. In other words, it is the prior of two actions, both of which are future in relation to the main verb. See EE, 92 and note NIV, "what would happen."[30]

Step 3: Interpretive Translation

In light of the decisions you have made in your analysis, provide an interpretive, paraphrastic translation of Jonah 4:1–5.

_____

_____

_____

_____

_____

_____

_____

_____

_____

Step 4: Structural Outline

Outline the narrative structure of Jonah 4:1–5. Carefully delineate the narrative mainline (initiated and extended by wayyiqtol forms), offline (nonstandard) constructions, and quotations. Using the categories listed in the appendix (cf. EE, 120–27), classify all wayyiqtol and disjunctive clauses that are in the narrative framework. You need not classify clauses within quotations.

_____

_____

_____

_____

_____

_____

_____

_____

---

30. See also GKC, 316, §107l.

God sent Jonah to warn the Ninevites that he was ready to judge their evil deeds (רָעָה). The Ninevites changed, prompting God to relent from sending disaster (רָעָה again). Rather than celebrating God's mercy, Jonah got angry. The statement "Jonah was greatly displeased" literally reads "Jonah was displeased (with) great displeasure." The Hebrew term רָעָה is used again, this time to describe Jonah's displeasure. Ironically, at the beginning of the story the word characterized the evil Ninevites; by the end of the story it applies to Jonah.

Jonah now reveals why he disobeyed God's orders and fled for Tarshish (v. 2). He suspected that God, because of his merciful nature, would give the Ninevites another chance, if they repented. Jonah had a double standard. He knew God was merciful because he had extended his compassion to sinful Israel in the past and to the disobedient prophet himself. But Jonah did not think the Ninevites deserved mercy. He decided he would rather die than see Nineveh spared, so he asked God to take his life (v. 3). In response to the Lord's simple, probing question, Jonah sat down outside the city and waited to see what would happen (v. 5). Apparently he could not accept the Lord's merciful decision as final.

Scene 4: Jonah 4:6–11: A Prophet Gets an Object Lesson

Assignment

Step 1: Initial View

Read Jonah 4:6–11 in the Hebrew text, using an interlinear if you desire. Underline any words or forms you do not recognize. Try to identify verbal forms and label them as follows:

- wayyiqtol verbal forms: wc-y (the so-called *waw* consecutive with the yiqtol, usually identified as a preterite or imperfect)
- weqatal forms: wc-q (the so-called *waw* consecutive with the qatal, that is, perfect)
- simple perfects (without *waw*): pf.
- simple imperfects (without *waw*): impf.
- imperatives: impv.
- jussives: juss.
- cohortatives: coh.
- infinitives construct: inf. const.
- infinitives absolute: inf. abs.
- participles: part.

Step 2: Analyzing the Text

4:6

וַיְמַן יְהוָה־אֱלֹהִים קִיקָיוֹן וַיַּעַל מֵעַל לְיוֹנָה לִהְיוֹת צֵל עַל־רֹאשׁוֹ לְהַצִּיל לוֹ מֵרָעָתוֹ וַיִּשְׂמַח יוֹנָה עַל־הַקִּיקָיוֹן שִׂמְחָה גְדוֹלָה:

1. וַיַּעַל—Parse this verb. The form can be either Qal or Hiphil, but syntax requires the Qal here ("it grew up"), rather than the Hiphil ("he caused to grow")(cf. BDB, 748). Note that the verb is intransitive here; it has no object. See NASB, in contrast to NIV, KJV, NRSV, and NET.

_____

_____

2. מֵעַל לְיוֹנָה—The construction מֵעַל לְ-, literally, "from upon to," has the force of "over, above" (BDB, 759; *HALOT*, 827).

3. לִהְיוֹת—Parse this form. How do you determine the root? How is the infinitive construct functioning in relation to the main verb? See PVP, 241–47;[31] W-OC, 605–10.[32] The translations suggest that it indicates purpose; this works well if one takes the main verb as causative, but וַיַּעַל is Qal, not Hiphil. See note 1 above. If one reads the main verb correctly as Qal, "it grew up," does purpose make the best sense? Or does result fit better, "so that it provided shade, so as to provide shade"? If one connects the plant's growth with God's action conceptually, it is possible to see the infinitive as indicating purpose. The plant's growth, which resulted from God's intervention, was for the purpose of giving Jonah shade. The logic is best seen if one translates the second clause as relative: "Yahweh God provided a plant, which grew up over Jonah, to provide shade over his head."

_____

_____

_____

_____

4. לְהַצִּיל—Parse this form. How do you determine the *(a)* stem, and *(b)* root? How is the infinitive functioning? (See the discussion in note 3 above.) The verb נָצַל means "be delivered, deliver oneself" in the Niphal; the Hiphil has a causative nuance, "cause to be delivered" (i.e., "deliver").

_____

_____

_____

_____

---

31. Fut., 121–22 (20.7–20.8); Gar., 212 (36.B.2); Kel., 181–83 (56.2); Ross, 164 (22.4); Seow, 258–59 (3).
32. See also AC, 67–73; BHRG, 154–55; GKC, 348–51; Joüon, 436–38; WHS, 192–200.

5. מֵרָעָתוֹ—This form consists of what elements? In this case רָעָה appears to refer to Jonah's physical discomfort, but see the discussion below in the concluding comments.

_____

_____

6. שִׂמְחָה—Note that this noun, "joy," is from the same root as the verb וַיִּשְׂמַח, "and he rejoiced." When a verb and its accusative have a common derivation, grammarians sometimes call the latter a "cognate accusative" (see 1:10). However, cognate accusatives actually function as direct objects or in an adverbial manner. In this passage how is שִׂמְחָה functioning?

_____

_____

7. עַל־הַקִּיקָיוֹן—In this phrase the preposition has a causal force, "on account of."

4:7

וַיְמַן הָאֱלֹהִים תּוֹלַעַת בַּעֲלוֹת הַשַּׁחַר לַמָּחֳרָת וַתַּךְ אֶת־הַקִּיקָיוֹן וַיִּיבָשׁ:

1. בַּעֲלוֹת—Parse this form. How do you determine the root? How is the preposition -בְּ functioning? See PVP, 241–47 (20.10–20.13).[33] How is הַשַּׁחַר functioning in relation to the infinitive?

_____

_____

_____

2. וַתַּךְ—Parse this verb. The root is נָכָה. Note that only one root letter is visible. The final _he_ has apocopated, while the initial _nun_ has assimilated into the _kaph_. The a-class vowel under the prefix indicates that the form is a Hiphil, for the Qal would take an i-class vowel, unless it was a I-guttural verb, which it is not. How do you determine the P-G-N of this verb? What is its subject? With the exception of two passages, the verb נָכָה occurs in the Hiphil/Hophal with the meaning "strike, attack."

_____

_____

_____

_____

33. Fut., 122 (20.9); Gar., 212 (36.B.2); Kel., 182 (56.2); Ross, 163 (22.4); Seow, 259 (3.e).

3. וַיִּיבָשׁ—Parse this verb. How do you determine the root?

_____

_____

4:8

וַיְהִי כִּזְרֹחַ הַשֶּׁמֶשׁ וַיְמַן אֱלֹהִים רוּחַ קָדִים חֲרִישִׁית וַתַּךְ הַשֶּׁמֶשׁ עַל־רֹאשׁ יוֹנָה וַיִּתְעַלָּף
וַיִּשְׁאַל אֶת־נַפְשׁוֹ לָמוּת וַיֹּאמֶר טוֹב מוֹתִי מֵחַיָּי:

1. כִּזְרֹחַ—Parse this form. How is the preposition -כְּ functioning? See PVP, 241–47 (20.10–20.13).[34] How is הַשֶּׁמֶשׁ functioning in relation to the infinitive? What does וַיְהִי indicate about the temporal framework of the infinitive? See PVP, 196, 245; Ful., 121–22 (20.3).

_____

_____

_____

_____

2. וַיְמַן—For the fourth time the verb מָנָה, "appoint, send," appears with the LORD/God as its subject (cf. 2:1; 4:6–7). The first two times the verb is used, God acts to bring Jonah physical relief. He appointed a fish to rescue Jonah from drowning and a plant to bring him relief from his discomfort. The last two times the verb is used, God's actions bring Jonah discomfort, but are designed to teach him an important lesson.

3. קָדִים—This noun functions here as a genitive after רוּחַ, which must be understood as construct. (Technically the masculine form קָדִים is not an adjective; an adjectival modifier of רוּחַ, a feminine noun, would most likely need to be feminine as well. The noun is functioning here as an attributive genitive, "an east wind.") חֲרִישִׁית is an adjective, modifying רוּחַ (note the feminine ending *taw*). The term appears only here; apparently it means "sharp, scorching" (*HALOT*, 353).

4. שֶׁמֶשׁ—The noun is feminine here (note the preceding 3fs verb, וַתַּךְ). It is attested as both feminine and masculine in biblical Hebrew. See *HALOT*, 1589–90.

5. וַיִּתְעַלָּף—Parse this verb. How do you determine the stem? The verb עָלַף occurs in only the Pual and Hithpael stems. In the latter it means "cover oneself" (Gen. 38:14) or "faint" (Amos 8:13). The second nuance fits well here.

_____

_____

6. נַפְשׁוֹ—This is an accusative of specification, "regarding, with respect to his life."[35] Normally after שָׁאַל the accusative sign introduces the one to whom a request is made or, less often, the object requested. It

---

34. AC, 109–10; Fut., 122 (20.9); Gar., 212 (36.B.2); Kel., 182 (56.2); Ross, 163 (22.4); Seow, 259 (3.e).

35. On this use of the accusative sign, see BDB, 85.

is also uncommon for שָׁאַל to be followed by the preposition -לְ and an infinitive construct (other than the epexegetical לֵאמֹר, "saying"), but the same collocation used here (וַיִּשְׁאַל אֶת־נַפְשׁוֹ לָמוּת) also occurs in 1 Kings 19:4, where the discouraged Elijah asks to die.

4:9–10

וַיֹּאמֶר אֱלֹהִים אֶל־יוֹנָה הַהֵיטֵב חָרָה־לְךָ עַל־הַקִּיקָיוֹן וַיֹּאמֶר הֵיטֵב חָרָה־לִי עַד־מָוֶת:
וַיֹּאמֶר יְהוָה אַתָּה חַסְתָּ עַל־הַקִּיקָיוֹן אֲשֶׁר לֹא־עָמַלְתָּ בּוֹ וְלֹא גִדַּלְתּוֹ
שֶׁבִּן־לַיְלָה הָיָה וּבִן־לַיְלָה אָבָד:

1. עַד־מָוֶת—Some call this otherwise unattested phrase, meaning "unto death," an idiom, as in the English expression "bored to death" (see W-OC, 269). See the note in NET, which translates "I am as angry as I could possibly be." But in light of verse 8b it may be better to take the expression more literally, unless, of course, that statement is also idiomatic. See verse 8, note 6.

2. חַסְתָּ—Parse this verb. How do you determine the (a) root, and (b) P-G-N? How is the perfect functioning? Contrast NET ("You were upset") with NRSV ("You are concerned"). The verb has the meaning "be troubled about" (HALOT, 298), "be concerned about" (NIV, NRSV).

_____

_____

_____

_____

3. עָמַלְתָּ בּוֹ—The collocation עָמַל בְּ- means "work for, labor over" (see Ps. 127:1; Eccl. 2:21). The suffix on the preposition is resumptive, referring back to the relative pronoun that precedes the verb. (See W-OC, 333–34.) One may translate, "over which you did not labor."

4. גִדַּלְתּוֹ—The verb form is a Piel (note the _hireq_). How can you tell this from the form? It is a 2ms form with a 3ms suffix. On the _taw_ ending, see GKC, 158, §59a. On the form of the suffix, see GKC, 155, §58a, d. The suffix is resumptive, referring back to the relative pronoun. One may translate, "and which you did not grow." In the Qal stem the verb גָּדַל is intransitive, meaning "grow up." In the Piel it is transitive and has a causative nuance, "make grow."

_____

_____

5. שֶׁבִּן—This form is comprised of the relative pronoun -שֶׁ and בִּן, an alternate form of בֵּן, "son" (see GKC, 285, §96). The relative pronoun is here in apposition to אֲשֶׁר, which appears earlier in the verse.

6. בִּן־לַיְלָה—This phrase, which means literally, "son of a night," reflects a Hebrew idiom in which "son of" precedes a noun that functions as an attributive genitive. See BDB, 121, no. 8.[36] The point is that the plant grew up overnight and perished just as quickly. It was short-lived (cf. NLT) and did not merit a great deal of concern.

_____

36. See also GKC, 417–18, §128s, v; Joüon, 468–69, §129j.

4:11

וַאֲנִי לֹא אָחוּס עַל־נִינְוֵה הָעִיר הַגְּדוֹלָה
אֲשֶׁר יֶשׁ־בָּהּ הַרְבֵּה מִשְׁתֵּים־עֶשְׂרֵה רִבּוֹ אָדָם אֲשֶׁר לֹא־יָדַע בֵּין־יְמִינוֹ לִשְׂמֹאלוֹ וּבְהֵמָה רַבָּה:

1. וַאֲנִי—The initial וַאֲנִי marks a shift in focus from Jonah's perspective (v. 10) to God's and introduces the main point he wants to make.

2. אָחוּס—Parse this verb. How do you determine the (a) root, and (b) P-G-N? How is the imperfect functioning? It is best to treat this as a rhetorical question, despite the lack of a formal interrogative indicator.[37]

_____

_____

_____

_____

3. בָּהּ—The suffix on בָּהּ is resumptive, referring back to the relative pronoun that precedes יֵשׁ. One may translate, "in which there are."

4. הַרְבֵּה—Parse this form. How do you determine the stem? How does this form differ from the infinitive construct? You may need to review the diagnostics for the Hiphil stem of III-he verbs. See PVP, 358–59 (31.8–9); Ful., 149–51 (24.2–24.3).[38] The infinitive absolute here functions in an adverbial manner. Combined with the comparative מִן on the following number, it can be translated, "more than."

_____

_____

_____

5. שְׁתֵּים־עֶשְׂרֵה רִבּוֹ—The compound number consists of (1) a contracted form of the feminine dual שְׁתַּיִם,[39] (2) עֶשְׂרֵה, the feminine form of "ten" used in combination with the preceding numeral to make the cardinal number twelve,[40] and (3) רִבּוֹ, "ten thousand." So the number is literally, "two-ten [i.e., twelve], ten thousand," that is, twelve ten thousands, or 120,000.

6. אָדָם—The collective singular noun follows the number, indicating the enumerated item. See W-OC, 281. In the relative clause that follows, the verb (יָדַע) and the pronominal suffixes (יְמִינוֹ לִשְׂמֹאלוֹ) are singular, agreeing with the collective noun. Used here with בֵּין, "between," the verb here has the meaning "discern" (KJV), "know the difference" (NASB).

---

37. See the translations, as well as GKC, 473, §150a; Joüon, 609, §161a.
38. Fut., 214–15 ; Gar., 286 (49.D); Kel., 287 (72.3); Ross, 263 (36.4); Seow, 283 (4–5).
39. See GKC, 289–90, §97d.
40. See BDB, 797; GKC, 289, §97d; Joüon, 325, §100g.

7. וּבְהֵמָה—This noun is compounded with אָדָם; it is also a collective singular, as the modifying adjective רַבָּה, "many," indicates.[41] What is the gender of רַבָּה? How can you tell this?

_____

_____

Step 3: Interpretive Translation

In light of the decisions you have made in your analysis, provide an interpretive, paraphrastic translation of Jonah 4:6–11.

_____

_____

_____

_____

_____

_____

_____

Step 4: Structural Outline

Outline the narrative structure of Jonah 4:6–11. Carefully delineate the narrative mainline (initiated and extended by wayyiqtol forms), offline (nonstandard) constructions, and quotations. Using the categories listed in the appendix (cf. EE, 120–27), classify all wayyiqtol and disjunctive clauses that are in the narrative framework. You need not classify clauses within quotations.

_____

_____

_____

_____

_____

_____

_____

_____

_____

41. The phrase obviously does not mean "a great beast." See Joüon, 497–98, §135b.

Now that Nineveh had repented, the Lord turned his attention to angry Jonah. He caused a large plant to grow up over Jonah's shelter so he could ease the prophet's discomfort (v. 6). The word רָעָה has a double meaning here. English "discomfort" is the translation for רָעָה, the same term used earlier to describe the Ninevites' evil (1:2; 3:8) and Jonah's displeasure with God's decision to spare the city (4:1). On the surface the word seems to refer in verse 6 to Jonah's physical discomfort. But if this were God's primary concern, he would not have destroyed the plant so quickly (v. 7). God used the plant as an object lesson designed to deliver Jonah from his morally wrong attitude. On a deeper level the word refers to Jonah's "evil" attitude.[42]

When Jonah pouted over the loss of the plant, God asked him if it was right for him to be so angry. Jonah replied that he had every right to be angry. Jonah's answer played right into God's hands. Using an argument from the lesser to the greater, God explained that Jonah was saddened over the loss of a plant that he did not create or grow (v. 10). If Jonah could feel this way about losing a plant, how much more should God have the right to feel regret over losing a great city filled with people and animals (v. 11).

There were 120,000 people in Nineveh who could not "tell their right hand from their left," a reference to their moral ignorance. Though responsible for their evil deeds (see 1:2), the Ninevites did not have the advantage of special divine revelation concerning God's moral will; they were like mere children in this respect. Their relative ignorance, though not an excuse for their behavior, prompted God to be merciful to them when they repented.

---

42. See EE, 51–52.

Vocabulary for the Book of Jonah

This glossary lists all words found in Jonah with the exception of commonly used particles, prepositions, and pronouns. Numbers in parentheses are the BDB/*HALOT* page numbers where the discussion of the word appears or begins. If only one passage is listed in the right hand column, this means the word occurs only in this text in Jonah. In cases where a word occurs in more than one passage, the first passage where it is used is listed, as well as some others. But one should not assume that the lists are exhaustive. Words marked "PN" are proper nouns.

א

אָבַד	perish (1/2)	1:6, 14; 3:9
אָדָם	man, people (9/14)	3:7, 8; 4:11
אֲדָמָה	land (9/15)	4:2
אַדֶּרֶת	robe (12/17)	3:6
אוּלַי	perhaps (19/21)	1:6
אֶחָד	one (25/29)	3:4
אִישׁ	a man, each one (35/43)	1:5, 7, etc.
אַךְ	surely (36/45)	2:5
אֵל	God, god (42/48)	4:2
אֱלֹהִים	God, god (43/52)	1:5, 6, etc.
אָמַן	believe (52/63)	3:5
אָמַר	say (55/65)	1:1, 6, etc.
אֲמִתַּי	Amittai (PN)(54/69)	1:1
אָנָּה	ah, please (58/69)	1:14; 4:2
אֲנִיָּה	ship (58/71)	1:3, 4, 5
אַף	anger, nostril (60/76)	3:9; 4:2
אָפַף	surround, overwhelm (67/79)	2:6
אֵפֶר	ashes (68/80)	3:6
אַרְבָּעִים	forty (917/83)	3:4
אֶרֶךְ	(construct of אָרֵךְ*) long (74/88)	4:2
אֶרֶץ	land, earth (75/90)	1:8; 2:7

ב

בְּהֵמָה	beast, animal (96/112)	3:7, 8; 4:11
בּוֹא	come, go (97/112)	1:3, 8; 2:8; 3:4
בֶּטֶן	belly (105/121)	2:3
בָּלַע	to swallow (118/134)	2:1
בֵּן	son (119/137)	1:1; 4:10
בַּעַד	behind (126/141)	2:7
בָּקָר	cattle, herd (133/151)	3:7
בָּרַח	flee (137/156)	1:3, 10; 4:2
בְּרִיחַ	bar (138/157)	2:7

ג

גָּדוֹל	great, important (152/177)	1:2, 4, etc.
גָּדַל	be great, grow (152/178)	4:10
גּוֹרָל	lot (174/185)	1:7
גַּל	wave (plural)(164/190)	2:4
גָּרַשׁ	drive out (176/204)	2:5

ד

דִּבֶּר	speak (180/210)	3:2, 6, 10
דָּבָר	word (182/211)	1:1; 3:1, 3; 4:2
דָּג	fish (185/213)	2:1, 11
דָּגָה	fish (185/213)	2:2
דָּם	blood (196/224)	1:14
דֶּרֶךְ	way, behavior (202/231)	3:8, 10

ה

הֶבֶל	vanity, idol (plural)(210/236)	2:9
הָיָה	be (224/243)	1:1, etc.
הֵיכָל	temple (228/244)	2:5, 8
הָלַךְ	go (229/246)	1:2, 7, etc.
הָפַךְ	overthrow, overturn (245/253)	3:4
הַר	mountain (plural)(249/254)	2:7

ז

זָבַח	to sacrifice (256/261)	1:16; 2:10
זֶבַח	sacrifice (noun: 257/262)	1:16
זָכַר	remember (269/269)	2:8
זַעַף	storming, raging (277/277)	1:15
זָעַק	cry out (277/277)	1:5; 3:7
זָרַח	rise, shine (280/281)	4:8

ח

חֹבֵל	sailor (287/287)	1:6
חָבַשׁ	bind, wrap (289/289)	2:6
חוּס	look with compassion (299/298)	4:10, 11
חָזְקָה	strength (306/304)	3:8
חַיִּים	life (313/307)	2:7; 4:3, 8
חָלַל	begin (320/319)	3:4
חָמָס	violence (329/329)	3:8
חַנּוּן	merciful, kind (337/333)	4:2
חֶסֶד	loyalty (338/336)	2:9; 4:2
חָפֵץ	to delight, desire (342/339)	1:14
חָרָה	be angry (354/351)	4:1, 4, 9
חָרוֹן	anger (354/351)	3:9
חֲרִישִׁית	scorching (362/353)	4:8
חָשַׁב	think (362/359)	1:4

חָתַר	dig, row (369/365)	1:13

ט

טוֹב	good (adjective: 373/370)	4:3, 8
טוּל	throw (376/373)	1:4, 5, 12, 15
טָעַם	to taste (380/377)	3:7
טַעַם	decree (381/377)	3:7

י

יָבֵשׁ	dry up, wither (386/384)	4:7
יַבָּשָׁה	dry land (387/384)	1:9, 13; 2:11
יָדַע	know (393/390)	1:7, 10, etc.
יְהוָה	Yahweh (PN)(217/394)	1:1, etc.
יוֹם	day (398/399)	2:1; 3:3, 4
יוֹנָה	Jonah (PN)(402/402)	1:1, etc.
יָטַב	be good (405/408)	4:4, 9
יָכֹל	be able (407/410)	1:13
יָם	sea (410/413)	1:4, 5, etc.
יָמִין	right hand (411/415)	4:11
יָסַף	add, do again (414/418)	2:5
יָצָא	go out (422/425)	4:5
יָפוֹ	Joppa (PN)(421/424)	1:3
יָרֵא	to fear (431/432)	1:5, 9, 10, 16
יִרְאָה	fear (noun: 432/433)	1:10, 16
יָרַד	go down (432/434)	1:3, 5; 2:7
יַרְכָה	inner part (438/439)	1:5
יֵשׁ	there is (441/443)	4:11
יָשַׁב	sit (442/444)	3:6; 4:5
יְשׁוּעָה	salvation (447/446)	2:10

כ

כֹּל	all (481/474)	2:4
כְּלִי	cargo (plural)(479/478)	1:5
כִּסֵּא	throne (490/487)	3:6
כָּסָה	to cover (491/487)	3:6, 8
כַּף	hand (496/491)	3:8

ל

לֵבָב	heart (523/516)	2:4
לָבֵשׁ	wear, put on (527/519)	3:5
לַיְלָה	night (538/528)	2:1; 4:10
לָקַח	take (542/534)	4:3

מ

מְאוּמָה	anything, something (548/539)	3:7
מַהֲלָךְ	walk, journey (237/552)	3:3, 4
מוּת	die (559/562)	4:8

מָוֶת	death (560/563)	4:3, 8
מָחֳרָת	the following day (564/572)	4:7
מַיִם	water (565/576)	2:6; 3:7
מְלָאכָה	occupation, work (521/586)	1:8
מַלָּח	sailor (572/588)	1:5
מֶלֶךְ	king (572/591)	3:6, 7
מָנָה	appoint (584/599)	2:1; 4:6, 7, 8
מֵעֶה	insides (plural)(588/609)	2:1, 2
מַעֲשֶׂה	work, deed (795/616)	3:10
מָצָא	find (592/619)	1:3
מְצוּלָה	deep (noun: 846/623)	2:4
מִשְׁבָּר	breaker, wave (plural)(991/642)	2:4

נ

נָבַט	to look (613/661)	2:5
נָגַד	tell (616/665)	1:8, 10
נֶגֶד	in front of, before (617/666)	2:5
נָגַע	reach, touch (619/668)	3:6
נָדַר	to vow (623/674)	1:16; 2:10
נֶדֶר	vow (noun: 623/674)	1:16
נָהָר	river, current (625/676)	2:4
נָחַם	relent (636/688)	3:9, 10; 4:2
נִינְוֵה	Nineveh (PN)(644/696)	1:2, etc.
נָכָה	strike, destroy (645/697)	4:7, 8
נָפַל	to fall (656/709)	1:7
נֶפֶשׁ	life, throat (659/711)	1:14; 2:6, etc.
נָצַל	deliver, give relief (664/717)	4:6
נָקִיא	innocent (667/720)	1:14
נָשָׂא	lift up (669/724)	1:12, 15
נָתַן	give, pay (678/733)	1:3, 14

ס

סָבַב	surround, overwhelm (685/738)	2:4, 6
סוּף	reed(s) (693/747)	2:6
סֻכָּה	hut, shelter (697/753)	4:5
סָעַר	be stormy (704/762)	1:11, 13
סַעַר	storm (noun: 704/762)	1:4, 12
סְפִינָה	ship, hold (706/764)	1:5

ע

עָבַר	pass over, remove (Hiphil) (716/778)	2:4; 3:6
עִבְרִי	Hebrew (720/782)	1:9
עוֹד	still, yet, more (728/795)	3:4
עוֹלָם	perpetuity, forever (761/798)	2:7
עָזַב	forsake, abandon (736/806)	2:9
עָטַף	be faint (742/814)	2:8

עַיִן	eye (dual)(744/817)	2:5
עִיר	city (746/821)	1:2; 3:2, etc.
עַל־כֵּן	therefore (487/826)	4:2
עָלָה	go up (748/828)	1:2; 2:7; 4:6, 7
עָלַף	be faint (763/836)	4:8
עַם	people, nation (766/837)	1:8
עָמַד	to stand, stand still (763/840)	1:15
עָמַל	to work, toil (765/845)	4:10
עָנָה	to answer (772/851)	2:3
עָשָׂה	make, do (793/889)	1:9, 10, etc.
עָשַׁת	think, recollect (799/898)	1:6
עַתָּה	now (773/901)	4:3

פ

| פָּלַל | pray (813/933) | 2:2; 4:2 |

צ

צֹאן	sheep, flock (838/992)	3:7
צוֹם	fast (noun: 847/1012)	3:5
צֵל	shade (853/1024)	4:5, 6
צָרָה	distress (865/1053)	2:3

ק

קָדִים	east (870/1067)	4:8
קָדַם	act beforehand (869/1068)	4:2
קֶדֶם	front, east (869/1069)	4:5
קֹדֶשׁ	holiness (871/1076)	2:5, 8
קוֹל	voice (876/1083)	2:3, 10
קוּם	arise (877/1086)	1:2, 3, 6; 3:2, 3
קָטֹן	small (882/1093)	3:5
קִיא	to vomit (883/1096)	2:11
קִיקָיוֹן	a type of plant (884/1099)	4:6, 7, 9, 10
קָלַל	be light (886/1103)	1:5
קֶצֶב	extremity (plural)(891/1120)	2:7
קָרָא	cry out, proclaim (894/1128)	1:2, 6, etc.
קָרַב	draw near (897/1132)	1:6
קְרִיאָה	proclamation (896/1141)	3:2

ר

רָאָה	see (906/1157)	3:10; 4:5, 8
רֹאשׁ	head (910/1164)	2:6; 4:6
רַב	chief (noun: 913/1172)	1:6
רַב	great, many (adjective: 912/1170)	4:2, 11
רָבָה	be many (915/1176)	4:11
רִבּוֹ	multitude (914/1178)	4:11
רָדַם	to sleep (922/1191)	1:5, 6

99

רוּחַ	wind (924/1197)	1:4; 4:8
רַחוּם	compassionate (933/1214)	4:2
רַע	evil (adjective: 948/1250)	3:8, 10
רֵעַ	friend, another (945/1253)	1:7
רָעָה	eat, graze (944/1258)	3:7
רָעָה	evil, calamity, distress (949/1262)	1:2, 7, 8; 4:1, 2
רָעַע	be displeased (949/1269)	4:1

שׂ

שָׂכָר	fare (969/1331)	1:3
שְׂמֹאל	left hand (969/1332)	4:11
שָׂמַח	rejoice (970/1333)	4:6
שִׂמְחָה	joy (970/1336)	4:6
שַׂק	sackcloth (plural)(974/1349)	3:5, 6, 8

שׁ

שְׁאוֹל	Sheol, underworld (982/1368)	2:3
שָׁאַל	ask (981/1371)	4:8
שָׁבַר	to break (990/1402)	1:4
שָׁוְא	emptiness, worthless (996/1425)	2:9
שׁוּב	return (996/1427)	1:13; 3:8, 9, 10
שָׁוַע	cry out (1002/1443)	2:3
שַׁחַר	dawn (1007/1466)	4:7
שַׁחַת	pit (1001/1472)	2:7
שָׁכַב	lie down, sleep (1011/1486)	1:5
שָׁלַךְ	throw (1020/1527)	2:4
שָׁלֵם	be complete (1022/1532)	2:10
שְׁלֹשָׁה	three (1025/1544)	2:1; 3:3
שָׁם	there (1027/1546)	4:5
שָׁמַיִם	heaven (1029/1559)	1:9
שָׁמַע	hear (1033/1570)	2:3
שָׁמַר	watch (1036/1581)	2:9
שֶׁמֶשׁ	sun (1039/1589)	4:8
שֵׁנִית	second (1041/1604)	3:1
שָׁתָה	to drink (1059/1667)	3:7
שְׁתֵּים עֶשְׂרֵה	twelve (literally, "two-ten")(1041/1606)	4:11
שָׁתַק	be quiet, silent (1060/1671)	1:11, 12

ת

תְּהוֹם	deep (noun: 1062/1690)	2:6
תּוֹדָה	thanksgiving (392/1695)	2:10
תּוֹלַעַת	worm (1069/1702)	4:7
תְּפִלָּה	prayer (813/1776)	2:8
תַּרְשִׁישׁ	Tarshish (PN)(1076/1797)	1:3, 4:2

Part 2

ANALYSIS OF THE BOOK OF RUTH

Looking at the Whole

The book of Ruth has four distinct acts, corresponding to the book's chapter divisions. Each of the first three acts contains three scenes; the fourth act has two scenes, followed by an epilogue (genealogy).[1]

In act one, Naomi's family moves to Moab and then, following the death of her husband and two sons, Naomi returns to Bethlehem with her daughter-in-law Ruth. As she enters the town, the ladies meet her. Naomi expresses her pain and sorrow, arguing that the Lord has opposed her and brought her bitterness. Despite the fact that loyal Ruth stands at her side, she laments that she has returned empty-handed.

In act two, Ruth goes out to find food for herself and Naomi. She meets Boaz, who permits her to glean in his field and goes out of his way to show her kindness because of the loyalty she has demonstrated to Naomi. After a long day of hard work, Ruth returns to Naomi, who is delighted that she has met Boaz.

In act three, Naomi suggests that Ruth should go to the threshing floor and let Boaz know that she is available for marriage. Ruth aggressively carries out Naomi's instructions and proposes marriage to Boaz, challenging him to raise up offspring for the deceased Elimelech's family line. Boaz agrees to do so, but he must first iron out certain legal complications. Ruth returns to Naomi, who assures her that Boaz will take care of the matter.

In the final act, Boaz confronts the nearer kinsman, who declines to marry Ruth. Boaz then marries Ruth in the presence of the elders and people of the town. They pronounce a blessing upon him, asking the Lord to give him and Ruth an unbroken line of male descendants who will bring his family fame and prosperity. The Lord answers the prayer by giving Boaz a son, who will also serve as Naomi's protector in her old age. The women of the town extol the virtues of Ruth, who has proven to be of more value to Naomi than seven sons. The epilogue shows the extent of God's blessing by tracing Boaz's line of descent to David, the great king.

Note Regarding the Hebrew Text

The Hebrew text is presented without its cantillation marks/accents, with the exception of *soph pasuq* (meaning "end of verse") at the end of each verse and *athnaq* (meaning "rest"), which, in most cases, marks the major break in thought within a verse.

---

1. This outline essentially follows that of Frederic W. Bush, *Ruth, Esther*, WBC (Dallas: Word Books, 1996), 56. Bush calls 4:18–22 a "scene," but it is better labeled an epilogue for it is simply a genealogical list, not a narrative with a plot line.

Act 1

Ruth 1

Scene 1: Ruth 1:1–6: Famine and Death

Assignment

Step 1: Initial View

Read Ruth 1:1–6 in the Hebrew text, using an interlinear if you desire. Underline any words or forms you do not recognize. Try to identify verbal forms and label them as follows:

- wayyiqtol verbal forms: wc-y (the so-called *waw* consecutive with the yiqtol, usually identified as a preterite or imperfect)
- weqatal forms: wc-q (the so-called *waw* consecutive with the qatal, that is, perfect)
- simple perfects (without *waw*): pf.
- simple imperfects (without *waw*): impf.
- imperatives: impv.
- jussives: juss.
- cohortatives: coh.
- infinitives construct: inf. const.
- infinitives absolute: inf. abs.
- participles: part.

Step 2: Analyzing the Text

1:1

וַיְהִי בִּימֵי שְׁפֹט הַשֹּׁפְטִים וַיְהִי רָעָב בָּאָרֶץ
וַיֵּלֶךְ אִישׁ מִבֵּית לֶחֶם יְהוּדָה לָגוּר בִּשְׂדֵי מוֹאָב הוּא וְאִשְׁתּוֹ וּשְׁנֵי בָנָיו:

1. וַיְהִי—The book begins with a wayyiqtol form (from the verb הָיָה).[1] It has an introductory function and is followed by a temporal clause that provides the setting for the story to follow. See EE, 120.
2. בִּימֵי—The form בִּימֵי consists of the preposition בְּ- followed by the construct form of יָמִים, which is the plural of יוֹם. How can you tell the form is construct? See PVP, 103 (10.5); Ful., 62–63 (11.4).[2] The form

---

1. See Joüon, 390, §118c.
2. Fut., 75 (13.1); Gar., 97 (17.E.2); Kel., 59 (26.4); Ross, 100 (12.3); Seow, 118 (2.c).

develops as follows: בְּיְמֵי* < בְּיְמֵי* < בְּיְמֵי. On the contraction that occurs, see PVP, 51, note 3; Ful., 35 (8.2).[3]

_____

_____

3. שְׁפֹט—Parse this verb. Note that the infinitive construct (which is a verbal noun) is filling a genitival slot after the construct form. See EE, 78; W-OC, 601.[4]

_____

_____

4. הַשֹּׁפְטִים—Parse this form. How can you tell this is an active participle? How is the participle functioning here? (Is it attributive, predicative, or substantival?) See EE, 67.[5]

_____

_____

_____

5. וַיְהִי—This next וַיְהִי introduces additional background for the story. רָעָב, "famine," functions as the subject here, "a famine was," or the subject may be understood as indefinite, "there was a famine."

6. וַיֵּלֶךְ—This next wayyiqtol clause initiates the action of the story. Parse וַיֵּלֶךְ. A prefix vowel _tsere_ usually signals a I-_yod_ verb, but the verb הָלַךְ follows the I-_yod_ pattern in the imperfect/wayyiqtol. See PVP, 182–83 (16.16); Ful., 241 (35.5).[6]

_____

_____

7. לָגוּר—Parse this form. How is the infinitive functioning in relation to the main verb "went"? See PVP, 241–47;[7] W-OC, 605–10.[8]

_____

_____

The verb גוּר means "to live temporarily in a place (as a resident alien)." The translation "to sojourn" (KJV, NASB) is archaic, while "to live" (NRSV, NLT) fails to bring out the technical meaning of the verb. It is better to translate "to live for a while" (NIV) or "to live as a resident alien" (NET).

---

3. Gar., 74 (13.A.3); Kel., 31 (16.3); Ross, 63 (6.1); Seow, 56 (3.a).
4. See also AC, 68; GKC, 347, §114b; Joüon, 433; WHS, 194.
5. See also AC, 77–83; BHRG, 162–63; GKC, 355–62; Joüon, 409–14; WHS, 213–22; W-OC, 614–28.
6. Fut., 109 (18.3); Gar., 229 (40.A); Kel., 340 (75.2); Ross, 254 (35.4); Seow, 218 (5.c).
7. Fut., 122 (20.8); Gar., 212 (36.B.2); Kel., 181–83 (56.2); Ross, 164 (22.4); Seow, 258–59 (3).
8. See also AC, 67–73; BHRG, 154–55; GKC, 348–51; Joüon, 436–38; WHS, 192–200.

8. בִּשְׂדֵי—The form consists of a construct plural form of שָׂדֶה, "field, region, land," and a prefixed preposition. On the plural form see Joüon, 272, §90e. How can you tell the form is construct?

_____

_____

9. הוּא—The independent pronoun הוּא is resumptive, referring back to אִישׁ. The resumptive pronoun is necessary because a prepositional phrase (note . . . מִבֵּית) appears before the second element of the compound subject (the following וְאִשְׁתּוֹ). See W-OC, 295.[9] Note that the verb, which comes first in the sentence, is singular, even though the subject is compound.[10]

10. וּשְׁנֵי בָנָיו—This phrase is better translated "his two sons" here, rather than "two of his sons" (as if there were more). When the construct of שְׁנַיִם is followed by a suffixed noun, it can occasionally refer to two out of a larger number (see Gen. 22:3; 40:2; Num. 22:22; 2 Kings 5:23), but it can also refer to two items which comprise exclusively a given category (see Gen. 9:22; 48:1, 5; Exod. 18:3, 6; 32:15; 1 Sam. 2:34; Song 4:5; 7:4 [Eng. v. 3]; Ezek. 15:4). The context in Ruth 1 leads us to believe that Mahlon and Kilion were Elimelech's only sons. One gets the impression that their deaths robbed Naomi of all the men in her life (see v. 21).

1:2

וְשֵׁם הָאִישׁ אֱלִימֶלֶךְ וְשֵׁם אִשְׁתּוֹ נָעֳמִי וְשֵׁם שְׁנֵי־בָנָיו מַחְלוֹן וְכִלְיוֹן אֶפְרָתִים מִבֵּית לֶחֶם יְהוּדָה
וַיָּבֹאוּ שְׂדֵי־מוֹאָב וַיִּהְיוּ־שָׁם׃

1. וְשֵׁם—Note the disjunctive structure at the beginning of verse 2 (with the subject placed at the front of the sentence). Such clauses, especially when they have no stated verb (as here), are descriptive and provide background for the story; they do not further the action. How would you classify the clause? See the appendix (cf. EE, 124–27).[11]

_____

_____

2. הָאִישׁ—How is the article functioning on הָאִישׁ. (Note the indefinite אִישׁ in the preceding verse.) See EE, 72–73, as well as W-OC, 242.[12]

_____

_____

3. וְשֵׁם שְׁנֵי־בָנָיו—One might expect the plural "names" before "his two sons," but Hebrew tends to use the singular (cf. שֵׁם) when individuals have in common the item in view. See Joüon, 504, §136l.

---

9. See also Joüon, 541, §146c.
10. See GKC, 468, §146f; Joüon, 552, §150b; W-OC, 294.
11. See also BHRG, 346–50; W-OC, 650–52.
12. See also AC, 28–32; BHRG, 190–91; GKC, 404–10; Joüon, 505–13; WHS, 82–93.

4. אֶפְרָתִים—The form "Ephrathites" is appositional to the individuals mentioned prior to this (Elimelech, Naomi, Mahlon, and Kilion). On apposition see AC, 21–24; W-OC, 226–34.

5. וַיָּבֹאוּ—The wayyiqtol וַיָּבֹאוּ brings us back to the story line after the parenthesis. Parse this verb. How do you determine the *(a)* stem, *(b)* root, and *(c)* P-G-N?

_____

_____

6. שְׂדֵי—The form is an adverbial accusative; one must supply a preposition. See EE, 64–65.[13]

7. וַיִּהְיוּ־שָׁם—The final clause reads literally "and they were there." It is better style to translate "they remained there" (cf. NASB, NRSV). See the collocation of the wayyiqtol of הָיָה with שָׁם in Joshua 4:9; Judges 19:2; 2 Samuel 4:3; 13:38; 1 Kings 8:8; 1 Chronicles 12:40 (Eng. v. 39); 2 Chronicles 5:9; and Nehemiah 2:11.

1:3

וַיָּמָת אֱלִימֶלֶךְ אִישׁ נָעֳמִי וַתִּשָּׁאֵר הִיא וּשְׁנֵי בָנֶיהָ:

1. וַיָּמָת—Parse this verb. How do you determine the *(a)* stem, and *(b)* root?

_____

_____

_____

_____

2. אִישׁ—How is אִישׁ, "husband," syntactically related to the preceding proper name? See 1:2, note 4.

_____

_____

3. וַתִּשָּׁאֵר—Parse this verb. How do you determine the *(a)* stem, and *(b)* P-G-N? The verb is singular, despite the fact that the following subject is compound.[14] With one exception, this verb occurs in the Niphal/Hiphil. In the Niphal it means "be left, remain."

_____

_____

_____

_____

---

13. See also AC, 18–21; BHRG, 244; GKC, 372–76, §118; WHS, 50–60; W-OC, 169–73.
14. See GKC, 468, §146g; Jouön, 552, §150b; W-OC, 294.

1:4

וַיִּשְׂאוּ לָהֶם נָשִׁים מֹאֲבִיּוֹת שֵׁם הָאַחַת עָרְפָּה וְשֵׁם הַשֵּׁנִית רוּת וַיֵּשְׁבוּ שָׁם כְּעֶשֶׂר שָׁנִים:

1. וַיִּשְׂאוּ לָהֶם—Parse וַיִּשְׂאוּ. How do you determine the P-G-N? The root is difficult to spot here because the *dagesh,* indicating *nun* assimilation, does not appear in the letter *sin.* This often occurs in certain letters when they have vocal *shewa* beneath them. See PVP, 316 (26.16).[15] In the following prepositional phrase, -לְ is used reflexively, "for themselves." See BDB, 515.

2. נָשִׁים—How is נָשִׁים, "wives," related syntactically to the preceding verb? Why is there no אֵת before the word? See PVP, 56 (6.7); Ful., 33 (7.7).

3. מֹאֲבִיּוֹת—This form is feminine plural. How can you tell this from the form? It is a gentilic adjective (מֹאָבִי [ms]/מֹאֲבִיָּה [fs]), "Moabite" (cf. the noun מֹואָב, "Moab"). The *hireq yod* ending is a gentilic marker, indicating ethnicity. See W-OC, 92–93, 115.

4. שֵׁם—The form introduces an asyndetic (no conjunction) disjunctive clause that provides parenthetical information. See EE, 124–25. הָאַחַת functions here as a substantival ordinal number, "the first." Note הַשֵּׁנִית, "the second," later in the verse.

5. וַיֵּשְׁבוּ—Parse this verb. How do you determine the *(a)* stem, *(b)* root, and *(c)* P-G-N?

6. כְּעֶשֶׂר—When used with a numeral (cf. כְּעֶשֶׂר), the preposition -כְּ means "about, approximately." See BDB, 453; *HALOT,* 454.[16]

---

15. See also the last two sentences on p. 184 of PVP. See also Ross, 243 (34.2.1); Seow, note on p. 217.
16. See also Joüon, 490, §133g; W-OC, 202–3.

1:5

וַיָּמוּתוּ גַם־שְׁנֵיהֶם מַחְלוֹן וְכִלְיוֹן וַתִּשָּׁאֵר הָאִשָּׁה מִשְּׁנֵי יְלָדֶיהָ וּמֵאִישָׁהּ׃

1. וַיָּמוּתוּ—Parse this verb. How do you determine the *(a)* stem, *(b)* root, and *(c)* P-G-N?

2. גַם־שְׁנֵיהֶם—The adverb גַם here means "also, even." The form שְׁנֵיהֶם consists of what elements? How is מַחְלוֹן וְכִלְיוֹן related syntactically to שְׁנֵיהֶם? See 1:2, note 4.

3. וַתִּשָּׁאֵר—After the verb וַתִּשָּׁאֵר, "she was left," the preposition מִן (note מִשְּׁנֵי and מֵאִישָׁהּ) is privative, indicating what was missing or unavailable. See AC, 118; W-OC, 214. Note NIV "without."

4. יְלָדֶיהָ—This form consists of what elements? Naomi's sons are called יְלָדִים here (rather than בָּנִים). This is the only place where יֶלֶד is used of married men. Perhaps this reflects Naomi's motherly perspective.

1:6

וַתָּקָם הִיא וְכַלֹּתֶיהָ וַתָּשָׁב מִשְּׂדֵי מוֹאָב
כִּי שָׁמְעָה בִּשְׂדֵה מוֹאָב כִּי־פָקַד יְהוָה אֶת־עַמּוֹ לָתֵת לָהֶם לָחֶם׃

1. וַתָּקָם—Parse this verb. How do you determine the *(a)* stem, *(b)* root, and *(c)* P-G-N? Once more a singular verb is used before a compound subject (see 1:3b).

2. וְכַלֹּתֶיהָ—This form consists of what elements? How can you tell the form is feminine plural? See PVP, 85 (9.7); Ful., 77 (13.2).

_____

_____

3. וַתָּשָׁב—Parse this verb. How do you determine the (a) stem, (b) root, and (c) P-G-N?

_____

_____

_____

_____

In the discourse structure of the story, this verb summarizes what the remainder of the story is about—Naomi's return to her homeland.[17] (Note the use of this same verb form in v. 22, which provides a summarizing conclusion to what has preceded.) Verse 7 begins a more detailed account of her return.

4. כִּי שָׁמְעָה—What type of dependent clause is . . . כִּי שָׁמְעָה? See AC, 171–86; EE, 113–17; W-OC, 632–46. How is the perfect verbal form functioning here? (What is the temporal relationship between the action expressed by this verb and that of the main verb, "she returned"?) See AC, 54–56; EE, 86–89; W-OC, 486–95.

_____

_____

5. כִּי פָקַד—What type of dependent clause is . . . כִּי פָקַד? See AC, 171–86; EE, 113–17; W-OC, 632–46. How is the perfect verbal form functioning here? (What is the temporal relationship between the action expressed by this verb and that of the preceding verb, "she had heard"?) See AC, 54–56; EE, 86–89; W-OC, 486–95.

_____

_____

The verb פָקַד has the primary meaning "pay attention to, observe with care, interest." Here it refers by metonymy to the consequence of the Lord's attention and has the connotation "visit graciously" (see Gen. 21:1; 50:24–25). The next clause explains more specifically that he brought relief from the famine and restored Israel's crops.

---

17. Another option is that the wayyiqtol has an ingressive function here, perhaps in conjunction with the preceding verb ("she arose"): "she began to return." Note that the preceding clause states that she and her daughters-in-law arose, perhaps implying that all three went back to Judah. But the following story clearly indicates this was not the case. Orpah turned back; only Ruth did in fact return with Naomi.

6. לָחֶת—Parse this form. For help with this highly irregular form, see PVP, 430–31; Ful., 232 (34.4).[18] How is the infinitive construct functioning in relation to the verb פָּקַד? Discuss at least two options. See PVP, 241–47;[19] W-OC, 605–10.[20] One of the options is reflected in NIV ("by providing"; cf. NLT as well).

_____

_____

_____

7. לָהֶם—Note how the 3mp suffix (cf. לָהֶם) refers back to the collective singular noun עַם (cf. עַמּוֹ, "his people"), which has implied plurality.

Step 3: Interpretive Translation

In light of the decisions you have made in your analysis, provide an interpretive, paraphrastic translation of Ruth 1:1–6.

_____

_____

_____

_____

_____

_____

_____

_____

Step 4: Structural Outline

Outline the narrative structure of Ruth 1:1–6. Carefully delineate the narrative mainline (initiated and extended by wayyiqtol forms), offline (nonstandard) constructions, and quotations. Using the categories listed in the appendix (cf. EE, 120–27), classify all wayyiqtol and disjunctive clauses that are in the narrative framework. You need not classify clauses within quotations.

_____

_____

_____

_____

_____

---

18. Fut., 121 (20.6); Gar., 207 (35.B.4); Kel., 305 (73.2); Ross, 245 (34.2.3); Seow, 258 (2.d).
19. Fut., 122 (20.8); Gar., 212 (36.B.2); Kel., 181–83 (56.2); Ross, 164 (22.4); Seow, 258–59 (3).
20. See also AC, 67–73; BHRG, 154–55; GKC, 348–51; Joüon, 436–38; WHS, 192–200.

_____

_____

_____

_____

_____

Scene 2: Ruth 1:7–19a: Ruth Returns with Naomi

To facilitate classroom use, this longer scene is divided into three assignments, covering verses 7–10, 11–14, and 15–19a.

Assignment 1

Step 1: Initial View

Read Ruth 1:7–10 in the Hebrew text, using an interlinear if you desire. Underline any words or forms you do not recognize. Try to identify verbal forms and label them as follows:

- wayyiqtol verbal forms: wc-y (the so-called *waw* consecutive with the yiqtol, usually identified as a preterite or imperfect)
- weqatal forms: wc-q (the so-called *waw* consecutive with the qatal, that is, perfect)
- simple perfects (without *waw*): pf.
- simple imperfects (without *waw*): impf.
- imperatives: impv.
- jussives: juss.
- cohortatives: coh.
- infinitives construct: inf. const.
- infinitives absolute: inf. abs.
- participles: part.

Step 2: Analyzing the Text

1:7

וַתֵּצֵא מִן־הַמָּקוֹם אֲשֶׁר הָיְתָה־שָׁמָּה וּשְׁתֵּי כַלֹּתֶיהָ עִמָּהּ וַתֵּלַכְנָה בַדֶּרֶךְ לָשׁוּב אֶל־אֶרֶץ יְהוּדָה׃

1. וַתֵּצֵא—Parse this verb. How do you determine the *(a)* stem, and *(b)* root? As noted above, this verb begins a more detailed account of Naomi's return. On this specifying or focusing use of a wayyiqtol form, see the appendix (cf. EE, 122).

_____

_____

_____

_____

2. הָיְתָה—Parse this verb. How do you determine the P-G-N? For help with the ending see PVP, 154 (14.7); Ful., 265 (37.4).[21] How is the perfect verbal form functioning here? (How does it relate to the main verb, "she went out"?)

_____

_____

_____

3. שָׁמָּה—The form is the adverb שָׁם with a terminative ending, but here the form is not used with a verb of motion and is simply equivalent to שָׁם. See BDB, 1027. The collocation of the relative pronoun אֲשֶׁר and שָׁמָּה indicates location, "where."

4. וּשְׁתֵּי כַלֹּתֶיהָ עִמָּהּ—This construction is either a compound subject ("and she and her two daughters-in-law along with her went out") or a disjunctive, parenthetical clause ("Now her two daughters-in-law were with her"). שְׁתֵּי is the construct of שְׁתַּיִם, the feminine dual form of the number two (BDB, 1040–41; HALOT, 1605).

5. וַתֵּלַכְנָה—Parse this verb. How do you determine the P-G-N? The prefix vowel _tsere_ usually signals a I-_yod_ verb, but the verb הָלַךְ follows the I-_yod_ pattern in the imperfect/wayyiqtol. See PVP, 182–83 (16.16); Ful., 241 (35.5).[22]

_____

_____

6. לָשׁוּב—Parse this form. How is the infinitive construct functioning in relation to the main verb? See PVP, 241–47;[23] W-OC, 605–10.[24]

_____

_____

1:8

וַתֹּאמֶר נָעֳמִי לִשְׁתֵּי כַלֹּתֶיהָ לֵכְנָה שֹּׁבְנָה אִשָּׁה לְבֵית אִמָּהּ
יַעֲשֶׂה יְהוָה עִמָּכֶם חֶסֶד כַּאֲשֶׁר עֲשִׂיתֶם עִם־הַמֵּתִים וְעִמָּדִי׃

1. לֵכְנָה שֹּׁבְנָה—Parse שֹּׁבְנָה and לֵכְנָה.[25] How do you determine the (a) P-G-N and (b) root of each form? How are the imperatives functioning here? See EE, 105–6.[26]

---

21. Fut., 89–90 (15.6); Gar., 165 (27.E); Kel., 288 (72.3); Ross, 260 (36.2); Seow, 161 (3.a).

22. Fut., 109 (18.3); Gar., 229 (40.A); Kel., 340 (75.2); Ross, 254 (35.4); Seow, 218 (5.c).

23. Fut., 122 (20.8); Gar., 212 (36.B.2); Kel., 181–83 (56.2); Ross, 164 (22.4); Seow, 258–59 (3).

24. See also AC, 67–73; BHRG, 154–55; GKC, 348–51; Joüon, 436–38; WHS, 192–200.

25. Note the presence of a _dagesh forte_ in the first letter of שֹּׁבְנָה. On the use of this so-called conjunctive _dagesh,_ see PVP, 317 (26.17), as well as GKC, 71, §20f.

26. See also AC, 63–65; BHRG, 150–51; GKC, 324–25, §110; Joüon, 378–79; W-OC, 571–73.

2. אִשָּׁה—The form is functioning here in a distributive sense, "each one." See BDB, 61.

3. יַעֲשֶׂה—As Brotzman explains, the *kethib* (which would be vocalized יַעֲשֶׂה) is an imperfect, while the *qere* (vocalized יַעַשׂ) is a jussive.[27] How do we know the *qere* form is distinctively jussive? See PVP, 216; Ful., 266–67 (37.4).[28] The jussive form is more likely here (cf. 2 Sam. 2:6), expressing Naomi's prayer of blessing upon her daughters-in-law.

4. עִמָּכֶם—The pronominal suffix on עִמָּכֶם appears to be a second masculine plural form, but this is likely a preservation of an archaic common dual form.[29]

5. חֶסֶד—The word חֶסֶד frequently means "loyalty, devotion, commitment." When collocated with עָשָׂה it normally refers to fair or benevolent treatment as a reward for good deeds rendered, usually as an act of allegiance. (See Gen. 40:14; 47:29; Josh. 2:12, 14; Judg. 8:35; 1 Sam. 20:14; 2 Sam. 2:6; 9:1, 3, 7.) The remainder of the prayer (see v. 9) suggests Naomi has the security of marriage in mind here. She asks God to reward the girls for their past devotion by giving them new husbands.

6. עֲשִׂיתֶם—Parse this verb. How do you determine the root? See PVP, 154 (14.7); Ful., 266 (37.4).[30] The form appears to be second masculine plural, but this is odd since two women are being addressed. The form is probably an archaic common dual. See note 4 above.

7. וְעִמָּדִי—The form עִמָּדִי is an alternate form of עִמִּי, "with me." See BDB, 767; *HALOT,* 842.

1:9

יִתֵּן יְהוָה לָכֶם וּמְצֶאןָ מְנוּחָה אִשָּׁה בֵּית אִישָׁהּ וַתִּשַּׁק לָהֶן וַתִּשֶּׂאנָה קוֹלָן וַתִּבְכֶּינָה׃

1. יִתֵּן—Parse this verb. How do you determine the root? This is probably a jussive continuing Naomi's prayer of blessing. (Recall that with most verbs there is formal overlap between the imperfect and jussive. One must determine the sense from context.)

---

27. Ellis R. Brotzman, *Old Testament Textual Criticism: A Practical Introduction* (Grand Rapids: Baker, 1994), 135–36.
28. Fut., 151 (24.8); Gar., 226 (39.B); Kel., 292 (72.8); Ross, 261 (36.2.1); Seow, 235 (1.a).
29. See Frederic W. Bush, *Ruth, Esther,* WBC (Dallas: Word Books, 1996), 75–76.
30. Fut., 89 (15.5); Gar., 165 (27.E); Kel., 288 (72.3); Ross, 260 (36.1); Seow, 161 (3.a).

2. וּמְצֶאןָ—Parse this verb. How do you determine the P-G-N? (Note that the ending נָ- is defectively written here, without the final *he.*) How is this form functioning after the jussive? See EE, 108–10, especially p. 110.[31] It is difficult to bring out the force of the construction in English; most translations simply use "that" here.

3. מְנוּחָה—In this context (note "in the home of another husband") מְנוּחָה, "rest," refers to the security that comes from marriage (see 3:1 as well).

4. בֵּית—The noun is an adverbial accusative; one must supply the preposition "in." See Joüon, 487, §113c.

5. וַתִּשַּׁק—Parse this verb. How do you determine the root? Why is the stem not Niphal (despite the *i* + *dagesh* + *a* pattern)? For help you may want to review PVP, 184 (16.18) and 288 (24.6); Ful., 231–32 (34.3–34.4).[32]

6. לָהֶן—The preposition on לָהֶן introduces the object. See BDB, 517; *HALOT,* 509–10.[33]

7. וַתִּשֶּׂאנָה—Parse this verb. How do you determine the *(a)* root, and *(b)* P-G-N? The expression "lifted their voice(s)" is best translated as an adverb modifying the following verb. Note NIV "wept aloud" (cf. NRSV) and NET, "wept loudly." On the idiomatic use of the singular "voice" (one expects the plural) see Joüon (504, §136l), as well as 1:2, note 3.

8. וַתִּבְכֶּינָה—Parse this verb. How do you determine the *(a)* P-G-N, and *(b)* root? For help see PVP, 176–77 (16.6–7); Ful., 265–66 (37.4).[34]

---

31. See also GKC, 325, §110i; Joüon, 384, §116f. Joüon calls this an object clause (651, §177h).
32. Fut., 88 (15.3) and 226 (36.2); Gar., 179 (30.C) and 246 (43.D); Kel., 307 (73.2); Ross, 243 (34.2.1) and 246 (34.3); Seow, 216 (4.a) and 292 (4.a).
33. See also Joüon, 447–48, §125k; W-OC, 210–11.
34. Fut., 89 (15.5); Gar., 187 (31.E); Kel., 288 (72.3); Ross, 260 (36.1); Seow, 216 (3).

1:10

וַתֹּאמַרְנָה־לָּהּ כִּי־אִתָּךְ נָשׁוּב לְעַמֵּךְ׃

1. וַתֹּאמַרְנָה—Parse this verb. How do you determine the P-G-N? אָמַר is one of a handful of I-*aleph* verbs that has a *holem* prefix vowel in the Qal prefixed verbal form. See GKC, 184, §68b.

_____

_____

2. כִּי—כִּי appears at the beginning of the quotation and is not subordinate to a preceding verb. It can be translated "no, on the contrary" (*HALOT,* 470; cf. NASB, NRSV, NET) or "surely" (KJV; cf. the texts listed in BDB, 472, 1.e, though our passage is not included there).[35]

3. אִתָּךְ—The form אִתָּךְ consists of what elements? See PVP, 90 (9.14); Ful., 83–84 (14.3).[36]

_____

_____

4. נָשׁוּב—Parse this verb. How do you recognize the *(a)* stem, and *(b)* P-G-N? How is the imperfect functioning here?

_____

_____

_____

_____

Step 3: Interpretive Translation

In light of the decisions you have made in your analysis, provide an interpretive, paraphrastic translation of Ruth 1:7–10.

_____

_____

_____

_____

_____

_____

_____

_____

---

35. According to BDB, כִּי here introduces a direct quotation. See pp. 471–72 (1.b).
36. Gar., 83 (14.A.4); Kel., 69 (27.1); Ross, 123 (15.7); Seow, 95 (2.a).

Step 4: Structural Outline

Outline the narrative structure of Ruth 1:7–10. Carefully delineate the narrative mainline (initiated and extended by wayyiqtol forms), offline (nonstandard) constructions, and quotations. Using the categories listed in the appendix (cf. EE, 120–27), classify all wayyiqtol and disjunctive clauses that are in the narrative framework. You need not classify clauses within quotations.

_____

_____

_____

_____

_____

_____

_____

_____

_____

_____

Assignment 2

Step 1: Initial View

Read Ruth 1:11–14 in the Hebrew text, using an interlinear if you desire. Underline any words or forms you do not recognize. Try to identify verbal forms and label them as follows:

- wayyiqtol verbal forms: wc-y (the so-called *waw* consecutive with the yiqtol, usually identified as a preterite or imperfect)
- weqatal forms: wc-q (the so-called *waw* consecutive with the qatal, that is, perfect)
- simple perfects (without *waw*): pf.
- simple imperfects (without *waw*): impf.
- imperatives: impv.
- jussives: juss.
- cohortatives: coh.
- infinitives construct: inf. const.
- infinitives absolute: inf. abs.
- participles: part.

Step 2: Analyzing the Text

1:11

וַתֹּאמֶר נָעֳמִי שֹׁבְנָה בְנֹתַי לָמָּה תֵלַכְנָה עִמִּי הַעוֹד־לִי בָנִים בְּמֵעַי וְהָיוּ לָכֶם לַאֲנָשִׁים:

1. בְנֹתַי—This form consists of what elements? How is the form functioning in the sentence? See AC, 7; EE, 61.

2. תֵלַכְנָה—How is the imperfect form תֵלַכְנָה functioning here in this rhetorical question?

3. הַעוֹד־לִי—What function does the *he* prefixed to עוֹד have? See PVP, 75–76 (8.10); Ful., 42 (9.3).[37] The prepositional phrase לִי, "to me," is possessive. See W-OC, 206–7.[38] The Hebrew text reads literally, "Still to me sons?" One may translate, "Do I still have sons?"

4. בְּמֵעַי—This form consists of what elements? How can you tell the noun is plural? See PVP, 83–84 (9.4–9.5); Ful., 71 (12.2).[39]

5. וְהָיוּ—Parse this verb. How do you determine the P-G-N? This is a case of the perfect with *waw* consecutive expressing a logical consequence of the preceding statement. Usually this construction follows an imperfect, but in this case it is preceded by a verbless interrogative sentence. See W-OC, 534; GKC, 333, §112p.

6. לָכֶם—The prepositional phrase לָכֶם "to you," is possessive (see AC, 112–13; W-OC, 206–7); it may be translated, "your." The apparent masculine suffix is probably an archaic common dual form. See 1:8, note 4.

---

37. Fut., 171 (27.5); Gar., 158–59 (26.C); Kel., 94 (34.1); Ross, 146 (19.5); Seow, 109 (6.b).
38. See also AC, 112–13; Joüon, 487, §133d.
39. Fut., 114 (19.1); Gar., 87–88 (16.B); Kel., 59 (26.4); Ross, 115 (14.4); Seow, 118 (2.c).

7. לָאֲנָשִׁים—The preposition -לְ (cf. לָאֲנָשִׁים), when collocated with הָיָה, indicates a transition into a new state or condition. See BDB, 512. The last clause may be translated, "that they may become your husbands" (NRSV).

1:12

שֹׁבְנָה בְנֹתַי לֵכְןָ כִּי זָקַנְתִּי מִהְיוֹת לְאִישׁ
כִּי אָמַרְתִּי יֶשׁ־לִי תִקְוָה גַּם הָיִיתִי הַלַּיְלָה לְאִישׁ וְגַם יָלַדְתִּי בָנִים:

1. לֵכְןָ—The form לֵכְןָ is a defectively written form of לֵכְנָה (cf. v. 8), with *qamets* at the end of the form rather than the usual *qamets he*.

2. כִּי זָקַנְתִּי—What type of dependent clause is . . . כִּי זָקַנְתִּי? How is the perfect verbal form functioning?

_____

_____

3. מִהְיוֹת—Parse this form. How do you determine the root? How is the preposition מִן (prefixed to the form) functioning here? See PVP, 53–54 (6.6); Ful., 165 (26.4), as well as AC, 116–19; W-OC, 214; BDB, 582–83.

_____

_____

4. לְאִישׁ—The prepositional phrase לְאִישׁ, "for a man," is possessive: "(I am too old to be) a man's." See AC, 112–13; W-OC, 206–7.

5. כִּי אָמַרְתִּי—The כִּי at the beginning of verse 12b has either a conditional or concessive sense, "even if."[40] A perfect verbal form (cf. אָמַרְתִּי, "I said, thought") can appear in such clauses. See GKC, 313, §107p; 497, §159aa.[41]

6. יֶשׁ־לִי—The construction יֶשׁ־לִי, literally, "there is to me," is possessive: "I have (hope)." See PVP, 253–54 (21.7).[42]

7. גַּם—The two clauses that follow (cf. גַּם . . . וְגַם) are parenthetical and specify what it would mean for Naomi to have hope. In each case גַּם is intensive, "even if."[43]

8. הַלַּיְלָה—When used with temporal terms, the article can have a demonstrative force, so הַלַּיְלָה may be translated "this night, tonight."

9. לְאִישׁ—The preposition -לְ (cf. לְאִישׁ), when collocated with הָיָה, indicates a transition into a new state or condition. See BDB, 512. The clause may be translated, "(Even if) I became . . . a man's" (i.e., even if I got married).

---

40. See Bush, *Ruth, Esther,* 78.
41. See also Joüon, 630, §167i.
42. Fut., 142 (23.1); Gar., 108 (19.A); Ross, 109–10 (13.3); Seow, 108 (3.c).
43. See Bush, *Ruth, Esther,* 78–79, as well as GKC, 483, §153.

1:13

הֲלָהֵן תְּשַׂבֵּרְנָה עַד אֲשֶׁר יִגְדָּלוּ הֲלָהֵן תֵּעָגֵנָה לְבִלְתִּי הֱיוֹת לְאִישׁ
אַל בְּנֹתַי כִּי־מַר־לִי מְאֹד מִכֶּם כִּי־יָצְאָה בִי יַד־יְהוָה:

1. הֲלָהֵן—This word, which appears twice in the verse, is problematic. The form may consist of the interrogative particle followed by the Aramaized conjunction לָהֵן, "therefore" (see Dan. 2:6, 9; 4:24, as well as BDB, 530; GKC, 302, §103 note 4). In this case one may translate, "Would you, therefore, (wait)?" (see NASB; cf. NRSV). Another option is to understand לָהֵן as a suffixed preposition (cf. KJV, NLT), but why would a feminine suffix be used to refer to the hypothetical sons born to Naomi? The suffix may be a masculine dual form borrowed from Moabite,[44] though some prefer to emend the text to read לָהֶם (see *HALOT*, 521).

2. תְּשַׂבֵּרְנָה—Parse this verb. How do you determine the *(a)* stem, and *(b)* P-G-N? This verb occurs exclusively in the Piel stem, which may have a frequentative function here.[45]

_____

_____

_____

3. עַד אֲשֶׁר יִגְדָּלוּ—The construction is temporal, "until." The imperfect is functioning as an anterior future (EE, 92), indicating a condition that, though future from the speaker's perspective, is viewed as preceding the action of the main clause ("would you wait?").

4. תֵּעָגֵנָה—Parse this verb. How do you determine the *(a)* stem, and *(b)* P-G-N? Explain why the prefix vowel is *tsere* rather than *hireq*. See PVP, 299 (25.6–25.7); Ful., 190 (29.4).[46] This is the only occurrence of this verb in the Hebrew Bible. Apparently, it means "to shut oneself in" (reflexive use of the stem). One expects to see a *dagesh forte* in the *nun* (representing the juxtaposition of the third root letter and the *nun* of the ending), but it is omitted (see GKC, 139, §51m).

_____

_____

_____

5. לְבִלְתִּי הֱיוֹת—The negative particle לְבִלְתִּי is used before infinitives. See PVP, 241 (20.11).[47] How is the infinitive construct הֱיוֹת functioning in relation to the main verb? See PVP, 241–47;[48] W-OC, 605–10.[49] Note once more the possessive idiom: "to be for a man" = "to be a man's," i.e., "to be married."

---

44. See Robert L. Hubbard Jr., *The Book of Ruth*, NICOT (Grand Rapids: Eerdmans, 1988), 111, note 31.
45. On this function of the Piel stem see Joüon, 155; W-OC, 414–16.
46. Fut., 232; Gar., 245 (43.D.1); Kel., 224 (66.3); Ross, 232–33 (33.1.1); Seow, 292 (4.b).
47. Fut., 122 (20.8); Gar., 212 (36.B.2); Kel., 183 (56.2); Ross, 164 (22.5); Seow, 259 (4.a).
48. Fut., 122 (20.8); Gar., 212 (36.B.2); Kel., 181–83 (56.2); Ross, 164 (22.4); Seow, 258–59 (3).
49. See also AC, 67–73; BHRG, 154–55; GKC, 348–51; Joüon, 436–38; WHS, 192–200.

_____

_____

6. אַל בְּנֹתַי כִּי—The כִּי following אַל בְּנֹתַי, "no, my daughters," is either directly causal ("for") or emphatic ("surely"). (The latter would be indirectly causal.) The logic of Naomi's statement is not entirely clear. If אַל בְּנֹתַי is the answer to the preceding questions (v. 13a), then Naomi is saying that they would not be willing to wait around for her to raise up new husbands for them because her suffering would be too much for the girls to bear and they would be unwilling to stay with her that long. It seems more likely, however, that אַל בְּנֹתַי is Naomi's response to their stated intention of returning with her (cf. v. 10). In this case, she tells them they must not stay with her because her suffering is too much for them to bear.[50]

7. מַר—Parse this verb. How do you determine the root? (For help see PVP, 156 [14.10]; Ful., 280 [38.5].) How is the perfect functioning here? (See AC, 54–56; EE, 86–89.) The subject is impersonal ("it").[51] The verb refers primarily to Naomi's emotional pain over the loss of her husband and sons, but it may also encompass the economic distress that resulted from their deaths.

_____

_____

_____

8. מִכֶּם—How is the preposition מִן functioning here? (Note that the verb has an adjectival meaning—"it is bitter.") See PVP, 53–54 (6.6); Ful., 165 (26.4).[52] Naomi seems to be saying that her pain exceeds that of Orpah and Ruth; after all she lost a husband and two sons, while they each lost a husband. However, her argument may be more nuanced than this. Perhaps her point is that her suffering is too great a burden for them to attempt to bear. In this case the preposition has the force of "too much for."[53] See the NET note. On the apparent masculine suffix, see 1:8, note 4.

_____

_____

_____

9. יָצְאָה—Parse this verb. How do you determine the P-G-N? How is the perfect functioning here? (See AC, 54–56; EE, 86–89.)

_____

_____

_____

_____

50. There is an implied jussive. See Joüon, 606, §160j.
51. See Joüon, 559, §152d.
52. Gar., 70 (12.B.2); Kel., 30 (15.3); Ross, 82–83 (9.3); Seow, 73 (5.a).
53. See Joüon, 523–24, §141i.

10. בִּי—In this context the preposition -בְּ (cf. בִי) has the sense of "against." See W-OC, 197; BDB, 89, II.4 .a. The Lord's "hand" is here a symbol of his power, which Naomi feels he has exerted to her detriment. Most translations render the expression literally, "has gone out against" (cf. NIV), but some try to be more idiomatic: "has caused me to suffer" (NLT), "is afflicting me" (NET).

1:14

וַתִּשֶּׂנָה קוֹלָן וַתִּבְכֶּינָה עוֹד וַתִּשַּׁק עָרְפָּה לַחֲמוֹתָהּ וְרוּת דָּבְקָה בָּהּ׃

1. וַתִּשֶּׂנָה—In the form וַתִּשֶּׂנָה the quiescent third root letter *aleph* is not written. See GKC, 206, §74k,[54] as well as PVP, 22 (3.9).[55] For the same form with the *aleph* written, see 1:9.

2. לַחֲמוֹתָהּ—The preposition on לַחֲמוֹתָהּ introduces the object after the verb "kissed." See 1:9, note 6. The form consists of the preposition, the noun חֲמוֹת, "mother-in-law," and a 3fs pronominal suffix.

    After לַחֲמוֹתָהּ, "to her mother-in-law," the Septuagint adds, "and she returned to her people," which, when retroverted to Hebrew, would read וַתָּשָׁב אֶל־עַמָּהּ (see *BHS* note a). (The verb form is a Qal wayyiqtol 3fs from שׁוּב.) This may be an interpretive addition in the Septuagint. In this case the translator (or his source) made the implicit explicit and harmonized the text of verse 14 with verse 15. However, it is also possible that the extra clause was accidentally omitted. A scribe's eye could have jumped from the initial *waw* on וַתָּשָׁב to the initial *waw* on וְרוּת in the following clause, leaving out all of the intervening words: ותשב אל עמה ורות. Or his eye could have jumped from the final *he* on לַחֲמוֹתָהּ to the final *he* on עַמָּהּ, leaving out the intervening words: לחמותה ותשב אל עמה. See Brotzman, 137–38.

4. וְרוּת—What type of clause is . . . .וְרוּת? How can you tell this from the form? How is the clause functioning here? See the appendix (cf. EE, 124–27).[56]

___

5. בָּהּ—The preposition -בְּ (cf. בָּהּ) here introduces the object of the verb דָּבְקָה. See W-OC, 198–99; *HALOT*, 104, no. 11. Elsewhere the idiom -דָּבַק בְּ has several meanings:

   a. cling to, stay close to, stick to (Gen. 2:24; Num. 36:7, 9; Deut. 13:18 [Eng. v. 17]; 28:60; Ruth 2:23; 2 Kings 5:27; Job 19:20; 31:7; Ps. 101:3; Ezek. 29:4)
   b. be bound to emotionally (Gen. 34:3)
   c. be loyal to (Deut. 4:4; 10:20; 11:22; 13:4; 30:20; Josh. 22:5; 23:8; 2 Sam. 20:2; 1 Kings 11:2; 2 Kings 18:6; Pss. 63:8; 119:31)
   d. form alliances with (Josh. 23:12)

   In verse 14 Ruth's action contrasts with Orpah's goodbye kiss, so a hug is apparently in view (cf. NET). This hug was an expression of her deep emotional attachment and loyalty to Naomi.

___

54. See also Joüon, 202, §78f.
55. Fut., 82–84 (14.7–14.9); Gar., 164 (27.D); Kel., 275 (71.3); Ross, 63 (6.1); Seow, 13 (11).
56. See also BHRG, 346–50; W-OC, 650–52.

Step 3: Interpretive Translation

In light of the decisions you have made in your analysis, provide an interpretive, paraphrastic translation of Ruth 1:11–14.

_____

_____

_____

_____

_____

_____

_____

_____

Step 4: Structural Outline

Outline the narrative structure of Ruth 1:11–14. Carefully delineate the narrative mainline (initiated and extended by wayyiqtol forms), offline (nonstandard) constructions, and quotations. Using the categories listed in the appendix (cf. EE, 120–27), classify all wayyiqtol and disjunctive clauses that are in the narrative framework. You need not classify clauses within quotations.

_____

_____

_____

_____

_____

_____

_____

_____

_____

Assignment 3

Step 1: Initial View

Read Ruth 1:15–19a in the Hebrew text, using an interlinear if you desire. Underline any words or forms you do not recognize. Try to identify verbal forms and label them as follows:

- wayyiqtol verbal forms: wc-y (the so-called _waw_ consecutive with the yiqtol, usually identified as a preterite or imperfect)
- weqatal forms: wc-q (the so-called _waw_ consecutive with the qatal, that is, perfect)

- simple perfects (without *waw*): pf.
- simple imperfects (without *waw*): impf.
- imperatives: impv.
- jussives: juss.
- cohortatives: coh.
- infinitives construct: inf. const.
- infinitives absolute: inf. abs.
- participles: part.

Step 2: Analyzing the Text

1:15

וַתֹּאמֶר הִנֵּה שָׁבָה יְבִמְתֵּךְ אֶל־עַמָּהּ וְאֶל־אֱלֹהֶיהָ שׁוּבִי אַחֲרֵי יְבִמְתֵּךְ׃

1. שָׁבָה—Parse this verb. How do you determine the *(a)* root, and *(b)* P-G-N? Notice the placement of the accent on the first syllable. How does this help identify the form? (See PVP, 158 and, especially, 261; Ful., 255 [36.5].)[57]

_____

_____

_____

_____

2. יְבִמְתֵּךְ—This form consists of what elements? How can you tell the noun is feminine? See PVP, 85 (9.7); Ful., 77–78 (13.2).

_____

_____

3. אֱלֹהֶיהָ—The form may be translated "her gods," since Orpah was probably a polytheist, but it is also possible to translate "her god," since the Moabites worshiped Chemosh as their national patron deity. In the latter case the plural is one of respect; the suffixed form of אֱלֹהִים can be used as a plural of respect for foreign gods (see, e.g., Judg. 9:27; 1 Sam. 5:7; 1 Kings 18:24), including Chemosh (Judg. 11:24; cf also 1 Kings 11:33).

4. שׁוּבִי—Parse this verb. What does the *hireq yod* ending indicate? See PVP, 206–7; Ful., 111 (18.4).[58]

_____

_____

---

57. Gar., 202–3 (34.B.5); Kel., 318 (74.3); Ross, 276 (38.2.2); Seow, 163 (4).
58. Fut., 149 (24.5); Gar., 215 (37.A); Kel., 165 (48.1), 167 (48.2); Ross, 149–50 (20.2); Seow, 237 (3).

1:16

וַתֹּאמֶר רוּת אַל־תִּפְגְּעִי־בִי לְעָזְבֵךְ לָשׁוּב מֵאַחֲרָיִךְ
כִּי אֶל־אֲשֶׁר תֵּלְכִי אֵלֵךְ וּבַאֲשֶׁר תָּלִינִי אָלִין עַמֵּךְ עַמִּי וֵאלֹהַיִךְ אֱלֹהָי:

1. תִּפְגְּעִי—Parse this verb. How do you determine the P-G-N? The presence of אַל before תִּפְגְּעִי indicates the verb is a negated jussive. The preposition -בְּ (cf. בִי) introduces the object. See *HALOT,* 104, no. 11.

2. לְעָזְבֵךְ—Parse this form. How do you determine the stem? On the vowel pointing under the *ayin,* see PVP, 240 (20.9); Ful., 180–81 (28.4).[59] How is the preposition functioning in relation to the preceding verb? (See AC, 68–69; W-OC, 606.) How is the pronominal suffix functioning in relation to the infinitive? See PVP, 240 (20.9); Ful., 181 (28.4).

3. לָשׁוּב—Parse this form. How is the preposition functioning in relation to the preceding infinitive? See PVP, 241–47;[60] W-OC, 605–10.[61] Note: The translations use "to/and" before their translation of this form, but there is no conjunction in the Hebrew text. Is mere coordination all that is involved here?

4. מֵאַחֲרָיִךְ—This form consists of what elements?

5. כִּי—What type of subordinate clause does כִּי introduce here? Explain the logical relationship of this clause to the preceding negated jussive.

---

59. Fut., 120 (20.5); Gar., 211 (36.A); Kel., 183 (56.2); Ross, 161–62 (22.2); Seow, 255 (1.b).
60. Fut., 122 (20.8); Gar., 212 (36.B.2); Kel., 181–83 (56.2); Ross, 164 (22.4); Seow, 258–59 (3).
61. See also AC, 67–73; BHRG, 154–55; GKC, 348–51; Joüon, 436–38; WHS, 192–200.

6. אֶל־אֲשֶׁר—This construction, meaning "to which," may be translated, "to the place which." The phrase בַּאֲשֶׁר, "in which," later in the verse may be translated, "in the place where." On both constructions, see BDB, 82, 4.b.

7. תֵּלְכִי אֵלֵךְ—Parse תֵּלְכִי and אֵלֵךְ. How do you determine the *(a)* root and *(b)* P-G-N of these forms? The *tsere* prefix vowel normally indicates a I-*yod* verb, but הָלַךְ follows this pattern in the imperfect. See PVP, 182–83 (16.16); Ful., 241 (35.5).[62]

_____

_____

8. תָּלִינִי אָלִין—Parse תָּלִינִי and אָלִין. How do you determine the stem of these forms? Theoretically there are two options. Imperfect forms of hollow verbs with middle *yod* (like שִׂים, as opposed to קוּם and בּוֹא) have the *a* + *i* vowel pattern in both the Qal and Hiphil stems (see PVP, 182 and 361; Ful., 259).[63] So one has to determine the stem from the semantic sense. Does the basic meaning or a causative nuance fit better here?

_____

_____

_____

9. . . . עַמֵּךְ—The juxtapositioning of the suffixed nouns with no intervening verb is a way of equating the two items: "your people, my people" = "your people (will be) my people," and "your God, my God" = "your God (will be) my God."

1:17

בַּאֲשֶׁר תָּמוּתִי אָמוּת וְשָׁם אֶקָּבֵר כֹּה יַעֲשֶׂה יְהוָה לִי וְכֹה יֹסִיף כִּי הַמָּוֶת יַפְרִיד בֵּינִי וּבֵינֵךְ:

1. תָּמוּתִי אָמוּת—Parse תָּמוּתִי and אָמוּת. How do you determine the *(a)* stem and *(b)* root of each form?

_____

_____

_____

---

62. Fut., 109 (18.3); Gar., 229 (40.A); Kel., 340 (75.2); Ross, 254 (35.4); Seow, 218 (5.c).
63. Fut., 156 (24.2), 215; Gar., 185 (31.C), 278 (48.B.6); Kel., 319 (74.3), 324 (74.5); Ross, 276 (38.2.3), 280 (38.7); Seow, 219–20 (7), 278–79 (1.j).

2. אֶקָּבֵר—Parse this verb. How do you determine the *(a)* P-G-N, and *(b)* stem? How is the stem functioning here? (See AC, 38–41; EE, 79.)

_____

_____

_____

3. כֹּה—The second half of the verse contains an oath. The first part of the oath, consisting of two clauses, each introduced by כֹּה, "thus," describes the punishment for breaking the promise. The second part of the oath, introduced by כִּי, gives the condition of the oath. This structure is formulaic, appearing with slight variations in 1 Samuel 14:44; 20:13; 2 Samuel 3:9; 1 Kings 2:23; 19:2.

The description of the punishment is vague and stereotypical. It reads literally, "Thus will the LORD do to me, and thus will he add." The presence of כֹּה, "thus," seems to assume the presence of a more specific form of punishment, but this element is implied, rather than stated. One may paraphrase the formula as follows: "The LORD will punish me severely" (cf. NET). The first verb (יַעֲשֶׂה) is a Qal imperfect from עָשָׂה. See PVP, 185–86 (16.20–16.21); Ful., 197.[64] The second verb (יֹסִיף) is a Hiphil imperfect from יָסַף. Normally the Hiphil imperfect of I-*yod* verbs has a *holem waw* as the prefix vowel (see PVP, 360; Ful., 244),[65] but here the vowel is written defectively as *holem* (without the consonantal element *waw*).

Based on the usage of כִּי in the other examples of this oath formula, it appears that the final clause, introduced by כִּי, affirms what will or must happen for the punishment to be averted. Consequently כִּי may be understood as an emphasizer, "indeed, certainly."[66] One may paraphrase Ruth 1:17b as follows: "Indeed death (alone) will separate me and you." Note NIV (cf. also NASB, NLT), "anything but death"; KJV, "if ought but death"; and NET, "nothing but death." NRSV, "if even death," understands כִּי in the sense of "certainly not, if even," but this would require כִּי־אִם. See 2 Samuel 3:35.

4. הַמָּוֶת—The article on מָוֶת indicates the uniqueness of the referent. See W-OC, 242. Since the referent in this case is intrinsically unique, the article may make הַמָּוֶת the equivalent of a proper name. See W-OC, 249, as well as AC, 30–31.

5. יַפְרִיד—Parse this verb. How do you determine the stem? In this stem the verb appears to be causative ("cause/make a separation").

_____

_____

_____

6. בֵּינִי—When Hebrew expresses the idea "between X and Y," the term בֵּין, "between," is repeated before the Y element.

---

64. Fut., 91 (15.8, 15.10); Kel., 290 (72.6); Ross, 267 (37.2.1).
65. Fut., 208; Gar., 278 (48.B.5); Kel., 343 (75.2); Ross, 253 (35.2.5); Seow, 278 (1.f).
66. See Bush, *Ruth, Esther*, 83.

1:18

וַתֵּרֶא כִּי־מִתְאַמֶּצֶת הִיא לָלֶכֶת אִתָּהּ וַתֶּחְדַּל לְדַבֵּר אֵלֶיהָ׃

1. וַתֵּרֶא—Parse this verb. Normally in a Qal wayyiqtol form, a *tsere* prefix vowel indicates a I-*yod* verb, but occasionally III-*he* verbs take it as well, especially in forms with prefixed *taw*. See GKC, 211, §75p.[67]

2. כִּי—What type of subordinate clause is . . . כִּי? See AC, 171–86; EE, 113–17.

3. מִתְאַמֶּצֶת—Parse this form. How can you tell this is a participle? How is the participle functioning? (Remember: Participles are verbal adjectives.) What is the temporal nuance of the participle here? (See AC, 79–81; EE, 67.) How do you determine the stem? How is the stem functioning here? How do you determine the gender and number of the form?

4. לָלֶכֶת—Parse this form. Normally the suffixed *taw* characterizes the infinitive construct form of I-*yod* or I-*nun* verbs, but הָלַךְ follows the I-*yod* pattern in this case. See PVP, 238–39 (20.6),[68] especially note 5, as well as parsing chart 7 below. See as well Ful., 241 (35.5). How is the infinitive functioning in relation to the preceding participle?

5. אִתָּהּ—This form consists of what elements? See PVP, 90 (9.14); Ful., 42 (9.3).[69]

---

67. See also Joüon, 207, §79i.
68. Fut., 121 (20.6); Gar., 229 (40.A); Kel., 341 (75.2); Ross, 254 (35.4); Seow, 256–57 (2.c).
69. Gar., 83 (14.A.4); Kel., 69 (27.1); Ross, 123 (15.7); Seow, 95 (2.a).

6. לְדַבֵּר—Parse this form. How do you determine the stem? How is the infinitive functioning in relation to the preceding verb ("she stopped")? See W-OC, 606.

_____

_____

_____

7. אֵלֶיהָ—This form consists of what elements? See PVP, 96 (9.19); Ful., 85 (14.4).[70]

_____

_____

1:19a

וַתֵּלַכְנָה שְׁתֵּיהֶם עַד־בֹּאָנָה בֵּית לָחֶם

1. שְׁתֵּיהֶם—What is the gender of the suffix on שְׁתֵּיהֶם? Does this strike you as odd? (To whom does the suffix refer? Note the preceding verb form. What is its gender?) Many medieval Hebrew manuscripts have a feminine suffix (see *BHS* textual note 19a), but it is more likely that the suffix is an archaic dual form. See 1:8, note 4.

_____

_____

_____

_____

2. בֹּאָנָה—This form is a Qal infinitive construct with a rare form of the 3fp suffix. See GKC, 256, §91f.[71] How is the suffix functioning in relation to the infinitive? See PVP, 240 (20.9); Ful., 181 (28.4).[72]

_____

_____

Step 3: Interpretive Translation

In light of the decisions you have made in your analysis, provide an interpretive, paraphrastic translation of Ruth 1:15–19a.

_____

_____

---

70. Fut., 136 (22.1); Gar., 91 (16.F); Kel., 70 (27.1); Ross, 123 (15.8); Seow, 97 (2.c).
71. See also Joüon, 289, §94h.
72. Gar., 212 (36.B.1); Kel., 183 (56.2); Ross, 162 (22.3); Seow, 255–56 (1.c).

_____

_____

_____

_____

_____

_____

Step 4: Structural Outline

Outline the narrative structure of Ruth 1:15–19a. Carefully delineate the narrative mainline (initiated and extended by wayyiqtol forms), offline (nonstandard) constructions, and quotations. Using the categories listed in the appendix (cf. EE, 120–27), classify all wayyiqtol and disjunctive clauses that are in the narrative framework. You need not classify clauses within quotations.

_____

_____

_____

_____

_____

_____

_____

_____

_____

_____

Scene 3: Ruth 1:19b–22: Naomi Laments Her Bitter Condition

Assignment

Step 1: Initial View

Read Ruth 1:19b–22 in the Hebrew text, using an interlinear if you desire. Underline any words or forms you do not recognize. Try to identify verbal forms and label them as follows:

- wayyiqtol verbal forms: wc-y (the so-called *waw* consecutive with the yiqtol, usually identified as a preterite or imperfect)
- weqatal forms: wc-q (the so-called *waw* consecutive with the qatal, that is, perfect)
- simple perfects (without *waw*): pf.
- simple imperfects (without *waw*): impf.
- imperatives: impv.

- jussives: juss.
- cohortatives: coh.
- infinitives construct: inf. const.
- infinitives absolute: inf. abs.
- participles: part.

Step 2: Analyzing the Text

1:19b

וַיְהִי כְּבֹאָנָה בֵּית לֶחֶם וַתֵּהֹם כָּל־הָעִיר עֲלֵיהֶן וַתֹּאמַרְנָה הֲזֹאת נָעֳמִי:

1. וַיְהִי—The וַיְהִי in verse 19b signals the transition to a new scene. See EE, 120. The following temporal clause is introduced by the preposition -כְּ with the infinitive construct. See PVP, 241 (20.10); Ful., 122 (20.4).[73] This clause repeats the description of their arrival in Bethlehem (cf. v. 19a) and provides a transitional link between the former scene and this new one.

2. וַתֵּהֹם—This verb is a Niphal wayyiqtol 3fs (note the *taw* prefix; the subject is the feminine noun עִיר), from the hollow verb הום (see BDB, 223; *HALOT*, 242). Normally the Niphal imperfect/wayyiqtol has an *i + dagesh + a* pattern with the first root letter (e.g., קוּם < יִקּוֹם). But here the first root letter is a guttural, so the form exhibits compensatory lengthening of the *hireq yod* to *tsere*. (Without the doubling of the first root letter the initial syllable remains open and, being unaccented, prefers a long vowel.) The *holem waw* theme vowel is written defectively, making the form more difficult to identify. In this stem the verb may be translated "was stirred, excited."

3. עֲלֵיהֶן—This form consists of what elements? See PVP, 87–88 (9.10–9.11); Ful., 85 (14.4).[74] How is the preposition functioning here? See AC, 120–24; W-OC, 218; BDB, 754; *HALOT*, 826, as well as NIV, NASB, and NRSV.

   _____

   _____

4. הֲזֹאת—What is the function of the prefixed *he* on הֲזֹאת? See PVP, 75–76 (8.10); Ful., 42 (9.3).[75] What part of speech is זֹאת? See PVP, 72–74 (8.7); Ful., 55 (10.9).

   _____

   _____

1:20

וַתֹּאמֶר אֲלֵיהֶן אַל־תִּקְרֶאנָה לִי נָעֳמִי קְרֶאןָ לִי מָרָא כִּי־הֵמַר שַׁדַּי לִי מְאֹד:

---

73. Ful., 122 (20.9); Gar., 212 (36.B.2); Kel., 182 (56.2); Ross, 163 (22.4); Seow, 259 (3.e).
74. Ful., 136 (22.1); Gar., 91 (16.F); Ross, 123 (15.8); Seow, 97 (2.c).
75. Ful., 171 (27.5); Gar., 158–59 (26.C); Kel., 94 (34.1); Ross, 146 (19.5); Seow, 109 (6.b). According to Joüon (609–10, §161b), the statement is exclamatory here: "This is indeed Naomi!"

1. אֲלֵיהֶן—This form consists of what elements? See PVP, 96; Ful., 85 (14.4).[76]

_____

_____

2. תִּקְרֶאנָה—Parse this verb. How do you determine the P-G-N? The negative particle אַל before the form indicates the verb is a jussive. The idiom קָרָא לְ- here means "give a name to" (see BDB, 896). The name נָעֳמִי is derived from a verbal root meaning "be lovely, pleasant." Naomi felt this name was inappropriate, given the hardship she was enduring. She wanted a new name, מָרָא, meaning "bitter," because she was convinced God had brought bitterness into her life.

_____

_____

_____

3. קְרֶאןָ—Parse this verb. How do you determine the P-G-N? (The ending is a defectively written form of נָה-.) How is the imperative functioning here?

_____

_____

_____

4. כִּי—What type of subordinate clause does כִּי introduce here?

_____

_____

5. הֵמַר—Parse this verb. For help see chart 9. The _tsere_ prefix vowel is characteristic of the Hiphil perfect of hollow verbs, but a hollow verb would have a _hireq yod_ theme vowel (e.g., הֵקִים; see PVP, 361; Ful., 259).[77] Geminate verbs also take a _tsere_ prefix vowel in the Hiphil perfect, but they typically take a tone long or short theme vowel (e.g., סָבַב < הֵסֵב). When a verb is both geminate and III-guttural (recall that _resh_ acts like a guttural in some respects), a _pathaq_ will appear as the theme vowel, as in the form מָרַר < הֵמַר, "be bitter, distressed, grieved, pained" (cf. Ruth 1:13). The Hiphil is causative here, meaning "make bitter."

_____

_____

The Hiphil of מָרַר also appears in Job 27:2, where Job accuses God of making his soul bitter by denying him justice, and in Zechariah 12:10, where it describes the bitter grief one feels over the loss

---

76. Fut., 136 (22.1); Gar., 91 (16.F); Kel., 70 (27.1); Ross, 123 (15.8); Seow, 97 (2.c).
77. Fut., 215; Gar., 276 (48.A.6); Kel., 324 (74.5); Ross, 280 (38.7); Seow, 278–79 (1.j).

of an only child. Naomi accuses God of causing her grief by taking away the men in her life (see v. 21). She even adds the adverb מְאֹד, "very," to emphasize the depth of her pain.

6. שַׁדַּי—This word, transliterated *Shaddai*, is a divine name or title emphasizing God's sovereign position. The derivation of the name is debated, but it may be related to an Akkadian word meaning "mountain," in which case it may designate God as the "one of the mountain" and depict him as ruling from a mountain (cf. Ps. 48:2), like Canaanite deities are sometimes pictured doing (cf. Isa. 14:13; Ezek. 28:16, 18). This divine title depicts God as the judge of the world who both gives and takes away life. The patriarchs knew God primarily as El (meaning "God") Shaddai (Exod. 6:3). When the title is used in Genesis, God appears as the source of fertility and life (see Gen. 17:1–8; 28:3; 35:11; 48:3). The name is especially prominent in the book of Job, where it occurs thirty-one times. Job and his friends regard Shaddai as the sovereign king of the world (11:7; 37:23a) who is the source of life (33:4b) and promotes justice (8:3; 34:10–12; 37:23b). He provides blessings, including children (22:17–18; 29:4–6), but he also disciplines and judges (5:17; 6:4; 21:20; 23:16). Psalm 91:1 pictures Shaddai as his people's protector, while Psalm 68:15 (Eng. v. 14); Isaiah 13:6; and Joel 1:15 portray him as a warrior. Naomi uses the name as she laments the death of her husband and sons.

1:21

אֲנִי מְלֵאָה הָלַכְתִּי וְרֵיקָם הֱשִׁיבַנִי יְהוָה לָמָּה תִקְרֶאנָה לִי נָעֳמִי וַיהוָה עָנָה בִי וְשַׁדַּי הֵרַע לִי׃

1. אֲנִי מְלֵאָה—The use of the pronoun אֲנִי at the beginning of verse 21 highlights the speaker. The adjective מְלֵאָה, "full," follows. What gender and number is the adjective? How can you tell this from the form? See PVP, 61 (7.2); Ful., 51 (10.3). How has the addition of the ending affected the vowel pointing under the *mem?* See PVP, 68 (7.10); Ful., 52 (10.3). By placing the adjective before the verb, Naomi draws attention to her former condition and sets up the contrast to follow in the next clause. See GKC, 374–75, §118n. Technically the adjective is substantival and functions as an adverbial accusative of state (see EE, 65, as well as AC, 20, 26), "as a full one I went."[78] Naomi refers to the fact that she had a husband and two sons when she left Bethlehem for Moab.

_____

_____

_____

2. וְרֵיקָם—This word contrasts with מְלֵאָה, "full." רֵיקָם is an adverb, formed by placing the adverbial ending ָם on the adjective רֵיק, "empty."[79] She refers to the fact that she returned to Bethlehem without her husband and sons. Ruth apparently counts for nothing in Naomi's eyes, but this changes by the end of the book, where the women of the town correct Naomi's oversight (see 4:15).

3. הֱשִׁיבַנִי—This verb is a Hiphil perfect 3ms from שׁוּב with a 1cs pronominal suffix. Normally the prefix vowel of the Hiphil perfect of hollow verbs is *tsere* (e.g., הֵשִׁיב, see PVP, 361; Ful., 259).[80] However the addition of the pronominal suffix (which functions as the object of the verb) causes an accent shift that

_____

78. See Joüon, 455, §126a; W-OC, 171–72.
79. See GKC, 295, §100g; W-OC, 93.
80. Fut., 215; Gar., 276 (48.A.6); Kel., 324 (74.5); Ross, 280 (38.7); Seow, 278–79 (1.j).

leaves the hypothetical *tsere* in an open, propretonic syllable. Under these conditions the *tsere* reduces to *shewa*, in this case a compound *shewa* because of the guttural letter *he*.[81] The stem is causative here ("cause to return, bring back").

4. תִּקְרֶאנָה—Parse this verb. How is the imperfect functioning?

---

5. וַיהוָה—This introduces a disjunctive clause within the quotation. It probably has a circumstantial-causal nuance here: "Why do you call me Naomi, seeing that/since the LORD has testified against me?" See KJV, NASB, NET.

6. עָנָה—This verb is a Qal perfect. Collocated with the preposition -בְּ, it has a legal connotation, "testify against" (see BDB, 772–73, 3.a; *HALOT*, 852). Some translations, following the Greek Septuagint, have "afflicted me" (see NIV; cf. NRSV, NLT). This reading assumes an emendation of the Hebrew text to עִנָּה, a Piel form of a homonymic root meaning "afflict" (see BDB, 776; *HALOT*, 853). For a defense of the Qal reading see EE, 36–37; and Brotzman, 141–42.

7. The style here is semi-poetic: שַׁדַּי is parallel to יהוָה, and the collocation הֵרַע לִי corresponds to עָנָה בִי. The repetition emphasizes Naomi's point: God has actively opposed her.

8. הֵרַע—Parse this verb. How do you determine the *(a)* stem, and *(b)* root? (On the form see 1:20, note 5, above.) In the Hiphil stem this verb has the basic idea "do harm to" (Gen. 19:9; 43:6; Exod. 5:22–23), but in some contexts it carries the nuance "judge, punish" (Num. 11:11; Josh. 24:20; Jer. 25:6; Zech. 8:14), or even "treat unfairly" (Num. 20:15; 1 Sam. 26:21).[82] It is not clear if Naomi has one of these connotations in mind, but it is apparent she regarded God as directly responsible for her misery. However, the narrator does not attribute the death of her husband and sons to God. On the contrary, in this story God emerges as Naomi's ally and savior, not her enemy. While all that happens in the world ultimately falls under the umbrella of God's sovereign dominion, this hardly means that the death of loved ones is an act of divine judgment.

1:22

וַתָּשָׁב נָעֳמִי וְרוּת הַמּוֹאֲבִיָּה כַלָּתָהּ עִמָּהּ הַשָּׁבָה מִשְּׂדֵי מוֹאָב
וְהֵמָּה בָּאוּ בֵּית לֶחֶם בִּתְחִלַּת קְצִיר שְׂעֹרִים:

1. וַתָּשָׁב—The wayyiqtol clause at the beginning of verse 22 has a summarizing/concluding function (see

---

81. Ross, 281 (38.8); Seow, 279 (1.j).
82. The basic sense of the Hiphil is causative; cf. the Qal meaning "be injured."

the appendix and EE, 123).[83] In combination with the same verb in verse 6 (וַתָּשָׁב), it forms a bracket around the story of Naomi's return to her homeland.

2. וְרוּת—What type of clause is . . . וְרוּת? How can you tell this? How is it functioning here?

_____

_____

_____

3. הַמּוֹאֲבִיָּה—This form is a feminine singular (note the ה ָ - ending) adjective; note the gentilic *hireq yod* ending (see W-OC, 92–93, 115). With the article it is substantival and stands in apposition to רוּת.

4. כַּלָּתָהּ—This form consists of what elements? Explain the *taw* before the pronominal suffix. See PVP, 85 (9.7); Ful., 77 (13.2).[84]

_____

_____

5. עִמָּהּ—This form consists of what elements? See PVP, 90–91 (9.15); Ful., 83–84 (14.3).[85]

_____

_____

6. הַשָּׁבָה—This form is difficult to analyze. Based on the placement of the accent (under the *shin*), it appears to be a Qal perfect 3fs from שׁוּב, with a prefixed article. See PVP, 261; Ful., 255 (36.5).[86] However, it is rare for a perfect verbal form to appear with an article. For examples, see GKC, 447, §138k; W-OC, 339. According to GKC (447), Joüon (538, §146e), and W-OC (339–40), apparent examples with hollow verbs should probably be read as participles. The article on the form functions like a relative pronoun (W-OC, 338–39). Actually the form is substantival and appositional to "Ruth . . . her daughter-in-law," and can be translated, "the one who returned."

7. וְהֵמָּה—What type of clause is . . . וְהֵמָּה? How can you tell this? How is it functioning here?

_____

_____

_____

Once more an apparent masculine form is used with reference to women. (One would expect the pronoun to be הֵנָּה. See PVP, 71 [8.3]; Ful., 103 [17.2].)[87] Again the form is best taken as an archaic common dual. See 1:8, note 4, as well as Bush, *Ruth, Esther*, 94–95.

83. See also Joüon, 392, §118i.
84. Fut., 96 (16.3); Gar., 89 (16.C); Kel., 72 (28.1); Ross, 114 (14.3); Seow, 133 (1.b).
85. Fut., 135–36 (22.1); Gar., 83 (15.A.3); Kel., 69 (27.1); Ross, 123 (15.7); Seow, 95 (2.a).
86. Gar., 202–3 (34.B.5); Kel., 318 (74.3); Ross, 276 (38.2.2); Seow, 163 (4.a).
87. Fut., 24 (5.1); Gar., 78 (14.C); Kel., 52 (23.2); Ross, 94 (11.1); Seow, 92 (1.a).

8. בָּאוּ—Parse this verb. How do you determine the *(a)* root, and *(b)* P-G-N?

_____

_____

_____

9. בִּתְחִלַּת—This form consists of what elements? How do you explain the *hireq* under the prepositional prefix? See PVP, 51–52 (6.4); Ful., 35 (8.2).[88] How can you tell from the form of the noun that it is in the construct state? See PVP, 104; Ful., 63 (11.5).[89] The *dagesh* in the *lamed* reflects the geminate root from which the noun is derived (חלל).

_____

_____

_____

_____

10. קְצִיר—This form is also in the construct state. How can you tell this? See PVP, 102–3; Ful., 61–62 (11.3).[90] (Note that the absolute form of this noun is קָצִיר.) As the middle term in this construct chain, the form is genitival in relation to the preceding word.

_____

_____

11. שְׂעֹרִים—The final term in the construct chain is שְׂעֹרִים, an absolute plural form. (Recall that only the last word in a chain is in the absolute state. See PVP, 98–99; Ful., 61 [11.1].)[91] The form looks masculine, but this is an irregular feminine plural, like עָרִים, "cities," or נָשִׁים, "women." The singular form is שְׂעֹרָה; see BDB, 972. According to W-OC (119), the plural form is used to "indicate composition" and, with "vegetable nouns," it "refers to the gathered, measured, cooked or sewn material."[92]

Step 3: Interpretive Translation

In light of the decisions you have made in your analysis, provide an interpretive, paraphrastic translation of Ruth 1:19b–22.

_____

_____

_____

_____

---

88. Fut., 50 (9.8); Gar., 74 (13.A.1); Kel., 28 (15.1); Ross, 46 (3.5); Seow, 56 (3.a).
89. Fut., 71 (12.7); Gar., 96 (17.E.2); Kel., 62–63 (26.4); Ross, 100 (12.3); Seow, 133 (1.b).
90. Fut., 70 (12.6); Gar., 96 (17.E.2); Kel., 61–62 (26.4); Ross, 101 (12.4); Seow, 118 (2.d).
91. Fut., 68 (12.1); Gar., 99 (17.F.2); Kel., 58–59 (26.1–4); Ross, 99 (12.2); Seow, 116–17 (1).
92. See also GKC, 400, §124m; Joüon, 500, §136b.

_____

_____

_____

_____

Step 4: Structural Outline

Outline the narrative structure of Ruth 1:19b–22. Carefully delineate the narrative mainline (initiated and extended by wayyiqtol forms), offline (nonstandard) constructions, and quotations. Using the categories listed in the appendix (cf. EE, 120–27), classify all wayyiqtol and disjunctive clauses that are in the narrative framework. You need not classify clauses within quotations.

_____

_____

_____

_____

_____

_____

_____

_____

_____

_____

Act 2
Ruth 2

Scene 1: Ruth 2:1–3: Ruth Seeks Food

Assignment

Step 1: Initial View

Read Ruth 2:1–3 in the Hebrew text, using an interlinear if you desire. Underline any words or forms you do not recognize. Try to identify verbal forms and label them as follows:

- wayyiqtol verbal forms: wc-y (the so-called *waw* consecutive with the yiqtol, usually identified as a preterite or imperfect)
- weqatal forms: wc-q (the so-called *waw* consecutive with the qatal, that is, perfect)
- simple perfects (without *waw*): pf.
- simple imperfects (without *waw*): impf.
- imperatives: impv.
- jussives: juss.
- cohortatives: coh.
- infinitives construct: inf. const.
- infinitives absolute: inf. abs.
- participles: part.

Step 2: Analyzing the Text

2:1

וּלְנָעֳמִי מוֹדַע לְאִישָׁהּ אִישׁ גִּבּוֹר חַיִל מִמִּשְׁפַּחַת אֱלִימֶלֶךְ וּשְׁמוֹ בֹּעַז׃

1. וּלְנָעֳמִי—What type of clause does וּלְנָעֳמִי introduce? How can you tell this from the form? How is the clause functioning here? (Note that it is purely descriptive and does not carry along the action of the story.)

   _____

   _____

   _____

2. מוֹדַע—The ungrammatical and unreadable form מוֹדַע is a *kethib-qere.* The vowels inserted in the form belong with the consonants provided in the left margin of the text above the *qoph* (an abbreviation for "*qere*," meaning "what is to be read"): מוֹדָע. Note how this set of consonants differs from the set in

the text. To construct the *qere* reading, one must take the vowels from the text and insert them into the marginal reading: מוֹדַע. This form is a noun meaning "kinsman" (see BDB, 396; *HALOT*, 550). The *BHS* note (2,1 a) gives the vocalization of the *kethib* ("what is written"): מְיֻדָּע. This form is a substantival Pual participle meaning "known (one), acquaintance." On the Pual form, which is passive, see PVP, 336; Ful., 141 (23.2).[1] For further discussion of the text critical issue, see Brotzman, 142.

3. לְאִישָׁהּ—This form consists of what elements? The preposition indicates reference or possession here. See AC, 112–13; W-OC, 209; BDB, 512–13.

_____

_____

4. אִישׁ גִּבּוֹר חַיִל—אִישׁ is in apposition to מוֹדַע *(qere)*. What part of speech is גִּבּוֹר? How is it functioning in relation to אִישׁ? What part of speech is חַיִל? How is it functioning in relation to גִּבּוֹר? (What case is it? How would you classify its use here? See AC, 8–13; EE, 62–64 and W-OC, 143–54.)[2] The expression גִּבּוֹר חַיִל is often used of warriors, referring to their military courage and/or prowess. However, this does not appear to be the focus here. The phrase seems to refer to Boaz as being wealthy and/or important. Perhaps the phrase is applied to Boaz because, as a prominent leader in the community, he may have been a military officer in the local militia, responsible for supplying soldiers in case of battle. See *HALOT*, 311.

_____

_____

_____

_____

5. מִשְׁפַּחַת—This is a construct form. How can you tell this? See PVP, 104; Ful., 63 (11.5).

_____

_____

6. וּשְׁמוֹ—This form consists of what elements? What type of clause is וּשְׁמוֹ בֹּעַז? How can you tell? How is it functioning here?

_____

_____

_____

---

1. Fut., 237–38; Gar., 265 (46.E); Kel., 196 (59.5); Ross, 200–201 (28.1); Seow, 321 (1.c).
2. See also BHRG, 197–200; Joüon, 465–73; WHS, 36–49; GKC, 416–19.

2:2

וַתֹּאמֶר רוּת הַמּוֹאֲבִיָּה אֶל־נָעֳמִי אֵלְכָה־נָּא הַשָּׂדֶה וַאֲלַקֳטָה בַשִּׁבֳּלִים אַחַר אֲשֶׁר אֶמְצָא־חֵן בְּעֵינָיו
וַתֹּאמֶר לָהּ לְכִי בִתִּי:

1. וַתֹּאמֶר—The wayyiqtol clause at the beginning of verse 2 picks up the action of the story after the descriptive material in verse 1 and initiates the next scene.

2. אֵלְכָה—Parse this verb. What do the הָ - ending (in combination with the *aleph* prefix) and the particle נָּא indicate about the form? See PVP, 214–15 (18.13); Ful., 110–11 (18.4).[3] How is the form functioning here? See EE, 107.[4] (Note Naomi's response later in the verse: לְכִי.)

3. הַשָּׂדֶה—How is הַשָּׂדֶה functioning in relation to the preceding verb? In other words, identify its case and case function. See AC, 13–21; EE, 64–65. (Note that it is necessary to supply a preposition in English when translating the form.)

4. וַאֲלַקֳטָה—Parse this verb. How do you determine the stem? Note: The *dagesh* is sometimes omitted when there is a vocal *shewa* (here it is the compound variety) beneath a letter that is typically doubled. See PVP, 316 (26.16).[5] The verb לָקַט occurs in the Qal stem with the meaning "pick up, gather." Here the Piel is probably frequentative.[6] What does the הָ- ending indicate about the form? How is this verb functioning in relation to the preceding verb? See EE, 108–10. (Consider the following question: Does Naomi have the authority to give Ruth permission to glean? Note her response to Ruth in the second half of the verse, and see as well v. 7.) Note also NLT ("to gather") and NET ("so I can gather").

5. אֲשֶׁר—The relative pronoun אֲשֶׁר collocates with בְּעֵינָיו and may be translated, "in whose eyes." On the use of the resumptive pronoun after the relative, see W-OC, 333–34.

---

3. Fut., 148 (24.3); Gar., 226 (39.A) and 110 (19.B.4); Kel., 131–32 (41.1–2); Ross, 151 (20.4–20.5); Seow, 241 (4) and 210 (6).
4. See also AC, 65–66; BHRG, 151–52; GKC, 319–20; Joüon, 374–76; W-OC, 573–75.
5. Ross, 195 (27.1); Seow, 264 (1.a).
6. On this use of the Piel stem, see Joüon, 155; W-OC, 414–16.

6. אֶמְצָא—Parse the verb. How is the imperfect functioning here?

_____

_____

7. לְךָ—This form consists of what elements? See PVP, 88; Ful., 83 (14.2).[7]

_____

_____

8. לְכִי—Parse this verb. How do you determine the root? Normally an imperatival verbal form displaying two root letters with a *shewa* under the first is either III-*he*, I-*yod*, or I-*nun*, but הָלַךְ follows I-*yod* patterns. See PVP, 213 (18.11); Ful., 241 (35.5).[8] What does the *hireq yod* ending indicate about the gender and number of the form? What is the function of the imperative here? See EE, 105–6.[9]

_____

_____

_____

_____

9. בִתִּי—This form consists of what elements?

_____

_____

2:3

וַתֵּלֶךְ וַתָּבוֹא וַתְּלַקֵּט בַּשָּׂדֶה אַחֲרֵי הַקֹּצְרִים
וַיִּקֶר מִקְרֶהָ חֶלְקַת הַשָּׂדֶה לְבֹעַז אֲשֶׁר מִמִּשְׁפַּחַת אֱלִימֶלֶךְ׃

1. וַתֵּלֶךְ—The three wayyiqtols in verse 3a summarize what happened after Ruth left Naomi and went on her mission to find food. Verses 3b–17 give a more detailed account of what transpired. Verse 3a says she "gleaned in the field behind the reapers." However, in verse 7–8 she asks for and receives permission to glean in the field. Verse 17 observes that she "gleaned in the field until evening." The discourse structure (introductory summary—detailed account—concluding summary) is similar to that of chapter 1 (introductory summary in 1:6; detailed account in 1:7–21; concluding summary in 1:22).

---

7. Fut., 135 (22.1); Gar., 82 (15.A.1); Kel., 68 (27.1); Ross, 108 (13.1); Seow, 94 (2.a).
8. Fut., 150 (24.6); Gar., 229 (40.A); Kel., 341 (75.2); Ross, 254 (35.4); Seow, 239 (3.e).
9. See also AC, 63–65; BHRG, 150–51; GKC, 324–25; Joüon, 378–79; WHS, 188–91; W-OC, 571–73.

2. וַתְּלַקֵּט—Parse this verb. How do you determine the *(a)* stem, and *(b)* P-G-N?

_____

_____

_____

3. הַקֹּצְרִים—Parse this form. How can you tell the form is a participle? See PVP, 258–59 (22.2–22.3); Ful., 115 (19.2). How is the participle functioning here? Note the article and see PVP, 262–63 (22.5); Ful., 115–16 (19.2), as well as AC, 82. How do you determine the gender and number of the form?

_____

_____

_____

4. וַיִּקֶר—Parse this verb. How do you determine the root? What happened to the final root letter? See PVP, 198 (17.4); Ful., 266–67 (37.4). This wayyiqtol clause begins a more detailed, specific account of Ruth's day in the field.

_____

_____

_____

5. מִקְרֶהָ—This form consists of what elements? (For help with the suffix see PVP, 82 [9.3].) Note that this noun is derived from the verbal root that precedes. The expression וַיִּקֶר מִקְרֶהָ is difficult to translate literally. The verb means "encounter, meet, befall," while the noun means "incident, chance." The idea seems to be that she just happened to end up in Boaz's portion of the field, seemingly by chance, not by any design or plan on her part. While ancient Israelite culture made room for seemingly chance occurrences (see 1 Sam. 6:9), it is unlikely the narrator really believed Ruth arrived at Boaz's field by sheer coincidence. Throughout the book prayers are offered to the Lord and then answered in the course of events, often through the instrumentality of worthy characters (see 1:9; 2:12, 20; 3:10; 4:11–12, 14–15). As far as the narrator is concerned, God's hand, however invisible it might be, is always superintending events. For this reason the statement in verse 3b probably reflects Ruth's limited perspective. Rather than promoting a theology of chance, the narrator makes it clear this encounter with Boaz was not something that Ruth or Naomi engineered. From Ruth's perspective she just randomly picked a field, but God was steering her to just the right one. For further discussion of this passage see Bush, *Ruth, Esther*, 104; and Daniel I. Block, *Judges, Ruth*, NAC (Nashville: Broadman & Holman, 1999), 653. For a discussion of the literary technique involved here, see Robert B. Chisholm Jr., "A Rhetorical Use of Point of View in Old Testament Narrative," *BSac* 159 (2002): 404–14.

_____

_____

6. חֶלְקַת—How can you tell this form is construct?

_____

_____

7. לִבְעַז—How is the preposition on לִבְעַז functioning here? See AC, 112–13; W-OC, 206–7.

_____

_____

Step 3: Interpretive Translation

In light of the decisions you have made in your analysis, provide an interpretive, paraphrastic translation of Ruth 2:1–3.

_____

_____

_____

_____

_____

_____

_____

_____

Step 4: Structural Outline

Outline the narrative structure of Ruth 2:1–3. Carefully delineate the narrative mainline (initiated and extended by wayyiqtol forms), offline (nonstandard) constructions, and quotations. Using the categories listed in the appendix (cf. EE, 120–27), classify all wayyiqtol and disjunctive clauses that are in the narrative framework. You need not classify clauses within quotations.

_____

_____

_____

_____

_____

_____

_____

_____

_____

Scene 2: Ruth 2:4–17a: Boaz Extends Kindness to Ruth

Since this is a relatively long scene, it is divided into three assignments, covering verses 4–7, 8–13, and 14–17a.

Assignment 1

Step 1: Initial View

Read Ruth 2:4–7 in the Hebrew text, using an interlinear if you desire. Underline any words or forms you do not recognize. Try to identify verbal forms and label them as follows:

- wayyiqtol verbal forms: wc-y (the so-called *waw* consecutive with the yiqtol, usually identified as a preterite or imperfect)
- weqatal forms: wc-q (the so-called *waw* consecutive with the qatal, that is, perfect)
- simple perfects (without *waw*): pf.
- simple imperfects (without *waw*): impf.
- imperatives: impv.
- jussives: juss.
- cohortatives: coh.
- infinitives construct: inf. const.
- infinitives absolute: inf. abs.
- participles: part.

Step 2: Analyzing the Text

2:4

וְהִנֵּה־בֹעַז בָּא מִבֵּית לֶחֶם וַיֹּאמֶר לַקּוֹצְרִים יְהוָה עִמָּכֶם וַיֹּאמְרוּ לוֹ יְבָרֶכְךָ יְהוָה׃

1. וְהִנֵּה—What type of clause is . . . וְהִנֵּה? How is it functioning here? See the appendix (cf. EE, 124–27).

_____

_____

2. בָּא—Parse this form. Theoretically there are two options for this form. See PVP, 261; Ful., 255–56 (36.6).[10] When הִנֵּה is followed by a nominal subject and the verb בּוֹא, the verb can be a participle (Gen. 24:63; 1 Sam. 2:31) or a perfect (Josh. 2:2). When הִנֵּה is followed by a proper name (as subject) and a verb, the participle is far more common than the perfect.

_____

_____

---

10. Fut., 157–58 (24.6–24.7); Gar., 202–3 (34.B.5); Kel., 317–18 (74.3); Ross, 276 (38.2.2); Seow, 163 (4.a).

3. עִמָּכֶם—This form consists of what elements? See PVP, 90–91; Ful., 83–84 (14.3).[11] Boaz's statement to the reapers is probably a prayer of blessing, "The LORD (be) with you."[12]

_____

_____

4. יְבָרֶכְךָ—Parse this form. How do you determine the stem? Why is the vowel under the *beth* a *qamets*, rather than the usual *pathaq*? See PVP, 322–23 (27.10–27.11); Ful., 207 (31.4).[13] Apart from the Qal passive participle, the verb בָּרַךְ appears almost exclusively in the Piel stem with the meaning "bless." Their response to Boaz is probably a prayer of blessing, so the prefixed verb form should be understood as a jussive, rather than an imperfect. (Recall that the imperfect and jussive overlap in most verb types.) How is the pronominal suffix functioning in relation to the verb? See PVP, 222 (19.1); Ful., 169 (27.1).

_____

_____

_____

_____

2:5

וַיֹּאמֶר בֹּעַז לְנַעֲרוֹ הַנִּצָּב עַל־הַקּוֹצְרִים לְמִי הַנַּעֲרָה הַזֹּאת:

1. לְנַעֲרוֹ—This form consists of what elements?

_____

_____

2. הַנִּצָּב—Parse this form. How do you determine the stem? How can you tell the form is a participle? How is the participle used here? (Note the article.) How does the form function in relation to the preceding noun? The verb נָצַב occurs in the Niphal and Hiphil/Hophal. The Niphal can be reflexive ("station oneself, take one's stand") or passive ("be stationed, appointed"). Since the foreman works for Boaz, the passive nuance fits better here.

_____

_____

_____

_____

---

11. Fut., 135–36 (22.1); Gar., 83 (15.A.3); Kel., 69 (27.1); Ross, 123 (15.7); Seow, 95 (2.a).
12. See Joüon, 615, §163b.
13. Fut., 182 (29.1); Gar., 257 (45.B.1); Kel., 250–51 (69.2); Ross, 234–35 (33.2.1); Seow, 264 (1.b).

3. לְמִי—This form consists of what elements? On the translation of the form see BDB, 566, b., and *HALOT*, 575, no. 1. How is the preposition functioning? See AC, 112–13; W-OC, 206–7.

_____

_____

4. הַזֹּאת—How is this form functioning in relation to the preceding noun? See PVP, 72–73 (8.7); Ful., 55–56 (10.9).[14]

_____

_____

2:6

וַיַּעַן הַנַּעַר הַנִּצָּב עַל־הַקּוֹצְרִים וַיֹּאמַר נַעֲרָה מוֹאֲבִיָּה הִיא הַשָּׁבָה עִם־נָעֳמִי מִשְּׂדֵה מוֹאָב:

1. וַיַּעַן—Parse this verb. Theoretically the form can be either Qal (the *a* prefix vowel due to I-guttural) or Hiphil, but the sense requires the Qal ("he answered"), rather than a causative.

_____

_____

2. נַעֲרָה—How is this form functioning in the sentence?

_____

_____

3. מוֹאֲבִיָּה—This form is a feminine singular (note the ה ָ- ending) gentilic adjective (see 1:22, note 3), modifying נַעֲרָה. One may translate, "a Moabite girl."

4. הִיא—What part of speech is הִיא? How is it functioning in the sentence?

_____

_____

5. הַשָּׁבָה—On this form see 1:22, note 6. Here the form is appositional to נַעֲרָה.

2:7

וַתֹּאמֶר אֲלַקֳטָה־נָּא וְאָסַפְתִּי בָעֳמָרִים אַחֲרֵי הַקּוֹצְרִים
וַתָּבוֹא וַתַּעֲמוֹד מֵאָז הַבֹּקֶר וְעַד־עַתָּה זֶה שִׁבְתָּהּ הַבַּיִת מְעָט:

1. אֲלַקֳטָה—Parse this form. (See 2:2, note 4.) What does the attached particle נָּא indicate about the form? See PVP, 214 (18.13). How is the form functioning here? See AC, 65–66; EE, 107.

_____

14. Fut., 102–3 (17.4); Gar., 77 (14.B); Kel., 53 (24.3); Ross, 95 (11.3); Seow, 104–5 (1.b).

2. וְאָסַפְתִּי—Parse this form. How do you determine the P-G-N? Following the cohortative, the *waw* is regarded as consecutive. The *waw* has no special vowel pointing to indicate this, but the accent shift on the verb form is characteristic of this construction. Normally the accent on the 1cs form of the perfect is on the middle syllable, but with the *waw* consecutive it is on the ending. See PVP, 200; Ful., 121, note 2.[15] The perfect consecutive normally follows an imperfect, but it can also follow a volitional form.[16] It expresses a consequence of the preceding action. See W-OC, 529–30.

3. בָּעֳמָרִים—This prepositional phrase is normally understood to mean, "among the sheaves," but the action of gathering grain among the sheaves is already implied in her request to glean. Bush (*Ruth, Esther*, 117) makes a good case for the phrase meaning "in bundles."

4. וַתָּבוֹא—This form resumes the narratival sequence of the servant's report, after his brief quotation of what Ruth said to him earlier.

5. וַתַּעֲמוֹד—Parse this verb. How do you determine the *(a)* P-G-N, and *(b)* stem? (Why is the prefix vowel *pathaq* instead of *hireq*? See PVP, 177–78 [16.8–16.9]; Ful., 191–92 [29.6].)

6. מֵאָז הַבֹּקֶר—This form consists of the preposition מִן and the adverb אָז, "then." The form may be translated, "from then, from that time." The following form, הַבֹּקֶר, "the morning," specifies what time is in view.

7. זֶה . . .—The meaning of the last clause is uncertain; the text may suffer from corruption. See Brotzman, 143–45. The individual words are clear:

   a. זֶה is the masculine singular demonstrative,
   b. שִׁבְתָּהּ is a Qal infinitive construct from יָשַׁב (note the suffixed *taw*; see PVP, 238–39; Ful., 240 [35.4])[17] with a 3fs pronominal suffix functioning as the subject of the infinitive,
   c. הַבַּיִת = "the house," and
   d. מְעָט is a noun functioning as an adverb, "a little." How these words fit together is not clear.

---

15. Fut., 163 (26.2); Gar., 114 (20.E); Kel., 212 (63.2); Ross, 138–39 (18.3); Seow, 227 (3.a).
16. See AC, 88–89; Joüon, 398–400; GKC, 333, §112q.
17. Fut., 121 (20.6); Gar., 207 (35.B.3); Ross, 252 (35.2.3); Seow, 256 (2.c).

Step 3: Interpretive Translation

In light of the decisions you have made in your analysis, provide an interpretive, paraphrastic translation of Ruth 2:4–7.

_____
_____
_____
_____
_____
_____
_____
_____

Step 4: Structural Outline

Outline the narrative structure of Ruth 2:4–7. Carefully delineate the narrative mainline (initiated and extended by wayyiqtol forms), offline (nonstandard) constructions, and quotations. Using the categories listed in the appendix (cf. EE, 120–27), classify all wayyiqtol and disjunctive clauses that are in the narrative framework. You need not classify clauses within quotations.

_____
_____
_____
_____
_____
_____
_____
_____
_____
_____
_____
_____

Assignment 2

Step 1: Initial View

Read Ruth 2:8–13 in the Hebrew text, using an interlinear if you desire. Underline any words or forms you do not recognize. Try to identify verbal forms and label them as follows:

- wayyiqtol verbal forms: wc-y (the so-called *waw* consecutive with the yiqtol, usually identified as a preterite or imperfect)
- weqatal forms: wc-q (the so-called *waw* consecutive with the qatal, that is, perfect)
- simple perfects (without *waw*): pf.
- simple imperfects (without *waw*): impf.
- imperatives: impv.
- jussives: juss.
- cohortatives: coh.
- infinitives construct: inf. const.
- infinitives absolute: inf. abs.
- participles: part.

Step 2: Analyzing the Text

2:8

וַיֹּאמֶר בֹּעַז אֶל־רוּת הֲלוֹא שָׁמַעַתְּ בִּתִּי אַל־תֵּלְכִי לִלְקֹט בְּשָׂדֶה אַחֵר וְגַם לֹא תַעֲבוּרִי מִזֶּה וְכֹה תִדְבָּקִין עִם־נַעֲרֹתָי׃

---

2. שָׁמַעַתְּ—Parse this verb. How do you determine the P-G-N? The question makes it sound as if Boaz had already made an announcement with which Ruth should have been familiar (cf. 1 Kings 1:11; 2 Kings 19:25). Since the announcement actually follows, the question is rhetorical here (see v. 9 as well). The point seems to be: "Listen carefully!" See the translations, which (with the exception of KJV) treat the form as if it were an imperative.[18]

---

3. בִּתִּי—This form consists of what elements? How is the form functioning in the sentence? See AC, 7; W-OC, 77.

---

4. תֵּלְכִי—Parse this verb. How do you determine the *(a)* root, and *(b)* P-G-N? Note the negative particle אַל; the form must be understood as a jussive, rather than a simple imperfect.

---

18. According to Joüon (359, §112a), the perfect is used in a present sense here, "you hear."

5. לְלַקֵּט—Parse this form. How is the form functioning in relation to the preceding verb? The verb לָקַט occurs twelve times in Ruth 2 (cf. vv. 2–3, 7, 8, 15–19, 23), but only here in the Qal stem. The significance of this is not clear. For a discussion of the issue, see Robert L. Hubbard Jr., *The Book of Ruth*, NICOT (Grand Rapids: Eerdmans, 1988), 154–55.

6. תַעֲבוּרִי—Parse this verb. How do you determine the *(a)* P-G-N, and *(b)* stem? Why is there a *pathaq* prefix vowel, instead of *hireq*? One expects a *pathaq* under the *ayin* and a *shewa* in the theme vowel position (after the *beth*), but instead the combination vocal *shewa* + *shureq* appears.[19] Note the negative particle לֹא before the verb, indicating the latter is an imperfect.

7. מִזֶּה—This form consists of what elements? The antecedent of זֶה, which is masculine, must be שָׂדֶה, which is also masculine.

8. כֹּה—This term normally indicates manner, "thus," but here it appears to have a locative sense, "here." See AC, 135; BDB, 462, no. 2; W-OC, 657–58.

9. תִדְבָּקִין—Parse this verb. How is the imperfect functioning? Note the so-called paragogic *nun* on the end of the form.[20] On the possible significance of these paragogic forms, see W-OC, 516–17. Following Hoftijzer, they suggest that these forms may indicate "contrastivity," that is, exceptions to or deviations from normal practice.[21] In the Hebrew Bible, the verb דָּבַק is collocated with the preposition עִם only here and in verse 21. Apparently it means "keep close to" (NRSV) or "stay here with" (NIV, NASB).

10. נַעֲרֹתַי—This form consists of what elements? What gender is the noun?

---

19. On this oddity, see GKC, 127, §47g; Joüon, 136, §44c.
20. See GKC, 129, §47o; Joüon, 136–37, §44e–f.
21. J. Hoftijzer, *The Function and Use of the Imperfect Forms with Nun Paragogicum in Classical Hebrew* (Assen, Netherlands: Van Gorcum, 1985).

2:9

עֵינַיִךְ בַּשָּׂדֶה אֲשֶׁר־יִקְצֹרוּן וְהָלַכְתְּ אַחֲרֵיהֶן הֲלוֹא צִוִּיתִי אֶת־הַנְּעָרִים לְבִלְתִּי נָגְעֵךְ
וְצָמִת וְהָלַכְתְּ אֶל־הַכֵּלִים וְשָׁתִית מֵאֲשֶׁר יִשְׁאֲבוּן הַנְּעָרִים׃

1. עֵינַיִךְ בַּשָּׂדֶה—This clause has no verb; in this context it is best translated with a jussive nuance, continuing the instruction begun in verse 8: "Let your eyes be on the field," that is, "Watch" (NIV) or "Take note of" (NET).

2. יִקְצֹרוּן—Parse this verb. How do you determine the P-G-N? (On the paragogic *nun* ending, see 2:8, note 9.) Who is the subject?

   _____

   _____

3. וְהָלַכְתְּ—Parse this verb. How do you determine the P-G-N? The *waw* should be understood as consecutive following the implied jussive of the previous main clause (see note 1). Boaz continues his instructions.

   _____

   _____

4. אַחֲרֵיהֶן—This form consists of what elements? Note especially the gender of the suffix. To whom does it refer? (Note NIV and NET in this regard.)

   _____

   _____

5. צִוִּיתִי—Parse this verb. How do you determine the (a) stem, (b) root, and (c) P-G-N? The verb צָוָה occurs exclusively in the Piel/Pual with the meaning "command, instruct." The question (note הֲלוֹא) is rhetorical: Boaz emphasizes that this command to his servants is as good as done. Most of the translations give the impression that Boaz has already given this command: NIV ("I have told"), NASB ("I have commanded"), NRSV ("I have ordered"), and NLT ("I have warned"). Since Boaz has just met Ruth and given her permission to glean, it seems unlikely that he would have already issued such a command. NET, "I will tell" is better, or Joüon (363, §112g), "Behold, I order."

   _____

   _____

   _____

   _____

6. נָגְעֵךְ—Parse this form. (What does the *qamets hatuph* under the *nun* indicate about the form? See PVP, 240 [20.9]; Ful., 180 [28.4].)[22] How is the suffix functioning in relation to the verb? The preceding לְבִלְתִּי consists of the preposition -לְ and the negative particle בִּלְתִּי. The latter is used to negate the infinitive construct. See PVP, 241 (20.11).[23] When used with -לְ, it intervenes between the preposition and the infinitive. The preposition with infinitive here complements the verb, giving the content of his command to the servants.

7. וְצָמִת—This form is difficult. It is a Qal perfect 2fs (note the *taw* ending with no vowel beneath it) from צָמֵא, "to be thirsty." The *aleph* is not present in the form, which actually follows the pattern of a III-*he* verb (though the form is defectively written; one expects וְצָמִית).[24] The *waw* is consecutive; the form may be taken as temporal (cf. NASB)[25] or as the protasis ("if" part) of a conditional sentence (cf. NRSV), "when/if you are thirsty." We may call this a hypothetical future use (EE, 100).

8. וְהָלַכְתְּ—This verb is a Qal perfect 2fs with *waw* consecutive; it functions as the apodosis ("then" part) of the conditional sentence, "then you may go." It has an imperatival-permissive nuance. For other examples of the perfect with *waw* consecutive being used in both the protasis and apodosis of a conditional sentence, see GKC, 337, §112kk, and 494 (§159g).

9. וְשָׁתִית—Parse this verb. How do you determine the *(a)* root, and *(b)* P-G-N? The *waw* is consecutive; it continues the apodosis, "then you may go . . . and drink."

10. יִשְׁאֲבוּן—Parse this verb. How do you determine the P-G-N? How is the *nun* to be explained? (See 2:8, note 9.) How is the imperfect functioning here? The preceding מֵאֲשֶׁר consists of the preposition מִן and the relative pronoun, "from that which."

22. Fut., 121 (20.6); Gar., 211 (36.A); Kel., 183 (56.2); Ross, 161–62 (22.2); Seow, 255 (1.b).
23. Fut., 122 (20.8); Gar., 212 (36.B.2); Kel., 183 (56.2); Ross, 164 (22.5); Seow, 259 (4.a).
24. See GKC, 216, §75qq; Joüon, 202, §78g.
25. See also Joüon, 622, §106b.

2:10

וַתִּפֹּל עַל־פָּנֶיהָ וַתִּשְׁתַּחוּ אָרְצָה וַתֹּאמֶר אֵלָיו מַדּוּעַ מָצָאתִי חֵן בְּעֵינֶיךָ לְהַכִּירֵנִי וְאָנֹכִי נָכְרִיָּה:

1. וַתִּפֹּל—Parse this verb. How do you determine the *(a)* root, and *(b)* P-G-N?

2. פָּנֶיהָ—This form consists of what elements?

3. וַתִּשְׁתַּחוּ—This verb is a Hishtaphel wayyiqtol 3fs from the root חָוָה, "bow down, worship." See PVP, 400–401 (35.14),[26] as well as *HALOT*, 295–96.[27] The prefix תשׁת consists of the 3fs prefixed *taw* and a stem prefix; the *he* that is part of the stem prefix (cf. the perfect form הִשְׁתַּחֲוָה) has been lost by syncope.[28] חו are root letters; the third root letter *he* has apocopated. Despite the ו at the end of the form, the verb is not plural. Normally the ending would be וֶה-, but the apocopation of the *he* leaves the *waw* isolated. Under these conditions the *waw* is sometimes written as an unaccented "u" vowel. See GKC, 83, §24d.

4. אָרְצָה—What is the function of the *qamets he* ending on the form אָרְצָה? Note that it is unaccented. See PVP, 64 (7.6); Ful., 56–57 (10.11).

5. מָצָאתִי—Parse this verb. How do you determine the P-G-N? How is the perfect functioning here? The expression "find favor in the eyes of" means "to be an object of another's favorable disposition or action" or "to be a recipient of another's favor or kindness." The favor shown is typically deserved or at least prompted by the object's character, actions, or condition (see Gen. 6:8–9; 32:6 [Eng. v. 5]; 39:3–4; 1 Sam. 25:7–8; Prov. 3:3–4). Ruth assumed that Boaz's kindness had some basis, though she was unsure of the reason for it. Boaz explained that Ruth's kindness to her mother-in-law prompted him to reach out to her and meet her needs (vv. 11–12).

---

26. Fut., 244–45; Gar., 232 (40.D); Ross, 298–99 (40.4); Seow, 303 (7.f).
27. Traditionally this form was understood as a Hithpalel from the verbal root שָׁחָה. See BDB, 1005; GKC, 215, §75kk. Most now reject this view. See W-OC, 360–61, as well as Joüon, 170, §60g.
28. So hypothetical (*) וַתִּשְׁתַּחוּ < וַתִּהְשְׁתַּחוּ. One sees this same principle (syncope) at work elsewhere in biblical Hebrew, for example, when a preposition is prefixed to a definite noun: *בְּהַשָּׂדֶה < בַּשָּׂדֶה, "in the field"; or in the Hiphil imperfect: *יַהְקְטִיל < יַקְטִיל.

6. לְהַכִּירֵ֫ (a)—Parse this form. How do you determine the *(a)* stem, and *(b)* root? How is the pronominal suffix functioning in relation to the verb? How does the form relate to the preceding verb מָצָ֫אתִי?[29] With just a few exceptions, the verb נָכַר occurs in the Hiphil stem with the meaning "observe, recognize."

_____

_____

_____

7. וְאָנֹכִ֖י נָכְרִיָּ֑ה—This clause has a disjunctive structure and is probably circumstantial-concessive: "Why have I found favor in your sight, so that you show me special regard, *even though* I am a foreigner." נָכְרִיָּ֑ה is either a feminine (note the *qamets he* ending) noun or adjective (functioning sustantivally); in either case it has the gentilic ending. See 1:22, note 3.

2:11

וַיַּ֤עַן בֹּ֨עַז֙ וַיֹּ֣אמֶר לָ֔הּ הֻגֵּ֨ד הֻגַּ֜ד לִ֗י כֹּ֤ל אֲשֶׁר־עָשִׂית֙ אֶת־חֲמוֹתֵ֔ךְ אַחֲרֵ֖י מ֣וֹת אִישֵׁ֑ךְ
וַתַּֽעַזְבִ֞י אָבִ֣יךְ וְאִמֵּ֗ךְ וְאֶ֙רֶץ֙ מֽוֹלַדְתֵּ֔ךְ וַתֵּ֣לְכִ֔י אֶל־עַ֕ם אֲשֶׁ֥ר לֹֽא־יָדַ֖עַתְּ תְּמ֥וֹל שִׁלְשֽׁוֹם:

1. הֻגֵּ֨ד—This verb is a Hophal infinitive absolute from the verbal root נָגַד, which typically occurs in the Hiphil stem with the meaning "tell, relate." You will recall that the Hophal is the passive of the Hiphil. Normally the prefix vowel for the Hophal is *qamets hatuph,* but with I-*nun* verbs it is *qibbuts.* How can you tell this is a I-*nun* root? How is the infinitive absolute functioning in relation to the following finite verbal form? See EE, 76–77.[30] Note how the translations attempt to bring out the force of the infinitival construction: "I've been told all about" (NIV), "has been fully reported" (NASB), "has been fully told" (NRSV), "I have been given a full report" (NET).

_____

_____

2. הֻגַּ֜ד—Parse this form. How do you determine the *(a)* stem, and *(b)* root? See PVP, 378 (33.6–33.7); Ful., 231 (34.4).[31] This verbal stem indicates what voice? See PVP, 367 (32.2); Ful., 152 (24.5).[32] This verb occurs exclusively in the Hiphil/Hophal with the meaning "declare, tell." The verb may be related to the preposition נֶ֫גֶד, "in front of," and carry the basic idea "to act in front of."[33]

_____

_____

_____

---

29. See AC, 67–73; Jouon, 436, §124l; W-OC, 607.
30. See also AC, 73–77; BHRG, 158–59; GKC, 342–43; Jouon, 422, §123e; WHS, 205; W-OC, 584–88.
31. Gar., 289–91 (50); Kel., 307 (73.2); Ross, 247 (34.5); Seow, 322–23 (2).
32. Fut., 238; Gar., 289 (50); Kel., 112–13 (36.6); Ross, 219 (31.2); Seow, 322 (2).
33. See W-OC, 444.

3. כֹּל—How is כֹּל functioning in relation to the preceding verb?

_____

_____

4. עָשִׂית—Parse this verb. How do you determine the *(a)* root, and *(b)* P-G-N? The accusative sign that follows probably is used here to indicate reference, "regarding, with respect to." See BDB, 794, I.1.a.(4).

_____

_____

5. וַתַּעַזְבִי—Parse this verb. How do you determine the *(a)* P-G-N, and *(b)* stem? (Why is the prefix vowel *pathaq* instead of *hireq?*) The wayyiqtol clause here has a specifying function; it begins a description of what Ruth did for Naomi. (In other words, it fills in the content of the preceding כֹּל.) It may be translated, "how you left . . ."

_____

_____

_____

6. מוֹלַדְתֵּךְ—This form consists of the feminine singular noun מוֹלֶדֶת, "kin, relatives," and a 2fs suffix. How is the noun functioning in relation to אֶרֶץ?

7. אֲשֶׁר—How is the relative pronoun functioning in relation to the following verb יָדַעַתְּ? Parse this verb. How do you determine the P-G-N?

_____

_____

8. תְּמוֹל שִׁלְשׁוֹם—This is an idiomatic expression meaning "formerly, beforehand, previously." Literally, it means "yesterday, a third day." See BDB, 1070; *HALOT*, 1546.

2:12

יְשַׁלֵּם יְהוָה פָּעֳלֵךְ
וּתְהִי מַשְׂכֻּרְתֵּךְ שְׁלֵמָה מֵעִם יְהוָה אֱלֹהֵי יִשְׂרָאֵל אֲשֶׁר־בָּאת לַחֲסוֹת תַּחַת־כְּנָפָיו:

1. יְשַׁלֵּם—Parse this verb. How do you determine the stem? How is the stem functioning here? (See AC, 41–45; EE, 80, for categories. To determine the best category you will need to compare the meaning of the verb in the Qal with its meaning in the Piel. See BDB, 1022; *HALOT*, 1532–36.) The form is best taken as a jussive since this appears to be a prayer of blessing. Note the parallel verb וּתְהִי, clearly a jussive form, later in the verse.

_____

_____

_____

_____

2. פָּעֳלֵךְ—This form consists of what elements? How does the form relate to the preceding verb? Boaz appears to use a metaphor from the economic sphere; he asks that Yahweh repay Ruth for her labor. He recognized that her efforts were sacrificial, being motivated by her devotion to Naomi (see 3:10).

_____

_____

3. וּתְהִי—The verb וּתְהִי is a jussive from the root הָיָה, "to be." The form is shortened due to the apocopation of the III-*he*; the imperfect form would be תִּהְיֶה. (See PVP, 216.)[34] How do you determine the P-G-N?

_____

_____

4. מַשְׂכֻּרְתֵּךְ—This form consists of what elements? How is it functioning in the sentence?

_____

_____

5. שְׁלֵמָה—What part of speech is שְׁלֵמָה? How is it functioning in the sentence?

_____

_____

6. אֲשֶׁר—The relative pronoun collocates with תַּחַת־כְּנָפָיו and may be translated, "under whose wings." On the use of the resumptive pronoun after the relative, see W-OC, 333–34.

7. בָּאת—Parse this verb. How do you determine the P-G-N? Who is the subject?

_____

_____

8. לַחֲסוֹת—Parse this form. How do you determine the root? How does the form relate to the preceding verb? The metaphor is that of a young bird finding shelter under its mother's protective wings. When Ruth committed herself to Naomi, she abandoned her homeland and its god(s) and placed herself under the authority and care of Naomi's God (see 1:17).

_____

_____

_____

---

34. Fut., 151 (24.8); Gar., 226 (39.B); Kel., 291 (72.7); Ross, 261–62 (36.2.1); Seow, 235 (1.a).

2:13

וַתֹּאמֶר אֶמְצָא־חֵן בְּעֵינֶיךָ אֲדֹנִי כִּי נִחַמְתָּנִי וְכִי דִבַּרְתָּ עַל־לֵב שִׁפְחָתֶךָ
וְאָנֹכִי לֹא אֶהְיֶה כְּאַחַת שִׁפְחֹתֶיךָ:

1. אֶמְצָא—Parse this verb. How do you determine the P-G-N? How is the imperfect functioning here? Note: The form is not a cohortative, but some (cf. KJV; NIV; NRSV) treat it as a virtual cohortative, since III-*aleph* verbs only rarely have the cohortative ending.[35] However, the imperfect makes excellent sense here if this statement recognizes Boaz's continuing kindness to her (cf. NET). He extended kindness to her initially by permitting her to work in the field (vv. 8–10). Now he continues to extend kindness to her by praying that Yahweh would bless her for her efforts. NASB's "I have found favor" is problematic; the form is not a perfect.

2. כִּי נִחַמְתָּנִי—What type of clause is this? Parse נִחַמְתָּנִי. How do you determine the P-G-N? The Niphal perfect and Piel perfect of נָחַם overlap in form, but the form in verse 13 has to be Piel because of the pronominal objective suffix, "you have comforted me." The Niphal of this verb is intransitive and would not take an objective suffix. In the Piel this verb can mean "to console, comfort" someone who has experienced loss (Gen. 37:35; 2 Sam. 10:2; 12:24), but it can also carry the idea "to encourage, reassure" (Gen. 50:21; Ps. 23:4), which seems to be the nuance here (cf. NET).

3. וְכִי דִבַּרְתָּ . . .—The idiom "speak to the heart" can have a romantic connotation (Gen. 34:3; Hos. 2:14), but that concept would be premature here, where the expression simply means "encourage, reassure" (see Gen. 50:21; 2 Sam. 19:8 [Eng. v. 7]; 2 Chron. 30:22; Isa. 40:2).

4. שִׁפְחָתֶךָ—The term שִׁפְחָה, used here with a suffix, views a female servant as a laborer and can be used to emphasize subservience. In 1 Samuel 25:41 Abigail states that she is willing to stoop to this level and wash the feet of David's servants. In so doing she highlights her humility and her willingness to serve. Ruth uses the term because she has been given permission to work with Boaz's laborers, as if she were a female servant. Later, when she approaches Boaz to propose marriage, she uses a different term. See 3:9, and EE, 42–44.

5. וְאָנֹכִי—The clause . . . וְאָנֹכִי has a disjunctive structure and is probably circumstantial-concessive, "even though I could never be . . ."

---

35. See Joüon, 202, §78h; 374.

6. אֶהְיֶה—Parse this verb. The imperfect is either present or future. Usage of the imperfect of הָיָה elsewhere suggests that the sense is future here, "I will never be."[36]

_____

_____

7. שִׁפְחֹתֶיךָ—This form consists of what elements? How can you tell the noun is plural?

_____

_____

Step 3: Interpretive Translation

In light of the decisions you have made in your analysis, provide an interpretive, paraphrastic translation of Ruth 2:8–13.

_____

_____

_____

_____

_____

_____

_____

_____

Step 4: Structural Outline

Outline the narrative structure of Ruth 2:8–13. Carefully delineate the narrative mainline (initiated and extended by wayyiqtol forms), offline (nonstandard) constructions, and quotations. Using the categories listed in the appendix (cf. EE, 120–27), classify all wayyiqtol and disjunctive clauses that are in the narrative framework. You need not classify clauses within quotations.

_____

_____

_____

_____

_____

_____

36. See Frederic W. Bush, *Ruth, Esther,* WBC (Dallas: Word Books, 1996),124–25.

_____

_____

_____

_____

Assignment 3

Step 1: Initial View

Read Ruth 2:14–17a in the Hebrew text, using an interlinear if you desire. Underline any words or forms you do not recognize. Try to identify verbal forms and label them as follows:

- wayyiqtol verbal forms: wc-y (the so-called *waw* consecutive with the yiqtol, usually identified as a preterite or imperfect)
- weqatal forms: wc-q (the so-called *waw* consecutive with the qatal, that is, perfect)
- simple perfects (without *waw*): pf.
- simple imperfects (without *waw*): impf.
- imperatives: impv.
- jussives: juss.
- cohortatives: coh.
- infinitives construct: inf. const.
- infinitives absolute: inf. abs.
- participles: part.

Step 2: Analyzing the Text

2:14

וַיֹּאמֶר לָה בֹעַז לְעֵת הָאֹכֶל גֹּשִׁי הֲלֹם וְאָכַלְתְּ מִן־הַלֶּחֶם וְטָבַלְתְּ פִּתֵּךְ בַּחֹמֶץ
וַתֵּשֶׁב מִצַּד הַקּוֹצְרִים וַיִּצְבָּט־לָהּ קָלִי וַתֹּאכַל וַתִּשְׂבַּע וַתֹּתַר׃

1. לָה—The *mappiq,* marking the 3fs suffix, is omitted in לָה, "to her."[37]
2. לְעֵת—The preposition -לְ has a temporal force here, "at the time of." See AC, 111; W-OC, 206.
3. גֹּשִׁי—This verb is a Qal imperative 2fs from נָגַשׁ. On the loss of the initial *nun,* see PVP, 210–11 (18.9); Ful., 232 (34.4).[38] The vocalization of the first syllable is odd; one expects the form to be גְּשִׁי. See GKC, 173, §66c. How do you determine the P-G-N?

_____

_____

4. הֲלֹם—The form is an adverb, meaning "to here." See BDB, 240–41; *HALOT,* 249.

---

37. See GKC, 302, §103g; Joüon, 93, §25a.
38. Gar., 217 (37.B.3); Kel., 304 (73.2); Ross, 243–44 (34.2.2); Seow, 239–40 (3.f).

5. וְאָכַלְתְּ—Parse this verb. How do you determine the P-G-N? After the preceding imperative how is the *waw* to be classified and how is the form functioning? See PVP, 218;[39] EE, 99–101.[40]

_____

_____

_____

6. וְטָבַלְתְּ—On this form see the preceding note.

7. וַתֵּשֶׁב—Parse this verb. How do you determine the *(a)* root, and *(b)* P-G-N?

_____

_____

8. מִצַּד—In the phrase מִצַּד the preposition has the force of "at " (see BDB, 841). On this use of מִן to indicate location see W-OC, 212.

9. וַיִּצְבָּט—Parse this verb. How do you determine the P-G-N? Who is the subject? One expects the theme vowel to be *holem* (long *o*), but the form is joined by a *maqqeph* to the following prepositional phrase, which takes the accent. This leaves the final syllable of the verb closed and unaccented, necessitating a short vowel, in this case *qamets hatuph* (short *o*). This verb occurs only here in the Hebrew Bible; it apparently means "reach, hold out."

_____

_____

_____

10. וַתֹּאכַל . . .—Notice the shift in subject once more; Ruth is the subject of the three 3fs verbs that conclude the verse. The last form (וַתֹּתַר) is difficult; it is Hiphil wayyiqtol 3fs from יָתַר, "be left, remain" (usually in the Niphal stem). In the causative stem it means "to leave over, have left over." One expects the form to be וַתּוֹתֵר (cf. the 3ms form in 2 Sam. 8:4). The imperfect form is תּוֹתִיר (see PVP, 360; Ful., 244),[41] but in the wayyiqtol the theme vowel is normally *tsere*. However, here in a pausal position (at the end of the verse) with the guttural-like *resh*, it is *pathaq*. See GKC, 147, §53n; 191, §69v. The prefix vowel, normally *holem waw*, is written defectively as *holem*.

2:15

וַתָּקָם לְלַקֵּט וַיְצַו בֹּעַז אֶת־נְעָרָיו לֵאמֹר גַּם בֵּין הָעֳמָרִים תְּלַקֵּט וְלֹא תַכְלִימוּהָ:

1. וַתָּקָם—Parse this verb. How do you determine the *(a)* stem, *(b)* root, and *(c)* P-G-N?

_____

---

39. Gar., 114–15 (20.E); Kel., 214–15 (63.3); Ross, 138–39 (18.3); Seow, 243 (8.b).
40. See also AC, 88–89; BHRG, 168–71; GKC, 330–39; Joüon, 399–400, §119l; W-OC, 519–39 (especially 529–30).
41. Fut., 208; Gar., 278 (48.B.5); Kel., 343 (75.2); Ross, 253 (35.2.5); Seow, 278 (1.f).

2. לְלַקֵּט—Parse this form. How do you determine the stem? How is the form functioning in relation to the preceding verb?

3. וַיְצַו—Parse this verb. How do you determine the *(a)* stem, and *(b)* root? What happened to the third root letter? On the omission of the *dagesh* in the *yod* prefix due to the *shewa*, see PVP, 316 (26.16).[42] The *dagesh* in the second root letter *waw* is omitted because the letter stands at the end of the form (the III-*he* apocopates in the wayyiqtol form).[43]

4. תְּלַקֵּט—Parse this verb. How do you determine the *(a)* stem, and *(b)* P-G-N? The form could be an imperfect. If so, how is it functioning? It may also be taken as a jussive. In this case, how is it functioning?

5. תַכְלִימוּהָ—Parse this verb. How do you determine the *(a)* stem, and *(b)* P-G-N? How is the pronominal suffix functioning in relation to the verb? How is the imperfect functioning? (Note the preceding negative particle.) In the Niphal stem the verb כָּלַם means "be humiliated, ashamed." The Hiphil is causative.[44]

---

42. Gar., 258 (45.D.1); Ross, 263 (36.4).
43. See Gar., 258 (45.D.1); Kel., 292 (72.8); Ross, 263 (36.4); Seow, 265–66 (2.a).
44. On the mixture of the Niphal and Hiphil stems see W-OC, 394.

2:16–17a

וְגַם שֹׁל־תָּשֹׁלּוּ לָהּ מִן־הַצְּבָתִים וַעֲזַבְתֶּם וְלִקְּטָה וְלֹא תִגְעֲרוּ־בָהּ׃
וַתְּלַקֵּט בַּשָּׂדֶה עַד־הָעָרֶב

1. שֹׁל—This form appears to be an infinitive construct from שָׁלַל, but it is functioning like an infinitive absolute here—note the following finite form תָּשֹׁלּוּ.[45] One would expect the infinitive absolute to be שָׁלוֹל. At any rate the infinitive has an emphasizing function before the finite form. One may translate, "make sure you pull out" (NET). There is a well-attested verb שָׁלַל, meaning "plunder, rob," but this meaning does not fit in verse 16. The verb here is probably a homonym meaning "pull out." See BDB, 1021; *HALOT,* 1531.

2. תָּשֹׁלּוּ—Parse this verb. How do you determine the *(a)* stem, *(b)* root, and *(c)* P-G-N? How is the imperfect functioning here?

_____

_____

_____

3. צְבָתִים—This term appears only here in the Hebrew Bible; apparently it refers to bundles or sheaves of grain. See BDB, 841; *HALOT,* 1000.

4. וַעֲזַבְתֶּם—Parse this verb. How do you determine the P-G-N? How do you classify the *waw*? How is the form functioning here? (Note the preceding imperfect.)

_____

_____

_____

5. וְלִקְּטָה—Parse this verb. How do you determine the *(a)* stem, and *(b)* P-G-N? The verb sequence begins with an imperfect (תָּשֹׁלּוּ), so the *waw* should be taken as consecutive. There is a shift in subject with this verb; in this case the construction probably indicates consequence, "so she can gather" (NET). The closest syntactical parallel to this text is in 1 Samuel 6:8b, where an imperfect of command (תָּשִׂימוּ, a 2mp form, like תָּשֹׁלּוּ in Ruth 2:16) is followed by a *waw* consecutive with the perfect functioning as a command (וְשִׁלַּחְתֶּם, a 2mp form, like וַעֲזַבְתֶּם in Ruth 2:16) and then by a *waw* consecutive with the perfect indicating consequence (וְהָלַךְ, a third singular form, like וְלִקְּטָה in Ruth 2:16). NASB translates 1 Samuel 6:8b: "put . . . Then send it away that it may go." See KJV as well. Another option is to take the final verb in the sequence as equivalent to a jussive. NRSV translates 1 Samuel 6:8b: "put . . . Then send it off, and let it go its way." Understanding the syntax this way in Ruth 2:16 would yield a translation: "Pull out . . . leave and let her gather" (cf. NLT). It should be noted, however, that NRSV does not translate

---

45. See GKC, 345, §113x; Jouön, 426, §123q. Jouön suggests a textual corruption here.

the final verb as jussive in Ruth 2:16. It reads: "pull out . . . and leave them for her to glean," taking the final verb as indicating purpose or consequence.

_____

_____

_____

6. תִּגְעֲרוּ—Parse this verb. How do you determine the P-G-N? This negated imperfect continues Boaz's instuctions to his workers (note תָּשֹׁלּוּ . . . וַעֲזַבְתֶּם). After the verb גָּעַר, the preposition -בְּ (cf. בָהּ) introduces the object (cf. the 3fs pronominal suffix). See W-OC, 198–99.

_____

_____

7. וַתְּלַקֵּט—Parse this verb. How do you determine the (a) stem, and (b) P-G-N?

_____

_____

Step 3: Interpretive Translation

In light of the decisions you have made in your analysis, provide an interpretive, paraphrastic translation of Ruth 2:14–17a.

_____

_____

_____

_____

_____

_____

_____

_____

Step 4: Structural Outline

Outline the narrative structure of Ruth 2:14–17a. Carefully delineate the narrative mainline (initiated and extended by wayyiqtol forms), offline (nonstandard) constructions, and quotations. Using the categories listed in the appendix (cf. EE, 120–27), classify all wayyiqtol and disjunctive clauses that are in the narrative framework. You need not classify clauses within quotations.

_____

_____

_____
_____
_____
_____
_____
_____
_____
_____

Scene 3: Ruth 2:17b–23: Ruth Returns with Good News

Assignment

Step 1: Initial View

Read Ruth 2:17b–23 in the Hebrew text, using an interlinear if you desire. Underline any words or forms you do not recognize. Try to identify verbal forms and label them as follows:

- wayyiqtol verbal forms: wc-y (the so-called *waw* consecutive with the yiqtol, usually identified as a preterite or imperfect)
- weqatal forms: wc-q (the so-called *waw* consecutive with the qatal, that is, perfect)
- simple perfects (without *waw*): pf.
- simple imperfects (without *waw*): impf.
- imperatives: impv.
- jussives: juss.
- cohortatives: coh.
- infinitives construct: inf. const.
- infinitives absolute: inf. abs.
- participles: part.

Step 2: Analyzing the Text

2:17b

וַתַּחְבֹּט אֵת אֲשֶׁר־לִקֵּטָה וַיְהִי כְּאֵיפָה שְׂעֹרִים:

1. וַתַּחְבֹּט—Parse this verb. How do you determine the *(a)* stem, and *(b)* P-G-N? Why is the prefix vowel *pathaq* instead of *hireq?* See PVP, 177–78 (16.8–16.9); Ful., 191–92 (29.6).

_____
_____
_____

2. אֲשֶׁר—Within its clause the relative pronoun is the object of the following verb (on the verb, see note 3 below). Yet the clause in its entirety (אֲשֶׁר לִקֵּטָה) is an accusative noun clause, functioning as the object of the verb "she beat out." Note the accusative sign אֵת before the relative.

3. לִקֵּטָה—Parse this verb. How do you determine the *(a)* stem, and *(b)* P-G-N? One would expect a *shewa* beneath the *qoph,* but in pause a *tsere* appears. See GKC, 142, §52l. How is the perfect functioning here? (Hint: What is the chronological relationship between this action and that of the main verb?)

---

4. וַיְהִי—This introduces a brief parenthetical note telling how much Ruth actually gleaned from the field. See EE, 122–23. The subject is indefinite, "now there was . . ."

5. כְּאֵיפָה—The preposition -כְּ is usually understood in the sense of "about, approximately."[46] However, Bush (*Ruth, Esther,* 132–33) and Hubbard (*The Book of Ruth,* 179, note 3) suggest that the preposition may be used to indicate an exact amount here. On this use of the preposition, see W-OC, 203. They explain that in this use the preposition indicates "*correspondence* or identity" (emphasis theirs). They add: "The agreement of the things compared is complete."

6. שְׂעֹרִים—This term, "barley," is in apposition to the preceding אֵיפָה, "ephah." After the unit of measure (an ephah), it indicates the substance measured. See W-OC, 231.[47] On the significance of the plural form, see 1:22, note 11.

2:18

וַתִּשָּׂא וַתָּבוֹא הָעִיר וַתֵּרֶא חֲמוֹתָהּ אֵת אֲשֶׁר־לִקֵּטָה וַתּוֹצֵא וַתִּתֶּן־לָהּ אֵת אֲשֶׁר־הוֹתִרָה מִשָּׂבְעָהּ׃

1. וַתִּשָּׂא—Parse this verb. How do you determine the *(a)* root, and *(b)* P-G-N? (Note: Despite the *i* + *dagesh* + *a* vocalization pattern, the verb is not a Niphal because the *sin* is not the first root letter. How do you explain the *dagesh* in the *sin*? How do you explain the *qamets* under the *sin*? See PVP, 175–76; Ful., 223 [33.3].)[48] The object of the verb is implied here; she lifted up the barley mentioned in the previous verse. On the occasional omission of the object with this verb see Hubbard, *The Book of Ruth,* 180, note 1.

---

46. Joüon, 490, §133g.
47. See also AC, 23; Joüon, 479, §131e.
48. Fut., 83 (14.9); Gar., 180–81 (30.F); Kel., 175 (71.3); Ross, 237 (33.4); Seow, 215 (2).

164

2. הָעִיר—How is this noun functioning in relation to the preceding verb? In other words, identify the case and case function of the noun. (Note: There is no preposition in the Hebrew text; one has to supply a preposition in translation.)

_____

_____

3. וַתֵּרֶא—This verb is a Qal wayyiqtol from רָאָה. How do you determine the P-G-N? The prefix vowel _tsere_ usually indicates a I-_yod_ verb, but occasionally it appears with III-_he_ verbs. See 1:18, note 1. Who is the subject of the verb? In this regard, how is the following חֲמוֹתָה functioning in relation to the verb? A few medieval Hebrew manuscripts, supported by some ancient versions, have וַתַּרְא, a Hiphil wayyiqtol (note the _pathaq_ prefix vowel in this case) from רָאָה. In this case Ruth would be the subject of the verb, which would then have a double accusative: "and she showed her mother-in-law what she had gleaned." See NLT. For a discussion of the textual issue, see Brotzman, 145–46.

_____

_____

4. אֵת אֲשֶׁר לִקֵּטָה—Within this clause the relative pronoun אֲשֶׁר is the object of the following verb. Yet the clause in its entirety is an accusative noun clause (note אֵת), functioning as the object of the verb "saw." How is the perfect verbal form functioning in relation to the main verb?

_____

_____

5. וַתּוֹצֵא—Parse this verb. How do you determine the _(a)_ stem, _(b)_ root, and _(c)_ P-G-N? Who is the subject of the verb? How is the stem functioning?

_____

_____

_____

_____

6. וַתִּתֶּן—Parse this verb. How do you determine the _(a)_ stem, and _(b)_ root?

_____

_____

7. אֵת אֲשֶׁר־הוֹתִרָה—Within this clause the relative pronoun אֲשֶׁר is the object of the following verb. Yet the clause in its entirety is an accusative noun clause (note אֵת), functioning as the object of the verb "gave."

8. הֹוֹתִרָה—Parse this verb. How do you determine the *(a)* stem, *(b)* root, and *(c)* P-G-N? Who is the subject of the verb? For help with the stem and root, see PVP, 360 (31.12–31.13); Ful., 244.[49] The theme vowel is normally *hireq yod*, but it is written defectively here as *hireq*. How is the perfect verbal form functioning in relation to the main verb? On the function of the stem, see 2:14, note 10.

_____

_____

_____

_____

9. מִשָּׂבְעָהּ—The dictionaries understand this form as a suffixed verbal noun, שָׂבַע, "satiation" (BDB, 959–60; *HALOT*, 1304). However, one could take the form as a Qal infinitive construct from the verb שָׂבַע. (On the form see PVP, 240 [20.9]; Ful., 180–81 [28.4]).[50] The preposition מִן is prefixed to the form. (Note the *dagesh* in the following letter, indicating the assimilated *nun*. See PVP, 52 [6.5]; Ful., 41 [9.2].)[51] In this context it has a temporal function, "after, when." See AC, 117; W-OC, 212–13; BDB, 583, 7.c; *HALOT*, 597–98. Identify the P-G-N of the pronominal suffix. Who is its antecedent? How is the suffix functioning in relation to the noun/infinitive?

_____

_____

2:19

וַתֹּאמֶר לָהּ חֲמוֹתָהּ אֵיפֹה לִקַּטְתְּ הַיּוֹם וְאָנָה עָשִׂית יְהִי מַכִּירֵךְ בָּרוּךְ
וַתַּגֵּד לַחֲמוֹתָהּ אֵת אֲשֶׁר־עָשְׂתָה עִמּוֹ וַתֹּאמֶר שֵׁם הָאִישׁ אֲשֶׁר עָשִׂיתִי עִמּוֹ הַיּוֹם בֹּעַז:

1. לִקַּטְתְּ—Parse this verb. How do you determine the *(a)* stem, and *(b)* P-G-N? How is the perfect verbal form functioning here?

_____

_____

_____

2. הַיּוֹם—With יוֹם, "day," the article is often demonstrative, "this day, today." See PVP, 48 (5.11);[52] W-OC, 246.

3. וְאָנָה—Like אֵיפֹה earlier in the verse, the interrogative particle אָנָה has a locative sense, "Where?" See BDB, 33; *HALOT*, 69; W-OC, 329.

---

49. Fut., 208; Gar., 276 (48.A.5); Kel., 343 (75.2); Ross, 253 (35.2.5); Seow, 185 (8.a).
50. Fut., 120 (20.5); Gar., 211–12 (36.A–B); Kel., 183 (56.2); Ross, 161–62 (22.2); Seow, 255 (1.b).
51. Fut., 50–51 (9.12); Gar., 70 (12.B.1); Kel., 30 (15.3); Ross, 78–79 (8.4); Seow, 57 (5.b).
52. Ross, 59 (5.7).

4. עָשִׂית—Parse this verb. How do you determine the (a) root, and (b) P-G-N?

_____

_____

5. יְהִי—This form is a Qal jussive 3ms from הָיָה. The form is distinctly jussive (note the apocopated _he_). See PVP, 216–17 (18.14).[53] How is the jussive functioning here? See EE, 103–5.[54]

_____

_____

6. מַכִּירֵךְ—Parse this form. What tips you off that this may be a participle? How do you determine the (a) stem, and (b) root? How is the participle functioning here? (What is its relationship to the preceding jussive?) How does the pronominal suffix relate to the participle?

_____

_____

_____

_____

7. בָּרוּךְ—Parse this form. How is the form functioning here? (What is its relationship to the preceding jussive?) See W-OC, 628, as well as PVP, 265–66 (22.9).[55]

_____

_____

8. וַתַּגֵּד—Parse this verb. How do you determine the (a) stem, (b) root, and (c) P-G-N?

_____

_____

_____

9. אֲשֶׁר עָשְׂתָה—The relative pronoun collocates with עִמּוֹ and may be translated, "with whom." On the use of the resumptive pronoun after the relative, see W-OC, 333–34. The entire clause is an accusative noun clause (note אֵת), functioning as the object of the verb "she told."

10. עָשְׂתָה—Parse this verb. How do you determine the (a) root, and (b) P-G-N? See PVP, 154 (14.7); Ful., 265 (37.4).[56] How is the perfect verbal form functioning here? (How does it relate to the main verb?)

_____

53. Fut., 151 (24.8); Gar., 226 (39.B); Kel., 292 (72.8); Ross, 261 (36.2.1); Seow, 235 (1.a).
54. See also AC, 61–63; BHRG, 152–53; GKC, 321–23; Joüon, 376–78; W-OC, 568–70.
55. Fut., 237 (38.2); Gar., 63–65 (11.A, D); Kel., 199–200 (60.1); Ross, 157–58 (21.3); Seow, 85 (5.c).
56. Fut., 89–90 (15.6); Gar., 165 (27.E); Kel., 288 (72.3); Ross, 260 (36.2); Seow, 161 (3.a).

_____

_____

_____

11. וַתֹּאמֶר—The wayyiqtol form has a specifying function here. See EE, 122. The preceding clause informs us that Ruth told Naomi the identity of the man with whom she worked. This clause now tells us specifically what she said.

12. עָשִׂיתִי—Parse this verb. How do you determine the (a) root, and (b) P-G-N? How is the perfect verbal form functioning here?

_____

_____

_____

_____

13. בֹּעַז—How is the proper name בֹּעַז functioning in the sentence?

_____

_____

2:20

וַתֹּאמֶר נָעֳמִי לְכַלָּתָהּ בָּרוּךְ הוּא לַיהוָה אֲשֶׁר לֹא־עָזַב חַסְדּוֹ אֶת־הַחַיִּים וְאֶת־הַמֵּתִים
וַתֹּאמֶר לָהּ נָעֳמִי קָרוֹב לָנוּ הָאִישׁ מִגֹּאֲלֵנוּ הוּא:

1. הוּא—How is the pronoun functioning in relation to the preceding passive participle?

_____

_____

2. לַיהוָה—In this formal prayer of blessing, לַיהוָה indicates the agent of blessing, "by Yahweh." On this use of the preposition -לְ with passive verbs see AC, 114; GKC, 389, §121f; Joüon, 483–84, §132f.[57]

3. אֲשֶׁר—Theoretically the relative pronoun could modify יְהוָה or הוּא (i.e., Boaz). Elsewhere when אֲשֶׁר follows בָּרוּךְ it introduces the reason why the one being blessed deserves to be rewarded. This suggests that it refers here to הוּא (Boaz), for otherwise the reason for the blessing would be omitted.

   The fact that יְהוָה appears immediately before אֲשֶׁר is not determinative, as 2 Samuel 2:5 demonstrates:

$$\text{בְּרֻכִים אַתֶּם לַיהוָה אֲשֶׁר עֲשִׂיתֶם} \ldots$$

_____

57. See also W-OC, 210. Note, however, that W-OC interprets the use of the preposition in this passage in a different manner. See pp. 206–7. For a critique of this view, see Bush, _Ruth, Esther,_ 136.

In this case, as in Ruth 2:20, the relative pronoun immediately follows יְהוָה, but the appearance of the second masculine plural verb after אֲשֶׁר makes it clear that the relative modifies the second masculine pronoun אַתֶּם, not יְהוָה. For a fuller discussion see EE, 72. KJV, NASB, and NRSV misinterpret the syntax here. NIV and NLT opt for ambiguity. NET uses the causal "because" to make it clear that Boaz is in view.

4. חַסְדֹּו—How is this form functioning in relation to the preceding verb?

5. אֶת—This form (used twice here) is the preposition "with," not the accusative sign. For other examples of the collocation of חֶסֶד and אֶת, "with," see Genesis 24:49; 2 Samuel 16:17; Zechariah 7:9.
6. הַחַיִּים—If Naomi refers to Boaz's faithfulness to the widows ("the living") and their deceased husbands ("the dead"), it seems odd that the masculine plural form (הַחַיִּים) is used of the women. One might expect the feminine plural form חַיֹּות. However, the feminine noun חַיֹּות is used exclusively of nonhuman beings (cherubim) or animals in the Hebrew Bible, while the feminine plural form of the adjective חַי, "living," is used but once, as an attributive modifying "birds" (Lev. 14:4).[58]
7. קָרֹוב—How is the adjective קָרֹוב functioning in the sentence? (How does it relate to הָאִישׁ?)

8. מִגֹּאֲלֵנוּ—This form consists of what elements? (The suffix is defectively written without the *yod*: יִנוּ- > נוּ-. The noun should be understood as plural, "our kinsmen," not singular. See PVP, 81–83 [9.2–9.4]; Ful., 71 [12.2].)[59] The prepositional phrase is collocated with the following pronoun, not with what precedes. (Note the disjunctive accent *zaqeph parvum* above הָאִישׁ, indicating a syntactical break at that point.) The preposition מִן has a partitive function here, introducing the larger entity of which the subject (הוּא) is a part, "(he is one) of our near kinsmen." See BDB, 580, 3.b.*(b)*.

2:21

וַתֹּאמֶר רוּת הַמֹּואֲבִיָּה
גַּם כִּי־אָמַר אֵלַי עִם־הַנְּעָרִים אֲשֶׁר־לִי תִּדְבָּקִין עַד אִם־כִּלּוּ אֵת כָּל־הַקָּצִיר אֲשֶׁר־לִי:

1. גַּם כִּי—Following the adverb גַּם, כִּי has an emphasizing force. See BDB, 472, 1.d., and Bush, *Ruth, Esther*, 138–39. Bush translates, "he even said" (cf. NIV, NRSV, NET).
2. אֲשֶׁר־לִי—The construction אֲשֶׁר־לִי, "who are to me," has a possessive meaning, "who belong to me."[60]

58. See Bush, *Ruth, Esther*, 135.
59. Fut., 114 (19.1); Gar., 87–89 (16.B); Kel., 72 (28.2); Ross, 115–16 (14.4); Seow, 132 (1.a).
60. See GKC, 439, §135, note 3; Joüon, 475, §130e.

3. תִּדְבָּקִין—Parse this verb. How do you determine the P-G-N? (On the paragogic *nun* ending see 2:8, note 9.) How is the imperfect functioning here? (See v. 8.)

_____

_____

4. עַד אִם—This construction is temporal, "until." See Genesis 24:19, 33; Isaiah 30:17.

5. כִּלּוּ—Parse this verb. How do you determine the *(a)* stem, *(b)* root, and *(c)* P-G-N? How is the perfect functioning in relation to the preceding main verb? How is the stem functioning?

_____

_____

_____

2:22

וַתֹּאמֶר נָעֳמִי אֶל־רוּת כַּלָּתָהּ טוֹב בִּתִּי כִּי תֵצְאִי עִם־נַעֲרוֹתָיו וְלֹא יִפְגְּעוּ־בָךְ בְּשָׂדֶה אַחֵר:

1. טוֹב—How is טוֹב functioning in the sentence? To answer this you must determine how the clause כִּי תֵצְאִי . . . is functioning. It appears to be a noun clause serving as the subject of the sentence: "That you go out . . . (is) good."

_____

_____

2. בִּתִּי—This form consists of what elements? How is it functioning in the sentence?

_____

_____

3. תֵצְאִי—Parse this verb. How do you determine the *(a)* root, and *(b)* P-G-N? How is the imperfect functioning?

_____

_____

_____

4. נַעֲרוֹתָיו—This form consists of what elements? Note the gender and number of the noun. How does it differ from הַנְּעָרִים (v. 21) in this regard? Perhaps Naomi, in response to Ruth's exuberance, is reminding Ruth to be careful—she must stay close to the *female* servants.

_____

5. יִפְגְּעוּ—Parse this verb. How do you determine the P-G-N? The negated imperfect probably indicates result here, "that way they will not harm you in another field" (cf. NET). After the verb פָּגַע, the preposition בְּ- introduces the object. See W-OC, 198–99; BDB, 803.

_____

_____

2:23

וַתִּדְבַּק בְּנַעֲרוֹת בֹּעַז לְלַקֵּט עַד־כְּלוֹת קְצִיר־הַשְּׂעֹרִים וּקְצִיר הַחִטִּים וַתֵּשֶׁב אֶת־חֲמוֹתָהּ:

1. וַתִּדְבַּק בְּנַעֲרוֹת—On the meaning of the collocation דָּבַק בְּ- see 1:14, note 5.
2. כְּלוֹת—Parse this form. How do you determine the root? How is the form functioning here? See AC, 67–73; EE, 77–78.[61]

_____

_____

_____

3. קְצִיר־הַשְּׂעֹרִים—On this construction see 1:22, notes 10–11.
4. הַחִטִּים—On the use of the plural see 1:22, note 11.
5. וַתֵּשֶׁב—Parse this verb. How do you determine the (a) root, and (b) P-G-N? How is the following אֶת functioning in relation to the verb? (Note the textual variant here; see *BHS*, note a-a. A few medieval Hebrew manuscripts read וַתָּשָׁב אֶל, "and she returned to." The verb is a Qal wayyiqtol 3fs from the hollow verb שׁוּב, as the *qamets* prefix vowel indicates.)

_____

_____

_____

Step 3: Interpretive Translation

In light of the decisions you have made in your analysis, provide an interpretive, paraphrastic translation of Ruth 2:17b–23.

_____

_____

_____

_____

_____

---

61. See also BHRG, 153–57; GKC, 347–52; Joüon, 432–39; WHS, 192–200; W-OC, 600–611.

_____

_____

_____

Step 4: Structural Outline

Outline the narrative structure of Ruth 2:17b–23. Carefully delineate the narrative mainline (initiated and extended by wayyiqtol forms), offline (nonstandard) constructions, and quotations. Using the categories listed in the appendix (cf. EE, 120–27), classify all wayyiqtol and disjunctive clauses that are in the narrative framework. You need not classify clauses within quotations.

_____

_____

_____

_____

_____

_____

_____

_____

_____

_____

Act 3
Ruth 3

Scene 1: Ruth 3:1–5: Naomi Plays the Role of Matchmaker

Assignment

Step 1: Initial View

Read Ruth 3:1–5 in the Hebrew text, using an interlinear if you desire. Underline any words or forms you do not recognize. Try to identify verbal forms and label them as follows:

- wayyiqtol verbal forms: wc-y (the so-called *waw* consecutive with the yiqtol, usually identified as a preterite or imperfect)
- weqatal forms: wc-q (the so-called *waw* consecutive with the qatal, that is, perfect)
- simple perfects (without *waw*): pf.
- simple imperfects (without *waw*): impf.
- imperatives: impv.
- jussives: juss.
- cohortatives: coh.
- infinitives construct: inf. const.
- infinitives absolute: inf. abs.
- participles: part.

Step 2: Analyzing the Text

3:1

וַתֹּאמֶר לָהּ נָעֳמִי חֲמוֹתָהּ בִּתִּי הֲלֹא אֲבַקֶּשׁ־לָךְ מָנוֹחַ אֲשֶׁר יִיטַב־לָךְ:

1. בִּתִּי—How is this form functioning in Naomi's statement to Ruth?

_____

_____

2. הֲלֹא—This form consists of what elements?

_____

_____

3. אֲבַקֶּשׁ—Parse this verb. How do you determine the (a) stem, and (b) P-G-N? How is the imperfect functioning in this rhetorical question? This verb occurs exclusively in the Piel/Pual with the meaning "seek."

_____

_____

_____

4. מָנוֹחַ—How is this noun functioning in the sentence?

_____

_____

5. יִיטַב—Parse this verb. How do you determine the root? The idiom "will be good for you" here means "will be for your benefit."

_____

_____

3:2

וְעַתָּה הֲלֹא בֹעַז מֹדַעְתָּנוּ אֲשֶׁר הָיִית אֶת־נַעֲרוֹתָיו הִנֵּה־הוּא זֹרֶה אֶת־גֹּרֶן הַשְּׂעֹרִים הַלָּיְלָה:

1. מֹדַעְתָּנוּ—This form consists of what elements?[1] How is it functioning in the sentence?

_____

_____

2. אֲשֶׁר—The relative pronoun modifies Boaz. It collocates with the preposition אֵת and the suffix on נַעֲרוֹתָיו; the construction may be translated, "with whose." On the use of the resumptive pronoun after the relative, see W-OC, 333–34.

3. הָיִית—Parse this verb. How do you determine the (a) root, and (b) P-G-N? How is the perfect verbal form functioning here?

_____

_____

_____

4. זֹרֶה—Parse this form. How can you tell the form is an active participle? How is the participle functioning in the sentence? What temporal nuance does it have? See AC, 79–82; EE, 67.[2] Your answer to this

---

1. On the apparent feminine noun form referring to a man, see Joüon, 266–67, §89b. On the form of the suffix, see Joüon, 289, §94h.
2. See also BHRG, 162; GKC, 359–60; Joüon, 409–13; WHS, 213–14; W-OC, 623–28.

question is related to how you understand הַלַּיְלָה, "tonight." Has nighttime already arrived, or is Naomi anticipating the arrival of nightfall later in the day? Unfortunately we cannot be sure. The participle is only rarely used with הַלַּיְלָה. In 1 Samuel 19:11, Michal urged David to escape during the night because Saul's men were outside waiting to kill him when morning arrived. Though David's escape took place at night, it is not clear if Michal warned him at night or earlier in the day.

_____

_____

_____

5. אֶת־גֹּרֶן—The function of the accusative sign following זֹרֶה is not clear. It may introduce the direct object, if גֹּרֶן, "threshing floor," stands by metonymy for the barley gathered on the floor. However, it may be better to understand גֹּרֶן as an accusative of location, "at the threshing floor." The accusative sign occasionally appears before adverbial accusatives of place. See W-OC, 181 (though our text is not cited).

3:3

וְרָחַצְתְּ וָסַכְתְּ וְשַׂמְתְּ שִׂמְלֹתַ֫יִךְ עָלַיִךְ וְיָרַדְתְּ הַגֹּרֶן אַל־תִּוָּדְעִי לָאִישׁ עַד כַּלֹּתוֹ לֶאֱכֹל וְלִשְׁתּוֹת:

1. וְרָחַצְתְּ—This verb begins a series of instructions. It is logically dependent on the preceding clause: "Look! He is winnowing at the barley threshing floor tonight, so wash . . ." The form is a Qal perfect 2fs with *waw* consecutive. One might expect the sequence of instructions to begin with an imperative or imperfect, but occasionally such sequences commence with the perfect and *waw* consecutive. See GKC, 335, §112aa. Note that the following three verbs in the sequence of instructions are also perfects with *waw* consecutive. This is typical in procedural discourse, where a routine is rehearsed. See Robert E. Longacre, "Weqatal Forms in Biblical Hebrew Prose," pp. 52–54, in Robert D. Bergen, ed., *Biblical Hebrew and Discourse Linguistics* (Winona Lake: Eisenbrauns, 1994).

2. וָסַכְתְּ—Parse this verb. How do you determine the *(a)* root, and *(b)* P-G-N? In translation the verb appears to be reflexive, "anoint yourself," but actually it is an elliptical construction with the object implied. See as well 2 Samuel 12:20. Sometimes the object (שֶׁמֶן, "oil") is stated. See 2 Samuel 14:2. One could translate: "wash and put on (oil)." On the pointing *(qamets)* of the conjunction before the accented syllable, see GKC, 306–7, §104g.[3]

_____

_____

_____

---

3. See also Joüon, 348–49, §105d.

3. וְשַׂמְתְּ—Parse this verb. How do you determine the *(a)* root, and *(b)* P-G-N? (Note that the pattern is the same as the preceding verb.)

_____

_____

_____

4. שִׂמְלֹתֵ ךְ—This unreadable form involves a *kethib/qere* variant.[4] The consonantal text (*kethib,* "what is written") combines the singular noun שִׂמְלָה with a 2fs suffix. The form would be vocalized שִׂמְלָתֵךְ. See *BHS* note (a). Recall that feminine nouns ending in ָה- have a *taw* ending before suffixes. See PVP, 84–85 (9.6–9.7); Ful., 77 (13.2).[5]

    The vowels that appear in the text go with the consonants given in the left margin above the *qoph* (an abbreviation for "*qere*"). This set of consonants differs from the *kethib* in that a *yod* appears before the final *kaph.* When the vowels are combined with these consonants, the resulting form (the *qere,* "what is to be read") is שִׂמְלֹתַיִךְ, a plural form of שִׂמְלָה with a 2fs suffix. One can tell the form is plural by the *-ot* ending before the suffix and the presence of *yod* in the suffix. See PVP, 81–82 (9.2–9.3), and 84–85 (9.6–9.7); Ful., 77 (13.2).[6]

5. עָלַיִךְ—This form consists of what elements? See PVP, 87–88 (9.10); Ful., 85 (14.4).[7]

_____

_____

6. וְיָרַדְתִּי—This unreadable form involves another *kethib/qere* variant. The consonantal text *(kethib)* has a *yod* at the end, suggesting a vocalization וְיָרַדְתִּי (see *BHS* note b). The vocalization in the text *(qere)* goes with the consonants in the left margin above the *qoph.* This set of consonants omits the *yod* and when combined with the vowels in the text yields the form וְיָרַדְתְּ, which you should recognize as a Qal perfect 2fs from יָרַד with *waw* consecutive. The *kethib* form appears to be a first common singular perfect, but this would make no sense here. Naomi is instructing Ruth what to do, not telling her what she herself intends to do. The *kethib* actually preserves an archaic form of the 2fs perfect ending תִּי-. See GKC, 121, §44h; Joüon, 132, §42f. This ending is still observable when the 2fs perfect takes pronominal suffixes. See PVP, 224–26 (19.4); Ful., 169 (27.2).[8]

7. הַגֹּרֶן—How is this form functioning in relation to the preceding verb? (Note that you must supply a preposition when translating.)

_____

_____

8. תִּוָּדְעִי—Parse this verb. (Note the negative particle אַל before the form, indicating this is a jussive.) How do you determine the *(a)* stem, and *(b)* P-G-N? The *waw* is the original first root letter of this verb. See

---

4. The form is unreadable in that a *hireq* is placed between the *taw* and final *kaph* with no accompanying consonant.
5. Fut., 96 (16.3); Gar., 89 (16.C); Kel., 72 (28.1); Ross, 114 (14.3); Seow, 133 (1.b).
6. Fut., 115 (19.2); Gar., 90 (16.D); Kel., 72–73 (28.2); Ross, 116 (14.5); Seow, 133 (1.b).
7. Fut., 136 (22.1); Gar., 91 (16.F); Ross, 123 (15.8); Seow, 97 (2.c).
8. Gar., 309 (54.A.2); Ross, 173 (24.3); Seow, 194 (1.a.iii).

PVP, 301–2 (25.10–11); Ful., 244. The Niphal stem might be causative-reflexive here, "(do not) make yourself known, reveal yourself" (W-OC, 390–91), but one wonders if it is not tolerative, "(do not) allow yourself to be known, recognized."[9]

9. כַּלֹּתוֹ—Parse this form. How do you determine the (a) stem, and (b) root? How is the stem functioning here? (Compare the meaning of the verb in the Qal with its meaning in the Piel and then consider the options for the latter. See EE, 80.)[10] How is the pronominal suffix functioning in relation to the verb?

10. לֶאֱכֹל וְלִשְׁתּוֹת—How are the two infinitives construct with -לְ functioning in relation to כַּלֹּתוֹ? See W-OC, 606.

11. וְלִשְׁתּוֹת—Parse this form. How do you determine the root?

3:4

וִיהִי בְשָׁכְבוֹ וְיָדַעַתְּ אֶת־הַמָּקוֹם אֲשֶׁר יִשְׁכַּב־שָׁם וּבָאת וְגִלִּית מַרְגְּלֹתָיו וְשָׁכָבְתְּ וְהוּא יַגִּיד לָךְ אֵת אֲשֶׁר תַּעֲשִׂין׃

1. וִיהִי—This form is a Qal jussive (note the apocopated he) 3ms from הָיָה with a *waw* conjunctive prefixed to the form. The usual form of the jussive is יְהִי, but when the conjunction -וְ is prefixed to the form, the following series of vocalization changes occurs: *וְיְהִי* > *וִיְהִי* > וִיהִי. The jussive continues Naomi's instructions, "and let it be."

2. בְשָׁכְבוֹ—Parse this form. How do you determine the stem? How is the prefixed preposition functioning? See PVP, 244–46.[11] How is the pronominal suffix functioning in relation to the verb?

3. וְיָדַעַתְּ—Parse this verb. How do you determine the P-G-N? Once more the *waw* consecutive with the perfect is used to begin a series of instructions. See 3:3, note 1.

4. אֲשֶׁר יִשְׁכַּב־שָׁם—The collocation of the relative pronoun אֲשֶׁר and שָׁם indicates location, "where."

---

9. For this category of the stem see W-OC, 389–90, as well as AC, 40–41; GKC, 137, §51c; Joüon, 150–51.
10. See also W-OC, 400–416.
11. Fut., 122 (20.9); Gar., 212 (36.B.2); Kel., 182 (56.2); Ross, 163 (22.4); Seow, 259 (3.e).

5. יִשְׁכַּב—How is the imperfect יִשְׁכַּב functioning?

_____

_____

6. וּבָאת—Parse this verb. How do you determine the P-G-N? On the use of the *waw* consecutive, see 3:3, note 1.

_____

_____

7. וְגִלִּית—Parse this verb. How do you determine the *(a)* stem, *(b)* root, and *(c)* P-G-N? This is probably a resultative use of the Piel stem (on this function of the stem, see W-OC, 404–9). The Qal means "to uncover"; the Piel, "to make uncovered."

_____

_____

_____

8. מַרְגְּלֹתָיו—This form consists of a feminine plural noun, functioning as the object of the preceding verb, and a 3ms pronominal suffix. The noun means "the place of his feet" (see BDB, 920; *HALOT*, 631). The word is used elsewhere only in Daniel 10:6, where it refers to the lower body or legs.[12] Since Hebrew רַגְלַיִם, "feet, legs," can be used as a euphemism for the genitals (Isa. 7:20), some see Ruth's action as being of a bold sexual nature. But the word used in Ruth 3:4 is different. Ruth's action was probably a symbolic gesture by which she invited Boaz to take her as his wife (see v. 9).

Some have suggested that the Piel verb (see note 7 above) has a reflexive nuance here and that מַרְגְּלֹתָיו is an adverbial accusative of place: "and uncover yourself (at) the place of his feet." The absence of the accusative sign before the suffixed (and therefore definite) noun appears to favor this. In this case Ruth was to disrobe in front of Boaz, inviting him to take her sexually. However, this interpretation is problematic, for one would expect the Niphal or Hithpael form of the verb גָּלָה in this case. In 2 Samuel 6:20 the Niphal form (נִגְלָה) is used of David exposing himself in public as he celebrated the return of the ark to Jerusalem. In Genesis 9:21 the Hithpael form (וַיִּתְגַּל) is used of drunken Noah exposing himself. In Isaiah 57:8 the Piel has no object stated, but it is better to supply one than to take the verb in a reflexive manner (some prefer to read a Qal in this passage, see *BHS*, note a). The Piel form of גָּלָה is usually followed by a direct object; the accusative sign is not consistently used before the object when the latter is a suffixed noun (see Lev. 18:7, 9–11, 15, 17–19), though examples in narratival texts are rare. In the book of Ruth, the accusative sign does not consistently appear before suffixed nouns functioning as objects. See Ruth 1:9, 14; 2:11–12, 14, 20; 3:3, 9–10; 4:4, 7–8, 17. For a fuller discussion of this issue see Bush, *Ruth, Esther*, 153.

9. וְשָׁכַבְתִּי—This unreadable form involves a *kethib/qere* variant. As with the form וְיָרַדְתִּי in verse 3, the *kethib* preserves the archaic 2fs form of the perfect, while the *qere* has the later/usual form. See 3:3, note 6.

---

12. See Frederic W. Bush, *Ruth, Esther*, WBC (Dallas: Word Books, 1996), 152.

10. וְהוּא יַגִּיד ...—This final clause in the verse has a disjunctive structure, perhaps to highlight the shift in subject. Prior to this Naomi has told Ruth "do this, do that, etc." Now she informs Ruth how Boaz will respond once she finishes carrying out her instructions.

11. יַגִּיד—Parse this verb. How do you determine the *(a)* stem, and *(b)* root?

_____

_____

12. אֵת אֲשֶׁר—The relative clause functions as the object (note אֵת) of the verb "he will tell."

13. תַּעֲשִׂין—Parse this verb. How do you determine the P-G-N? Note the paragogic *nun* at the end of the form. See 2:8, note 9. In III-*he* verbs the *he* is not present before an ending. See PVP, 176–77 (16.6–16.7); Ful., 266 (37.4).[13] The prefix vowel *pathaq* is present because of the guttural letter in first position. See PVP, 178 (16.9); Ful., 191–92 (29.6).[14] How is the imperfect functioning here?

_____

_____

3:5

וַתֹּאמֶר אֵלֶיהָ כֹּל אֲשֶׁר־תֹּאמְרִי __ אֶעֱשֶׂה:

1. אֵלֶיהָ—This form consists of what elements? See PVP, 96 (9.19); Ful., 85 (14.4).[15]

_____

_____

2. כֹּל—How is כֹּל functioning in relation to the verb אֶעֱשֶׂה?

_____

_____

3. תֹּאמְרִי—Parse this verb. On the *holem* prefix vowel see PVP, 178–79 (16.10–16.11); Ful., 201 (30.3).[16] How do you determine the P-G-N? How is the imperfect functioning here?

_____

_____

4. The appearance of the vowels __ without any accompanying consonants looks strange, but this is another *kethib/qere* variant. There is no *kethib per se*; the vowels belong with the consonants אלי that appear in the left margin. Combining the vowels with the consonants produces the form אֵלַי, "to me." See *BHS* note a.

---

13. Fut., 90 (15.7); Gar., 187–88 (31.E); Kel., 290 (72.6); Ross, 260 (36.2); Seow, 216 (3).
14. Fut., 82 (14.6); Gar., 178 (30.A); Kel., 225 (66.3); Ross, 227 (32.2.1); Seow, 214 (1).
15. Fut., 136 (22.1); Gar., 91 (16.F); Kel., 70 (27.1); Ross, 123 (15.8); Seow, 97 (2.c).
16. Fut., 109–10 (18.4); Gar., 192 (32.C); Kel., 237–38 (67.2, 67.4); Ross, 228–29 (32.3.1); Seow, 214 (1.c).

5. אֶעֱשֶׂה—Parse this verb. How do you determine the P-G-N? Actually this form can be understood as an imperfect (specific future) or as a cohortative (of resolve), since III-*he* verbs do not have a distinctive cohortative form.[17]

_____

_____

Step 3: Interpretive Translation

In light of the decisions you have made in your analysis, provide an interpretive, paraphrastic translation of Ruth 3:1–5.

_____

_____

_____

_____

_____

_____

_____

_____

Step 4: Structural Outline

Outline the narrative structure of Ruth 3:1–5. Carefully delineate the narrative mainline (initiated and extended by wayyiqtol forms), offline (nonstandard) constructions, and quotations. Using the categories listed in the appendix (cf. EE, 120–27), classify all wayyiqtol and disjunctive clauses that are in the narrative framework. You need not classify clauses within quotations.

_____

_____

_____

_____

_____

_____

_____

_____

_____

17. See GKC, 210, §75l; Joüon, 209, §79o.

Scene 2: Ruth 3:6–15: Encounter at the Threshing Floor

Since this scene is relatively longer, it is divided into two assignments, covering verses 6–10 and 11–15.

Assignment 1

Step 1: Initial View

Read Ruth 3:6–10 in the Hebrew text, using an interlinear if you desire. Underline any words or forms you do not recognize. Try to identify verbal forms and label them as follows:

- wayyiqtol verbal forms: wc-y (the so-called *waw* consecutive with the yiqtol, usually identified as a preterite or imperfect)
- weqatal forms: wc-q (the so-called *waw* consecutive with the qatal, that is, perfect)
- simple perfects (without *waw*): pf.
- simple imperfects (without *waw*): impf.
- imperatives: impv.
- jussives: juss.
- cohortatives: coh.
- infinitives construct: inf. const.
- infinitives absolute: inf. abs.
- participles: part.

Step 2: Analyzing the Text

3:6

וַתֵּ֖רֶד הַגֹּ֑רֶן וַתַּ֕עַשׂ כְּכֹ֥ל אֲשֶׁר־צִוַּ֖תָּה חֲמוֹתָֽהּ׃

1. וַתֵּרֶד—Parse this verb. How do you determine the *(a)* root, and *(b)* P-G-N?

   _____

   _____

2. הַגֹּרֶן—How is this form functioning in relation to the preceding verb? (Note that you must supply a preposition when translating.)

   _____

   _____

3. וַתַּעַשׂ—Parse this verb. How do you determine the root? The form can be either Qal (*a* prefix vowel due to I-guttural) or Hiphil, but the sense requires the Qal ("she did"), rather than a causative.

   _____

   _____

4. צִוַּתָּה—This form is a Piel perfect 3fs from צָוָה with a 3fs pronominal suffix functioning as the object of the verb. The *hireq* under the first letter *(tsade)*, as well as the *dagesh forte* in the second root letter

181

(waw), mark the form as Piel. Before a suffix the 3fs perfect has a *taw* ending. See PVP, 225 (19.4); Ful., 169 (27.2).[18] This ending combines with the 3fs suffix to form the ending תָּה-.[19] How is the perfect verbal form functioning in this relative clause?

_____

_____

5. חֲמוֹתָהּ—How is this form functioning in relation to the preceding verb?

_____

_____

3:7

וַיֹּאכַל בֹּעַז וַיֵּשְׁתְּ וַיִּיטַב לִבּוֹ וַיָּבֹא לִשְׁכַּב בִּקְצֵה הָעֲרֵמָה וַתָּבֹא בַלָּט וַתְּגַל מַרְגְּלֹתָיו וַתִּשְׁכָּב:

1. וַיֵּשְׁתְּ—Parse this verb. Normally in a Qal wayyiqtol form, a *tsere* prefix vowel indicates a I-*yod* verb, but occasionally III-*he* verbs have it as well. See GKC, 211, §75p–q; workbook note 1 on 1:18.

_____

_____

2. וַיִּיטַב—Parse this verb. How do you determine the root?

_____

_____

3. לִבּוֹ—How is this form functioning in relation to the preceding verb? The idiom יִיטַב לֵב, literally, "(the) heart is good," refers to happiness and/or contentment (cf. Judg. 18:20; 19:6; 1 Kings 21:7; Eccl. 7:3).

_____

_____

4. וַיָּבֹא—Parse this verb. How do you determine the (a) stem, and (b) root?

_____

_____

5. לִשְׁכַּב—Parse this form. How is the form functioning in relation to the preceding verb?

_____

_____

18. Gar., 309 (54.A.2); Kel., 156 (46.4); Ross, 173 (24.3); Seow, 194 (1.a.i).
19. See GKC, 160, §59g; Joüon, 175, §63d, as well as 1 Samuel 1:6; Isaiah 34:17; Jeremiah 49:24; Ezekiel 14:15.

6. בִּקְצֵה—The preposition -בְּ prefixed to קְצֵה is functioning in a locative sense here, "at." See W-OC, 196. The form קְצֵה is a construct of קָצֶה. "end." The *qamets* in the open unaccented syllable reduces to *shewa* (see PVP, 102 [10.5]; Ful., 61–62 [11.3]),[20] while the ending ה ָ - changes to ה ֵ - (see PVP, 105 [10.5]).[21]

7. וַתָּבֹא—Parse this verb. How do you determine the P-G-N?

8. בַּלָּט—This form consists of the preposition -בְּ and the noun לָט, "secrecy." The preposition introduces the condition that accompanied the action. On this use of the preposition, see W-OC, 196–97; BDB, 89, III.1.c; *HALOT*, 105. In this case the prepositional phrase is a functional equivalent of an adverb, "secretly."

9. וַתְּגַל—Parse this verb. How do you determine the *(a)* stem, *(b)* root, and *(c)* P-G-N?

10. וַתִּשְׁכָּב—This verb is a Qal wayyiqtol. Intransitive verbs (those that take no direct object) sometimes take an *a*-class theme vowel in the imperfect/wayyiqtol (rather than the usual *holem*). See PVP, 168–69 (15.6); Ful., 109 (18.2).[22] *Pathaq* usually appears, but in this case it is lengthened to a *qamets* because the form, being at the end of the verse, is in pause. See PVP, 406 (36.3).[23]

3:8

וַיְהִי בַּחֲצִי הַלַּיְלָה וַיֶּחֱרַד הָאִישׁ וַיִּלָּפֵת וְהִנֵּה אִשָּׁה שֹׁכֶבֶת מַרְגְּלֹתָיו:

1. וַיְהִי—This form signals movement within the scene from dusk to midnight. The following prepositional phrase specifies the temporal setting of what follows.

2. וַיֶּחֱרַד—After the temporal clause, the wayyiqtol form וַיֶּחֱרַד resumes the story line. On the vocalization of the I-guttural verb see PVP, 177–78 (16.8–16.9); Ful., 191–92 (29.6).[24]

3. הָאִישׁ—How is this noun functioning in relation to the verb? How is the article functioning?

20. Fut., 70 (12.6); Gar., 26 (4.A) and 96 (17.E.2); Kel., 61 (26.4); Ross, 76 (8.1) and 101 (12.4); Seow, 20 (2.a.i) and 118 (2.b).
21. Gar., 96 (17.E.2); Ross, 100 (12.3); Seow, 119 (2.e).
22. Fut., 63–64 (11.4); Gar., 240 (42.A); Kel., 129 (39.6); Ross, 144–45 (19.4); Seow, 205–6 (2).
23. Gar., 159 (26.D); Kel., 17 (8.3); Ross, 158 (21.4); Seow, 67 (5.a).
24. Fut., 82 (14.6); Kel., 225 (66.3); Ross, 227 (32.2.1); Seow, 214–15 (1).

4. וַיִּלָּפֵת—Parse this verb. How do you determine the stem? The verb is rare; it appears to mean either "grope around" or "turn over" in this context. The stem is probably functioning in a middle or reflexive manner. For a helpful discussion of the meaning of this verb, see Bush, *Ruth, Esther,* 163.

---

5. וְהִנֵּה—This form interrupts the narrative sequence and dramatically invites the reader to step into Boaz's shoes and see through his eyes. See EE, 126–27.

6. אִשָּׁה—Using the indefinite form of the noun ("a woman") is a vague way of referring to Ruth. After all, the reader knows who this woman is because the narrator has already revealed her identity. But the narrator purposely writes from Boaz's perspective to heighten the drama of the scene. See EE, 127, 159–60.

7. שֹׁכֶבֶת—Parse this form. How can you tell the form is a participle? How do you determine the gender and number of the form? How does the form relate to the preceding noun?

---

8. מַרְגְּלֹתָיו—How does this form relate to the preceding participle? (Note that the verb שָׁכַב is intransitive and that one must supply a preposition to translate the form.) See W-OC, 169–70.[25]

3:9

וַיֹּאמֶר מִי־אָתְּ וַתֹּאמֶר אָנֹכִי רוּת אֲמָתֶךָ וּפָרַשְׂתָּ כְנָפֶךָ עַל־אֲמָתְךָ כִּי גֹאֵל אָתָּה:

1. אָתְּ—The 2fs pronoun has a *shewa* missing in Codex L; it should be written אָתְּ (see *BHS,* note 9b). The form is pausal, so *qamets* appears under the *aleph.*

2. אֲמָתֶךָ—This form consists of what elements? (For help identifying the form, recall that feminine nouns ending in הָ - have a *taw* before suffixes.) How does the form relate to the preceding proper name? Earlier Ruth used the noun שִׁפְחָה to describe her humble state (2:13). But here she switches and uses a different term for a female servant. Though these terms appear to be interchangeable, usage elsewhere suggests a distinction. The term שִׁפְחָה views a female servant as a laborer, while אָמָה focuses on gender. Consequently שִׁפְחָה can be used to emphasize subservience, while אָמָה can be used to draw attention to a servant's vulnerability and need for protection. Since אָמָה focuses on gender, it is also the preferred term when one wants to make the point that a female servant is marriageable or married. (See Richard

---

25. See also Joüon, 457–58, §126h.

Schultz, *NIDOTTE*, 1:418–21; 4:211–13.) Ruth's use of the term is appropriate for she was about to confront Boaz with his obligations as a kinsman-redeemer and propose that he marry her.

_____

_____

3. וּפָרַשְׂתָּ—This verb is a Qal perfect 2ms form with a *waw* consecutive prefixed. In this case one can tell the *waw* is consecutive because of the accent shift. Normally the 2ms perfect has the middle syllable accented, but here the accent appears on the 2ms ending. See PVP, 200 (17.5); Ful., 121, note 2.[26] This is a case of the perfect with *waw* consecutive expressing a logical consequence of the preceding statement. Usually this construction follows an imperfect, but in this case it is preceded by a verbless sentence. It introduces an invitation or command here. See W-OC, 534–35; GKC, 335, §112aa.[27]

4. כְנָפֶךָ—This reading reflects two variants within the Masoretic tradition. See *BHS* note c, as well as Brotzman, 153. The vocalization suggests the reading כְנָפֶיךָ, a dual form of the noun with a 2ms suffix, "your wings." The consonantal text would be vocalized כְנָפְךָ, a singular form with a 2ms suffix, "your wing."

5. כִּי גֹאֵל אָתָּה—What type of clause is this?

_____

_____

6. גֹאֵל—How is the participle גֹאֵל functioning here?

_____

_____

3:10

וַיֹּאמֶר בְּרוּכָה אַתְּ לַיהוָה בִּתִּי הֵיטַבְתְּ חַסְדֵּךְ הָאַחֲרוֹן מִן־הָרִאשׁוֹן
לְבִלְתִּי־לֶכֶת אַחֲרֵי הַבַּחוּרִים אִם־דַּל וְאִם־עָשִׁיר׃

1. בְּרוּכָה—Parse this form. How do you determine the gender and number? How is the form functioning in the sentence? For help here see PVP, 265–66 (22.9); Ful., 116–17 (19.3);[28] W-OC, 619–20. The statement should probably understood as a prayer, "May you be blessed."

_____

_____

2. לַיהוָה—In this formal prayer of blessing, לַיהוָה indicates the agent of blessing, "by Yahweh." See 2:20, note 2.

---

26. Fut., 163 (26.2); Gar., 114 (20.E); Kel., 212 (63.2); Ross, 138–39 (18.3); Seow, 227 (3.a).
27. Joüon (403, §119w) understands the form as equivalent to an imperfect of obligation, "you must spread."
28. Fut., 237; Gar., 63–65 (11.A, D); Kel., 199–200 (60.1); Ross, 157–58 (21.3); Seow, 85 (5.c).

3. בִּתִּי—How is this form functioning in the sentence?

_____

_____

4. הֵיטַבְתְּ—Parse this verb. How do you determine the *(a)* stem, *(b)* root, and *(c)* P-G-N? In this stem the verb is causative, meaning literally, "make, cause to be good."

_____

_____

_____

5. חַסְדֵּךְ—How is this form functioning in relation to the preceding verb? What type of genitive is the pronominal suffix?

_____

_____

6. הָאַחֲרוֹן—This form consists of the article and the adjective אַחֲרוֹן. The adjective is attributive, modifying חַסְדֵּךְ. It has the article because חַסְדֵּךְ is definite by reason of the pronominal suffix. The expression may be translated, "your latter act of faithfulness." This refers to Ruth's proposal of marriage so that she might raise up offspring for her deceased husband.

7. מִן—The preposition is comparative here. Combined with the verb הֵיטַבְתְּ, which has an inherent adjectival idea, it carries the idea "better than." One may translate the sentence: "You made your latter act of faithfulness better than the first."

8. הָרִאשׁוֹן—This form consists of the article and the adjective רִאשׁוֹן. The adjective is substantival, "the former (one)," i.e., the former act of faithfulness. This refers to Ruth's decision to stay with Naomi and look out for her well-being.

9. לְבִלְתִּי—This form consists of the preposition -לְ and the negative particle בִּלְתִּי. See PVP, 241 (20.11).[29] In relation to the preceding main verb ("make good"), the preposition is explanatory, specifying the way in which her latter act of faithfulness exceeds the earlier one. One may translate, "by not . . ." See PVP, 243–44 (20.12); W-OC, 608–9.[30]

10. לֶכֶת—Parse this form. Normally the segholate vowel pattern with suffixed *taw* is characteristic of a I-*nun* or I-*yod* pattern, but הָלַךְ follows the I-*yod* pattern in this regard. See PVP, 238–39 (20.6),[31] including note 5; Ful., 241 (35.5).

_____

_____

---

29. Fut., 122 (20.8); Gar., 212 (36.B.2); Kel., 183 (56.2); Ross, 164 (22.5); Seow, 259 (4.a).
30. Gar., 212 (36.B.2); Ross, 164 (22.4); Seow, 258 (3.b–d).
31. Fut., 121 (20.6); Gar., 229 (40.A); Kel., 340 (75.2); Ross, 254 (35.4); Seow, 256–57 (2.c).

11. אִם—The double וְאִם . . . אִם can be translated, "whether . . . or." See BDB, 50, 1.b. The expression is a merism, with the polar opposites within the category בַּחוּרִים, "young men," standing for the members of the category in its entirety.

Step 3: Interpretive Translation

In light of the decisions you have made in your analysis, provide an interpretive, paraphrastic translation of Ruth 3:6–10.

Step 4: Structural Outline

Outline the narrative structure of Ruth 3:6–10. Carefully delineate the narrative mainline (initiated and extended by wayyiqtol forms), offline (nonstandard) constructions, and quotations. Using the categories listed in the appendix (cf. EE, 120–27), classify all wayyiqtol and disjunctive clauses that are in the narrative framework. You need not classify clauses within quotations.

Assignment 2

Step 1: Initial View

Read Ruth 3:11–15 in the Hebrew text, using an interlinear if you desire. Underline any words or forms you do not recognize. Try to identify verbal forms and label them as follows:

- wayyiqtol verbal forms: wc-y (the so-called *waw* consecutive with the yiqtol, usually identified as a preterite or imperfect)
- weqatal forms: wc-q (the so-called *waw* consecutive with the qatal, that is, perfect)
- simple perfects (without *waw*): pf.
- simple imperfects (without *waw*): impf.
- imperatives: impv.
- jussives: juss.
- cohortatives: coh.
- infinitives construct: inf. const.
- infinitives absolute: inf. abs.
- participles: part.

Step 2: Analyzing the Text

3:11

וְעַתָּה בִּתִּי אַל־תִּירְאִי כֹּל אֲשֶׁר־תֹּאמְרִי אֶעֱשֶׂה־לָּךְ כִּי יוֹדֵעַ כָּל־שַׁעַר עַמִּי כִּי אֵשֶׁת חַיִל אָתְּ׃

1. תִּירְאִי—Parse this verb. How do you determine the *(a)* root, and *(b)* P-G-N? What does the negative particle אַל indicate about the form?

   _____

   _____

   _____

2. כֹּל—How is this form functioning in its sentence? See 3:5, note 2.

   _____

   _____

3. תֹּאמְרִי—Parse this verb. How is the imperfect functioning here? See 3:5, note 3.

   _____

   _____

4. אֶעֱשֶׂה—On this form see 3:5, note 5. The following prepositional phrase (לָּךְ) indicates interest or advantage. See AC, 112; W-OC, 207–8.

5. כִּי יוֹדֵעַ—What type of clause does this introduce here?

_____

_____

6. יוֹדֵעַ—Parse this form. How is the form functioning here?

_____

_____

7. כָּל—How does this form relate to the preceding verb? (What case is it?)

_____

_____

8. כָּל־שַׁעַר עַמִּי—In the construct chain כָּל־שַׁעַר עַמִּי the second and third terms are genitival because each follows a construct form. After כָּל, which is a term that quantifies in a general way, שַׁעַר is a genitive of measure (or thing measured). See W-OC, 152, as well as AC, 12. The form עַמִּי is difficult to classify; perhaps "people" is a genitive of relation. See W-OC, 145. שַׁעַר cannot be taken in a literal sense, for a city gate cannot "know" something. "Gate" probably stands for those who oversee the business of the city at the gate (the town's elders, one of whom was probably Boaz).

9. כִּי אֵשֶׁת—What type of clause is this introducing?

_____

_____

10. חַיִל—What type of genitive is חַיִל? The basic idea of the Hebrew word is "strength," but it can be used of ability and character as well as physical strength. The phrase "woman of noble character" appears elsewhere in Proverbs 12:4, where such a woman brings honor to her husband, and in Proverbs 31:10 at the beginning of a passage that extols the value of such a wife and gives a lengthy character profile of this kind of woman. It highlights her devotion to her family and others within her social circle, as well as her hard work. Ruth had demonstrated these character qualities. She swore to never leave Naomi's side and worked hard in the fields to provide food for her destitute mother-in-law.

_____

_____

3:12

וְעַתָּה כִּי אָמְנָם כִּי אִם גֹּאֵל אָנֹכִי וְגַם יֵשׁ גֹּאֵל קָרוֹב מִמֶּנִּי:

1. וְעַתָּה כִּי אָמְנָם כִּי אִם—This construction is textually and syntactically problematic. All of the terms after the temporal adverb עַתָּה can have an emphatic function.[32] The _qere_ omits אם; note the absence of a

_____

32. On the emphatic function of כִּי אם see GKC, 501, §163d.

vowel and see *BHS* note a. The entire sequence, with or without אִם, occurs only here in the Hebrew Bible. The various collocations within the construction are nonexistent elsewhere or rare. כִּי עַתָּה occurs four other places, but in each case the כִּי functions differently than in Ruth 3:12. Elsewhere it introduces the object of the verb "see" (Deut. 32:39; 1 Chron. 28:10), has a temporal function (Job 35:15, see NET), or is explanatory/causal (1 Sam. 9:12). כִּי אָמְנָם occurs only here and in Job 36:4, where the כִּי, unlike the use in Ruth 3:12, is explanatory/causal (see NET). אָמְנָם כִּי occurs only here and in Job 12:2, where, as in Ruth 3:12, it seems to have an emphatic function. The text seems to be overloaded with emphasizing particles. Unless Boaz is stammering in his effort to respond appropriately to Ruth's offer and to soften the impact of what he must say next (see v. 12b),[33] it would appear the text is suffering from dittography, as the repetition of the consonantal sequence כי אם/ם suggests: כִּי אָמְנָם כִּי אִם. The most likely scenario is that the text originally had either כִּי אָמְנָם, "indeed it is true," or אָמְנָם כִּי, "it is true, indeed."

2. וְגַם—The construction is contrastive here, "but also." The particle יֵשׁ can be translated "there is." See PVP, 253 (21.7).[34]

3. קָרוֹב—The adjective קָרוֹב, "near," is functioning attributively in relation to גֹּאֵל. The following preposition (see מִמֶּנִּי, "from me") has a comparative nuance after the adjective. We may translate verse 12b: "But also there is a kinsman nearer than I (am)."

3:13

לִינִי הַלַּיְלָה וְהָיָה בַבֹּקֶר אִם־יִגְאָלֵךְ טוֹב יִגְאָל וְאִם־לֹא יַחְפֹּץ לְגָאֳלֵךְ וּגְאַלְתִּיךְ אָנֹכִי חַי־יְהוָה שִׁכְבִי עַד־הַבֹּקֶר:

1. לִינִי—Parse this verb. How do you determine the *(a)* root, and *(b)* P-G-N?

_____

_____

2. וְהָיָה—This verb is a Qal perfect with *waw* consecutive; it literally means "and it will be," but one may translate, "and then." On this temporal use of וְהָיָה see W-OC, 538–39.

3. אִם—This introduces the protasis ("if" section) of a conditional sentence, which utilizes an imperfect verbal form.[35] The 3ms Qal imperfect of גָּאַל is יִגְאַל (see Ruth 4:4). But the addition of the pronominal suffix pulls the accent to the final syllable (ךְ-) and opens the pretonic syllable, resulting in a lengthening of the *pathaq* to *qamets*. The imperfect may be labeled a hypothetical future (see EE, 92), though it seems to carry a nuance of capability or desire as well (cf. 1 Sam. 21:10).[36] Note that the parallel protasis that follows (cf. וְאִם־לֹא יַחְפֹּץ) uses the verb חָפֵץ, "to desire."

4. טוֹב—The apodosis ("then" section) of the conditional sentence begins with an exclamatory טוֹב, "Good!" This is probably an abbreviated form of טוֹב הַדָּבָר, "the matter is good." See BDB, 374, no. 5. The exclamation is then followed by יִגְאָל, which may be a jussive, "let him redeem," or an imperfect of permission, "he may redeem." In either case, the use is rhetorical since Boaz does not actually have

---

33. For this view see Adele Berlin, *Poetics and Interpretation of Biblical Narrative* (Sheffield: Almond, 1983), 90.
34. Fut., 142 (23.1); Gar., 108 (19.A); Ross, 109–10 (13.3); Seow, 107 (3.a).
35. On this form of protasis, see GKC, 496, §159q; Joüon, 630, §167h.
36. See Joüon, 372, §113n; W-OC, 509

authority over the nearer kinsman in the matter. Of course, the form may also be taken as a hypothetical imperfect, "then (in that case) he will redeem." On this form of apodosis, see GKC, 496, §159r. The lengthened theme vowel *(qamets)* is due to the form being in pausal position. See PVP, 406 (36.3).[37]

5. וְאִם־לֹא יַחְפֹּץ—The first conditional sentence in the verse assumes the nearer kinsman's willingness to marry Ruth. The second condition gives the alternative, explaining what will happen if the nearer kinsman does not want to take on this responsibility. The imperfect יַחְפֹּץ is a hypothetical future. Why does the form have a *pathaq* prefix vowel instead of a *hireq*?

_____

_____

6. לְגָאֳלֵךְ—Parse this form. (For help see PVP, 240 [20.9]; Ful., 180–81 [28.4].)[38] How is the pronominal suffix functioning in relation to the verb? How does the form relate to the preceding verb?

_____

_____

_____

7. וּגְאַלְתִּיךְ—Parse this verb. How do you determine the P-G-N of the verb? How is the pronominal suffix functioning in relation to the verb? On the reduction of the *qamets* to *shewa* under the *gimel,* see PVP, 225–26 (19.4); Ful., 169–70 (27.3).[39] The *waw* is to be understood as consecutive, introducing the apodosis ("then" section) of the conditional sentence. On this form of apodosis see GKC, 496, §159s, as well as 336, §112ff.

_____

_____

8. אָנֹכִי—The pronoun is appositional to the first person ending on the preceding verb. It appears for emphasis. For a discussion of the use of independent personal pronouns with finite verbs (which are already marked for P-G-N and theoretically do not need a pronoun), see W-OC, 293–97.

9. חַי־יְהוָה—This is an oath formula that elevates Boaz's statement to the level of a solemn promise. The traditional interpretation understands חַי as a predicate adjective (BDB, 311), "(as surely as) the LORD is alive/lives." Some treat חַי as a noun, "(by) the life of the LORD." See W-OC, 679–80.

10. שִׁכְבִי—Parse this verb. How do you determine the P-G-N?

_____

_____

---

37. Gar., 159 (26.D); Kel., 17 (8.3); Ross, 158 (21.4); Seow, 67 (5.a).
38. Fut., 120 (20.5); Gar., 211–12 (36.A–B); Kel., 183 (56.2); Ross, 161–64 (22.1–4); Seow, 255–56 (1).
39. Fut., 221 (35.2); Gar., 310 (54.A.3); Kel., 155 (46.3); Ross, 174 (24.4); Seow, 196 (1.c).

3:14

וַתִּשְׁכַּב מַרְגְּלוֹתָו עַד־הַבֹּקֶר וַתָּקָם בְּטֶרוֹם יַכִּיר אִישׁ אֶת־רֵעֵהוּ
וַיֹּאמֶר אַל־יִוָּדַע כִּי־בָאָה הָאִשָּׁה הַגֹּרֶן:

1. מַרְגְּלֹתָו—This form involves a *kethib/qere* variant. As the consonantal form in the left margin indicates, a *yod* should be added before the final *waw*, yielding מַרְגְּלֹתָיו, the form that appears in verses 4, 7–8. With the intransitive verb שָׁכַב, the noun is an adverbial accusative of location. See 3:8, note 8.

2. וַתָּקָם—Parse this verb. How do you determine the *(a)* stem, *(b)* root, and *(c)* P-G-N?

_____

_____

_____

3. בְּטֶרוֹם—This unreadable form involves a *kethib/qere* variant. A *waw* has been accidentally added. If we place the vowels into the consonantal form in the left margin, we get the expected and correct reading בְּטֶרֶם, "before."

4. יַכִּיר—Parse this verb. How do you determine the stem and the root? After בְּטֶרֶם the prefixed verb often indicates a past action (W-OC, 513).[40] According to some, this is a past progressive use of the imperfect (see GKC, 314, §107c), but others argue for a preterite use, even though the longer, distinctly imperfect form sometimes appears, as here. (One expects the preterite form to be יַכֵּר.) For a discussion of this issue, see W-OC, 501. If one takes the verb as an imperfect, it is possible that it indicates capability ("before a man could recognize") or is an idiomatic expression for early morning ("before one can recognize").

_____

_____

_____

5. אִישׁ אֶת־רֵעֵהוּ—This expression, which means literally "a man . . . his neighbor," is idiomatic, meaning "one . . . another." See BDB, 945–46, no. 2.

6. יִוָּדַע—Parse this verb. How do you determine the stem? How is the stem functioning here? The negative particle אַל indicates this is a jussive, "let it not be known."

_____

_____

_____

7. כִּי־בָאָה—This introduces a noun clause functioning as the subject of the preceding passive verb. See EE, 113; W-OC, 644.

---

40. See also AC, 60; BHRG, 147; GKC, 314; Joüon, 370, §113j.

8. בָּאָה—Parse this verb. Note the accent on the initial syllable. How does this enable you to parse the form? See PVP, 157–58 (14.12) and 261 (22.4); Ful., 255 (36.5).[41]

_____

_____

_____

9. הָאִשָּׁה—The article on הָאִשָּׁה is probably dittographic; the *he* on the end of the preceding verb may have been accidentally repeated and interpreted as an article. If the article is retained, there appear to be two options.[42] Some interpret the article as generic. See NIV: "a woman" (cf. KJV, NLT). However, in none of the other 107 occurrences of הָאִשָּׁה in the Hebrew Bible does the article have this generic function. Others prefer to see the article as pointing specifically to Ruth ("the woman," cf. NASB). But this would be an odd way for Boaz to speak of Ruth if he were talking to her. Consequently proponents of this view understand this to be what Boaz thought. They take the verb וַיֹּאמֶר as indicating self-reflection, "he thought, said to himself." See Bush, *Ruth, Esther,* 177–78; Hubbard, *The Book of Ruth,* 220.

10. הַגֹּרֶן—How is this form functioning in the sentence? See 3:3, note 7.

_____

_____

3:15

וַיֹּאמֶר הָבִי הַמִּטְפַּחַת אֲשֶׁר־עָלַיִךְ וְאֶחֳזִי־בָהּ וַתֹּאחֶז בָּהּ וַיָּמָד שֵׁשׁ־שְׂעֹרִים וַיָּשֶׁת עָלֶיהָ וַיָּבֹא הָעִיר׃

1. הָבִי—This verb is a Qal imperative 2fs from יָהַב, "give." This verb occurs only in the Qal imperative (BDB, 396; *HALOT,* 236). One expects the form to be הֲבִי, but instead a *qamets* appears beneath the *he.*[43]

2. וְאֶחֳזִי—This verb is also a Qal imperative 2fs. The vowel pattern is rare;[44] the shortened theme vowel represents a reduction of a *holem.*

3. בָהּ—After the verb אָחַז, the preposition -בְּ (cf. בָהּ) introduces the object. See W-OC, 198–99. What is the antecedent of the pronominal suffix?

_____

_____

4. וַתֹּאחֶז—This verb is a Qal wayyiqtol 3fs from אָחַז, which is one of a handful of I-*aleph* verbs that has a *holem* prefix vowel in the Qal prefixed verbal form.[45]

---

41. Gar., 202–3 (34.B.5); Kel., 318 (74.3); Ross, 276 (38.2.2); Seow, 163 (4).
42. On the uses of the article see EE, 73; W-OC, 241–46.
43. See GKC, 190, §69o; Joüon, 196–97, §75k.
44. See GKC, 169, §64c; Joüon, 182, §69b.
45. See GKC, 184, §68b; Joüon, 188–90, §73.

5. וַיָּמָד—Parse this verb. How do you determine the stem? Theoretically the form could be from one of two roots—hollow (cf. וַיָּקָם) or geminate.[46] When there is morphological overlap, one must make a choice based on lexical and contextual considerations. Biblical Hebrew has no hollow verb מוד/מִיד, but the geminate verb מָדַד, "to measure," fits very well here.

_____

_____

_____

6. שֵׁשׁ־שְׂעֹרִים—This expression, "six, barley," is elliptical. The unit of measure (ephahs or seahs) is omitted. See W-OC, 278–79.[47] On the significance of the plural form of the noun, see 1:22, note 11.

7. וַיָּשֶׁת—Parse this verb. How do you determine the root? Because the verb is a hollow middle _yod_, theoretically the stem could be either Qal or Hiphil. In this case one must rely on lexical and contextual factors to make a decision. The Hiphil stem is not attested for the verb שִׁית, nor does a causative meaning fit the context. The Qal meaning, "put, place, set," makes good sense. Note, however, that the object (the shawl loaded with barley) is omitted since it is clear from the context.

_____

_____

8. וַיָּבֹא—Parse this verb. How do you determine the (a) stem, and (b) root?

_____

_____

9. הָעִיר—How is this noun functioning in relation to the preceding verb?

_____

_____

Step 3: Interpretive Translation

In light of the decisions you have made in your analysis, provide an interpretive, paraphrastic translation of Ruth 3:11–15.

_____

_____

_____

_____

_____

---

46. See Joüon, 213, §80b; 226, §82b.
47. See also GKC, 435, §134n; Joüon, 529, §142n.

_____
_____
_____
_____

Step 4: Structural Outline

Outline the narrative structure of Ruth 3:11–15. Carefully delineate the narrative mainline (initiated and extended by wayyiqtol forms), offline (nonstandard) constructions, and quotations. Using the categories listed in the appendix (cf. EE, 120–27), classify all wayyiqtol and disjunctive clauses that are in the narrative framework. You need not classify clauses within quotations.

_____
_____
_____
_____
_____
_____
_____
_____
_____
_____
_____

Scene 3: Ruth 3:16–18: Waiting for a Resolution

Assignment

Step 1: Initial View

Read Ruth 3:16–18 in the Hebrew text, using an interlinear if you desire. Underline any words or forms you do not recognize. Try to identify verbal forms and label them as follows:

- wayyiqtol verbal forms: wc-y (the so-called *waw* consecutive with the yiqtol, usually identified as a preterite or imperfect)
- weqatal forms: wc-q (the so-called *waw* consecutive with the qatal, that is, perfect)
- simple perfects (without *waw*): pf.
- simple imperfects (without *waw*): impf.
- imperatives: impv.
- jussives: juss.
- cohortatives: coh.
- infinitives construct: inf. const.
- infinitives absolute: inf. abs.
- participles: part.

Step 2: Analyzing the Text

3:16

וַתָּבוֹא אֶל־חֲמוֹתָהּ וַתֹּאמֶר מִי־אַתְּ בִּתִּי וַתַּגֶּד־לָהּ אֵת כָּל־אֲשֶׁר עָשָׂה־לָהּ הָאִישׁ:

1. וַתָּבוֹא—Parse this verb. How do you determine the P-G-N?

2. מִי־אַתְּ—This question ("Who are you?") cannot be taken literally because the addition of the vocative בִּתִּי, "my daughter," indicates that Naomi knows Ruth's identity. Furthermore, Ruth's answer has nothing to do with her identity.[48] The question is apparently used in an idiomatic manner here, "How did it go?" See W-OC, 320.

3. וַתַּגֶּד—Parse this verb. How do you determine the *(a)* stem, *(b)* root, and *(c)* P-G-N?

4. כָּל—How is this word functioning in the sentence?

5. עָשָׂה—How is this perfect verbal form functioning in relation to the main verb?

6. הָאִישׁ—How is this noun functioning within the relative clause?

---

48. See Bush, *Ruth, Esther*, 184–85.

3:17

וַתֹּאמֶר שֵׁשׁ־הַשְּׂעֹרִים הָאֵלֶּה נָתַן לִי כִּי אָמַר ... אַל־תָּבוֹאִי רֵיקָם אֶל־חֲמוֹתֵךְ:

1. הָאֵלֶּה—What part of speech is אֵלֶּה? How is it functioning here? See PVP, 72–74 (8.6–8.7); Ful., 55–56 (10.9).

_____

_____

2. כִּי אָמַר—What type of clause is this?

_____

_____

3. As in 3:5 (see note 4), the appearance of the vowels ◌ֵ without any accompanying consonants involves a *kethib/qere* variant. There is no *kethib per se;* the vowels belong with the consonants אלי that appear at the far right of the right margin. Combining the vowels with the consonants produces the form אֵלֵי, "to me." See *BHS* note b.

4. תָּבוֹאִי—Parse this verb. (Note the negative particle אַל before the form.)[49] How do you determine the *(a)* root, and *(b)* P-G-N?

_____

_____

_____

5. רֵיקָם—On this adverb see 1:21, note 2.

3:18

וַתֹּאמֶר שְׁבִי בִתִּי עַד אֲשֶׁר תֵּדְעִין אֵיךְ יִפֹּל דָּבָר כִּי לֹא יִשְׁקֹט הָאִישׁ כִּי־אִם־כִּלָּה הַדָּבָר הַיּוֹם:

1. שְׁבִי—Parse this verb. How do you determine the *(a)* root, and *(b)* P-G-N?

_____

_____

_____

---

49. See Joüon, 377, §114j.

2. עַד אֲשֶׁר תֵּדְעִין—On עַד אֲשֶׁר see 1:13, note 3. Parse תֵּדְעִין. How do you determine the (a) root, and (b) P-G-N? How is the imperfect functioning? (How does this action relate temporally to שְׁבִי?)

_____

_____

_____

_____

3. אֵיךְ—This adverb is normally interrogative or exclamatory. Here it is used in an indirect question that functions as the object of the verb "know."

4. יִפֹּל דָּבָר—This expression means literally, "a matter falls." It is not certain why the article is omitted on the noun since a definite "matter" is in view (cf. הַדָּבָר later in the verse).[50] Perhaps the expression is idiomatic or proverbial. Parse יִפֹּל. How do you determine the root? How is the imperfect functioning? (How does this action relate temporally to תֵּדְעִין?) One may translate, "(how) the matter turns out."

_____

_____

_____

_____

5. . . . כִּי לֹא יִשְׁקֹט—What type of clause is this?

_____

_____

6. כִּי־אִם—This construction may be translated "until," but it is actually exceptive, "unless, except." See BDB, 474; HALOT, 471; and, for a discussion of the probable origin of this use of the collocation, GKC, 500, §163c, note 1.

7. כִּלָּה—Parse this verb. How do you determine the stem? How is the perfect functioning in relation to יִשְׁקֹט? How is the stem functioning?

_____

_____

_____

_____

---

50. For other examples of this phenomenon, see Joüon, 512, §137p.

8. הַדָּבָר—How is this noun functioning in relation to the preceding verb?

_____

_____

Step 3: Interpretive Translation

In light of the decisions you have made in your analysis, provide an interpretive, paraphrastic translation of Ruth 3:16–18.

_____

_____

_____

_____

_____

_____

_____

Step 4: Structural Outline

Outline the narrative structure of Ruth 3:16–18. Carefully delineate the narrative mainline (initiated and extended by wayyiqtol forms), offline (nonstandard) constructions, and quotations. Using the categories listed in the appendix (cf. EE, 120–27), classify all wayyiqtol and disjunctive clauses that are in the narrative framework. You need not classify clauses within quotations.

_____

_____

_____

_____

_____

_____

_____

_____

_____

_____

Act 4
Ruth 4

Scene 1: Ruth 4:1–12: Events at the Town Gate

Since this scene is relatively long, it is divided into two assignments, covering verses 1–6 and 7–12.

Assignment 1

Step 1: Initial View

Read Ruth 4:1–6 in the Hebrew text, using an interlinear if you desire. Underline any words or forms you do not recognize. Try to identify verbal forms and label them as follows:

- wayyiqtol verbal forms: wc-y (the so-called *waw* consecutive with the yiqtol, usually identified as a preterite or imperfect)
- weqatal forms: wc-q (the so-called *waw* consecutive with the qatal, that is, perfect)
- simple perfects (without *waw*): pf.
- simple imperfects (without *waw*): impf.
- imperatives: impv.
- jussives: juss.
- cohortatives: coh.
- infinitives construct: inf. const.
- infinitives absolute: inf. abs.
- participles: part.

Step 2: Analyzing the Text

4:1

וּבֹעַז עָלָה הַשַּׁעַר וַיֵּשֶׁב שָׁם וְהִנֵּה הַגֹּאֵל עֹבֵר אֲשֶׁר דִּבֶּר־בֹּעַז וַיֹּאמֶר סוּרָה שְׁבָה־פֹּה פְּלֹנִי אַלְמֹנִי
וַיָּסַר וַיֵּשֵׁב:

1. וּבֹעַז עָלָה—What type of clause does this introduce? How is it functioning? How is the perfect verbal form עָלָה functioning?

_____

_____

_____

2. הַשַּׁעַר—How does this noun relate to the preceding verb?

_____

_____

3. וַיֵּשֶׁב—Parse this verb. How do you determine the root?

_____

_____

4. וְהִנֵּה הַגֹּאֵל—What type of clause does this introduce? How is it functioning?

_____

_____

5. עֹבֵר—What is the time frame of the participle עֹבֵר?

_____

_____

6. אֲשֶׁר—The relative pronoun modifies הַגֹּאֵל. One may translate, "about whom."

7. דִּבֶּר—How is the perfect verbal form functioning?

_____

_____

8. סוּרָה—The form is a Qal imperative 2ms from סור. An הָ- ending sometimes appears on the 2ms form of the imperative. See PVP, 207–8 (18.4); Ful., 111 (18.4).[1]

9. שְׁבָה—The form is a Qal imperative 2ms from יָשַׁב. Once more the alternative form with the הָ- ending is used (see the preceding note). The normal form of the 2ms imperative is שֵׁב, but the addition of the ending and the resulting accent shift cause the _tsere_ to reduce to _shewa_.

10. פְּלֹנִי אַלְמֹנִי—The Hebrew expression literally means "a certain one, so-and-so" (see 1 Sam. 21:3 and 2 Kings 6:8, where the phrase is used of a place). This form of address is not one of familiarity, as NIV suggests. In fact, Boaz probably used the man's name, but the narrator apparently substituted this expression because he wanted to suppress the name of the nearer kinsman, perhaps to protect the reputation of the man's family and descendants. From a literary standpoint, the omission of his name is appropriate, for this relative did nothing memorable. The omission is ironic, for the chapter ends with a genealogical record filled with names.[2]

11. וַיָּסַר—The verb is a Qal wayyiqtol 3ms from סור. For a hollow verb one expects the form to be *וַיָּסָר (see PVP, 198 [17.4]; Ful., 254 [36.4]),[3] but the quasi-guttural _resh_ takes a _pathaq_ (_a_-class vowel) instead of the usual _qamets hatuph_. See GKC, 199, §72t.

---

1. Gar., 109 (19.B.2); Kel., 172–73 (53); Ross, 150 (20.2); Seow, 241 (4).
2. Because the phrase is used elsewhere of a place, it is possible that it refers here to a specific location within the city gate. In this case, it may be translated "[in] such and such [a place]."
3. Fut., 162 (26.1); Gar., 197 (33.D); Ross, 277 (38.2.3); Seow, 229 (4.c).

4:2

וַיִּקַּח עֲשָׂרָה אֲנָשִׁים מִזִּקְנֵי הָעִיר וַיֹּאמֶר שְׁבוּ־פֹה וַיֵּשֵׁבוּ:

1. וַיִּקַּח—The form appears to be I-*nun* (note the *dagesh* in the *qoph*), but the verb לָקַח follows a I-*nun* pattern in the imperfect/wayyiqtol. See PVP, 185 (16.19); Ful., 233 (34.5).[4]

2. עֲשָׂרָה—How is this form functioning in relation to the preceding verb? The absolute form of cardinal numerals three through ten sometimes appears before an indefinite plural noun. See W-OC, 278–79. (The absolute form of the number ten is עֲשָׂרָה, while the construct form is עֲשֶׂרֶת.)

3. מִזִּקְנֵי—The preposition מִן is used in a partitive sense, introducing the entity (the group of town leaders) from which the part (the ten) was taken. For this use of the preposition see AC, 118; W-OC, 213–14; BDB, 580; *HALOT*, 598. One may translate, "from among."

4. שְׁבוּ—Parse this verb. How do you determine the *(a)* root, and *(b)* P-G-N?

5. וַיֵּשֵׁבוּ—Parse this verb. How do you determine the *(a)* root, and *(b)* P-G-N?

4:3

וַיֹּאמֶר לַגֹּאֵל חֶלְקַת הַשָּׂדֶה אֲשֶׁר לְאָחִינוּ לֶאֱלִימֶלֶךְ מָכְרָה נָעֳמִי הַשָּׁבָה מִשְּׂדֵה מוֹאָב:

1. חֶלְקַת הַשָּׂדֶה—How can you tell the form חֶלְקַת is a construct form? How is the genitive הַשָּׂדֶה functioning in relation to חֶלְקַת? See EE, 62–64; W-OC, 143–54.[5]

2. אֲשֶׁר לְאָחִינוּ—The expression אֲשֶׁר לְ-, "which (is) to," is an alternative to the construct indicating possession, "which belongs to."[6]

---

4. Fut., 89 (15.4); Gar., 230 (40.B); Kel., 307 (73.2); Ross, 247 (34.6); Seow, 217 (4.d).
5. See also AC, 8–13; BHRG, 197–200; GKC, 416–19; Joüon, 465–73; WHS, 36–49.
6. See GKC, 420, §129h.

3. לְאָחִינוּ לֶאֱלִימֶלֶךְ—The form לְאָחִינוּ consists of what elements? How is the phrase לֶאֱלִימֶלֶךְ functioning in relation to the preceding phrase?

_____

_____

4. מָכְרָה—Parse this verb. (Note: In this particular form one expects a *metheg* with the *qamets* under the first root letter, but it is omitted here. See PVP, 141 [13.6].)[7] How do you determine the P-G-N? According to W-OC, 489, this is a perfect of resolve. However, clear examples of this category seem difficult to find. It is better to label this use a simple present—Naomi is in the process of selling the land. The use of the perfect does not draw attention to the process, but to the simple fact. See EE, 87.

_____

_____

5. הַשָּׁבָה—On this form see 1:22, note 6.

4:4

וַאֲנִי אָמַרְתִּי אֶגְלֶה אָזְנְךָ לֵאמֹר קְנֵה נֶגֶד הַיֹּשְׁבִים וְנֶגֶד זִקְנֵי עַמִּי אִם־תִּגְאַל גְּאָל
וְאִם־לֹא יִגְאַל הַגִּידָה לִּי וְאֵדְעָ כִּי אֵין זוּלָתְךָ לִגְאוֹל וְאָנֹכִי אַחֲרֶיךָ וַיֹּאמֶר אָנֹכִי אֶגְאָל׃

1. וַאֲנִי אָמַרְתִּי—The pronoun אֲנִי before the first person verb form אָמַרְתִּי emphasizes Boaz's self-assertion. See W-OC, 294–97, especially 296.

2. אֶגְלֶה—This form may be understood as either an imperfect or cohortative, since III-*he* verbs do not have a distinctive cohortative form.[8] If the form is imperfect, how is it functioning? If it is cohortative, how is it functioning? The idiom "uncover the ear" means "reveal to, inform." See BDB, 163; *HALOT*, 191.

_____

_____

3. קְנֵה—Parse this verb. (For help see PVP, 211, [18.9]; Ful., 267 [37.4].)[9]

_____

_____

7. Gar., 48 (8.B); Kel., 84 (30.4); Ross, 87 (10.2); Seow, 146 (2).
8. See GKC, 210, §75l; Joüon, 209, §79o.
9. Fut., 151 (24.6); Gar., 216 (37.B.2); Kel., 287 (72.3); Ross, 259–61 (36.1–2); Seow, 238–39 (3.d).

4. הַיֹּשְׁבִים—Parse this form. How do you determine the gender and number? How is the participle functioning here?

_____

_____

5. זִקְנֵי עַמִּי—How can you tell זִקְנֵי is construct? How does the following genitive (cf. עַמִּי) function?

_____

_____

6. אִם תִּגְאַל—In the protasis ("if" section) of the conditional sentence (cf. אִם, "if") תִּגְאַל is a hypothetical future (EE, 92), but it also seems to have a nuance of capability or desire (see 3:13, note 3).[10]

7. גְּאָל—Parse this verb. One expects the imperatival form to be גְּאַל. The imperative is formed on the analogy of the imperfect; since the imperfect of this verb has a _pathaq_ as theme vowel (see the preceding תִּגְאַל), one expects to see this same vowel in the imperative. But this form is in pause, coming at the end of the clause. So the _pathaq_ is lengthened to _qamets_.

_____

_____

8. יִגְאַל—Parse this verb. Note especially the P-G-N. One expects instead a 2ms form (see the preceding 2ms forms in the initial conditional sentence). Many textual witnesses read the second person here (see _BHS_ note a), but it is possible that Boaz briefly addresses the crowd of witnesses before turning back to the unnamed kinsman. See Jack M. Sasson, _Ruth_ (Baltimore: Johns Hopkins, 1979), 118.

_____

_____

9. הַגִּידָה—Parse this verb. How do you determine the (a) stem, and (b) root? (For help analyzing the ה ֖- ending see 4:1, note 8.)

_____

_____

10. וְאֵדַע—This form involves a _kethib/qere_ variant. The _kethib_ (represented by the consonants in the text) is a Qal imperfect, vocalized וְאֵדַע (see _BHS_, note b). The _qere_, represented by the consonants in the right margin combined with the vowels in the text, is a Qal cohortative (note the ה ֖- ending): וְאֵדְעָה. What is the root of the form? How can you tell? Following the imperative (cf. הַגִּידָה), the imperfect/cohortative is most likely indicating purpose or result, "Tell me in order that I may know/Tell me and then I will know." For the use of the cohortative to indicate purpose/result after an imperative, see EE, 110; W-OC,

---

10. See also Joüon, 372, §113n.

575, 577–78.[11] For the use of the imperfect to indicate purpose/result after a volitional form, see W-OC, 562–63, 650.

_____

_____

11. כִּי אִין—What type of clause is this?

_____

_____

12. זוּלָתְךָ—This form consists of the preposition זוּלָה (which takes a *taw* ending before suffixes) and a 2ms pronominal suffix. One may translate, "except you."

13. לִגְאוֹל—Parse this form. (Note that the theme vowel, typically *holem,* is fully written here as *holem waw.* See PVP, 235 [20.2]; Ful., 117 [19.4].)[12] The infinitive (with prefixed preposition -לְ) is here used in a verbless clause (with אֵין) in a modal sense, indicating permission. See W-OC, 609–10. One may translate, "no one except you has the right to redeem."

_____

_____

14. אָנֹכִי אֶגְאָל—The unnamed kinsman uses the pronoun (cf. אָנֹכִי) before the first person verb אֶגְאָל (note the pausal form with *qamets* as theme vowel, rather than *pathaq*) to emphasize his self-assertion. See note 1 above.

4:5

וַיֹּאמֶר בֹּעַז בְּיוֹם־קְנוֹתְךָ הַשָּׂדֶה מִיַּד נָעֳמִי
וּמֵאֵת רוּת הַמּוֹאֲבִיָּה אֵשֶׁת־הַמֵּת קָנִיתִי לְהָקִים שֵׁם־הַמֵּת עַל־נַחֲלָתוֹ:

1. קְנוֹתְךָ—Parse this form. How do you determine the root? How is the pronominal suffix functioning in relation to the verb? The form is functioning as a genitive after יוֹם, literally, "in the day of your acquiring." It may be translated as a temporal clause, "When . . ."

_____

_____

_____

11. See also GKC, 320, §108d; Joüon, 381–82, §116b.
12. Fut., 120 (20.3); Gar., 74–75 (13.B.2); Ross, 161 (22.1); Seow, 255 (1.a).

2. הַשָּׂדֶה—How is this noun functioning in the clause?

_____

_____

3. וּמֵאֵת—As it stands the form וּמֵאֵת appears to consist of the conjunction, the preposition מִן, and the preposition אֵת, literally, "and from with." On the compound preposition see BDB, 86–87; *HALOT*, 101. This makes it sound as if Naomi and Ruth are co-owners and co-sellers of the field. However, it is clear from the following context (vv. 9–10) that the field is not acquired from Ruth; rather she is acquired with the field. Consequently, on the basis of the reading in verse 10, many emend the text here to וְגַם אֶת (conjunction + adverb + accusative sign), "and also Ruth." Another option is that וּמֵאֵת consists of the conjunction, an enclitic *mem*, and the accusative sign, with the enclitic *mem* having been misunderstood as a preposition. See W-OC, 648, note 2. For a discussion of enclitic *mem* in biblical Hebrew see W-OC, 158–60, as well as *HALOT*, 538.

4. אֵשֶׁת—How is this noun functioning in relation to "Ruth the Moabitess"?

_____

_____

5. הַמֵּת—This form consists of the article and a Qal participle masculine singular from מוּת. The participle is substantival and is genitival after the preceding construct, "the wife of the deceased." The Qal hollow participle typically has the vowel *qamets* (cf. קוּם > קָם, see PVP, 261; Ful., 255 [36.4]),[13] but intransitive verbs like מוּת, "to die," can take a *tsere*.[14]

6. קָנִיתִי—This ungrammatical form involves a *kethib/qere* variant. The *kethib* (represented by the consonants in the text) is a Qal perfect 1cs vocalized קָנִיתִי (see *BHS*, note b). The *qere*, represented by the consonants in the right margin combined with the vowels in the text, is a Qal perfect, 2ms: קָנִיתָה.[15] If one follows the *kethib*, then it sounds as if Boaz is asserting that he will purchase Ruth at the same time the nearer kinsman buys the land. But the context (see 3:11–12; 4:9–10) indicates that the land and Ruth are acquired together. This favors the *qere* reading. Boaz reminds the kinsman that if he purchases the land, he must also take Ruth with it.

7. לְהָקִים—Parse this form. How do you determine the *(a)* stem, and *(b)* root? How is the form functioning in relation to the preceding verb? How is the stem functioning?

_____

_____

_____

_____

_____

13. Fut., 158 (24.7); Gar., 202 (34.B.5); Kel., 317 (74.3); Ross, 276 (38.2.2); Seow, 80–81 (3.f).
14. See GKC, 195, §72c; Joüon, 214, §80d.
15. On the fully written form (with *he*) of the 2ms ending see GKC, 121, §44g; Joüon, 132, §42f.

8. לְהָקִים—The statement "raise up the name of the deceased on his inheritance" essentially means to provide a descendant who will carry on the family name and to whom the family's landed inheritance will pass.

4:6

וַיֹּאמֶר הַגֹּאֵל לֹא אוּכַל לִגְאָול־לִי פֶּן־אַשְׁחִית אֶת־נַחֲלָתִי
גְּאַל־לְךָ אַתָּה אֶת־גְּאֻלָּתִי כִּי לֹא־אוּכַל לִגְאֹל:

1. אוּכַל—This verb is a Qal imperfect 1cs from יָכֹל. This verb is irregular and has a distinctive pattern (with prefix vowel *shureq*) in the imperfect. See PVP, 191 (16.26); Ful., 243 (35.14).[16]

2. לִגְאָול—This unreadable form involves a *kethib/qere* variant. The *kethib* (represented by the consonants in the text) is לִגְאָול, a fully written (note the *holem waw*) form of the Qal infinitive construct. See 4:4, note 13. The *qere*, represented by the consonants in the right margin combined with the vowels in the text, is an alternative form of the infinitive לִגְאָל־; it shows the usual theme vowel *(holem)* reduced to *qamets hatuph* due to the accent shift produced by the form being combined with the following prepositional phrase. How is the infinitive functioning in relation to the preceding verb?

_____

_____

3. אַשְׁחִית—Parse this verb. How do you determine the stem? Within the negative purpose/result clause introduced by פֶּן, "lest, otherwise" (see EE, 116–17; W-OC, 639–40),[17] the imperfect may be classified as a contingent future (EE, 92–93). The stem is causative here—the Niphal means "be ruined, spoiled," and the Hiphil, "to ruin, spoil, destroy."

_____

_____

_____

4. גְּאַל־לְךָ אַתָּה—The nearer kinsman adds the 2ms pronoun אַתָּה after the 2ms imperative גְּאַל to emphasize that he is giving Boaz permission to acquire his right of redemption. See W-OC, 296–97.

5. כִּי לֹא־אוּכַל לִגְאֹל—What type of clause is this?

_____

_____

---

16. Kel., 341 (75.2); Ross, 251 (35.2.1); Seow, 220 (8).
17. See also GKC, 318, §107q; Joüon, 635, §168g.

Step 3: Interpretive Translation

In light of the decisions you have made in your analysis, provide an interpretive, paraphrastic translation of Ruth 4:1–6.

Step 4: Structural Outline

Outline the narrative structure of Ruth 4:1–6. Carefully delineate the narrative mainline (initiated and extended by wayyiqtol forms), offline (nonstandard) constructions, and quotations. Using the categories listed in the appendix (cf. EE, 120–27), classify all wayyiqtol and disjunctive clauses that are in the narrative framework. You need not classify clauses within quotations.

Assignment 2

Step 1: Initial View

Read Ruth 4:7–12 in the Hebrew text, using an interlinear if you desire. Underline any words or forms you do not recognize. Try to identify verbal forms and label them as follows:

- wayyiqtol verbal forms: wc-y (the so-called *waw* consecutive with the yiqtol, usually identified as a preterite or imperfect)

- weqatal forms: wc-q (the so-called *waw* consecutive with the qatal, that is, perfect)
- simple perfects (without *waw*): pf.
- simple imperfects (without *waw*): impf.
- imperatives: impv.
- jussives: juss.
- cohortatives: coh.
- infinitives construct: inf. const.
- infinitives absolute: inf. abs.
- participles: part.

Step 2: Analyzing the Text

4:7

וְזֹאת לְפָנִים בְּיִשְׂרָאֵל עַל־הַגְּאוּלָּה וְעַל־הַתְּמוּרָה לְקַיֵּם כָּל־דָּבָר שָׁלַף אִישׁ נַעֲלוֹ וְנָתַן לְרֵעֵהוּ וְזֹאת הַתְּעוּדָה בְּיִשְׂרָאֵל:

1. וְזֹאת לְפָנִים—What type of clause does this introduce? How is it functioning? (The statement is elliptical; one expects a predicate nominative after the demonstrative: "Now this was the legal proof . . ." Note the statement וְזֹאת הַתְּעוּדָה בְּיִשְׂרָאֵל at the end of v. 7.)

2. זֹאת—The demonstrative זֹאת refers to the custom that is described, beginning with שָׁלַף אִישׁ. For this use of the demonstrative, see W-OC, 311–12.

3. לְפָנִים—The prepositional phrase לְפָנִים, literally, "to (the) face," functions as a temporal adverb, "formerly, before." See BDB, 816, I.6; *HALOT,* 942.

4. עַל—The preposition is used here in the sense of "regarding, in connection with." See W-OC, 218; BDB, 754, II.1.f.*(h); HALOT,* 826.

5. לְקַיֵּם—This is a relatively rare Piel form (note the *dagesh forte* in the *yod*) of קוּם, "to arise." In this stem it means "establish, ratify."[18] The use of the Piel for hollow verbs with middle *shureq* appears to be a characteristic of relatively late texts. (One expects the Polel stem.)[19] While the grammar suggests that this explanatory gloss is relatively late, it is not necessarily an indicator of the date of the book as a whole.

6. כָּל־דָּבָר—This phrase may be translated "any thing" or "any (legal) matter." כָּל refers here to any individual representative of the class that follows (i.e., legal matter). See BDB, 482; *HALOT,* 474.

7. שָׁלַף—To describe a past customary action, one expects the imperfect rather than a perfect verbal form (cf. שָׁלַף). This use (see 1 Sam. 9:9 as well) appears to be an adaptation of the characteristic present (or gnomic) function (see EE, 87–88) to a past time frame. Perhaps the narrator assumes a dramatic perspective here and describes the past practice as if he were witnessing it (a rhetorical use of the simple present).

---

18. This is probably a resultative use of the Piel; on this function of the stem see W-OC, 404–9.
19. See GKC, 197–98, §72m; Joüon, 215, §80h; and Frederic W. Bush, *Ruth, Esther,* WBC (Dallas: Word Books, 1996), 27.

8. וְנָתַן—After the perfect (שָׁלַף) one expects a wayyiqtol form to describe the next action in the sequence, but the text uses instead a perfect with *waw* (cf. וְנָתַן). This may reflect later Hebrew style, where weqatal tends to replace wayyiqtol.[20] However, a weqatal form sometimes describes a complementary action, especially when procedural details are in view, as in this verse. See EE, 131–32, as well as 3:3, note 1 above.

4:8

וַיֹּאמֶר הַגֹּאֵל לְבֹעַז קְנֵה־לָךְ וַיִּשְׁלֹף נַעֲלוֹ:

1. קְנֵה—On this form see 4:4, note 3.
2. The Septuagint adds "and gave to him," which, when retroverted to Hebrew, would read וַיִּתֶּן לוֹ (see *BHS* note a). (The verb form is a Qal wayyiqtol 3ms from נָתַן.) Brotzman (p. 161) considers this to be an interpretive addition in the Septuagint. In this case the translator (or his source) harmonized the text of verse 8 with verse 7, which observes that the custom involved removing the sandal and handing it to the other party (note וְנָתַן). While this is certainly a reasonable explanation, it is also possible that the clause in question may have been accidentally omitted from the Hebrew text. A scribe's eye could have jumped from the initial *waw* on וַיִּתֶּן to the initial *waw* on וַיֹּאמֶר in the following clause (v. 9), leaving out the intervening letters: ויתן לו ויאמר. Or his eye could have jumped from the final *waw* on נַעֲלוֹ to the final *waw* on לוֹ, leaving out the letters that intervene: נעלו ויתן לו.

4:9

וַיֹּאמֶר בֹּעַז לַזְּקֵנִים וְכָל־הָעָם
עֵדִים אַתֶּם הַיּוֹם כִּי קָנִיתִי אֶת־כָּל־אֲשֶׁר לֶאֱלִימֶלֶךְ וְאֵת כָּל־אֲשֶׁר לְכִלְיוֹן וּמַחְלוֹן מִיַּד נָעֳמִי:

1. לַזְּקֵנִים וְכָל־הָעָם—The preposition לְ- takes a compound object here (לַזְּקֵנִים וְכָל־הָעָם). Note the disjunctive accent above the *ayin* in הָעָם, indicating a syntactical break at this point.
2. עֵדִים—This form begins a quotation of what Boaz said to the audience. How is the form functioning within the quotation?

_____

_____

_____

3. כִּי קָנִיתִי—What type of clause is this? (Note that עֵדִים, "witnesses," though a noun, carries an inherent verbal notion of seeing.)

_____

_____

_____

---

20. See Bush, *Ruth, Esther*, 27–28.

4. קָנִ֫יתִי—Parse this verb. How do you determine the P-G-N? According to W-OC (488), this is an instantaneous use of the perfect in which the situation is concurrent with the statement, "I acquire (here and now)."[21] The statement is a speech act and may therefore be classified as performative (see AC, 56).

4:10

וְגַ֣ם אֶת־ר֣וּת הַמֹּאֲבִיָּ֩ה אֵ֨שֶׁת מַחְל֜וֹן קָנִ֧יתִי לִ֣י לְאִשָּׁ֗ה לְהָקִ֤ים שֵׁם־הַמֵּת֙ עַל־נַ֣חֲלָת֔וֹ
וְלֹא־יִכָּרֵ֧ת שֵׁם־הַמֵּ֛ת מֵעִ֥ם אֶחָ֖יו וּמִשַּׁ֣עַר מְקוֹמ֑וֹ עֵדִ֥ים אַתֶּ֖ם הַיּֽוֹם׃

1. לְהָקִ֤ים—On this form see 4:5, note 7.
2. וְלֹא־יִכָּרֵת—The negated imperfect indicates consequence here, "so that the name of the deceased may not be cut off." Parse יִכָּרֵת. How do you determine the stem? How is the stem functioning here?

3. מֵעִם—This form is a compound preposition, meaning "from with." See BDB, 768–69; *HALOT*, 840.
4. מְקוֹמ֑וֹ—This form consists of what elements? How is the form functioning in relation to the preceding noun, שַׁ֫עַר?

4:11

וַיֹּ֨אמְר֜וּ כָּל־הָעָ֧ם אֲשֶׁר־בַּשַּׁ֛עַר וְהַזְּקֵנִ֖ים עֵדִ֑ים יִתֵּן֩ יְהוָ֨ה אֶֽת־הָאִשָּׁ֜ה הַבָּאָ֣ה אֶל־בֵּיתֶ֗ךָ כְּרָחֵ֤ל ׀ וּכְלֵאָה֙
אֲשֶׁר֩ בָּנ֨וּ שְׁתֵּיהֶ֜ם אֶת־בֵּ֣ית יִשְׂרָאֵ֗ל וַעֲשֵׂה־חַ֙יִל֙ בְּאֶפְרָ֔תָה וּקְרָא־שֵׁ֖ם בְּבֵ֥ית לָֽחֶם׃

1. הַזְּקֵנִים—How is this noun functioning in the sentence?

---

21. See also Joüon, 362, §112f.

2. יִתֵּן—Parse this verb. How do you determine the (a) stem, and (b) root? The form could be taken as either imperfect or jussive. Which fits better here? The verb נָתַן is typically glossed "give," but the verb often means "make, constitute." See BDB, 681, no. 3.

_____

_____

_____

3. הַבָּאָה—Parse this form. How do you determine the root? How do you determine the gender and number? How is the participle functioning in relation to the preceding noun? What is the time frame of the participle?

_____

_____

_____

_____

4. בָּנוּ—Parse this verb. How do you determine the P-G-N? The verb is from בָּנָה, "build," not בִּין, "discern." In addition to semantic considerations ("discern" makes no sense here), one can identify the root by the accent. In the Qal perfect 3cp of III-*he* verbs, the accent is on the final syllable, but in hollow verbs, it is on the first syllable. See PVP, 153, 158; Ful., 254 (36.4), 265 (37.4).[22]

_____

_____

5. שְׁתֵּיהֶם—This form, which consists of the feminine dual form of the number two and an apparent 3mp suffix, specifies that the relative pronoun אֲשֶׁר refers to both Rachel and Leah. The suffix, rather than being masculine, is probably another instance of the archaic common dual form. See 1:8, note 4.

6. וַעֲשֵׂה—Parse this verb. For help with the form see PVP, 213 (18.11); Ful., 267 (37.4).[23] How is the form functioning in relation to the preceding jussive יִתֵּן? See EE, 110; GKC, 325, §110i.

_____

_____

7. וַעֲשֵׂה חַיִל—The collocation עָשָׂה חַיִל, literally "do strength," is used elsewhere of many things:

   a. the mighty acts of God (Ps. 118:15–16)
   b. military success (Num. 24:18; 1 Sam. 14:48; Pss. 60:14 [Eng. v. 12]; 108:14 [Eng. v. 13])
   c. the numerous and impressive accomplishments of the ideal wife (Prov. 31:29), and
   d. the acquisition of wealth (Deut. 8:17–18; Ezek. 28:4)

---

22. Gar., 168 (28.A); Kel., 288 (72.3), 317 (74.3); Ross, 275–76 (38.2.1); Seow, 163 (4.a).
23. Kel., 290 (72.6); Ross, 267–68 (37.2.1); Seow, 238 (3.d).

In this context the fourth nuance seems to be in view. The people pray that the Lord would give Boaz many children, just as Rachel and Leah did Jacob, so that he might attain even greater wealth and fame (see the next clause). In this agrarian culture children were viewed as an economic asset.

8. וּקְרָא־שֵׁם—The collocation קָרָא שֵׁם normally means "assign a name," a nuance which does not fit here. Based on the context, the expression must here mean "achieve fame."[24]

4:12

וִיהִי בֵיתְךָ כְּבֵית פֶּרֶץ אֲשֶׁר־יָלְדָה תָמָר לִיהוּדָה מִן־הַזֶּרַע אֲשֶׁר יִתֵּן יְהוָה לְךָ מִן־הַנַּעֲרָה הַזֹּאת׃

1. וִיהִי—On this distinctively jussive form see 3:4, note 1. The jussive continues the prayer, "and may your house be." "House" is used here as a metonymy for "family, family tree." As the concluding genealogy indicates (vv. 18–22), Perez had an unbroken line of male descendants.

2. פֶּרֶץ אֲשֶׁר—How is the relative pronoun functioning in relation to the following verb יָלְדָה?

_____

_____

3. יָלְדָה—Parse this verb. How do you determine the P-G-N?

_____

_____

4. תָמָר—How is this proper noun functioning in relation to the verb?

_____

_____

Step 3: Interpretive Translation

In light of the decisions you have made in your analysis, provide an interpretive, paraphrastic translation of Ruth 4:7–12.

_____

_____

_____

_____

_____

_____

_____

---

24. See Bush, *Ruth, Esther,* 242–43.

Step 4: Structural Outline

Outline the narrative structure of Ruth 4:7–12. Carefully delineate the narrative mainline (initiated and extended by wayyiqtol forms), offline (nonstandard) constructions, and quotations. Using the categories listed in the appendix (cf. EE, 120–27), classify all wayyiqtol and disjunctive clauses that are in the narrative framework. You need not classify clauses within quotations.

_____

_____

_____

_____

_____

_____

_____

_____

_____

_____

Scene 2: Ruth 4:13–17: A Child Is Born

Assignment

Step 1: Initial View

Read Ruth 4:13–17 in the Hebrew text, using an interlinear if you desire. Underline any words or forms you do not recognize. Try to identify verbal forms and label them as follows:

- wayyiqtol verbal forms: wc-y (the so-called *waw* consecutive with the yiqtol, usually identified as a preterite or imperfect)
- weqatal forms: wc-q (the so-called *waw* consecutive with the qatal, that is, perfect)
- simple perfects (without *waw*): pf.
- simple imperfects (without *waw*): impf.
- imperatives: impv.
- jussives: juss.
- cohortatives: coh.
- infinitives construct: inf. const.
- infinitives absolute: inf. abs.
- participles: part.

Step 2: Analyzing the Text

4:13

וַיִּקַּח בֹּעַז אֶת־רוּת וַתְּהִי־לֹו לְאִשָּׁה וַיָּבֹא אֵלֶיהָ וַיִּתֵּן יְהוָה לָהּ הֵרָיֹון וַתֵּלֶד בֵּן:

1. וַיִּקַּח—On this form see 4:2, note 1.

2. וַתְּהִי—This verb is a Qal wayyiqtol from the root הָיָה, "to be." The form is shortened due to the apocopation of the III-*he;* the imperfect form would be תִּהְיֶה. (On the similarity in form between the wayyiqtol and the jussive see PVP, 216–17; Ful., 266–67 [37.4].)[25] How do you determine the P-G-N?

   _____

   _____

3. לֹו—The prepositional phrase לֹו, "to him," is possessive; it may be translated, "his."

4. לְאִשָּׁה—The preposition -לְ, when collocated with הָיָה, indicates a transition into a new state or condition. See BDB, 512. The clause may be translated, "and she became his wife."

5. וַיָּבֹא—On this form see 3:7, note 4. When the 3ms form of the verb is collocated with the preposition אֶל + 3fs suffix (cf. אֵלֶיהָ), the expression, literally, "he came to her," usually refers to sexual intimacy, as it does here. See Genesis 29:23; 30:4; 38:2, 18; Judges 16:1; 2 Samuel 12:24; Ezekiel 23:44. (Judg. 4:22 is an exception.)

6. וַיִּתֵּן—Parse this verb. How do you determine the root?

   _____

   _____

7. הֵרָיֹון—How is הֵרָיֹון, "conception," functioning in relation to וַיִּתֵּן? This noun is derived from the verbal root הָרָה, "conceive." The וֹן- ending often indicates an abstract noun. See W-OC, 92.

   _____

   _____

8. וַתֵּלֶד—Parse this verb. How do you determine the root?

   _____

   _____

---

25. Kel., 292–93 (72.8); Ross, 261 (36.2.1); Seow, 235 (1.a).

4:14

וַתֹּאמַרְנָה הַנָּשִׁים אֶל־נָעֳמִי בָּרוּךְ יְהוָה אֲשֶׁר לֹא הִשְׁבִּית לָךְ גֹּאֵל הַיּוֹם וְיִקָּרֵא שְׁמוֹ בְּיִשְׂרָאֵל:

1. וַתֹּאמַרְנָה—On this form see 1:10, note 1.
2. בָּרוּךְ—Parse this form. How is the form functioning here? Is it attributive, predicative, or substantival?

_____

_____

3. יְהוָה—How is the divine name functioning in relation to the preceding verb form?

_____

_____

4. אֲשֶׁר—Elsewhere when אֲשֶׁר follows בָּרוּךְ it introduces the reason why the one being blessed (in this case יְהוָה) deserves to be rewarded. See 2:20, note 3.

5. הִשְׁבִּית—Parse this verb. How do you determine the stem? How is the perfect verbal form functioning? In this context the verb, which is negated, means "allow to be missing, cause to fail" (causative use of the stem). See BDB, 991–92; *HALOT,* 1408.

_____

_____

_____

6. וְיִקָּרֵא—Parse this verb. How do you determine the stem? How is the stem functioning? In this prayer of blessing the form is best understood as a jussive of desire or wish (cf. Gen. 9:26; 2 Sam. 22:47; Ps. 72:19). When collocated with שֵׁם, "name," the Niphal of קָרָא can refer to someone being called by a particular name (see Gen. 35:10; Deut. 25:10), but no name is given here. The text simply says, "may his name be called in Israel." Most likely the expression refers here to one's name being perpetuated (see Gen. 48:16). One may translate, "may he be famous in Israel." See NIV, "become famous."

_____

_____

_____

7. שְׁמוֹ—The antecedent of the 3ms suffix on שְׁמוֹ, "his name," could be the Lord, who is being blessed/praised here, or it may refer to גֹּאֵל, "a redeemer," mentioned just before the verb. In favor of this view is the fact that the redeemer is obviously the subject of the next verb in the sequence (cf. וְהָיָה in v. 15). For a similar shift in subject in a blessing see Genesis 9:26, where the Lord is blessed (cf. בָּרוּךְ), but then Canaan becomes the subject of the following jussive (cf. וִיהִי כְנַעַן).

4:15

וְהָיָה לָךְ לְמֵשִׁיב נֶפֶשׁ וּלְכַלְכֵּל אֶת־שֵׂיבָתֵךְ
כִּי כַלָּתֵךְ אֲשֶׁר־אֲהֵבַתֶךְ יְלָדַתּוּ אֲשֶׁר־הִיא טוֹבָה לָךְ מִשִּׁבְעָה בָּנִים:

1. וְהָיָה—This verb (Qal perfect with *waw* consecutive) may be taken as equivalent to the preceding jussive (וְיִקְרָא), "and may he also be" (NASB) or as indicative in mood, "he will" (NIV). The גֹּאֵל, "redeemer," mentioned in the previous verse is the subject of the verb. As verse 15b makes clear (note especially יְלָדַתּוּ), this redeemer is not Boaz, but the son (cf. בֵּן, v. 13) born to Boaz and Ruth.

2. לָךְ—The prepositional phrase לָךְ, "to you," is possessive; it may be translated, "your."

3. לְמֵשִׁיב—The preposition -לְ, when collocated with הָיָה, indicates a transition into a new state or condition. See BDB, 512. The clause may be translated, "and he will become your restorer."

4. לְמֵשִׁיב—Parse this form. How do you determine the *(a)* stem, and *(b)* root? How can you tell the form is a participle? How is the participle functioning? (Note the prepositional prefix.)

   _____

   _____

   _____

5. נֶפֶשׁ—How is this noun functioning in relation to the participle מֵשִׁיב? (One may translate this sentence literally, "he will become for you one who restores life.")

   _____

   _____

6. וּלְכַלְכֵּל—This form consists of the conjunction, the preposition -לְ, and a Pilpel infinitive construct from the verbal root כּוּל. This is odd because one expects a participle after לְמֵשִׁיב. (The participial form would be מְכַלְכֵּל. See Mal. 3:2.) The Pilpel stem occurs with geminate and hollow verbs and is functionally equivalent to the Piel.[26] The Pilpel of כּוּל means "sustain, nourish." See BDB, 465; *HALOT*, 463. Here and in the previous clause reference is made to the fact that the child will provide for Naomi's economic and physical well-being.

7. שֵׂיבָתֵךְ—This form consists of what elements? Explain the *taw* ending before the suffix.

   _____

   _____

8. כִּי—The use of כִּי apparently has an explanatory or causal function here, but the logical connection is subtle. How does Ruth's giving birth to the child provide the basis for the affirmation (or prayer, see note 1 above) prior to this? The logic seems to be as follows: This child will sustain Naomi in her old age because, as Ruth's child, he will be obligated to do so. He is, as it were, the tangible proof of Ruth's devotion to Naomi and will be the living embodiment of her love in the days to come. BDB notes (473)

---

26. See GKC, 152, §55f; Joüon, 169, §59c.

that "the causal relation expressed by כִּי is sometimes subtle . . . and not apparent without careful study of a passage."

9. אֲהֵבָתֶךְ—This verb is a Qal perfect 3fs (note the *taw* ending before the suffix, see PVP, 225; Ful., 169 [27.2])[27] from אָהֵב with a 2fs suffix functioning as the object of the verb. The *qamets* that is normally under the *aleph* reduces with the addition of the suffix. How is the perfect verbal form functioning?

_____

_____

10. יְלָדַתּוּ—This verb is a Qal perfect 3fs from יָלַד with a 3ms suffix functioning as the object of the verb. The *qamets* that is normally under the *yod* has reduced with the addition of the suffix. The *qamets* under the second root letter (*lamed* in this case) is typical in suffixed third person forms of the perfect. See PVP, 224; Ful., 169–71 (27.4).[28] The *taw* ending is typical of the 3fs perfect before suffixes. See PVP, 225; Ful., 169 (17.2).[29] One expects the 3ms suffix to be הוּ- (PVP, 225; Ful., 173 [27.7]),[30] but the *he* is lost and the *taw* doubled.[31] The development may be analyzed as follows: דַתְהוּ* > -דַתּוּ-.

11. הִיא—Note how the 3fs pronoun is used to specify that the relative pronoun אֲשֶׁר refers to Ruth. For this same stylistic technique see 4:11, note 5.

12. טוֹבָה—What part of speech is טוֹבָה? How is it functioning here?

_____

_____

13. לָךְ—The preposition -לְ indicates advantage here, "for your benefit."

14. מִשִּׁבְעָה—After the adjective טוֹבָה, how is the preposition מִן functioning?

_____

_____

15. מִשִּׁבְעָה בָּנִים—On the use of the absolute form of the number with the following indefinite plural noun see W-OC, 278. On the lack of agreement in gender see PVP, 112;[32] GKC, 286–87, §97a; Joüon, 323, §100d.

27. Gar., 309 (54.A.2); Kel., 156 (46.4); Ross, 173 (24.3); Seow, 194 (1.a.i).
28. Fut., 221 (35.2); Gar., 310 (54.A); Kel., 155–56 (46.3–46.5); Ross, 174 (24.4); Seow, 196 (1.c).
29. Gar., 309 (54.A.2); Kel., 156 (46.4); Ross, 173 (24.3); Seow, 194 (1.a.i).
30. Gar., 309 (54.A); Kel., 155 (46.3); Ross, 172 (24.2); Seow, 197 (1.d).
31. See GKC, 160, §59g; Joüon, 175, §63d.
32. Fut., 188–89 (30.1); Gar., 152 (25.D); Kel., 97 (35.1); Ross, 180–81 (25.1); Seow, 269 (6.a).

4:16

וַתִּקַּח נָעֳמִי אֶת־הַיֶּלֶד וַתְּשִׁתֵהוּ בְחֵיקָהּ וַתְּהִי־לוֹ לְאֹמֶנֶת׃

1. וַתִּקַּח—Parse this verb. How do you determine the P-G-N? The verb appears to be I-*nun* (note the *dagesh* in the *qoph*), but the verb לָקַח follows a I-*nun* pattern in the imperfect and wayyiqtol. See PVP, 185 (16.19); Ful., 233 (34.5).[33]

_____

_____

2. וַתְּשִׁתֵהוּ—This verb is a Qal wayyiqtol 3fs from שִׁית with a 3ms pronominal suffix functioning as the object of the verb, "and she placed him." One expects a *qamets* under the *taw* prefix, but the addition of the suffix causes an accent shift and a reduction of the *qamets* to *shewa*. See PVP, 229 (19.7).[34] The *hireq* under the *shin* is a defectively written *hireq yod*. The *shewa* + *hireq* (*yod*) vowel pattern could be either Qal or Hiphil; hollow verbs of the middle *yod* variety exhibit formal overlap in this regard. The form should be taken as Qal because the context demands the basic meaning "put, place, set," not a causative nuance. The Hiphil does not occur with this verb.

3. וַתְּהִי—On this form see 4:13, note 2.

4. לוֹ—How is the preposition on לוֹ functioning? See 4:13, note 3.

_____

_____

5. לְאֹמֶנֶת—How is the preposition on לְאֹמֶנֶת functioning? See 4:13, note 4. How can you tell that the form אֹמֶנֶת is a participle? How is the participle functioning here? Note that *HALOT* (64) derives the word from a root אמן II, which is distinct from אמן I, "be firm." BDB (52) does not make such a distinction; they assume there is only one root.

_____

_____

_____

4:17

וַתִּקְרֶאנָה לוֹ הַשְּׁכֵנוֹת שֵׁם לֵאמֹר יֻלַּד־בֵּן לְנָעֳמִי וַתִּקְרֶאנָה שְׁמוֹ עוֹבֵד הוּא אֲבִי־יִשַׁי אֲבִי דָוִד׃

1. וַתִּקְרֶאנָה—Parse this verb. How do you determine the P-G-N?

_____

_____

---

33. Fut., 89 (15.4); Gar., 230 (40.B); Kel., 307 (73.2); Ross, 247 (34.6); Seow, 217 (4.d).
34. Ross, 278 (38.3).

2. שֵׁם . . . לֹו—The collocation קָרָא + לְ- + שֵׁם, literally, "call to . . . a name," means "to give, assign a name." See Genesis 26:18.

3. הַשְּׁכֵנוֹת—How is this form functioning in the sentence? What is the gender and number of the form?

_____

_____

4. יֻלַּד—This verb appears to be a Pual perfect 3ms from יָלַד. Some prefer to call this an old Qal passive.[35] The following observations favor this identification:

   a. the alleged Pual of יָלַד occurs only in the perfect, not the imperfect,
   b. the Piel meaning, "assist as a midwife," appears to differ from that of the Pual, and
   c. the Pual appears to be the passive of the Qal, "give birth."

5. לְנָעֳמִי—Elsewhere when the preposition לְ- follows a passive form of יָלַד (whether Qal passive/Pual or Niphal), it almost always introduces the father. But here Naomi's name follows. The preposition probably indicates advantage, "for (the benefit of) Naomi." Note לָנוּ, "for our (benefit)," in Isaiah 9:5 (Eng. v. 6).

6. וַתִּקְרֶאנָה—This final wayyiqtol clause has a specifying function. See EE, 122. Verse 17a informs us that the women gave the child a name as they observed that he had been born for Naomi's benefit. Verse 17b then tells us exactly what they named him.

Step 3: Interpretive Translation

In light of the decisions you have made in your analysis, provide an interpretive, paraphrastic translation of Ruth 4:13–17.

_____

_____

_____

_____

_____

_____

_____

_____

---

35. See GKC, 140–41, §52e; Joüon, 167, §58a; W-OC, 373–76.

Step 4: Structural Outline

Outline the narrative structure of Ruth 4:13–17. Carefully delineate the narrative mainline (initiated and extended by wayyiqtol forms), offline (nonstandard) constructions, and quotations. Using the categories listed in the appendix (cf. EE, 120–27), classify all wayyiqtol and disjunctive clauses that are in the narrative framework. You need not classify clauses within quotations.

Epilogue
Ruth 4:18–22

From This Union Comes David

Bush (*Ruth, Esther*, 565) calls this scene three, but it is hardly a scene in a dramatic sense. His additional designation of these verses as an epilogue is closer to the mark. This genealogical list is introduced with a disjunctive clause (note . . . וְאֵלֶּה, "These are the generations of Perez"). The pattern is then subject (proper name of father) + verb + accusative sign and direct object (proper name of son).

וְאֵ֣לֶּה תּוֹלְד֣וֹת פָּ֔רֶץ פֶּ֖רֶץ הוֹלִ֥יד אֶת־חֶצְרֽוֹן׃

וְחֶצְרוֹן֙ הוֹלִ֣יד אֶת־רָ֔ם וְרָ֖ם הוֹלִ֥יד אֶת־עַמִּֽינָדָֽב׃

וְעַמִּֽינָדָב֙ הוֹלִ֣יד אֶת־נַחְשׁ֔וֹן וְנַחְשׁ֖וֹן הוֹלִ֥יד אֶת־שַׂלְמָֽה׃

וְשַׂלְמוֹן֙ הוֹלִ֣יד אֶת־בֹּ֔עַז וּבֹ֖עַז הוֹלִ֥יד אֶת־עוֹבֵֽד׃

וְעוֹבֵד֙ הוֹלִ֣יד אֶת־יִשָׁ֔י וְיִשַׁ֖י הוֹלִ֥יד אֶת־דָּוִֽד׃

1. הוֹלִיד—The verb used in the list is הוֹלִיד. Parse this form. How do you determine the stem and the root? How is the stem functioning?

_____

_____

_____

_____

At first the genealogy seems to be an anticlimactic way for the story to end, but it illustrates the extent of the blessing that came to Boaz and Ruth. In response to the prayer of the people (4:11–12), the Lord gave Boaz an unbroken line of male descendants, culminating in the great king David.

Vocabulary for the Book of Ruth

This glossary lists all words found in Ruth with the exception of commonly used particles, prepositions, and pronouns. Numbers in parentheses are the BDB/*HALOT* page numbers where the discussion of the word appears or begins. If only one passage is listed in the right hand column, this means the word occurs only in this text in Ruth. In cases where a word occurs in more than one passage, the first passage where it is used is listed, as well as some others. But one should not assume that the lists are exhaustive. Words marked "PN" are proper nouns.

אֵ

אָב	father (3/1)	2:11; 4:17
אָדוֹן	lord, master (10/12)	2:13
אָהֵב	to love (12/17)	4:15
אָז	then (23/26)	2:7
אֹזֶן	ear (23/27)	4:4
אָח	brother (26/29)	4:3, 10
אָחַז	grasp, hold (28/31)	3:15
אַחֵר	another (29/35)	2:8, 22
אַחֲרוֹן	latter (30/36)	3:10
אַחַת	one (feminine)(25/29)	1:4; 2:13
אֵיךְ	how (32/39)	3:18
אֵיפָה	ephah (35/43)	2:17
אֵיפֹה	where? (33/43)	2:19
אִישׁ	man, husband, each one (35/43)	1:1, 2, etc.
אָכַל	eat (37/46)	2:14; 3:3, 7
אֹכֶל	food, eating (38/47)	2:14
אֱלֹהִים	God, god (43/52)	1:15, 16; 2:12
אֱלִימֶלֶךְ	Elimelech (PN)(45/56)	1:2, etc.
אַלְמֹנִי	someone (48/58)	4:1
אֵם	mother (51/61)	1:8; 2:11
אָמָה	female servant (51/61)	3:9
אָמְנָם	surely, truly (53/65)	3:12
אֹמֶנֶת	nurse, guardian (root אָמַן; 52/64)	4:16
אָמֵץ	be strong (54/65)	1:18
אָמַר	say (55/65)	1:8, etc.
אָנָה	where? (33/69)	2:19
אָסַף	gather (62/74)	2:7
אֶפְרָתָה	Ephrathah (PN)(68/81)	4:11
אֶפְרָתִי	Ephrathite (68/81)	1:2
אֶרֶץ	land, ground (75/90)	1:1, 7; 2:10, 11
אִשָּׁה	woman, wife, each one (61/93)	1:1, 2, etc.

ב

בּוֹא	come, go (97/112)	1:2, 19, etc.
בָּחוּר	young man (104/118)	3:10
בְּטֶרֶם	before (382/379)	3:14 (*qere*)
בַּיִת	house, home (108/124)	1:8, 9, etc.
בֵּית לֶחֶם	Bethlehem (PN)(111/127)	1:1, etc.
בָּכָה	weep (113/129)	1:9, 14
בֵּן	son (119/137)	1:1, 2, etc.
בָּנָה	build (124/139)	4:11
בֹּעַז	Boaz (PN)(126/142)	2:1, etc.
בֹּקֶר	morning (133/151)	2:7; 3:13, 14
בָּקַשׁ	seek (134/152)	3:1
בָּרַךְ	bless (138/159)	2:4, 19, etc.
בַּת	daughter (123/165)	1:11, 12, etc.

ג

גָּאַל	redeem (145/169)	2:20; 3:9, etc.
גְּאֻלָּה	right of redemption (145/170)	4:6, 7
גִּבּוֹר	strong, prominent (150/172)	2:1
גָּדַל	be great, grow (152/178)	1:13
גּוּר	live as a resident alien(157/184)	1:1
גָּלָה	uncover (162/191)	3:4, 7; 4:4
גַּם	also (168/195)	1:5, 12, etc.
גָּעַר	to rebuke, insult (172/199)	2:16
גֹּרֶן	threshing-floor (175/203)	3:2, 3, 6, 14

ד

דָּבַק	cling to, stick close (179/209)	1:14; 2:8, 21, 23
דָּבַר	speak (180/210)	1:18; 2:13; 4:1
דָּבָר	matter (182/211)	3:18; 4:7
דָּוִד	David (PN)(187/215)	4:17, 22
דַּל	poor (195/221)	3:10
דֶּרֶךְ	way (202/231)	1:7

ה

הוּם	be stirred up (223/242)	1:19
הָיָה	be (224/243)	1:1, etc.
הָלַךְ	go (229/246)	1:1, 7, etc.
הֲלֹם	to here (240/249)	2:14
הִנֵּה	behold, look (243/252)	1:15; 2:4; 3:2, 8
הֵרָיוֹן	conception, pregnancy (248/256)	4:13

ז

זוּלָה	except, besides (265/267)	4:4
זָקֵן	be old (278/278)	1:12
זָקֵן	elder (278/278)	4:2, 4, 9, 11

| זָרָה | winnow (279/280) | 3:2 |
| זֶרַע | offspring (282/282) | 4:12 |

ח

חָבַט	beat out (286/285)	2:17
חָדַל	cease (292/292)	1:18
חָוָה¹	bow down (1005/295)	2:10
חִטָּה	wheat (334/307)	2:23
חַי	living (311/308)	2:20; 3:13
חַיִל	strength, ability (298/311)	2:1; 3:11; 4:11
חֵיק	lap, chest (300/312)	4:16
חֶלְקָה	portion, plot of ground (324/324)	2:3; 4:3
חָמוֹת	mother-in-law (327/327)	1:14; 2:11, etc.
חֹמֶץ	vinegar (330/329)	2:14
חֵן	favor (336/332)	2:2, 10, 13
חֶסֶד	loyalty (338/336)	1:8; 2:20; 3:10
חָסָה	seek protection (340/337)	2:12
חָפֵץ	to delight, desire (342/339)	3:13
חֲצִי	half (345/343)	3:8
חֶצְרוֹן	Hezron (PN)(348/345)	4:18
חָרַד	tremble, shake (353/350)	3:8

ט

טָבַל	dip (371/368)	2:14
טוֹב	good (adjective: 373/370)	2:22; 3:13; 4:15
טֶרֶם	*see* בְּטֶרֶם	3:14 (*qere*)

י

יְבָמָה/יְבֶמֶת	sister-in-law (386/383)	1:15
יָד	hand (388/386)	1:13; 4:5, 9
יָדַע	know (393/390)	2:1 (*kethib*), 11, etc.
יָהַב	give (396/236)	3:15
יְהוּדָה	Judah (PN)(397/394)	1:1, etc.
יְהוָה	Yahweh (PN)(217/394)	1:6, etc.
יוֹם	day (398/399)	1:1; 2:19, etc.
יָטַב	be good (405/408)	3:1, 7, 10
יָכֹל	be able (407/410)	4:6
יָלַד	give birth (408/411)	1:12; 4:12, etc.
יֶלֶד	boy, son (409/412)	1:5; 4:16
יָסַף	add, do again (414/418)	1:17
יָצָא	go out (422/425)	1:7, 13; 2:18, 22
יָרֵא	to fear (431/432)	3:11
יָרַד	go down (432/434)	3:3, 6

---

1. BDB derives the form from שָׁחָה, but recent research suggests the root is חָוָה, though not all scholars concur with the modern consensus. For discussion and bibliography, see W-OC, 360–61.

יִשְׂרָאֵל	Israel (975/442)	2:12
יֵשׁ	there is (441/443)	1:12; 3:12
יָשַׁב	live, sit (442/444)	1:4; 2:7, etc.
יִשַׁי	Jesse (PN)(445/446)	4:17, 22
יָתַר	be left, remain (451/451)	2:14, 18

כ

כֹּה	thus, so (462/461)	1:17; 2:8
כּוּל	sustain (465/463)	4:15
כֹּל	all (481/474)	2:11, 21, etc.
כָּלָה	be finished (477/476)	2:21, 23, etc.
כַּלָּה	daughter-in-law (483/477)	1:6, 7, etc.
כְּלִי	jar (479/478)	2:9
כִּלְיוֹן	Kilion (PN)(479/479)	1:2
כָּלַם	be humiliated (483/480)	2:15
כָּנָף	wing, edge (489/486)	2:12; 3:9
כָּרַת	cut off (503/500)	4:10

ל

לֵאָה	Leah (PN)(521/513)	4:11
לֵב	heart (524/513)	2:13; 3:7
לִין/לוּן	spend the night, lodge (533/529)	1:16; 3:13
לֶחֶם	bread, food (536/526)	1:6; 2:14
לָט	secrecy (532/527)	3:7
לַיְלָה	night (538/528)	1:12; 3:2, 8, 13
לְפָנִים	before (816/942)	4:7
לָפַת	turn over, grope around (542/533)	3:8
לָקַח	take (542/534)	4:2, 13, 16
לָקַט	glean (544/535)	2:2, 3, etc.

מ

מְאֹד	very, exceedingly (547/538)	1:13, 20
מָדַד	to measure (551/547)	3:15
מַדּוּעַ	why? (396/548)	2:10
מֹדַעַת	relative (396/550)	3:2
מוֹאָב	Moab (PN)(555/554)	1:1, etc.
מוֹאֲבִיָּה	Moabitess (feminine)(555/554)	1:4, 22, etc.
מוֹדַע	relative (396/550)	2:1(qere)
מוֹלֶדֶת	birth, descent (409/556)	2:11
מוּת	die (559/562)	1:3, 5, etc.
מָוֶת	death (560/563)	1:17; 2:11
מַחְלוֹן	Mahlon (PN)(563/569)	1:2, etc.
מִטְפַּחַת	cloak, shawl (381/574)	3:15
מָכַר	sell (569/581)	4:3
מָלֵא	full (fs מְלֵאָה)(570/584)	1:21
מָנוֹחַ	resting place (629/600)	3:1

מְנוּחָה	resting place (629/600)	1:9
מֵעֶה	insides (plural)(588/609)	1:11
מְעַט	a little, short time (589/611)	2:7
מָצָא	find (592/619)	1:9; 2:2, 10, 13
מָקוֹם	place (879/626)	1:7; 3:4; 4:10
מִקְרֶה	incident, chance (899/629)	2:3
מָרָא	bitter (600/630)	1:20
מַרְגְּלוֹת	place of the feet (920/631)	3:4, 7, 8, 14
מָרַר	be bitter (600/638)	1:13, 20
מַשְׂכֹּרֶת	wage, pay (969/641)	2:12
מִשְׁפָּחָה	clan, extended family (1046/651)	2:1, 3

נ

נָגַד	tell (616/665)	2:11, 19, etc.
נֶגֶד	in front of, before (617/666)	4:4
נָגַע	touch, harm (619/668)	2:9
נָגַשׁ	to approach (620/670)	2:14
נַחֲלָה	property, inheritance (635/687)	4:5, 6, 10
נָחַם	comfort, console (636/688)	2:13
נַחְשׁוֹן	Nahshon (PN)(638/691)	4:20
נָכַר	recognize (647/699)	2:10, 19; 3:14
נָכְרִי	foreigner (fs נָכְרִיָּה)(648/700)	2:10
נַעַל	sandal (653/705)	4:7, 8
נָעֳמִי	Naomi (PN)(654/706)	1:2, etc.
נַעַר	young man, servant (654/707)	2:5, 6, 9, 15, 21
נַעֲרָה	young woman (655/707)	2:5, 6, etc.
נָפַל	to fall (656/709)	2:10; 3:18
נֶפֶשׁ	life (659/711)	4:15
נָצַב	to stand (662/714)	2:5, 6
נָשָׂא	lift up, take (669/724)	1:4, 9, 14; 2:18
נָשַׁק	to kiss (676/730)	1:9, 14
נָתַן	give, pay (678/733)	1:6, 8, etc.

ס

| סוּךְ | anoint oneself (691/745) | 3:3 |
| סוּר | turn aside (693/747) | 4:1 |

ע

עָבַר	pass by, leave (716/778)	2:8; 4:1
עָגַן	hinder, lock in (723/785)	1:13
עֵד	witness (729/788)	4:9, 10, 11
עוֹבֵד	Obed (PN)(714/794)	4:17, 21, 22
עוֹד	still, yet, more, again (728/795)	1:11, 14
עָזַב	forsake, abandon, leave (736/806)	1:16; 2:11, etc.
עַיִן	eye (dual)(744/817)	2:2, 9, 10, 13
עִיר	city (746/821)	1:19; 2:18, etc.

עָלָה	go up (748/828)	4:1
עַם	people, nation (766/837)	1:6, 10, etc.
עָמַד	to stand, stand still (763/840)	2:7
עִמָּדִי	with me (767/842)	1:8
עַמִּינָדָב	Amminadab (PN)(770/844)	4:19, etc.
עֹמֶר	sheaf, heap of grain (771/849)	2:7, 15
עָנָה	to answer, reply, testify (772/851)	1:21; 2:6, 11
עֶרֶב	evening, sunset (787/877)	2:17
עֲרֵמָה	heap (790/887)	3:7
עָרְפָּה	Orpah (PN)(791/888)	1:4, 14
עָשָׂה	make, do (793/889)	1:8, 17, etc.
עֶשֶׂר	ten (796/894)	1:4
עֲשָׂרָה	ten (796/895)	4:2
עָשִׁיר	rich (799/896)	3:10
עֵת	time (773/899)	2:14
עַתָּה	now (773/901)	3:11, 12

פ

פָּגַע	urge, force, hurt (803/910)	1:16; 2:22
פֹּה	here (805/916)	4:1, 2
פְּלֹנִי	a certain one (811/934)	4:1
פֶּן	lest (814/936)	4:6
פָּנִים	face (815/938)	2:10
פֹּעַל	work (noun: 821/951)	2:12
פָּקַד	visit (823/955)	1:6
פָּרַד	to separate (825/962)	1:17
פֶּרֶץ	Perez (PN)(829/973)	4:12, 18
פָּרַשׂ	spread out (831/975)	3:9
פַּת	fragment, morsel of food (837/983)	2:14

צ

צָבַט	reach, hold out (840/997)	2:14
צְבָתִים	bundles of grain (841/1000)	2:16
צַד	side (841/1000)	2:14
צָוָה	to command, instruct (Piel: 845/1010)	2:9, 15; 3:6
צָמֵא	be thirsty (854/1032)	2:9

ק

קָבַר	bury (868/1064)	1:17
קוֹל	voice (876/1083)	1:9, 14
קוּם	arise (877/1086)	1:6; 2:15, etc.
קָלִי	roasted grain (885/1102)	2:14
קָנָה	buy, acquire (888/1111)	4:4, 5, 8, 9, 10
קָצֶה	end (892/1120)	3:7
קָצִיר	harvest (894/1122)	1:22; 2:21, 23
קָצַר	reap (894/1126)	2:3, 4, etc.

קָרָא	call, cry out (894/1128)	1:20, 21, etc.
קָרָה	encounter, meet (809/1137)	2:3
קָרוֹב	near (898/1139)	2:20; 3:12

ר

רָאָה	see, look (906/1157)	1:18; 2:18
רִאשׁוֹן	former (911/1168)	3:10
רוּת	Ruth (PN)(946/1209)	1:4, etc.
רָחֵל	Rachel (PN)(932/1216)	4:11
רָחַץ	wash, bathe (934/1220)	3:3
רֵיקָם	emptily (adverb: 938/1229)	1:21; 3:17
רָם	Ram (PN)(928/1238)	4:19
רֵעַ	friend, another (945/1253)	3:14; 4:7
רָעָב	famine (944/1257)	1:1
רָעַע	be injured, harmed (949/1269)	1:21

שׂ

שָׂבַע	be full, satisfied (959/1302)	2:14, 18 (?)
שׂבַע	satiation (959–60/1304)	2:18 (?)
שָׂבַר	wait (960/1304)	1:13
שָׂדֶה	field (961/1307)	1:1, 2, etc.
שֵׂיבָה	old age (966/1318)	4:15
שִׂים	put, place (962/1321)	3:3
שַׂלְמָה	Salmah (PN)(969/1332)	4:20
שַׂלְמוֹן	Salmon (PN)(969/1332)	4:21
שִׂמְלָה	garment (971/1337)	3:3
שְׂעֹרִים	barley (singular שְׂעֹרָה)(972/1345)	1:22; 2:17, etc.

שׁ

שָׁאַב	draw water (980/1367)	2:9
שָׁאַר	remain, be left (983/1375)	1:3, 5
שִׁבֹּלֶת	ear of grain (987/1394)	2:2
שִׁבְעָה	seven (987/1399)	4:15
שָׁבַת	cease, rest (991/1407)	4:14
שַׁדַּי	Shadday (994/1420)	1:20, 21
שׁוּב	return (996/1427)	1:6, 7, etc.
שָׁחַת	be ruined, spoiled (1007/1469)	4:6
שִׁית	put, place (1011/1483)	3:15; 4:16
שָׁכַב	lie down, sleep (1011/1486)	3:4, 7, 8, 13, 14
שְׁכֵנָה	female neighbor (1015/1500)	4:17
שָׁלַל	pull out (1021/1531)	2:16
שָׁלֵם	be complete (1022/1532)	2:12
שָׁלֵם	complete, full (fs שְׁלֵמָה)(adjective:1023/1538)	2:12
שָׁלַף	remove (1025/1543)	4:7, 8
שִׁלְשׁוֹם	three days ago (1026/1545)	2:11
שָׁם	there (1027/1546)	1:2, 4, 7, 17; 3:4

שֵׁם	name (1027/1548)	1:2, 4, etc.
שָׁמַע	hear (1033/1570)	1:6; 2:8
שָׁנָה	year (1040/1600)	1:4
שְׁנַיִם	two (1040/1605)	1:1, 2, etc.
שֵׁנִית	second (1041/1604)	1:4
שַׁעַר	gate (1044/1614)	3:11; 4:1, 10, 11
שִׁפְחָה	servant (1046/1620)	2:13
שָׁפַט	to judge (1047/1622)	1:1
שָׁקַט	be quiet, to rest (1052/1641)	3:18
שֵׁשׁ	six (995/1663)	3:15, 16
שָׁתָה	to drink (1059/1667)	2:9; 3:3, 7
שְׁתַּיִם	two (1040/1605)	1:19; 4:11

ת

תּוֹלְדוֹת	generations (410/1699)	4:18
תְּחִלָּה	beginning (321/1717)	1:22
תְּמוֹל	yesterday (1069/1746)	2:11
תְּמוּרָה	exchange (558/1747)	4:7
תָּמָר	Tamar (PN)(1071/1756)	4:12
תְּעוּדָה	confirmation (730/1767)	4:7
תִּקְוָה	hope (noun: 876/1781)	1:12

Part 3

PARSING HEBREW VERBS

Introduction

These charts are designed to facilitate the parsing of Hebrew verbs. To use the charts begin with the following process:

I. If the form is a wayyiqtol, use chart 10.

II. If the form has one of the following characteristic prefixes of the imperfect *(yod, taw, aleph),* use chart 10.

III. If the form has a *nun* prefix, it will be either a 1cp imperfect or a Niphal. Here's how to distinguish the two options:

   A. If the form has one of the following characteristic endings of the perfect, then it is a Niphal perfect. Use chart 1 (for second and first person forms) or chart 5 (for the 3cp form).

———	3ms
תָּ/תָ	2ms
תְּ/ת	2fs
תִי/תִּי	1cs
וּ	3cp
תֶּם/תֶם	2mp
תֶּן/תֶן	2fp
נוּ	1cp

   B. If the form has one of the plural endings for the participle, then it is a Niphal participle. Use chart 8.

־ִים	mp
־וֹת	fp

   C. If the ending is ־ָה, then theoretically the form could be Niphal perfect 3fs, Niphal participle fs, or a 1cp cohortative from any stem. However, in the regular verb patterns only the Qal cohortative presents a problem because it, like the Niphal forms, has a *hireq* prefix vowel followed by *shewa* under the first root letter:[1]

---

1. In other words, for regular verbs if the vowel under the *nun* is anything except *hireq* or if the vowel under the first root letter is anything but *shewa*, assume the form is a cohortative from a derived (non-Qal) stem and use chart 10. If the prefix vowel is *hireq* and a *qamets* appears under the first root letter, the form is a Niphal cohortative (see chart 10). If the *hireq* is followed by a *taw* prefix before the first root letter, the form is Hithpael.

- נִקְטְלָה could be Qal cohortative 1cp or Niphal perfect 3fs (context decides)
- נִקְטָלָה = Niphal participle feminine singular due to *qamets* under the second root letter

III-*he* verbs are tricky. In III-*he* verbs the Niphal perfect 3ms and participle feminine singular have an ה ָ - ending (נִבְנָה); the Niphal participle masculine singular and Qal imperfect/cohortative have an ה ֶ - ending (נִבְנֶה):

- נִבְנָה = Niphal perfect 3ms or participle fs
- נִבְנֶה = Niphal participle masculine singular or Qal imperfect/cohortative 1cp

In I-*nun* verbs the Qal cohortative 1cp and Niphal perfect 3fs overlap (נִגְּשָׁה).

In I-*yod* verbs the Qal cohortative has a *tsere* prefix vowel (נֵשְׁבָה), while the Niphal perfect 3fs has a *holem waw* (נוֹשְׁבָה).

In hollow verbs the forms overlap only in the *o*-classes (נָבוֹאָה); in the 1cp imperfect the *u* and *i*-classes have a *shureq* or *hireq yod* theme vowel, respectively.

D. If the ending ה ֶ - appears, a III-*he* verb is involved. As noted in *(c)* above, the form is either Qal imperfect/cohortative 1cp or Niphal participle ms: נִבְנֶה

E. If there is no ending, theoretically the options are Niphal perfect 3ms, Niphal participle ms, Niphal infinitive absolute, or a 1cp imperfect from any stem. In the regular verb only the Qal imperfect presents a problem because it, like Niphal forms, has a *hireq* prefix vowel followed by a *shewa* under the first root letter: With no ending, here is the basic rule:

- *Pathaq* theme vowel = Niphal perfect 3ms   נִקְטַל
- *Qamets* theme vowel = Niphal participle masculine singular   נִקְטָל
- *Holem* theme vowel = Qal imperfect 1cp   נִקְטֹל
- *Holem waw* theme vowel = Niphal infinitive absolute   נִקְטוֹל

Some Qal imperfects (statives, I/II/III-gutturals) have a *pathaq* theme vowel and consequently overlap in form with the Niphal perfect: נִשְׁלַח/נִבְחַר/נֶעֱזֹב/נִכְבַּד.

In III-*aleph* verbs the Qal imperfect 1cp, Niphal perfect 3ms, and Niphal participle masculine singular have the same form: נִמְצָא. The Niphal infinitive absolute has a *holem* theme vowel: נִמְצֹא:

- נִמְצָא = Qal imperfect 1cp or Niphal perfect 3ms or Niphal participle ms
- נִמְצֹא = Niphal infinitive absolute

In I-*yod* verbs the Qal imperfect has a *tsere* prefix vowel, while the Niphal forms have a *holem waw* prefix vowel.

In geminate and hollow verbs the distinguishing vowel is with the first root letter:

- נָסַב = Niphal perfect 3ms geminate
- נֹסֹב = Qal imperfect 1cp geminate
- נָקוֹם = Niphal perfect 3ms hollow
- נָקוּם = Qal imperfect 1cp hollow

IV. For forms not covered in the three preceding categories, look for an ending:
   A. If there is *no ending,* then use chart 9.
   B. If there is an ending, then use one of charts 1–8, depending on the precise ending involved:

   1. Ending of perfect (second or first person)
   2. הָ - ending
   3. ה -, ה -, ה - ending (III-*he* verb)
   4. נָה- ending (2fp impv.)
   5. וּ- ending (3cp perf. or 2mp impv.)
   6. י - ending (2fs impv.)
   7. ת -or ת - ending (fs part. or inf. constr.)
   8. ים - or וֹת- ending (plural part. or III-*he* inf. constr.)

Chart 1

Second or First Person
Ending of Perfect

Use this chart when the form has a second or first person ending of the perfect:[1]

תָ/תָ	2ms	תֶם/תֶּם	2mp
ת/תְּ	2fs[2]	תֶן/תֶּן	2fp
תִי/תִּי	1cs[3]	נוּ	1cp

1. *NO PREFIX* = Qal, Piel, or Pual, determined by the vowel under the first root letter

    Qamets = Qal   קְטַלְתָּ
        Two root letters, *yod* before ending = III-*he*   בָּנִיתָ

    Shewa = Qal   קְטַלְתֶּם
        Two root letters, *yod* before ending = III-*he*   בְּנִיתֶם

    Pathaq = Qal
        Two root letters = hollow   קַמְתָּ
        Two root letters, 2nd doubled = geminate   סַבּוֹתָ

    Hireq = Piel   קִטַּלְתָּ
        Two root letters, *yod* before ending = III-*he*   גִּלִּיתָ

    Tsere = Piel   בֵּרַכְתָּ

    Qibbuts = Pual   קֻטַּלְתָּ
        Two root letters, *yod* before ending = III-*he*   גֻּלֵּיתָ

    Holem = Pual   בֹּרַכְתָּ

2. *PREFIX* = Niphal, Hiphil, Hophal, or Hithpael, determined by prefix and prefix vowel

    Nun prefix = Niphal   נִקְטַלְתָּ
        Two root letters, *yod* before ending = III-*he*   נִבְנֵיתָ

---

1. The third person forms of the perfect do not have distinctive endings. The 3ms has no ending, while the 3fs ending הָ - and the 3cp ending וּ - can appear on forms other than the perfect. We will use different charts for these forms.
2. The Qal active participle feminine singular of III-*aleph* verbs also ends in *taw:* מֹצֵאת.
3. This ending can also appear on an infinitive construct of a I-*nun* or I-*yod* verb: גֶּשֶׁת < נגשׁ; שִׁבְתִּי < ישׁב. In this case the form consists of the root (with the first root letter omitted), a suffixed *taw*, and a 1cs pronominal suffix.

Chart 1

Two root letters, *dagesh* in 2nd letter[4] = I-*nun* נִצַּלְתָּ

Two root letters, *holem waw* prefix vowel = I-*yod* נוֹשַׁבְתָּ

Two root letters, *shewa* under prefix = hollow נְקוּמוֹתָ

Two root letters, 2nd doubled, *shewa* under prefix = geminate נְסַבּוֹתָ

He prefix = Hiphil, Hophal, Hithpael (Hithpael has a *taw* with the prefix; Hophal has a *shureq, qibbuts,* or *qamets hatuph;* all other patterns are Hiphil.)

+ *hireq/seghol* prefix vowel = Hiphil הֶעֱמַדְתָּ/הִקְטַלְתָּ

    Two root letters, *yod* before ending = III-*he* הִגְלִיתָ

    Two root letters, *dagesh* in 2nd letter = I-*nun* הִצַּלְתָּ

+ *tsere yod* prefix vowel = Hiphil, I-*yod* הֵיטַבְתָּ

+ *holem* prefix vowel = Hiphil, I-*yod* הוֹשַׁבְתָּ

+ *pathaq shewa* prefix vowel = Hiphil

    Two root letters, *hireq yod* in middle = hollow הֲקִימוֹתָ

    Two root letters, 2nd doubled = geminate הֲסַבּוֹתָ

+ *qibbuts* prefix vowel = Hophal הֻקְטַלְתָּ

    Two root letters, *dagesh* in 2nd root letter = I-*nun* הֻצַּלְתָּ

+ *qamets hatuph* prefix vowel = Hophal הָקְטַלְתָּ

    Two root letters, *yod* before ending = III-*he* הָגְלֵיתָ

+ *shureq* prefix vowel = Hophal

    Two root letters, no doubling = I-*yod*/hollow הוּקַמְתָּ/הוּשַׁבְתָּ

    Two root letters, 2nd doubled = geminate הוּסַבּוֹתָ

הִת prefix = Hithpael הִתְקַטַּלְתָּ

    Two root letters, *yod* before ending = III-*he* הִתְגַּלִּיתָ

---

4. We refer here to the actual second root letter (the first one visible in the form); the actual first root letter *(nun)* has assimilated, hence the *dagesh.*

Chart 2
Verbal Form with הָ - Ending

The *qamets he* ending appears on feminine singular nouns and adjectives, as well as on nouns and adverbs to indicate direction. It is also used with several verb forms, including:

1. the 3ms form of the perfect in III-*he* verbs,
2. the 3fs form of the perfect,
3. the feminine singular form of both active and passive participles,
4. cohortative forms, and
5. the alternative (so-called emphatic) 2ms form of the imperative.

This chart deals with the first three options. Cohortative forms (*nun* or *aleph* prefix) are in chart 10 (for the imperfect). For the emphatic imperative, this chart includes only the regular Qal form (קָטְלָה) and emphatic imperatives found in Jonah and Ruth. If you cannot find a form with הָ - ending in the chart below, it is a cohortative (if prefixed with *nun* or *aleph*) or an emphatic imperative.

1. *NO PREFIX* = Qal, Piel, or Pual, determined by the vowel under the first root letter

    Qamets = Qal (pf. 3fs unless otherwise noted)   קָטְלָה
         Two root letters, *taw* before ending = III-*he*   בָּנְתָה

         Two root letters, accent on 1st syllable = hollow   קָ֫מָה
         Two root letters, accent on ending = hollow part. fs   קָמָה
            or III-*he* pf. 3ms   בָּנָה

    Shewa = Qal (pass. part., fs)   קְטוּלָה
         Yod before ending = III-*he*   בְּנוּיָה

    Pathaq = Qal (pf. 3fs *or* part. fs), geminate   תַּמָּה

    Qamets hatuph = Qal (impv. 2ms)   קָטְלָה

    Hireq = Piel (pf.)   קִטְּלָה
         Two root letters = 3ms, III-*he*   גִּלָּה
         Two root letters, *taw* before ending = 3fs, III-*he*   גִּלְּתָה

    Tsere = Piel (pf. 3fs)   בֵּרְכָה

    Qibbuts = Pual (pf. 3fs)   קֻטְּלָה
         Two root letters = pf. 3ms, III-*he*   גֻּלָּה
         Two root letters, *taw* before ending = III-*he*   גֻּלְּתָה

Chart 2

Holem
    Qal act. part., fs   קְטֵלָה
    Pual pf. 3fs, II-guttural   בֹּרְכָה
    Two root letters = Qal act. part., fs, III-*he*   בֹּנָה

2. *PREFIX* = Niphal, Hiphil, Hophal, or Hithpael, determined by prefix and prefix vowel

Nun prefix = Niphal
    Shewa in theme vowel slot = pf. 3fs[1]   נִקְטְלָה
    Qamets theme vowel = part. fs   נִקְטָלָה
    Two root letters, *taw* with ending = pf. 3fs, III-*he*   נִבְנְתָה
    Two root letters = part. fs, III-*he*   נִבְנָה
        or pf. 3ms, III-*he*   נִבְנָה
    Two root letters, *dagesh* in 2nd[2] = pf. 3fs, I-*nun*   נִצְּלָה
    Two root letters, *holem* prefix vowel = pf. 3fs, I-*yod*   נוֹשְׁבָה
    Two root letters, *holem waw* theme vowel = pf. 3fs, hollow   נָקוֹמָה
    Two root letters, 2nd doubled = pf. 3fs, geminate   נָסַבָּה

He prefix = Hiphil, Hophal, Hithpael; pf. 3fs (unless noted otherwise)

    + *pathaq* prefix vowel = Hiphil emphatic impv. ms
        Two root letters, *dagesh* in 2nd letter = I-*nun*   הַגִּידָה

    + *hireq/seghol* prefix vowel = Hiphil pf.
        Three root letters   הֶעֱמִידָה/הִקְטִילָה
        Two root letters = 3ms, III-*he*   הִגְלָה
        Two root letters, *taw* before ending = III-*he*   הִגְלְתָה
        Two root letters, *dagesh* in 2nd letter = I-*nun*   הִצִּילָה

    + *holem waw* prefix vowel = Hiphil pf., I-*yod*   הוֹשִׁיבָה

    + *tsere* prefix vowel = Hiphil pf.
        Two root letters, *hireq yod* in middle = hollow   הֵקִימָה
        Two root letters, 2nd doubled = geminate   הֵסַבָּה

    + *tsere yod* prefix vowel = Hiphil pf., I-*yod*   הֵיטִיבָה

    + *qibbuts* prefix vowel = Hophal   הָקְטְלָה
        Two root letters, *dagesh* in 2nd root letter = I-*nun*   הֻצְּלָה

---

1. This form overlaps with the Qal cohortative 1cp. One must rely on context to determine what the form is. (Does the context demand a third or first person subject?)
2. We refer here to the actual second root letter (the first one visible in the form); the actual first root letter (*nun*) has assimilated, hence the *dagesh*.

Chart 2

+ *qamets hatuph* prefix vowel = Hophal　　　　　　　　　　　　　　הָעֳמְדָה
　　Two root letters = pf. 3ms, III-*he*　　　　　　　　　　　　　　הָגְלָה
　　Two root letters, *taw* before ending = III-*he*　　　　　　　　הָגְלְתָה

+ *shureq* prefix vowel = Hophal
　　Two root letters, no doubling = I-*yod*, hollow　　　　הוּקְמָה/הוּשְׁבָה
　　Two root letters, 2nd doubled = geminate　　　　　　　　　　　הוּסַבָּה

הְת prefix = Hithpael pf.　　　　　　　　　　　　　　　　　　　　הִתְקַטְּלָה
　　Two root letters = pf. 3ms, III-*he*　　　　　　　　　　　　　　הִתְגַּלָּה
　　Two root letters, *taw* before ending = III-*he*　　　　　　　הִתְגַּלְּתָה

Mem prefix = part. fs

　　+ *shewa* prefix vowel + *pathaq* under 1st root= Piel III-*he*　　　　מְגַלָּה

　　+ *shewa* prefix vowel + *qibbuts* under 1st root= Pual　　　　　　מְמֻצָּאָה
　　　　Two root letters = III-*he*　　　　　　　　　　　　　　　　　　מְגֻלָּה

　　+ *shewa* prefix vowel + *hireq yod* under 1st root= Hiphil hollow　　מְקִימָה

　　+ *pathaq* prefix vowel = Hiphil III-*he*　　　　　　　　　　　　　מַגְלָה

　　+ *qamets hatuph* = Hophal III-*he*　　　　　　　　　　　　　　　מָגְלָה

מְת prefix = Hithpael III-*he*　　　　　　　　　　　　　　　　　　מִתְגַּלָּה

Chart 3

Verbal Form with
הֹ -, הֶ -, or הֵ - Ending

III-*He* Verb

The *holem/seghol/tsere-he* endings appear with III-*he* verbs in the *(a)* imperfect (see chart 10), *(b)* 2ms imperative (הֵ -), *(c)* infinitive absolute (הֹ - or הֵ -), and *(d)* masculine singular participle (הֶ -). This chart deals with *(b)*, *(c)*, and *(d)*.

1. הֹ - ending = infinitive absolute

   No prefix, two root letters:
   > *Qamets* under 1st root letter = Qal — בָּנֹה
   > *Pathaq* under 1st root letter (w/2nd letter doubled) = Piel — גַּלֹּה

   Nun prefix = Niphal — נִבְנֹה

2. הֶ - ending = masculine singular participle

   No prefix, two root letters = Qal act. part. — בֹּנֶה

   Nun prefix = Niphal — נִבְנֶה

   Mem prefix:
   > *Shewa* prefix vowel, *pathaq* under 1st root = Piel — מְגַלֶּה
   > *Shewa* prefix vowel, *qibbuts* under 1st root = Pual — מְגֻלֶּה
   > *Pathaq* prefix vowel = Hiphil — מַגְלֶה
   > *Qamets hatuph* prefix vowel = Hophal — מָגְלֶה
   > מִת- prefix = Hithpael — מִתְגַּלֶּה

3. הֵ - ending

   No prefix, two root letters:
   > *Shewa* under 1st root letter = Qal impv. 2ms — בְּנֵה
   > *Pathaq* under 1st root letter = Piel impv. 2ms/inf. abs. — גַּלֵּה

   He prefix:
   > *Hireq* prefix vowel = Niphal impv. 2ms/inf. abs. — הִבָּנֵה
   > *Pathaq* prefix vowel = Hiphil impv. 2ms/inf. abs. — הַגְלֵה
   > הִת- prefix = Hithpael impv. 2ms — הִתְגַּלֵּה

Chart 4
Verbal Form with נָה- Ending

Second Person Feminine Plural Imperative

The *nun-qamets-he* ending appears with *(a)* the 2fp form of the imperative, and *(b)* 3fp/2fp forms of the imperfect. This chart deals with *(a)*. See chart 10 for *(b)*.

1. *NO PREFIX* = Qal or Piel, determined by the vowel under the first root letter

   Qamets = Piel II-guttural   בָּרֵכְנָה

   Pathaq
       Three root letters = Piel[1]   קַטֵּלְנָה
       Two root letters:
           No doubling = Qal I-*nun*, I-*yod,* or geminate   תַּמְנָה/רַשְׁנָה/סַעֶנָה
           Doubling of 2nd root letter = Piel III-*he*   גַּלֶּינָה

   Tsere = Qal I-*yod*[2]   שֵׁבְנָה

   Holem = Qal, hollow or geminate   סֹבְנָה/קֹמְנָה

   Shewa = Qal   קְטֹלְנָה
       Two root letters = III-*he*   בְּנֶינָה

2. *PREFIX* He = Niphal, Hiphil, or Hithpael[3]

   + *pathaq* prefix vowel = Hiphil   הַקְטֵלְנָה
       Two root letters = III-*he*   הַגְלֶינָה
       Two root letters, *dagesh* in 2nd letter = I-*nun*   הַצֵּלְנָה

   + *qamets* prefix vowel = Hiphil, hollow   הָקֵמְנָה

   + *hireq* prefix vowel = Niphal
       + *dagesh* and *qamets* with 1st root letter   הִקָּטֵלְנָה[4]
           + *dagesh* and *qamets* with two root letters = III-*he*   הִבָּנֶינָה
       + *dagesh* and *pathaq* with 1st root letter = geminate   הִסַּבֶּינָה

---

1. The characteristic doubling of the Piel is sometimes omitted; cf. II-guttural verbs.
2. The verb הָלַךְ also displays this pattern: לֵכְנָה; so does the I-*nun* verb נָתַן: תֵּנָּה.
3. We do not include prefixes of the imperfect here; see the imperfect chart.
4. If a doubled *waw* is in the first root letter position, the verb is I-*yod*: הִוָּשֵׁבְנָה.

242

Chart 4

+ *holem* prefix vowel = Hiphil I-*yod*   הוֹשֵׁבְנָה

+ *tsere* prefix vowel = Niphal   הֵעָזַבְנָה

+ *tsere yod* prefix vowel = Hiphil I-*yod*   הֵיטֵבְנָה

+ *shewa* = Hiphil geminate   הְסִבֶּינָה

הְת prefix = Hithpael   הִתְקַטֵּלְנָה
  Two root letters = III-*he*   הִתְגַּלֵּינָה

Chart 5

Verbal Form with וּ- Ending

Third Person Common Plural Perfect or
Second Person Masculine Imperative

The *shureq* ending appears with *(a)* the 3cp form of the perfect, *(b)* the 2mp form of the imperative, and *(c)* 3mp and 2mp forms of the imperfect. This chart deals with *(a)* and *(b)*; see chart 10 for *(c)*.

1. *NO PREFIX* = Qal, Piel, or Pual, determined by the vowel under the first root letter

   Qamets = Qal (pf. 3cp) or Piel (impv. 2mp)[1]   בָּרְכוּ/קָטְלוּ
       Two root letters, accent on ending = Qal pf. 3cp, III-*he*   בָּנוּ

       Two root letters, accent on 1st syllable = Qal pf. 3cp, hollow   קָמוּ

   Pathaq
       Three root letters = Piel impv. 2mp[2]   קַטְּלוּ
       Two root letters, 2nd doubled:
           Accent on 1st syllable = Qal pf. 3cp/impv. 2mp, geminate   תַּמּוּ
           Accent on ending = Piel impv. 2mp, III-*he*   גַּלּוּ

   Hireq
       Doubled 2nd root letter = Piel pf. 3cp, II-guttural   קִטְּלוּ
       Two root letters, 2nd doubled = Piel pf. 3cp, III-*he*   גִּלּוּ
       No doubling = Qal impv. 2mp[3]   קִטְלוּ

   Tsere = Piel pf. 3cp   בֵּרְכוּ

   Hireq yod = Qal impv. 2mp, hollow   שִׂימוּ

   Qibbuts = Pual pf. 3cp   קֻטְּלוּ
       Two root letters, 2nd doubled = III-*he*   גֻּלּוּ

---

1. The Piel imperative will have a *qamets* only if the verb is II-guttural/*resh*.
2. The characteristic doubling of the Piel is sometimes omitted, but in a form with three root letters visible, the *pathaq* under the first root letter distinguishes the form as Piel imperative, *unless* the verb is II-guttural, in which case it may be Qal; cf. בַּחֲרוּ (Qal) with נַחֲמוּ (Piel).
3. The *dagesh* is sometimes omitted in the Piel perfect, making the form indistinguishable from a Qal imperative 2mp. At this point one must base a decision on semantic and contextual factors.

244

Chart 5

Holem
    Three root letters = Pual pf. 3cp, II-guttural   בֹּרְכוּ
    Two root letters, 2nd doubled = Qal impv. 2mp, geminate   סֹבּוּ

Shureq = Qal impv. 2mp, hollow   קוּמוּ

Holem waw = Qal impv. 2mp, hollow   בֹּאוּ

Shewa = Qal impv. 2mp from one of three roots:[4]
    III-*he*   בְּנוּ
    I-*nun*   סְעוּ
    I-*yod*   שְׁבוּ

2. *PREFIX*[5]

Nun prefix = Niphal
    Shewa in theme vowel slot = pf. 3cp   נִקְטְלוּ
        Two root letters = III-*he*   נִבְנוּ
        Two root letters, *dagesh* in 2nd[6] = I-*nun*   נִצְּלוּ
        Two root letters, *holem waw* prefix vowel = I-*yod*   נוֹשְׁבוּ
    Two root letters, *holem waw* theme vowel = pf. 3cp, hollow   נָקוֹמוּ
    Two root letters, 2nd doubled = pf. 3cp, geminate   נָסַבּוּ

He prefix = Niphal, Hiphil, Hophal, Hithpael

    + *pathaq* prefix vowel = Hiphil impv. 2mp   הַקְטִילוּ
        Two root letters = III-*he*   הַגְלוּ
        Two root letters, *dagesh* in 2nd letter = I-*nun*   הַצִּילוּ

    + *qamets* = Hiphil
        Two root letters, *hireq yod* in middle = impv. 2mp, hollow   הָקִימוּ
        Two root letters, 2nd doubled = impv. 2mp, geminate   הָסֵבּוּ

    + *hireq*
        Dagesh and *qamets* with 1st root letter = Niphal impv. 2mp   הִקָּטְלוּ[7]
        Two root letters = III-*he*   הִבָּנוּ
        Two root letters, 2nd doubled = geminate   הִסַּבּוּ
        Dagesh and *holem waw* with 1st root letter = Niphal impv. 2mp, hollow   הִקּוֹמוּ
        Others with three root letters = Hiphil pf. 3cp[8]   הִקְטִילוּ

---

4. The verb הָלַךְ follows this pattern in the imperative: לְכוּ. See PVP, 213 (18.11); Ful., 241 (35.5).
5. We do not include prefixes of the imperfect here; see the imperfect chart for 3mp and 2mp imperfect forms.
6. We refer here to the actual second root letter (the first one visible in the form); the actual first root letter (*nun*) has assimilated, hence the *dagesh*.
7. If a doubled *waw* is in the first root letter position, the verb is I-*yod*: הִוָּשְׁבוּ.
8. With I-guttural verbs the prefix vowel of the Hiphil perfect 3cp will be *seghol*: הֶעֱמִידוּ.

Chart 5

Two root letters = III-*he*	הִגְלוּ
Two root letters, *dagesh* in 2nd letter = I-*nun*	הִצִּילוּ
+ *holem* prefix vowel = Hiphil pf. 3cp/impv. 2mp, I-*yod*	הוֹשִׁיבוּ
+ *tsere* prefix vowel	
Three root letters, *qamets* under 1st = Niphal impv. 2mp	הֵעָזְבוּ
Two root letters, *hireq yod* in middle = Hiphil pf. 3cp, hollow	הֵקִימוּ
Two root letters, 2nd doubled = Hiphil pf. 3cp, geminate	הֵסַבּוּ
+ *tsere yod* prefix vow = Hiphil pf. 3cp/impv. 2mp, I-*yod*	הֵיטִיבוּ
+ *qibbuts* prefix vowel = Hophal pf. 3cp	הֻקְטְלוּ
Two root letters, *dagesh* in 2nd root letter = I-*nun*	הֻצְּלוּ
+ *qamets hatuph* prefix vowel = Hophal pf. 3cp	הָקְטְלוּ
Two root letters = III-*he*	הָגְלוּ
+ *shureq* prefix vowel = Hophal	
Two root letters, no doubling = I-*yod* or hollow	הוּקְמוּ/הוּשְׁבוּ
Two root letters, 2nd doubled = geminate	הוּסַבּוּ
הִת prefix = Hithpael pf. 3cp/impv. 2mp	הִתְקַטְּלוּ
Two root letters = III-*he* (pf. 3cp/impv. 2mp)	הִתְגַּלּוּ

Chart 6
Verbal Form with יִ - Ending

Second Person Feminine
Singular Imperative

The *hireq yod* ending appears with (*a*) the 2fs form of the imperative and (*b*) the 2fs form of the imperfect. This chart deals with (*a*); see chart 10 for (*b*). This ending can also be a pronominal suffix on verb forms; such forms are not included in this chart.

1. *NO PREFIX* = Qal or Piel, determined by the vowel under the first root letter

   Qamets = Piel II-guttural   בָּרְכִי

   Pathaq
       Three root letters = Piel[1]   קַטְּלִי
       Two root letters, 2nd doubled:
           Accent on 1st syllable = Qal geminate   תַּמִּי
           Accent on ending = Piel III-*he*   גַּלִּי

   Hireq = Qal   קִטְלִי

   Hireq yod = Qal hollow   שִׂימִי

   Holem = Qal geminate   סֹבִּי

   Shureq = Qal hollow   קוּמִי

   Holem waw = Qal hollow   בּוֹאִי

   Shewa = Qal from one of three roots:[2]
       III-*he*   בְּנִי
       I-*nun*   סְעִי
       I-*yod*   שְׁבִי

---

1. The characteristic doubling of the Piel is sometimes omitted, but in a form with three root letters visible, the *pathaq* under the first root letter distinguishes the form as Piel imperative, *unless* the verb is II-guttural, in which case it may be Qal; cf. בַּחֲרִי (Qal) with נַחֲמִי (Piel).
2. The verb הָלַךְ follows the pattern of I-*yod*: לְכִי.

Chart 6

2. *PREFIX*[3]

He prefix = Niphal, Hiphil, Hithpael

    + *pathaq* prefix vowel = Hiphil   הַקְטִילִי
        Two root letters = III-*he*   הַגְלִי
        Two root letters, *dagesh* in 2nd letter = I-*nun*   הַצִּילִי

    + *qamets* = Hiphil
        Two root letters, *hireq yod* in middle = hollow   הָקִימִי
        Two root letters, 2nd doubled = geminate   הָסֵבִּי

    + *hireq* = Niphal
        + *dagesh* and *qamets* with 1st of three root letters   הִקָּטְלִי[4]
        Two root letters = III-*he*   הִבָּנִי
        + *dagesh* and *holem waw* with 1st root letter = hollow   הִקּוֹמִי
        + *dagesh* and *pathaq* with 1st root letter = geminate   הִסַּבִּי

    + *holem* prefix vowel = Hiphil I-*yod*   הוֹשִׁיבִי

    + *tsere* prefix vowel = Niphal   הֵעָזְבִי

    + *tsere yod* prefix vowel = Hiphil I-*yod*   הֵיטִיבִי

הִת prefix = Hithpael   הִתְקַטְּלִי
    Two root letters = III-*he*   הִתְגַּלִי

---

3. We do not include prefixes of the imperfect here; see the imperfect chart for 2fs imperfect forms.

4. If a doubled *waw* is in the first root letter position, the verb is I-*yod*: הוּשֵׁבִי.

Chart 7

Verbal Form with
◌ֶת - or ◌ַת - Ending

Feminine Singular Participle or
Infinitive Construct

The *seghol/pathaq-taw* endings occur primarily with feminine singular nouns. With verbal forms they occur with *(a)* feminine singular participles and *(b)* certain irregular infinitive construct forms.

1. *NO PREFIX* = Qal
   Three root letters = act. part. fs[1]   שֹׁלַחַת/קֹטֶלֶת
   Two root letters (1st letter omitted) = inf. const., I-*nun* or I-*yod*[2]   שֶׁבֶת/סַעַת

2. *NUN PREFIX* = Niphal participle   נִשְׁלַחַת/נֶעֱזֶבֶת
   Two root letters, *dagesh* in 2nd = I-*nun*   נִצֶּלֶת
   Holem waw prefix vowel = I-*yod*   נוֹשֶׁבֶת

3. *MEM PREFIX* = feminine singular participle[3]

   Shewa prefix vowel + *pathaq/qamets* = Piel   מְבָרֶכֶת/מְקַטֶּלֶת
   Shewa prefix vowel + *qibbuts/holem* = Pual   מְבֹרֶכֶת/מְקֻטֶּלֶת

   Pathaq prefix vowel = Hiphil   מַקְטֶלֶת
       Two root letters, *dagesh* in 2nd = I-*nun*   מַצֶּלֶת

   Holem waw prefix vowel = Hiphil I-*yod*   מוֹשֶׁבֶת

   Qibbuts/qamets hatuph prefix vowel = Hophal   מָקְטֶלֶת/מֻקְטֶלֶת
       Two root letters, *dagesh* in 2nd = I-*nun*   מֻצֶּלֶת

   Shureq prefix vowel = Hophal I-*yod*/hollow/geminate   מוּסַבֶּת/מוּקֶמֶת/מוּשֶׁבֶת

   מִת prefix = Hithpael   מִתְקַטֶּלֶת

---

1. The Qal active participle feminine singular of III-*aleph* verbs ends in *taw* preceded by *tsere* and quiescent *aleph*: מֹצֵאת.
2. The verb הָלַךְ follows the I-*yod* pattern in the infinitive construct: לֶכֶת.
3. The active participle/passive participle feminine singular of III-*aleph* verbs ends in *taw* preceded by *tsere* and quiescent *aleph*. See, for example, the Piel מְמַצֵּאת.

Chart 8

Verbal Form with
‎‑ ִים or ‑ וֹת Ending

Plural Participle or
III-*He* Infinitive Construct

The *hireq yod-mem* and *holem waw-taw* endings characteristically appear with plural nouns and adjectives. With verbal forms, they appear on participles and infinitives construct:

- ‎ ִים‑ occurs with masculine plural participles
- ‎ וֹת‑ occurs with *(a)* feminine plural participles and *(b)* the III-*he* infinitive construct

1. *NO PREFIX* = Qal or Piel, determined by the vowel with the first letter:

   Holem = Qal act. part.   קֹטְלִים/קֹטְלוֹת
       Two root letters = III-*he*   בֹּנִים/בֹּנוֹת

   Qamets = Qal act. part., hollow   קָמִים/קָמוֹת

   Shewa = Qal pass. part. or inf. const., III-*he*
       Three root letters = pass. part.   קְטוּלִים/קְטוּלוֹת
       Two root letters, *yod* before ending = pass. part.[1]   בְּנוּיִים/בְּנוּיוֹת
       Two root letters, ‎ וֹת‑ ending = inf. const.   בְּנוֹת

   Pathaq, ‎ וֹת‑ ending = Piel inf. const., III-*he*   גַּלּוֹת

2. NUN *PREFIX* = Niphal participle   נִקְטָלִים/נִקְטָלוֹת
   Two root letters = III-*he*   נִבְנִים/נִבְנוֹת
   Two root letters, *dagesh* in 2nd = I-*nun*   נִצָּלִים/נִצָּלוֹת
   Holem waw prefix vowel = I-*yod*   נוֹשָׁבִים/נוֹשָׁבוֹת
3. HE *PREFIX* = Niphal, Hiphil, or Hithpael infinitive construct, III-*he*
   Hireq prefix vowel = Niphal   הִבָּנוֹת
   Pathaq prefix vowel = Hiphil   הַגְלוֹת
   ‎ הִת‑ prefix = Hithpael   הִתְגַּלּוֹת

---

1. Of course, this refers to cases where the *yod* is in the third root letter slot after the characteristic *shureq* theme vowel of the passive participle. If the second root letter is *yod* and there is no *shureq* before it, then the form is a Qal infinitive construct of a III-*he* verb: הֱיוֹת.

Chart 8

4. MEM *PREFIX* = participle
   Shewa prefix vowel + *pathaq/qamets* = Piel   מְבָרְכִים/מְקַטְּלִים
   Shewa prefix vowel + *qibbuts/holem* = Pual   מְבֹרְכִים/מְקֻטָּלִים
   Shewa prefix vowel + *hireq yod* = Hiphil hollow   מְקִימִים

   Pathaq prefix vowel = Hiphil   מַקְטִילִים
      Two root letters, *dagesh* in 2nd = I-*nun*   מַצִּילִים

   Holem waw prefix vowel = Hiphil I-*yod*   מוֹשִׁיבִים

   Qibbuts/qamets hatuph prefix vowel = Hophal   מְקֻטָּלִים/מְקָטְלִים
      Two root letters, *dagesh* in 2nd = I-*nun*   מֻצָּלִים

   Shureq prefix vowel = Hophal I-*yod*/hollow/geminate   מוּסָבִים/מוּקָמִים/מוּשָׁבִים

   מִת prefix = Hithpael   מִתְקַטְּלִים

Chart 9

Verbal Form with No Ending

Verbal forms with no ending include:

a. the 3ms form of the perfect,
b. the 2ms form of the imperative,
c. most forms of the infinitive construct,
d. the infinitive absolute,
e. the masculine singular form of the participle, and
f. various forms (3ms, 3fs, 2ms, 1cs, 1cp) of the imperfect.

This chart deals with *(a–e)*. See chart 10 for *(f)*. When a verb form has no ending, first determine if the form has a prefix (excluding imperfect forms).

1. *NO PREFIX* = Qal, Piel, or Pual

   Two root letters = Qal

Vowel	Parsing	Example
Pathaq	impv. ms, I-*nun*[1]	סַע
	impv. ms, I-*yod* or geminate	רֵשׁ
	pf./act. part./impv., geminate	תַּם
Qamets	pf./act. part., hollow	קָם
Tsere	impv. ms,[2] I-*yod*	שֵׁב
Hireq yod	impv./inf. const., hollow *i*-class	שִׂים
Holem	impv./inf. const., geminate	סֹב
Holem waw	impv./inf. const., hollow *o*-class	בּוֹא[3]
	inf. abs., hollow	קוֹם
Shureq	impv./inf. const., hollow *u*-class	קוּם

   Three root letters = Qal, Piel, or Pual

First Vowel	Parsing	Example
Qamets		
+ *qamets*	Qal pf., III-*aleph*	מָצָא
+ *pathaq*	Qal pf.	קָטַל

---

1. The verb לָקַח also follows this pattern: קַח.
2. The verbs הָלַךְ and נָתַן also follow this pattern in the imperative (e.g., תֵּן; לֵךְ).
3. If the form has a prepositional prefix, it is infinitive construct.

Chart 9

+ *holem waw*	Qal inf. abs.	קָטוֹל
+ *shureq*	Qal pass. part.	קָטוּל
+ *tsere*	Qal pf./part.	יָרֵא/כָּבֵד
	Piel impv./inf. const., II-guttural	בָּרֵךְ
Pathaq	Piel impv./inf. const./inf. abs., doubling[4]	קַטֵּל
Tsere	Piel pf.	בֵּרֵךְ
Hireq	Piel pf., doubling[5]	קִטֵּל
Holem waw or *holem*	Qal act. part.	קֹטֵל/קוֹטֵל
	Pual pf., II-guttural[6]	בֹּרַךְ
Qibbuts	Pual pf., with or w/o doubling	נֻחַם/קֻטַּל
Qamets hatuph	Qal impv./inf. const., pronominal suffix	קָטְלִי/שָׁמְרֵם
Shewa	Qal impv./inf. const.[7]	קְטֹל

2. *PREFIX* (other than that of the imperfect) = Niphal, Hiphil, Hophal, or Hithpael

Nun prefix = Niphal
   Three root letters:
   + *pathaq* theme vowel = pf.   נִקְטַל
   + *qamets* theme vowel = part.[8]   נִקְטָל
   + *holem waw* theme vowel = inf. abs.   נִקְטוֹל
   Two root letters:
   + *dagesh* in 2nd, *pathaq* theme vowel = pf., I-*nun*   נִצַּל
   + *dagesh* in 2nd, *qamets* theme vowel = part., I-*nun*   נִצָּל
   + *dagesh* in 2nd, *holem waw* theme vowel = inf. abs., I-*nun*   נִצּוֹל
   + *holem waw* prefix vowel, *pathaq* theme vowel = pf., I-*yod*   נוֹשַׁב
   + *holem waw* prefix vowel, *qamets* theme vowel = part., I-*yod*   נוֹשָׁב
   + *qamets* prefix vowel + *holem waw* = pf./part., hollow   נָקוֹם
   + *qamets* prefix vowel + *pathaq* = pf., geminate   נָסַב
   + *holem waw* theme vowel = inf. abs., hollow   נָסוֹג

He prefix

   Hireq prefix vowel, three root letters:
      + *dagesh*/*qamets* w/1st root letter, *tsere* theme vowel = Niphal impv./inf. const.[9]   הִקָּטֵל
      + *dagesh*/*qamets* w/1st root letter, *holem waw* theme vowel = Niphal inf. abs.   הִקָּטוֹל
      + *shewa* = Hiphil pf. 3ms   הִקְטִיל

---

4. Doubling will not be present if the verb is II-guttural (e.g., נִחַם).
5. Doubling will not be present if the verb is II-guttural (e.g., נִחַם).
6. The Pual perfect can be distinguished from the Qal active participle by its *pathaq* theme vowel. The Qal active participle has a *tsere* theme vowel in the masculine singular.
7. If the form has a prepositional prefix, it is infinitive construct. In some irregular verbs the imperative masculine singular and infinitive construct are distinguished by the theme vowel: the imperative has *pathaq* or *qamets*, the infinitive construct has *holem*. This is true with I-guttural (in some cases), II-guttural, III-guttural, and III-*aleph* verbs.
8. In III-*aleph* verbs the perfect 3ms and participle masculine singular overlap: נִמְצָא.
9. If the form has a prepositional prefix it is infinitive construct. In III-*aleph*, I-*nun*, and I-*yod* verbs the Niphal infinitive absolute overlaps in form with the imperative 2ms and the infinitive construct; see, e.g., הִנָּשֵׁב/הִנָּצֵל/הִמָּצֵא. Note that a *waw* appears in the first root position with I-*yod* verbs.

Chart 9

Hireq prefix vowel, two root letters:

    + *dagesh* in 1st root letter, *hireq yod* theme vowel = Hiphil pf., I-*nun*   הִצִּיל

    + *dagesh* in 1st root letter = Niphal

        + *pathaq* theme vowel = impv., geminate   הִסַּב

        + *tsere* theme vowel = inf. const., geminate   הִסֵּב

        + *holem* theme vowel = inf. abs., geminate   הִסֹּב

        + *holem waw* theme vowel = inf. const./inf. abs./impv., hollow   הִקּוֹם

Seghol prefix vowel = Hiphil pf., I-guttural   הֶעֱמִיד

Tsere prefix vowel

    Three root letters = Niphal

    + *tsere* theme vowel = impv./inf. const., I-guttural   הֵעָזֵב

    + *holem waw* theme vowel = inf. abs., I-guttural   הֵעָזוֹב

    Two root letters = Hiphil

    + *tsere/pathaq* theme vowel = pf., geminate   הֵמַר/הֵסֵב

    + *hireq yod* theme vowel = pf., hollow   הֵקִים

Tsere yod prefix vowel = Hiphil

    + *tsere* theme vowel = inf. abs./impv. 2ms, I-*yod*   הֵיטֵב

    + *hireq yod* theme vowel = inf. const./pf. 3ms, I-*yod*   הֵיטִיב

Pathaq prefix vowel = Hiphil

    Three root letters

    + *tsere* theme vowel = impv./inf. abs.[10]   הַקְטֵל

    + *hireq yod* theme vowel = inf. const.   הַקְטִיל

    Two root letters:

    + *dagesh* in 2nd root letter, *tsere* theme vowel = impv./inf. abs., I-*nun*   הַצֵּל

    + *dagesh* in 2nd root letter, *hireq yod* theme vowel = inf. const., I-*nun*   הַצִּיל

Qamets prefix vowel = Hiphil

    + *tsere* theme vowel = impv./inf. abs., hollow   הָקֵם

       or impv./inf. abs./inf. const., geminate   הָסֵב[11]

    + *hireq yod* theme vowel = inf. const., hollow   הָקִים

Qibbuts prefix vowel = Hophal

    Three root letters   הֻקְטַל

    Two root letters = I-*nun*   הֻצַּל

Qamets hatuph prefix vowel, three root letters = Hophal pf.   הָקְטַל

Holem waw prefix vowel, two root letters = Hiphil

    + *hireq yod* theme vowel = pf./inf. const., I-*yod*   הוֹשִׁיב

    + *tsere* theme vowel = impv./inf. abs., I-*yod*   הוֹשֵׁב

---

10. In III-guttural verbs, the 2ms imperative will have a *pathaq* theme vowel: הַשְׁלַח.

11. If the form has a prepositional prefix, it is infinitive construct.

Chart 9

Shureq theme vowel, two root letters = Hophal pf., I-*yod*/hollow/geminate   הוּסַב/הוּקַם/הוּשַׁב

הִת- prefix = Hithpael pf./impv./inf. const./inf. abs.   הִתְקַטֵּל

Mem prefix = masculine singular participle

    + *shewa* prefix vowel + *pathaq/qamets* = Piel   מְבָרֵךְ/מְקַטֵּל
    + *shewa* prefix vowel + *qibbuts/holem* = Pual   מְבֹרָךְ/מְקֻטָּל

    + *pathaq* prefix vowel = Hiphil   מַקְטִיל
       Two root letters, *dagesh* in 2nd = I-*nun*   מַצִּיל

    + *tsere* prefix vowel = Hiphil
       + *hireq yod* theme vowel = hollow   מֵקִים
       + *tsere* theme vowel = geminate   מֵסֵב

    + *tsere yod* prefix vowel = Hiphil I-*yod*   מֵיטִיב

    + *holem waw* prefix vowel = Hiphil I-*yod*   מוֹשִׁיב

    + *qibbuts/qamets hatuph* prefix vowel = Hophal   מָקְטָל/מֻקְטָל
       Two root letters, *dagesh* in 2nd = I-*nun*   מֻצָּל

    + *shureq* prefix vowel = Hophal I-*yod*/hollow/geminate   מוּסָב/מוּקָם/מוּשָׁב

מִת prefix = Hithpael   מִתְקַטֵּל

Chart 10

Verbal Form with Prefix of the Imperfect

Includes Wayyiqtol Forms, Jussives, and Cohortatives

The forms of the imperfect, jussive, wayyiqtol, and cohortative can be summarized as follows:

- Imperfects usually equal jussive forms, while wayyiqtol has special form of *waw* prefixed
- Wayyiqtols = jussive with a special form of *waw* prefixed: imperfect = יִבְנֶה, jussive = יִבֶן, wayyiqtol = וַיִּבֶן
- Cohortative = first person imperfect + הָ - ending, except in III-*he* verbs where forms are the same (הָ - ending)
- Jussive differs from the imperfect in III-*he* uninflected forms (*he* apocopates)
- Jussive also differs in hollow and geminate verbs, as does wayyiqtol: imperfect = יָקוּם, jussive = יָקֹם, wayyiqtol = וַיָּקָם

These forms have one of the following prefixes: *yod, taw, aleph, nun.* Use this chart to determine person, gender, and number.

Ø-----יְ	3ms
Ø-----תְ	3fs/2ms
יְ-----תְ	2fs
Ø-----אְ	1cs
וְ-----יְ	3mp
תְ----נָה	3fp/2fp
וְ-----תְ	2mp
Ø-----נְ	1cp

Two Root Letters

Prefix Vowel	Parsing	Example
Pathaq		
+ *shewa/pathaq*	Hiphil III-*he*	יַעַל/יַגְלֶה/juss.[1]
+ doubled letter	Hiphil I-*nun*	יַצִּיל

---

1. If the verb is both I-guttural and III-*he,* this pattern can be Qal (*a* before the guttural letter) or Hiphil. See, for example, יַעַל/יַעֲלֶה. In such cases one must rely on semantics and contextual factors to determine the stem.

Chart 10

Qamets

+ *tsere*	Hiphil geminate	יָסֵב[2]
	Hiphil hollow juss./wayyiqtol)[3]	וַיָּבֵא/יָקֵם
+ *seghol*	Hiphil geminate/hollow wayyiqtol	וַיָּסֶב/וַיָּקֶם[4]
	Qal/Hiphil hollow *i*-class wayyiqtol	וַיָּבֶן/וַיָּשֶׂם
+ *hireq yod*[5]	Hiphil hollow *u/o*-class	יָבִיא/יָקִים
	Qal/Hiphil hollow *i*-class	יָשִׂים
+ *qamets hatuph*	Qal hollow/geminate wayyiqtol	וַיָּסָב/וַיָּקָם[6]
+ *holem*	Qal geminate	יָסֹב[7]
	Qal hollow juss./impf./wayyiqtol	יָבֹאוּ/יָקֹם
+ *holem waw*	Qal hollow *o*-class	יָבוֹא
+ *shureq*	Qal hollow *u*-class	יָקוּם

Seghol (see *Hireq*)

Tsere

+ *tsere/seghol/shewa*	Qal I-*yod*	יֵשֵׁב[8]
+ *pathaq*[9]	Qal 3/2fp, I-*yod*	תֵּשַׁבְנָה
	Qal geminate	יֵתַם
+ *holem waw*	Niphal hollow	יֵעוֹר

Hireq/seghol

+ doubled letter[10]		
+ *holem*	Qal I-*nun*/geminate	יִסֹּב/יִפֹּל
+ *holem waw*	Niphal hollow	יִקּוֹם
+ *pathaq*	Qal I-*nun*/Niphal geminate	יִסַּב/יִסַּע[11]
+ *qamets*	Niphal III-*he*	יִבָּנֶה/juss. יִבָּן
+ *shewa*	Qal I-*nun* (inflected form)	יִפְּלוּ
+ *tsere/seghol*	Qal I-*nun* (נתן)	וַתִּתֵּן/יִתֵּן

---

2. In uninflected forms the geminate Hiphil imperfect overlaps in form with the hollow Hiphil jussive. However, in inflected forms the geminate forms have doubling; cf. יָסֵבּוּ.
3. If the verb is a hollow *i*-class (like שִׂים), then Qal is also an option.
4. Inflected forms of the geminate have doubling; cf. וַיָּסֵבּוּ.
5. The vowel can be defectively written as *hireq*.
6. In inflected forms the geminate forms have doubling; cf. וַיָּסֵבּוּ.
7. The hollow *u*-class jussive (יָקֹם) overlaps with the geminate imperfect in uninflected forms, but in inflected forms the geminate verbs have doubling; cf. יָסֹבּוּ.
8. Recall that the verb הָלַךְ resembles a I-*yod* verb in the imperfect: יֵלֵךְ. See PVP, 183–84 (16.16–17); Ful., 241 (35.5). Occasionally III-*he* verbs will take a *tsere* prefix vowel in the wayyiqtol pattern; cf. וַיֵּשְׁתְּ < שָׁתָה.
9. I-*yod/waw* has a *pathaq* after *tsere* in the feminine plural forms (e.g., תֵּשַׁבְנָה), but this can be easily distinguished from geminate feminine plural forms, which have a *shewa* prefix vowel, a doubled geminate letter, and a helping vowel before the suffix (e.g., תִּתַּמֶּינָה).
10. In uninflected forms the geminate Qal (יִסֹּב) and geminate Niphal (יִסַּב) can overlap with I-*nun* Qals (e.g., יִסַּע/יִפֹּל). Inflected geminate Niphal forms can be distinguished by the doubling of the geminate letter before the ending (e.g., יִסַּבּוּ), but geminate Qal forms (e.g., יִסֹּבּוּ) look like I-*nun* Qal forms (e.g., יִפְּלוּ).
11. Recall that the verb לָקַח resembles a I-*nun* verb in the Qal imperfect: יִקַּח. See PVP, 185 (16.19); Ful., 233 (34.5).

Chart 10

+ *taw* prefix	Hithpael III-*he*	יִתְגַּל/juss. יִתְגַּלֶּה
+ *shewa*	Qal III-*he*[12]	יִבְנֶה
+ *seghol*	Qal juss./wayyiqtol, III-*he*	וַיִּבֶן/יִגֶל
	Hiphil juss., III-*he*	יֶגֶל[13]
Hireq yod	Qal I-*yod*[14]	יִירַשׁ
Tsere yod	Hiphil I-*yod*	יֵיטִיב
Qamets hatuph	Hophal III-*he*	יָגְלֶה
Holem	Qal 1cs, I-*aleph*	אֹכַל
Holem waw	Hiphil I-*yod*	יוֹשִׁיב
Qibbuts	Hophal I-*nun*	יֻצַּל
Shureq	Hophal I-*yod*	יוּשַׁב
	Hophal hollow	יוּקַם
	Hophal geminate	יוּסַב[15]
Shewa		
+ *pathaq*	Piel III-*he*	יְגַל/juss. יְגַלֶּה
	Qal 3/2fp, geminate	תְּתַמֶּינָה
+ *qibbuts*	Pual III-*he*	יְגֻלֶּה
	Qal 3/2fp, geminate	תְּסֻבֶּינָה
	Qal hollow (in forms w/paragogic *nun*)	יְמֻתוּן
+ *holem waw*	Qal 3/2fp, hollow *o*-class	תְּבוֹאנָה
+ *hireq yod/hireq*[16]	Qal 3/2fp, hollow *i*-class	תְּשִׂימֶינָה
	Hiphil 3/2fp, hollow *u/o*-class	תְּקִימֶינָה
+ *shureq*	Qal 3/2fp, hollow *u*-class	תְּקוּמֶינָה

Three Root Letters

Prefix Vowel	**Parsing**	**Example**
Pathaq		
+ *hireq yod/tsere*	Hiphil	תַּקְטֵלְנָה/יַקְטִיל
+ *holem/shewa*	Qal I-*guttural*	יַעַמְדוּ/יַעֲמֹד

---

12. Sometimes a I-*nun* verb will omit the *dagesh* (in consonants accompanied by vocal *shewa*) and overlap in form with III-*he* verbs: וַיִּשָּׂאוּ.
13. Note that the Qal form has a *hireq* prefix vowel, while the Hiphil has *seghol*.
14. Occasionally a I-*yod* verb (cf. יִיצֶר) will be written defectively, e.g., וַיִּצֶר.
15. The inflected geminate forms have a doubled geminate letter (cf. יוּסַּבּוּ) and can be distinguished from I-*yod* and hollow forms.
16. In addition to 3/2fp forms, as illustrated in the chart, this pattern will also occur with suffixed forms of hollow verbs in both the Qal and Hiphil, e.g., יְשִׂמֵנִי (Qal, 2 Sam. 15:4)/וַיְטִלֵהוּ (Hiphil, Jonah 1:15).

Chart 10

Seghol (*see* Hireq)

Tsere	Niphal I-guttural	יֵעָזֵב
Hireq/seghol		
+ *taw* prefix	Hithpael	יִתְקַטֵּל
+ *qamets* (with doubled letter)	Niphal	יִקָּטֵל
+ *shewa*	Qal	יֶחֱזַק/יִקְטֹל
Qamets hatuph	Hophal	יָקְטַל
Holem	Qal I-*aleph*	יֹאכַל
Qibbuts	Hophal	יֻקְטַל
Shewa		
+ *pathaq/qamets*	Piel	יְבָרֵךְ/יְקַטֵּל
+ *qibbuts/holem*	Pual	יְבֹרַךְ/יְקֻטַּל

Chart 11

Characteristic Stems and Roots of Imperfect Verbal Forms

This supplement to chart 10 allows one to quickly identify the stem and root of most imperfect (or jussive, cohortative, and wayyiqtol) verbal forms based on the prefix vowel (and theme vowel). For a more detailed analysis of options, which includes less common forms, see chart 10.

- *A-class prefix vowel (pathaq or qamets)* = Qal or Hiphil

  If the prefix vowel is an *a*-class vowel, the verb is either Qal or Hiphil, depending on the theme vowel (the vowel that occurs before the final root letter). If the prefix vowel is *qamets* then the verb is hollow or geminate. (See chart 10 for details; for other roots see chart 10.)

  $$a + i = \text{Hiphil}$$

  $$a + \text{non-}i = \text{Qal}$$

  If the theme vowel is an *i*-class *(hireq, seghol, tsere,* or *hireq yod),* then the verb is Hiphil. (Hollow *i*-class is an exception. For example, יָשִׂים can be either Qal or Hiphil.)

- *Holem waw* or *tsere yod* prefix vowel = I-*yod* Hiphil: יֵיטִיב, יוֹשִׁיב.

- *I-class prefix vowel (hireq, seghol, tsere, hireq yod)*

  If the prefix vowel is an *i*-class vowel, the verb is either Qal, Niphal, or Hithpael depending on what follows:

  i + *dagesh* (w/actual 1st root letter) + *a*-class vowel (or *holem waw*) = Niphal[1]
  i + *taw* (e.g., -יִתְ) = Hithpael (unless *taw* is the first root letter)
  i + any other pattern = Qal

  > Prefix vowel *hireq* with only two root letters visible = III-*he* or I-*nun* (with *dagesh* in following letter)
  > Prefix vowel *tsere* or *hireq yod* = I-*yod*

- *Qibbuts* or *qamets hatuph* prefix vowel = Hophal

---

1. If the first root letter is a guttural, the *dagesh* will not be present and the prefix vowel will be *tsere:* יֵעָזֵב.

Chart 11

- *Shewa* prefix vowel = usually Piel or Pual, although it may be Hiphil
    - *Shewa* + *pathaq/qamets* under the following letter = Piel
    - *Shewa* + *qibbuts* = Pual (almost always)
    - *Shewa* + *hireq/hireq yod* = Hiphil (usually)

Appendix
Hebrew Independent Clauses

The *main line* of a narrative is essentially the storyline—the sequence of actions that forms the backbone of the story.[1] Stories can begin in a variety of ways, but the story line proper is typically initiated and then carried along by clauses introduced by *wayyiqtol* (or past tense) verbal forms (often called *waw* consecutive with the imperfect). Most *wayyiqtol* clauses are sequential or consequential, but they can also have a variety of less common functions. The following list, though not exhaustive, identifies the primary functions of *wayyiqtol* clauses:

1. Introductory: Often a *wayyiqtol* clause (especially one consisting of וַיְהִי, lit. "and it was," and a temporal word or phrase) introduces an episode or scene by providing background for the story to follow.
2. Initiatory: Here the *wayyiqtol* clause sets the story proper in motion with a verb describing an action.
3. Sequential/Consequential: The clause describes an action that follows the preceding action temporally and/or logically.
4. Flashback: Sometimes the narrator interrupts the sequence of events and uses a *wayyiqtol* clause to refer to a prior action that now becomes relevant. The flashback can initiate an episode or scene, refer back to an action that preceded the episode or scene chronologically, or, more often than not, recall an event that occurred within the time frame of the story being related.
5. Focusing: A *wayyiqtol* clause often has a focusing or specifying function. It can focus on a particular individual involved in the event just described, give a more detailed account of the event or an aspect of the event, or provide a specific example of a preceding statement.
6. Resumptive: A *wayyiqtol* clause can serve a resumptive function. When used in this manner it follows a supplementary, focusing, or flashback statement; such examples can be labeled resumptive-(con)sequential. On a few occasions the resumptive *wayyiqtol* repeats a statement made prior to the embedded comment or scene that interrupted the narrative; these clauses can be labeled resumptive-reiterative.
7. Complementary: A *wayyiqtol* clause sometimes complements the preceding statement by giving the other side of the same coin or by describing an action that naturally or typically accompanies what precedes.
8. Summarizing or Concluding: A *wayyiqtol* clause occasionally makes a summarizing statement, often in relation to the preceding narrative, and/or can be used to conclude a narrative or scene, sometimes with a formulaic comment.

Note: A list of *wayyiqtol* clause functions also appears in EE, 120–23. The list appearing in this appendix makes some minor revisions of the list in EE:

---

1. For a helpful, up-to-date study of discourse structure in Hebrew narrative, see Roy L. Heller, *Narrative Structure and Discourse Constellations: An Analysis of Clause Function in Biblical Hebrew Prose*, Harvard Semitic Studies 55 (Winona Lake, Ind.: Eisenbrauns, 2004).

a. The appendix adds three new categories that do not appear in the EE list. These are "initiatory" (no. 2), "flashback" (no. 4), and "complementary" (no. 7).

b. The appendix defines the category "resumptive" (EE, no. 3, p. 121) in a more detailed and nuanced manner (see no. 6 above).

c. The appendix omits the categories "supplemental" (EE, no. 6, pp. 122–23) and "explanatory" (EE, no. 7, p. 123). Both are relatively rare.

Offline clauses deviate from the *wayyiqtol* pattern. Most often the conjunction is immediately followed by a non-verb, usually the subject of the clause (sometimes called a disjunctive clause). The predicate then follows, whether stated (typically a perfect verbal form or a participle) or implied (in equative sentences where a subject is connected to its predicate by an implied "to be" verb; for example, וְהָאִשָּׁה טוֹבַת מַרְאֶה מְאֹד, "the woman [was] very beautiful" (2 Sam. 11:2). Offline constructions often are descriptive and do not further the action of the story. In such cases they tend to provide background or supplemental information. Sometimes, however, they do contribute to the story line by describing a contrastive or oppositional action. In other cases they shift the dramatic focus from one character or participant to another. The following list, though not exhaustive, identifies the primary functions of offline clauses:

1. Introductory or Backgrounding: Offline clauses sometimes formally mark the beginning of a new scene or episode; in this case they typically provide background information for the story that follows.

2. Supplemental: Offline clauses very frequently give supplemental (or parenthetical) information that is embedded within a story.

3. Circumstantial: Offline clauses sometimes describe the circumstances attending to an action, such as time or manner.

4. Synchronic: Occasionally disjunctive clauses are juxtaposed to indicate synchronic actions.

5. Contrastive: Sometimes an offline clause describes an action that contrasts with what precedes or qualifies it in some way.

6. Dramatic: An offline clause, especially when introduced by וְהִנֵּה, "and look!," can have a dramatic function, inviting the audience to enter into the story as a participant or eyewitness. This device can also signal a shift in focus from one character or participant to another, sometimes involving a flashback.

7. Concluding: Offline clauses can be used to signal closure formally for an episode or scene.

Teacher's Guide to Jonah

Note: These teacher's guides contain suggested answers to the questions in the analysis sections (step 2) of the assignments. For guidance in the process of outlining the narrative structures (step 4), see EE, 119–42.

1:1

2. In the construct state *qamets* reduces to *pathaq* in a final closed syllable, while *qamets* reduces to vocal *shewa* in an open unaccented syllable. Both of these rules apply in the change דְּבָר > דְּבַר.

3. The Lord is the one who speaks the word, so this is a genitive of subject (or author, source). See EE, 62 (category 3).

1:2

1. Since the Lord is the superior party, these imperatives are best understood as expressing a command. See EE, 105 (category 1).

2. The article probably indicates uniqueness in this case, suggesting Nineveh is "the great city" *par excellence.* See EE, 73 (category 1). The article may indicate that this city is especially well-known. See EE, 73 (category 2).

3. The form is an adjective, functioning attributively. It follows הָעִיר and agrees with it in gender, number, and definiteness. Recall that עִיר, "city," is feminine, despite the fact that it does not have a feminine ending. See PVP, 30 (4.7).

5. This form consists of the preposition עַל and a 3fs pronominal suffix. Recall that some prepositions, such as עַל, take the suffixes that are used with plural nouns. The antecedent of the feminine singular pronoun is the feminine singular noun עִיר, "city."

6. The clause is probably causal (or explanatory), giving the reason why the prophet is to go and preach against the city. Another option is that כִּי here introduces a noun clause that serves as the object of the verb "cry out" and identifies the content of the cry ("and cry out against her *that* their evil has come up before me"). The closest syntactical parallel to this construction (imperative of קָרָא + preposition + pronominal suffix + כִּי + perfect verbal form) is in Isaiah 40:2: קִרְאוּ אֵלֶיהָ כִּי מָלְאָה צְבָאָהּ. This statement may be translated, "cry out to her *for/that* her time of warfare is over."

7. The perfect may be functioning as a present perfect ("has come up"), describing the present condition resulting from a past action (EE, 88, category 6). Another option is to understand this as a characteristic perfect (EE, 87–88, category 5), describing a situation that characteristically takes place—Nineveh's evil comes up before the Lord on a regular basis. However, if one chooses this option, it is important to note that the perfect focuses on the factuality of the situation, not its ongoing nature. To highlight the latter, the imperfect would have been used.

1:3

1. The form is a Qal wayyiqtol 3ms from the root קוּם. The parenthetical remarks in the text explain how to determine the stem and root. The *yod* prefix and absence of an ending indicate the form is 3ms (cf. יִקְטֹל).

2. The form is a Qal infinitive construct (with prepositional prefix) from the root בָּרַח. The infinitive, as is typical with prefixed -לְ, indicates purpose, "in order to flee." See PVP, 242.

3. The unaccented הָ- ending indicates direction. The form is classified as an accusative of direction (EE, 64, category 3).

5. The form is a Qal wayyiqtol 3ms from the root יָרַד. The parenthetical remarks in the text explain how to determine the stem and root. The *yod* prefix and absence of an ending indicate the form is 3ms (cf. יִקְטֹל).

6. The form is an adverbial accusative, indicating direction (EE, 64, category 3).

8. There is no accusative sign because the object is indefinite.

9. The form is a Qal participle feminine singular from the root בּוֹא. The *qamets he* ending indicates the form is feminine singular. The participle (a verbal adjective) is functioning attributively; it follows the noun it modifies and agrees with it in indefiniteness, gender, and number. One could translate literally, "a going-to-Tarshish ship," but a better rendering would be "a ship headed toward Tarshish."

11. The form is a Qal wayyiqtol 3ms from the root נָתַן. The form displays a *yod* prefix of the imperfect with two root letters visible. A *dagesh forte,* indicating doubling, appears in the first visible root letter and the theme vowel is *tsere.* According to chart 10, this pattern is distinctive of the Qal of the I-*nun* verb נָתַן; the *dagesh* indicates that the first root letter, *nun,* has assimilated. The *yod* prefix and absence of an ending indicate the form is 3ms (cf. יִקְטֹל).

12. The antecedent of the feminine singular pronominal suffix is the feminine singular noun אֳנִיָּה, "ship."

14. The form consists of the preposition -בְּ and a 3fs pronominal suffix.

15. The form is Qal infinitive construct (with prepositional prefix) from the root בּוֹא. The infinitive, as is typical with prefixed -לְ, indicates purpose, "in order to go."

1:4

1. Options for classifying this disjunctive clause include the following (which are not necessarily mutually exclusive):

   a. Introductory—the disjunctive clause may signal the beginning of a new episode in the scene;
   b. Contrastive—the clause may highlight the oppositional action taken by the Lord in response to Jonah's disobedient actions;
   c. Dramatic—like a shift in camera angle in a modern film, the clause may draw attention to the shift in focus from Jonah to the Lord. (Note that Jonah is the subject of the preceding five main verbs [cf. v. 3].)

2. The form is a Hiphil perfect 3ms from the root טוּל. Since the form has no ending, we consult chart 9. The form has a prefixed *he,* two root letters, and a prefix vowel *tsere,* so it is a Hiphil perfect. The *hireq yod* theme vowel indicates it is a hollow verb, not geminate. The perfect here indicates simple past action (EE, 86, category 1).

3. It is the direct object of the verb; the accusative sign does not appear because the form is indefinite.

4. It is an attributive adjective; it follows the noun it modifies and agrees with it in indefiniteness, gender, and number ("a great wind").

6. The noun סַעַר is technically the subject of the preceding verb. The adjective גָּדוֹל is attributive; it follows the noun it modifies and agrees with it in indefiniteness, gender, and number.

7. The form consists of the preposition -בְּ + the definite article (with syncope of the *he*) + the noun יָם, "sea." Though the *he* of the article is not visible, the article is apparent because of the vowel *pathaq* under the preposition and the *dagesh forte* in the *yod*. (If the preposition were not present, the form for "the sea" would be הַיָּם.)

8. The disjunctive clause is probably dramatic (EE, 126–27, category 6). The camera lens zooms in, as it were, on the personified ship in order to highlight the impact of the storm on those experiencing it.

9. The form is a Piel perfect 3fs from the root חָשַׁב. The form has no prefix, three root letters, and the vowel under the first root letter is *hireq*. According to chart 2, the form must be a Piel perfect. The doubled second root letter also suggests the Piel. The *qamets he* ending indicates the form is 3fs. The perfect here indicates simple past action.

10. The form is a Niphal infinitive construct (with prepositional prefix) from the root שָׁבַר. Since the form has no ending we use chart 9. The form has a prefixed *he* with a *hireq*, three root letters, a *dagesh forte* in the first root letter, and a *qamets* under the first root letter. The prefixed *he* with a *hireq* prefix vowel limits the stem options to Hiphil or Niphal. The *qamets* under the first root letter indicates the form is Niphal. The *tsere* theme vowel indicates it must be an imperative or infinitive construct; the prepositional prefix indicates the latter.

1:5

1. The *yod* prefix in combination with the *shureq* ending indicates the P-G-N is 3mp (cf. יִקְטְלוּ).

5. The form consists of the plural noun אֱלֹהִים, "god(s)," + 3ms pronominal suffix. Recall that יו- is the form of the 3ms suffix before plural nouns; וֹ- is used with singular nouns. See PVP, 81 (9.2); Ful., 71 (12.2).

6. The form is a Hiphil wayyiqtol 3mp from the root טוּל. Two root letters are visible, the prefix vowel is *qamets,* and the theme vowel is *hireq* (defectively written *hireq yod*). The *qamets* prefix vowel indicates that the stem must be Hiphil or Qal and that the root must be hollow or geminate. The *hireq* (defectively written *hireq yod*) theme vowel indicates the form is from a hollow root and, since the root is a middle *u*-class, the stem is Hiphil. The *a*- class + *i*-class vowel pattern is typical of the Hiphil stem and *qamets* is the typical prefix vowel in the imperfect/wayyiqtol of hollow verbs. (Recall that middle *i*-class hollow verbs, like שִׂים, have the *a* + *i* pattern in both Qal and Hiphil, but the middle *u*-class verbs have *a* + *u* in the Qal and *a* + *i* in the Hiphil. See chart 11.) The *yod* prefix in combination with the *shureq* ending indicates the P-G-N is 3mp (cf. יִקְטְלוּ).

7. The accusative sign appears before definite objects (note the article on הַכֵּלִים).

8. The form consists of the preposition -בְּ + the article (the *he* is not visible, however) + the noun אֳנִיָה. Before the guttural *aleph*, the article takes the vowel *qamets* rather than the usual *pathaq* (compensatory lengthening).

9. The form is a Hiphil infinitive construct (with prepositional prefix) from the root קַלַל. Since the form has no ending use chart 9. The form has a prefixed *he* with a *qamets*, two root letters, and a *tsere* theme vowel. The *he* prefix with *qamets* prefix vowel indicates that the verb is Hiphil and that the root must be

hollow or geminate. The prepositional prefix indicates it is an infinitive construct; this means the form must be a geminate verb since hollow infinitives construct have a *hireq yod* theme vowel. (The form could only be hollow if it were an imperative or infinitive absolute, but the prepositional prefix rules these options out.) The infinitive, as is typical with prefixed -לְ, indicates purpose, "in order to lighten." The Hiphil stem has a causative idea here: Qal "be light"; Hiphil "cause to be light, lighten."

11. The disjunctive clause is both dramatic and contrastive. It shifts the focus from the sailors back to Jonah, whose action (or inaction, as the case may be!) contrasts with that of the sailors. Note that Jonah has not been a participant in the action since verse 3. The focus has been on the Lord (v. 4a), the ship (v. 4b), and the sailors (v. 5a).

12. The perfect may be taken as a past perfect (EE, 87, category 2), indicating that Jonah had already gone below prior to the sailors' action(s) described earlier in the verse. For example, in Genesis 31:19a, the perfect הָלַךְ indicates an action that took place prior to Jacob's leaving Paddan Aram (cf. v. 18). Laban had gone down to shear his sheep; while he was there Rachel stole the idols. This happened prior to their departure (cf. vv. 20–21). Another option for understanding the perfect in Jonah 1:5b is to take it as indicating simple past action roughly concurrent with the sailors' action(s). For example, in Genesis 4:4 the reference to Abel bringing an offering complements the statement in Genesis 4:3b that Cain brought an offering. There is no indication that Abel presented his offering prior to Cain.

13. The *tsere yod* ending is the construct ending for masculine dual and plural nouns. The form יַרְכְּתֵי should be understood as dual; note the use of the absolute dual form יַרְכָתַיִם in Exodus 26:27 and elsewhere.

15. The form is a Niphal wayyiqtol 3ms from the root רדם. The prefix vowel is *tsere* and the vowel under the first root letter is *qamets*. This is the distinctive pattern for the Niphal imperfect/wayyiqtol in I-guttural verbs. Normally the Niphal pattern consists of *hireq* prefix vowel + *dagesh forte* in the first root letter + *qamets* under the first root letter (יִקָּטֵל). Since a guttural will not allow the *dagesh*, the preceding *hireq* lengthens to *tsere* in the open syllable.

1:6

1. The form is a Qal wayyiqtol 3ms from the root קרב.
2. The form consists of the preposition אֶל + 3ms pronominal suffix.
5. The form is a Niphal participle masculine singular from the root רדם. The prefixed *nun* indicates the stem is Niphal. The *qamets* theme vowel is typical of the participle. (The Niphal perfect has a *pathaq* as its theme vowel.)
7. The form consists of the plural noun אֱלֹהִים + 2ms pronominal suffix. The noun should probably be translated as singular—the plural of respect can be used of foreign gods (cf. 1:5, note 5) and the next statement refers to "the god" (i.e., the one responsible for sending the storm) taking notice of (singular verb) them.
8. The form is a Hithpael imperfect 3ms from the root עשת. The infixed *taw* after the prefixed *yod* indicates the stem is Hithpael. The preceding word, אוּלַי, "perhaps," suggests contingency, so the imperfect indicates possibility (EE, 93, category 10).
9. The article indicates definiteness, referring to the god responsible for sending the disaster.
10. The form consists of the preposition -לְ + 1cp pronominal suffix.
11. The *nun* prefix indicates that the verb is 1cp (cf. נִקְטֹל).

1:7

1. The form is a Qal wayyiqtol 3mp from the root אָמַר. The *yod* prefix in combination with the *shureq* ending indicates the P-G-N is 3mp (cf. יִקְטְלוּ).

3. The *shureq* ending indicates the form is 2mp (cf. קִטְלוּ).

4. The form is a Hiphil cohortative 1cp from the root נָפַל with a prefixed conjunction. The form has a prefix vowel *pathaq* and two root letters; the stem is therefore Hiphil. Note the *a + i* vowel pattern, which is characteristic of the Hiphil (see chart 11). The *dagesh forte* in the *pe* indicates an assimilated *nun,* so the verb is I-*nun.* The prefixed *nun* indicates the form is 1cp. In the Qal the verb נָפַל means "to fall." The Hiphil is causative, meaning "cause to fall, cast down."

5. The form is a Qal cohortative 1cp from the root יָדַע with a prefixed conjunction. The form has a *tsere* prefix vowel, *shewa* in the theme vowel position, and two root letters (see chart 10). The stem is therefore Qal and the root I-*yod.* In sequence with the preceding cohortative, this cohortative indicates purpose ("in order that we may know") or result ("then we will know").

7. The form consists of the article prefixed to the feminine singular demonstrative, which is functioning as an adjective here ("this disaster").

9. The form is a Hiphil wayyiqtol 3mp from the root נָפַל. The form has a prefix vowel *pathaq* and two root letters; the stem is therefore Hiphil. Note the *a + i* vowel pattern, characteristic of the Hiphil (see chart 11). The *dagesh forte* in the *pe* indicates an assimilated *nun,* so the verb is I-*nun.* The *yod* prefix in combination with the *shureq* ending indicates the P-G-N is 3mp (cf. יִקְטְלוּ).

10. It is the direct object of the preceding verb; the accusative sign is omitted because the noun is indefinite.

11. The form is a Qal wayyiqtol 3ms from the root נָפַל. The form has a prefix vowel *hireq,* a theme vowel *holem,* and two root letters; the stem is therefore Qal (see chart 10). With the *dagesh forte* in the first visible root letter, the root could be either geminate or I-*nun.* The I-*nun* verb נָפַל is clearly the correct choice in this context. (Furthermore, the geminate verb פָּלַל occurs only in the Piel and Hithpael.) The *yod* prefix and the absence of an ending indicate the form is 3ms (cf. יִקְטֹל).

12. It is the subject of the preceding verb ("the lot fell").

1:8

1. The form is a Hiphil imperative masculine singular (alternative form with ה ָ - ending) from the root נָגַד. The form has a prefixed *he,* prefix vowel *pathaq,* and two root letters visible. The stem must therefore be Hiphil. The *dagesh forte* in the first visible root letter indicates an assimilation of *nun,* so the verb is I-*nun* (see chart 2).

3. The noun is a predicate nominative, "What *is* your *occupation?*"

4. The verb is a Qal imperfect 2ms from the root בּוֹא. It has a prefix vowel *qamets,* a theme vowel *holem waw,* and two root letters visible. As chart 10 indicates, it must be a Qal form of a hollow root (the root בּוֹא is actually visible in the form). The *taw* prefix with no ending indicates the form is 2ms (cf. תִּקְטֹל). Though this form could theoretically be 3fs, in this context, where the sailors are addressing Jonah, it must be 2ms.

    If the sailors simply want to know from where Jonah is presently traveling, then the imperfect is present progressive in function (see EE, 91, category 5), "From where are you coming?" This seems to be the case in Judges 19:17 and Job 1:7. If they are asking strictly about his ethnic identity (note the next two questions they ask), then the imperfect is probably characteristic in function (EE, 91, category 4), "From where do you come (i.e., hail)?" It seems likely that the first option is the better one, at least at the surface level, but the question is probably designed to reveal his ethnicity as well, as the subsequent questions indicate. Note the use of this question in Joshua 9:8 and Judges 17:9.

5. The form consists of the noun אֶרֶץ + 2ms pronominal suffix. The noun is a predicate nominative, "What *is* your *land?*"

1:9

1. The form consists of the preposition אֶל + 3mp pronominal suffix.
3. The form is a Qal participle masculine singular from the root יָרֵא. The participle, which is a verbal adjective, is functioning as a predicate with the preceding independent pronoun as its subject, "I fear."

1:10

1. The form is a Qal wayyiqtol 3mp from the root יָרֵא. As chart 10 notes, the *hireq yod* prefix vowel indicates the verb is I-*yod*. The *yod* prefix in combination with the *shureq* ending indicates the P-G-N is 3mp (cf. יִקְטְלוּ). הָאֲנָשִׁים, "the men," functions as the subject of the verb.
3. It is an adjective (fs) and is functioning attributively in relation to the preceding noun, "great fear."
4. The form is a Qal perfect 2ms from the root עָשָׂה. The ending תָ- is characteristic of the perfect and indicates the form is 2ms. Chart 1 deals with such forms. In this case only two root letters are visible and the vowel under the first letter is *qamets*. As the chart observes, the *yod* before the ending indicates the verb is III-*he*. The perfect appears to be present perfect in function (see EE, 88, category 6), indicating a completed action with continuing results, "What is this you have done?"
5. The clause is causal (EE, 116), explaining why they asked this question, "because/for the men knew."
6. This is a noun clause, giving the content of what the men knew. It functions as the object of the verb "they knew." See EE, 113.
7. The participle (a verbal adjective) is functioning as a predicate with the preceding pronoun (הוּא) as its subject. The statement reflects the narrator's descriptive perspective, so the participle indicates continuous action in the past, "he was fleeing."
8. The clause is causal (EE, 116), explaining how they knew he was fleeing from the Lord.
9. The form is a Hiphil perfect 3ms from the root נָגַד. It has a *he* prefix, a *hireq* prefix vowel, a *hireq yod* theme vowel, and two root letters visible with a *dagesh forte* in the first of these. According to chart 9 the stem is Hiphil; the *hireq yod* theme vowel sets the form apart from a Niphal form. The *dagesh* in the *gimel* indicates *nun* assimilation; the root is I-*nun*. In this subordinate clause the perfect is functioning as a past perfect (EE, 87, category 2). It describes an action that occurred before that of the preceding causal clause, "for they knew . . . because he *had* (prior to their knowing) told them."
10. The form consists of the preposition לְ- + 3mp pronominal suffix.

1:11

1. The form is a Qal imperfect 1cp from the root עָשָׂה. The *nun* prefix indicates that the verb is 1cp (cf. נִקְטֹל). The prefix vowel *pathaq* is due to the fact that the first root letter is a guttural. The imperfect is used in a subjective manner here, probably in an obligatory sense (see EE, 93, category 13). The sailors want to know what the proper course of action is under the circumstances.

2. The definite noun הַיָּם, "the sea," functions as the subject of the preceding verb.
3. The form consists of the preposition מִן + preposition עַל + 1cp pronominal suffix, "from upon us."
4. The clause is causal, explaining why the sailors asked what they did.
5. These forms can be recognized as Qal active participles by the *holem waw/holem* after the first root letter (see chart 9). If the participles are part of the quotation, then they indicate present continuous action ("for the sea is continually raging"). If the causal clause is an observation of the narrator, then the participles indicate past continuous action ("for the sea was continually raging").

1:12

1. The *shureq* ending indicates the verb is 2mp (cf. קִטְלוּ). The pronominal suffix is functioning as the object of the imperative ("pick me up").
2. The form is a Hiphil imperative 2mp from the root נוּל with a 1cs pronominal suffix attached. The prefixed *he* in combination with the *hireq yod* theme vowel indicates this is a Hiphil form from a hollow root. The *qibbuts* ending (defectively written for *shureq*) indicates the verb is 2mp. The pronominal suffix is the object of the verb ("throw me").
3. In this volitional sequence (imperative + jussive/imperfect), the second form indicates the purpose ("in order that the sea may cease") or result ("and then the sea will cease") of the commanded action ("throw").
4. The clause is causal, explaining why Jonah recommends this action. The participle has a present temporal nuance ("for I know").
5. The clause is a noun clause, functioning as the object of the verb "I know." It gives the content of what Jonah knows.
6. The form הַסַּעַר consists of a noun with the article; הַגָּדוֹל is an adjective with the article, functioning attributively; הַזֶּה is a demonstrative with the article, functioning adjectivally. The sequence reads literally, "the storm, the great, the this," which must be rendered in English, "this great storm."
7. The form consists of the preposition עַל + 2mp pronominal suffix.

1:13

1. The form is a Qal wayyiqtol 3mp from the root חָתַר. The *pathaq* prefix vowel means the stem is either Hiphil or Qal, but the *shewa* in the theme vowel position indicates the form is Qal (Hiphil would have a *hireq yod* or *tsere* theme vowel). The prefix vowel is *pathaq* because the first root letter is a guttural. The *yod* prefix in combination with the *shureq* ending indicates the P-G-N is 3mp (cf. יִקְטְלוּ).
2. The form is a Hiphil infinitive construct (with prepositional prefix), from the root שׁוּב. Since the form has no ending, use chart 9. The form has a prefixed *he*, prefix vowel *qamets*, two root letters, and a *hireq yod* theme vowel. The *he* prefix with *qamets* prefix vowel indicates that the verb is Hiphil and that the root must be hollow or geminate. The prepositional prefix indicates it is an infinitive construct; this means the form must be hollow since hollow infinitives construct have a *hireq yod* theme vowel. (Geminate infinitives construct have a *tsere* theme vowel.) The infinitive, as is typical with prefixed -לְ, indicates purpose, "in order to return."
4. The clause is causal, explaining why they were unable to row back to dry land.
5. The statement reflects the narrator's perspective, so the participles indicate continuous action in the past ("for the sea was continually raging against them").

1:14

2. The form is a Qal cohortative 1cp from the root אָבַד. The *qamets he* ending, in combination with the *nun* prefix, indicates the form is cohortative. Since the men are praying to the Lord, the cohortative expresses a request or wish (EE, 107, category 1).

3. The preposition has a causal function here, "on account of." See AC, 105 (category f); W-OC, 198 (ex. 29); BDB, 90, no. 5; *HALOT*, 105, no. 19.

4. The form is a Qal jussive 2ms from the root נָתַן. A *dagesh forte* appears in the first visible root letter, indicating that the first root letter *nun* has assimilated. Since the sailors are praying to the Lord, the negated jussive is expressing a request or wish (EE, 104, category 3).

5. The noun דָּם is the direct object of the negated jussive ("do not place upon us blood"); the adjective נָקִיא is functioning attributively—it follows the noun it modifies and agrees with it in indefiniteness ("innocent blood").

6. This is a causal clause, explaining the basis for their petition that they not be held accountable for Jonah's death.

7. The psalms cited are hymns in which the psalmist is generalizing about God, but the sailors' concern seems to be more immediate and contextualized. So the verb forms, rather than being characteristic in function (see EE, 87–88, category 5), are better classified as simple present (EE, 87, category 4) or perhaps even present perfect (EE, 88, category 6). One could even take the first verb as present perfect and the second as simple present.

1:15

1. The form is Qal wayyiqtol 3mp from the root נָשָׂא. The *yod* prefix in combination with the *shureq* ending indicates the P-G-N is 3mp (cf. יִקְטְלוּ). Sometimes the assimilated *nun* is not indicated by *dagesh forte* when a vocal *shewa* appears beneath the letter (i.e., in 2fs, 3mp, and 2mp forms, all of which have vocalic endings).

2. The form is a Hiphil wayyiqtol 3mp from the root טול with a 3ms pronominal suffix functioning as the direct object of the verb ("and they threw him").

3. The form is a Qal wayyiqtol 3ms from the root עָמַד. Prefix vowel *pathaq* is characteristic of the Hiphil stem in the imperfect/wayyiqtol, but it also appears in the Qal of I-guttural verbs. One can distinguish Qal and Hiphil by looking at the theme vowel. When the theme vowel is *holem* (i.e., a non-*i*-class vowel) as it is here, the stem is Qal (see chart 10).

4. The antecedent of the 3ms suffix is הַיָּם, "the sea." The suffix is the subject of the action implied in the noun זַעַף, "raging" (see EE, 62, category 3).

1:16

3. The form is a Qal wayyiqtol 3mp from the root נָדַר. The form has two root letters visible with a *dagesh forte* in the first. It also has a *hireq* prefix vowel and a *shewa* under the doubled letter. The *hireq* prefix vowel is characteristic of both Qal and Niphal verbs, but to be Niphal, the form would need a *holem waw, qamets,* or *pathaq* under the doubled letter. Instead it has a *shewa*, which means the form is Qal (see chart 10). The *dagesh* indicates an assimilated *nun*, so the root is I-*nun*. The *yod* prefix in combination with the *shureq* ending indicates the P-G-N is 3mp (cf. יִקְטְלוּ).

2:1

1. The form is a Piel wayyiqtol 3ms from the root מָנָה. The *shewa* in the prefix vowel position followed by the *pathaq* under the first root letter indicates the stem is Piel (see chart 10).
2. The form is a Qal infinitive construct from the root בָּלַע with a prepositional prefix indicating purpose.
3. The *tsere yod* ending indicates the form is construct.

2:2

1. The form is a Hithpael wayyiqtol 3ms from the root פָּלַל. The –יִת indicates the stem (see chart 10).

2:3

1. The form is a Qal perfect 1cs from the root קָרָא. The –תִי ending indicates the P-G-N. The perfect is functioning as a simple past (perhaps recent past) here; Jonah is recalling his cry for help when he was in the water.
3. The form is a Qal wayyiqtol 3ms from the root עָנָה with a 1cs pronominal suffix.
6. The form is a Piel perfect 1cs from the root שָׁוַע. The *hireq* under the first root letter indicates the stem is Piel (see chart 1). (Note also the characteristic *dagesh forte* in the second root letter.) The –תִי ending marks the form as 1cs (cf. קָטַלְתִּי). The perfect is functioning as a simple past (see no. 1 above).
7. The form is a Qal perfect 2ms from the root שָׁמַע. The –תָ ending marks the form as 2ms (cf. קָטַלְתָּ).

2:4

1. The form is a Hiphil wayyiqtol 2ms from the root שָׁלַךְ with a 1cs pronominal suffix. The *pathaq* prefix vowel in combination with the *hireq yod* theme vowel indicates the stem is Hiphil (see chart 10). The *taw* prefix (with no ending infixed before the suffix) indicates the P-G-N is 2ms (3fs makes no sense in this context). The suffix is the object of the verb.
2. The noun is an adverbial accusative of direction. See EE, 64 (category 3).
7. The form consists of the preposition עַל + 1cs pronominal suffix.
8. The form is a Qal perfect 3cp from the root עָבַר. The *shureq* ending indicates the P-G-N (cf. קָטְלוּ). The subject is "all your breakers and waves."

2:5

3. The form is a Niphal perfect 1cs from the root גָּרַשׁ. Since the form is clearly a 1cs perfect (note the –תִי ending; cf. קָטַלְתִּי), the prefixed *nun* indicates the stem is Niphal. The stem indicates the passive here; the perfect functions as a simple present ("I am driven out") or a present perfect ("I have been driven out"). It expresses Jonah's sentiments at the time he was in the water. (Note "I said.")
4. The form is a Hiphil imperfect 1cs from the root יָסַף. The form has two root letters with prefix vowel *holem waw* so it is a Hiphil of a I-*yod* verb (see chart 10).
5. The form is a Hiphil infinitive construct from the root נָבַט with a prepositional prefix. The form has no ending, a prefixed *he*, and two root letters with *pathaq* under the first, so the stem is Hiphil (see chart 9) and the root I-*nun* (note the *dagesh forte* in the *beth*, indicating assimilation of the first root letter).

The *hireq yod* theme vowel (as well as the prepositional prefix) distinguishes the form as an infinitive construct.

6. It is a genitive of attribute, indicating a quality or characteristic of the temple (EE, 63, category 9).

2:6

1. The form is a Qal perfect 3cp from the root אָפַף with a 1cs pronominal suffix. The *shureq* ending infixed before the pronominal suffix indicates the P-G-N (cf. קְטָלוּ). The subject is the following noun מַיִם, "waters." The suffix is the direct object of the verb.

4. The form is a Qal passive participle masculine singular from the root חָבַשׁ. The form has no ending, three root letters, a *qamets* under the first root letter, and a *shureq* as its theme vowel, so it is a passive participle (see chart 9). The participle is the predicate in the clause; סוּף is its subject ("seaweed was wrapped").

5. The form consists of a prepositional prefix + noun רֹאשׁ + 1cs pronominal suffix.

2:7

2. The form consists of the plural form of the noun בְּרִיחַ, "bar" + 3fs pronominal suffix. The 3fs suffix is the form used with plural nouns (note the *yod* in the form: -ֶיהָ).

3. The form is a Hiphil wayyiqtol 2ms from the root עָלָה. The *taw* prefix indicates the P-G-N (cf. תִּקְטֹל).

4. If definite, the form would be written either מֵהַשַּׁחַת or מִן־הַשַּׁחַת.

5. The compound divine title is a vocative of direct address (cf. EE, 61).

2:8

1. The form is a Hithpael infinitive construct from the root עָטַף with a prepositional prefix. The prefixed הִת– indicates the stem (see chart 9). As is so often the case when an infinitive is prefixed with the preposition -בְּ, the construction may be translated as a temporal clause.

4. The form is a Qal wayyiqtol 3fs from the root בּוֹא. See chart 10. The form has two root letters visible and a *qamets* prefix vowel, so the options for the stem are Qal or Hiphil. When the theme vowel is an *i/e*-class, the verb is normally Hiphil, but when the theme vowel is an *o/u*-class, the form is invariably Qal. Since the theme vowel on our form is *holem waw* the stem is Qal and the root hollow. In this context the P-G-N is 3fs.

5. It is the subject of the preceding 3fs verb.

2:9

1. The form is a Piel participle masculine plural from the root שָׁמַר. The prefixed *mem* indicates the form may be (and is in this case) a participle. The form has *shewa* in the prefix vowel position followed by a *pathaq* under the first root letter, so the stem is Piel (see chart 8). The participle is substantival here, "(those who) watch intently."

2. The *tsere yod* ending indicates the noun is a plural construct form.

3. It is a genitive because it follows a construct form. It indicates an attribute here, but since it is a synonym of the preceding noun, one can label it a genitive of degree or emphasis. See EE, 64, category 13.

5. The form is a Qal imperfect 3mp from the root עָזַב. The *pathaq* prefix vowel, due to the I-guttural,

appears with both the Qal or Hiphil; when the theme vowel is non-*i*-class (usually *holem* or *shewa*) the form is Qal. The *yod* prefix in combination with the *shureq* ending is characteristic of the 3mp imperfect (cf. יִקְטְלוּ). Jonah seems to be generalizing here, so the imperfect has a characteristic or habitual present function (EE, 91, category 4).

2:10

2. It is a genitive of attribute, indicating a characteristic of the voice or sound. See EE, 63, category 9.

3. The form is a Qal cohortative 1cs from the root זָבַח. The *aleph* prefix indicates the P-G-N (cf. אֶקְטֹל) and the *qamets he* ending, in combination with the first person prefix, indicates cohortative. The cohortative here expresses Jonah's resolve or intention. See EE, 107, category 2.

4. The relative pronoun is the object of the following verb נָדַרְתִּי ("that which I have vowed"); the relative clause is the object (noun clause) of the verb אֲשַׁלֵּמָה ("that which I have vowed I will repay"). See EE, 113.

5. The form is a Piel cohortative 1cs from the root שָׁלֵם. The form has a *shewa* (composite because it is under a guttural) in the prefix vowel position and a *pathaq* under the first root letter, so the stem is Piel (note the *dagesh forte* in the second root letter). The stem is factitive—the Qal is stative/intransitive ("be complete"), while the Piel indicates production of the state ("make complete, fulfill"). See EE, 80. The cohortative expresses Jonah's resolve or intention. See EE, 107, category 2.

2:11

1. The form is a Hiphil wayyiqtol 3ms from the root קִיא (see *HALOT*, 1096). It has two root letters with a *qamets* prefix vowel and a *tsere* theme vowel. The stem is therefore Hiphil or Qal (see chart 10, including the appropriate footnote), and the root either hollow or geminate. In this case there is no verb קאא, so the root must be hollow.

3:1–2

3. The predicative participle could indicate one of three things:

   a. Imminent future action ("which I am about to speak"; NASB interprets this way)
   b. Continuous action in the present ("which I am speaking")
   c. Continuous action in the past ("which I was speaking"; NLT interprets this way, but gives the impression of completed action, which is not accurate)

3:3

2. The clause is disjunctive, as indicated by the word order: *waw* + subject + predicate. The clause is supplemental (EE, 124–25, category 2); it provides background information about Nineveh, Jonah's destination.

3. The form is a Qal perfect 3fs from the root הָיָה. The form has an הָ- ending (see chart 2). Since there is no prefix, the stem must be Qal, Piel, or Pual. The *qamets* under the first root letter indicates Qal. Since the form has two root letters with a *taw* before the ending, it is a perfect 3fs from a III-*he* root.

3:4

2. The form is a Qal infinitive construct from the root בּוֹא with a preposition prefixed.

5. The form is a Niphal participle feminine singular from the root הָפַךְ. The תֶ- ending is a characteristic ending of the feminine singular participle. The prefixed *nun* indicates the stem is Niphal. The stem function is passive and the participle is predicative, "Nineveh will *be destroyed*."

3:5

1. The form is a Hiphil wayyiqtol 3mp from the root אָמַן. The *pathaq* prefix vowel indicates that the verb must be either Qal or Hiphil; the *hireq yod* theme vowel is characteristic of the Hiphil (see chart 10). The *yod* prefix in combination with the *shureq* ending indicates the P-G-N is 3mp.

3:6

1. The form is a Qal wayyiqtol 3ms from the root נָגַע. The form has two root letters visible and a *hireq* prefix vowel so it must be Qal or Niphal. The presence of a *pathaq* (a-class vowel) under the first visible root letter might make one think this is a Niphal, but this could only be the case if the *gimel* was the actual first root letter and the verb was geminate, which it is not (there is no verb גָּעַע). The *dagesh forte* in the *gimel* indicates *nun* assimilation, but it is the first root letter *nun* that has done so. The verb is I-*nun*. The *pathaq* theme vowel is due to the guttural letter that appears after the *gimel*.

2. The form consists of the prefixed preposition מִן + noun כִּסֵּא + 3ms pronominal suffix ("from his throne").

3. The form is a Hiphil wayyiqtol 3ms from the root עָבַר. The *pathaq* prefix vowel indicates that the verb must be either Qal or Hiphil; the *tsere* theme vowel is characteristic of the Hiphil (see chart 10).

4. The form is a Piel wayyiqtol 3ms from the root כָּסָה. The *shewa* in the prefix vowel position followed by the *pathaq* under the first root letter indicates the stem is Piel (see chart 10).

5. The form is a Qal wayyiqtol 3ms from the root יָשַׁב. The form has only two root letters visible and the vowel pattern is *tsere + seghol*, so it is a Qal from a I-*yod* root (see chart 10).

3:7

1. The form is a Hiphil wayyiqtol 3ms from the root זָעַק. The *pathaq* prefix vowel indicates that the verb must be either Qal or Hiphil; the *tsere* theme vowel is characteristic of the Hiphil (see chart 10).

4. The article indicates genre or class (EE, 73, category 4) and the singular is representative (EE, 58).

5. Since the king is issuing a decree that his subjects must obey, the negated jussives should be understood as expressing commands or prohibitions (EE, 104, category 1).

6. Both verbs are III-*he*. In III-*he* verbs with endings, the *he* drops. See PVP, 216–17; Ful., 266 (37.4).

3:8

1. The form is a Hithpael wayyiqtol 3mp from the root כָּסָה. The *taw* infix after the prefixed *yod* indicates the stem is Hithpael (see chart 10). The third root letter *he* drops before the plural ending. The stem has a reflexive function here ("and let them cover themselves").

3. The form is a Qal jussive 3mp from the root שׁוּב with a prefixed nonconsecutive *waw*. The form has

two root letters with a *qamets* prefix vowel, so the stem must be Qal or Hiphil, and the root hollow or geminate (see chart 10). The *qibbuts* theme vowel (a defectively written *shureq*) indicates the stem is Qal and the root hollow. The *yod* prefix in combination with the *shureq* ending indicates the P-G-N is 3mp.

5. The form consists of the prefixed preposition מִן + noun דֶּרֶךְ + 3ms pronominal suffix ("from his way").

6. רָעָה is an adjective functioning attributively; it follows the noun it modifies and agrees with it in definiteness, as well as in gender and number. (The noun דֶּרֶךְ is sometimes understood as feminine.)

7. The form consists of the prefixed preposition -בְּ + noun כַּף + 3mp pronominal suffix ("in their hands"). Note the *yod* that precedes the 3mp suffix. This indicates the noun is plural or, in this case, dual. See PVP, 83; Ful., 71 (12.2).

3:9

1. The form is a Qal active participle (note the *holem waw* with the first root letter; see chart 9) masculine singular from the root יָדַע.

2. The imperfect indicates possibility here (EE, 93, category 10), "God *may* turn" (then again, he may not).

4. The article indicates previous reference (EE, 73), referring to the God mentioned in verse 8.

5. The form is a Qal perfect 3ms from the root שׁוּב with a *waw* consecutive prefixed. The form has two root letters with a *qamets* under the first, so the root must be hollow (see chart 9).

7. The form is a Qal imperfect 1cp from the root אָבַד. The prefixed *nun* indicates the form is 1cp (cf. נִקְטֹל).

3:10

3. The form is a Qal perfect 3cp from the root שׁוּב. The form has two root letters with a *qamets* under the first and an וּ- ending. According to chart 5, the root must be hollow or III-*he*, depending on the placement of the accent. Since the accent is on the first syllable, the root is hollow. The *shureq* ending indicates the form is 3cp (cf. קָטְלוּ).

4. The form is a Niphal wayyiqtol 3ms from the root נָחַם. The prefix vowel is *hireq* and there is a *dagesh forte* in the first root letter with a *qamets* under the letter, so the stem is Niphal (see chart 10).

5. The perfect is in a subordinate (relative) clause and describes an action that occurred prior to the action of the preceding main clause. Therefore, the perfect is functioning as a past perfect (EE, 87, category 2): "God relented concerning the calamity that *he had threatened* (lit., "had spoken")."

6. The form is a Qal infinitive construct from the root עָשָׂה with a prepositional prefix. The form has two root letters visible with a *shewa* under the first letter and an וֹ- ending. According to chart 8, it must be from a III-*he* root.

4:1

2. The form is a Qal wayyiqtol 3ms from the root חָרָה. The final *he* drops (apocopates) from the 3ms form of III-*he* verbs in the wayyiqtol.

4:2

2. The prefixed *he* is interrogative.
3. The form is a Qal infinitive construct from the root הָיָה with a 3ms pronominal suffix. The form has two root letters visible with a *shewa* under the first letter and an וֹ- ending. According to chart 8, it must be from a III-*he* root. The suffix indicates the subject of the infinitive ("when I was").
4. The form consists of the feminine singular noun אֲדָמָה + 1cs pronominal suffix ("my land"). Before pronominal suffixes feminine singular nouns have a *taw* ending in place of the ה ָ-.
5. The form is a Piel perfect 1cs. The *hireq* under the first root letter of this perfect form indicates the stem is Piel (see chart 1). (Note also the characteristic *dagesh forte* in the second root letter.) The תִּי- ending marks the form as 1cs (cf. קָטַלְתִּי).
6. The clause is causal, explaining why he fled toward Tarshish (EE, 116).
7. The clause is a noun clause functioning as the object (accusative) of the verb "I know." The clause gives the content of what he knew, "I know *that* you are . . ." (EE, 113).
8. Both forms are adjectives, functioning attributively in relation to אֵל, "a gracious and compassionate god."
10. The noun חֶסֶד is functioning as a genitive of specification, "great with respect to faithfulness" (EE, 63).
11. The form is a Niphal participle masculine singular from the root נָחַם. The *qamets* theme vowel indicates the form is a participle, as opposed to a 3ms perfect, the form of which would be נִחַם. (See chart 9.)

4:3

1. The form is a Qal imperative 2ms from the root לָקַח. The appended נָא- sometimes appears after imperatives. Since Jonah is praying to God, the imperative expresses a request or wish here (EE, 106, category 4).
2. The form consists of the preposition מִן + 1cs pronominal suffix, "from me."
3. The clause is causal, explaining why Jonah requested that the Lord take his life (EE, 116).
4. The preposition is used to indicate comparison: "good my dying from my living" > "better for me to die than to live."

4:4

1. The prefixed *he* is an interrogative marker.
2. The form is a Hiphil infinitive absolute from the root יָטַב with an interrogative *he* prefixed. The form has a *he* prefix, a *tsere yod* prefix vowel, and two root letters visible. According to chart 10, it must be a Hiphil form from a I-*yod* root. The perfect 3ms and infinitive construct have a *hireq yod* theme vowel; the imperative masculine singular and infinitive absolute have a *tsere* theme vowel. So the form in verse 4 must be imperative or infinitive absolute; only the latter fits this context syntactically. The interrogative *he* is prefixed to an infinitive absolute twenty-four times in the Old Testament, but it is never prefixed to an imperative.

4:5

1. Both forms are derived from I-*yod* roots, as indicated by the *tsere* prefix vowel that appears in both. As chart 10 indicates, a *tsere* prefix vowel can also appear in geminate and hollow (Niphal) forms

occasionally, but not with a *tsere* or *seghol* theme vowel. According to the footnote in chart 10, III-*he* wayyiqtol forms can sometimes have a *tsere* prefix vowel as well, but not with a *tsere* or *seghol* theme vowel.

3. The form is a Qal wayyiqtol 3ms from the root עָשָׂה. The form has two visible root letters with a *pathaq* prefix and theme vowel, indicating a III-*he* verb with the final *he* apocopated (as in the jussive form). See chart 10.

4. The pronominal suffix is 3fs; the antecedent is the feminine singular noun סֻכָּה, "hut, booth."

5. The imperfect is functioning here as an historical future. The action is historical (past) from the narrator's perspective, but still future in relation to the action of the main verb: "he sat down under it in the shade until *he should see*."

4:6

1. The form is a Qal wayyiqtol 3ms from the root עָלָה. (Note that the III-*he* of the root has apocopated [dropped].)

3. The form is a Qal infinitive construct from the root הָיָה with a prepositional prefix. The verbal form has no prefix with two root letters visible. There is a *shewa* under the first root letter and an ◌וֹת- ending. According to chart 8, the form must be from a III-*he* verb. As so often with the preposition -לְ, the infinitive construct indicates either purpose or result. (For a discussion of these options, see the workbook.)

4. The form is a Hiphil infinitive construct from the root נָצַל with a prepositional prefix. The verbal form has a prefixed *he* and no ending. There are two root letters visible and the prefix vowel is *pathaq*. The form must therefore be a Hiphil from a I-*nun* verb. See chart 9. (Note the *dagesh forte* in the *tsade*, indicating assimilation of the first root letter, *nun*. The *hireq yod* theme vowel, as well as the prefixed preposition, distinguishes the form as an infinitive construct.) The infinitival construction indicates either purpose ("in order to deliver") or result ("so as to deliver").

5. The forms consists of the preposition מִן + noun (fs) רָעָה + 3ms pronominal suffix, "from his discomfort." (Note the *taw* ending before the suffix; this is typical of feminine nouns ending in ◌ָה-. See PVP, 85 [9.7]; Ful., 77 [13.2].)

6. In this case the cognate accusative is functionally adverbially (lit., "Jonah rejoiced with joy"). The verb "rejoiced" is intransitive (it takes no object), so the accusative cannot be the direct object.

4:7

1. The form is a Qal infinitive construct from the root עָלָה with a prepositional prefix. The verbal form has no prefix with two root letters visible. It has a *shewa* (composite under the guttural letter) under the first root letter and an ◌וֹת- ending. According to chart 8, the form must be from a III-*he* verb. As is so often the case when an infinitive is prefixed with the preposition -בְּ, the construction may be translated as a temporal clause. The following noun functions as the subject of the infinitive. The text, which literally reads, "in the going up of the dawn," may be translated, "When [the] dawn arose."

2. The form is a Hiphil wayyiqtol 3fs from the root נָכָה. The *taw* prefix indicates the verb is either 3fs or 2ms (cf. תִּקְטֹל); in this context it is 3fs, agreeing with its subject, the feminine singular noun תוֹלַעַת, "worm."

3. The form is a Qal wayyiqtol 3ms from the root יָבַשׁ. The *hireq yod* prefix vowel is characteristic of I-*yod* verbs in the Qal stem. See chart 10.

4:8

1. The form is a Qal infinitive construct from the root זָרַח with a prepositional prefix. As is so often the case when an infinitive is prefixed with the preposition -כְּ, the construction may be translated as a temporal clause. The following noun functions as the subject of the infinitive. The text, which literally reads, "as the rising of the sun," may be translated, "When the sun arose." The verbal form וַיְהִי, literally, "and it was" (Qal wayyiqtol 3ms from the root הָיָה), indicates that the following action occurred in past time.

5. The form is a Hithpael wayyiqtol 3ms from the root עָלַף. The -יִת prefix indicates the stem. Note the infixed *taw* between the prefixed *yod* and the first root letter *ayin*. See chart 10.

4:9–10

2. The form is a Qal perfect 2ms from the root חוּס. The non-prefixed form has two root letters with a *pathaq* under the first root letter. According to chart 1, the root must be hollow or geminate, but the latter, which does not exist in Biblical Hebrew, would take the form חַסֹּתָ. The root must be hollow. The תָּ- ending indicates the form is 2ms (cf. קָטַלְתָּ). NET takes the perfect as simple past (perhaps recent past; cf. EE, 86, category 1), but it appears that God confronts him while he is still angry (cf. v. 9). Consequently it is better to understand the perfect as a simple present (EE, 87, category 4). It simply recognizes the fact of the action, without drawing attention to its continuing nature.

4. The form has three root letters with a *hireq* under the first and a *dagesh forte* in the second. These are the characteristic indicators of a Piel perfect.

4:11

2. The form is a Qal imperfect 1cs from the root חוּס. It has two root letters with a *qamets* prefix vowel, so the root must be hollow or geminate. The *shureq* theme vowel indicates it is a hollow *u*-class. See chart 10. The *aleph* prefix indicates the form is 1cs (cf. אֶקְטֹל). The imperfect may be taken as permissive ("May I not feel compassion?")(see EE, 93, category 12) or as obligatory ("Should I not feel compassion?") (see EE, 93, category 13).

4. The form is a Hiphil infinitive absolute from the root רָבָה. It has an הֵ- ending and a prefixed *he* with a *pathaq* prefix vowel. According to chart 3, it must be Hiphil imperative 2ms or an infinitive absolute of a III-*he* root. The latter fits better in this context (see the discussion in the workbook). A III-*he* infinitive construct would have an וֹת- ending (הַרְבּוֹת).

7. The adjective רַבָּה is feminine singular, as the הָ- ending indicates.

Teacher's Guide to Ruth

Note: These teacher's guides contain suggested answers to the questions in the analysis sections (step 2) of the assignments. For guidance in the process of outlining the narrative structures (step 4), see EE, 119–42.

1:1

2. The *tsere yod* ending indicates the form is construct.
3. The form is a Qal infinitive construct from שָׁפַט. See chart 9.
4. The form is a Qal active participle masculine plural from שָׁפַט. See chart 8. The *holem* with the first root letter is the key to recognizing the form as an active participle. With the article prefixed to the form, it is functioning substantivally, being equivalent to a noun, "the judges."
6. The verb is a Qal wayyiqtol 3ms from הָלַךְ.
7. This form is a Qal infinitive construct from גּוּר with prepositional prefix. See chart 9. The infinitive here indicates the purpose of the preceding action, "went in order to live temporarily."
8. The *tsere yod* ending indicates the form is in construct.

1:2

1. The disjunctive clause gives supplemental information that provides background for the story to follow. See EE, 124–25 (category 2).
2. The article indicates previous reference. See EE, 73 (category 3).
5. The verb is a Qal wayyiqtol 3mp from בּוֹא. See chart 10. The form has two root letters visible and a *qamets* prefix vowel, so the options for the stem are Qal or Hiphil. When the theme vowel is an *i/e*-class, the verb is normally Hiphil, but when the theme vowel is an *o/u*-class, the form is invariably Qal. Since the theme vowel on this form is *holem* (long *o*) the stem is Qal. The root is either geminate or hollow, but there is no geminate root בָאא, so this has to be the hollow verb בּוֹא (there is no בוא or בִיא). The P-G-N is 3mp, as the *yod* prefix in combination with the וּ- ending indicates (recall יִקְטְלוּ).

1:3

1. The verb is a Qal wayyiqtol 3ms from מוּת. See chart 10. The form has two root letters visible and a *qamets* prefix vowel, so the options for the stem are Qal or Hiphil. When the theme vowel is an *i/e*-class, the verb is normally Hiphil, but when the theme vowel is an *o/u*-class, the form is invariably Qal. Since the theme vowel on our form is *qamets hatuph* (short *o*) the stem is Qal. The root is either geminate or hollow, but there is no geminate root מתת, so this has to be the hollow verb מוּת (there is no מֹת or מִית).
2. The noun is in apposition to the preceding name, "Elimelech, the husband of Naomi."
3. The verb is a Niphal wayyiqtol 3fs from שָׁאַר. See chart 10. The form has three root letters visible and a *hireq* prefix vowel. There are three stem options listed, but the *qamets* under the first root letter indicates the stem is Niphal. The *nun* of the stem has assimilated: *תִּנְשָׁאֵר > תִּשָּׁאֵר. The prefixed *taw*

indicates the P-G-N; it can be either 3fs or 2ms (recall תִּקְטֹל), but in this context it is 3fs (note the following 3fs pronoun הִיא, referring to Naomi).

1:4

1. The verb is a Qal wayyiqtol 3mp from נָשָׂא. The prefixed *yod* in combination with the וּ- ending indicates the P-G-N is 3mp (recall יִקְטְלוּ), the subject being Naomi's sons.
2. The noun is functioning as the direct object of the verb וַיִּשְׂאוּ. The accusative sign is not used before indefinite nouns.
3. The וֹת- ending indicates the form is feminine plural.
5. The verb is a Qal wayyiqtol 3mp from יָשַׁב. See chart 10. The form has two root letters visible and a *tsere* prefix vowel, so the stem must be Qal or Niphal. (Niphal has a *tsere* as prefix vowel only if the verb is I-guttural, which is not the case here.) The *shewa* in the theme vowel position indicates the root is I-*yod*.[1] Recall that I-*yod* verbs typically have a *tsere* prefix vowel in the Qal. The prefixed *yod* in combination with the וּ- ending indicates the P-G-N is 3mp (recall יִקְטְלוּ).

1:5

1. The verb is a Qal wayyiqtol 3mp from מוּת. See chart 10. The form has two root letters visible and a *qamets* prefix vowel, so the options for the stem are Qal or Hiphil. When the theme vowel is an *i/e*-class, the verb is normally Hiphil, but when the theme vowel is an *o/u*-class, the form is invariably Qal. Since the theme vowel on our form is *shureq* the stem is Qal and the root is a hollow *u*-class. The P-G-N is 3mp, as the *yod* prefix in combination with the וּ- ending indicates (recall יִקְטְלוּ).
2. The form שְׁנֵיהֶם consists of the number "two" and a 3mp pronominal suffix. The names are appositional to the suffix.
4. The form consists of the plural form of יֶלֶד + 3fs pronominal suffix.

1:6

1. The verb is a Qal wayyiqtol 3fs from קוּם. See chart 10. The form has two root letters visible and a *qamets* prefix vowel, so the options for the stem are Qal or Hiphil. When the theme vowel is an *i/e*-class, the verb is normally Hiphil, but when the theme vowel is an *o/u*-class, the form is invariably Qal. Since the theme vowel on our form is *qamets hatuph* (short *o*) the stem is Qal. The root is either geminate or hollow, but there is no geminate root קמם, so this must be the hollow verb קוּם (there is no קֹם or קִים). The prefixed *taw* indicates the P-G-N; it can be either 3fs or 2ms (recall תִּקְטֹל), but in this context it is 3fs. (Note the 3fs pronoun that follows as subject of the verb.)
2. The form consists of the conjunction + plural form of כַּלָּה + 3fs pronominal suffix. One can tell the form is plural by the feminine ending וֹת - and by the *yod* present in the suffix.
3. The verb is a Qal wayyiqtol 3fs from שׁוּב. See chart 10. The form has two root letters visible and a *qamets* prefix vowel, so the options for the stem are Qal or Hiphil. When the theme vowel is an *i/e*-class, the verb is normally Hiphil, but when the theme vowel is an *o/u*-class, the form is invariably Qal. Since the

---

1. A stative geminate can have a *shewa* in this position (reduced from *pathaq*) but in this case the prefix vowel would be *hireq* and there would be doubling indicating gemination; cf. תמם >וַיִּתְּמוּ in Deuteronomy 34:8. Furthermore there is no geminate verb שׁבב.

theme vowel on our form is *qamets hatuph* (short *o*) the stem is Qal. The root is either geminate or hollow, but there is no geminate root שבב, so this has to be the hollow verb שוב (there is no שׁוֹב or שִׁיב). The prefixed *taw* indicates the P-G-N; it can be either 3fs or 2ms (recall תִּקְטֹל), but in this context it is 3fs. (Naomi is the subject, as the preceding clause makes clear).

4. This is a causal clause, explaining why Naomi decided to return to her homeland. See EE, 116. The perfect is a past perfect, describing an action (her hearing about the relief from the famine) that preceded the action (her returning) of the main clause. One may translate, "because she had [prior to that] heard." See EE, 87.

5. This is a noun clause, functioning as the direct object of the verb "heard." It tells us what she heard. See EE, 113. Once again the perfect is a past perfect, describing an action (the Lord's bringing relief to his people) that preceded the action (her hearing of the relief from the famine) of the clause before this. One may translate, "that the Lord had [prior to that] brought relief to his people." See EE, 87.

6. The form is a Qal infinitive construct from נָתַן. The infinitive indicates either purpose: "visited his people *in order to give* them food," or manner: "brought relief to his people *by giving* them food." See EE, 78.

1:7

1. The verb is a Qal wayyiqtol 3fs from יָצָא. See chart 10. The form has two root letters visible and a *tsere* prefix vowel, so the stem must be Qal or Niphal. The *tsere* following the prefix vowel indicates the stem is Qal. (Niphal has a *tsere* prefix vowel if the verb is I-guttural, which is clearly not the case here.) The prefix vowel *tsere* followed by another *tsere* indicates the root is I-*yod*.

2. The verb is a Qal perfect 3fs from הָיָה. See chart 2. The form has no prefix and a *qamets* under the first root letter, so it has to be a Qal. It is perfect 3fs. Recall that III-*he* verbs have a *taw* before the typical 3fs הָ- ending. The perfect is a past perfect, describing a state (her being in Moab) that preceded the action (her leaving Moab) of the main clause. See EE, 87.

5. The verb is a Qal wayyiqtol 3fp from הָלַךְ. The *taw* prefix in combination with the נָה- ending indicates that the form is 3fp (recall תִּקְטֹלְנָה).

6. The form is a Qal infinitive construct from שׁוּב. See chart 9. The infinitive here indicates purpose, "they went . . . *in order to return*."

1:8

1. Both forms (לֵכְנָה and שֹׁבְנָה) are Qal imperative 2fp. The נָה- ending is characteristic of the feminine plural in both the imperfect and the imperative. לֵכְנָה is from the root הָלַךְ. Normally a 2fp imperatival form with no prefix and a *tsere* under the first root letter is I-*yod* (see chart 4), but הָלַךְ follows I-*yod* patterns in the imperative. שֹׁבְנָה is from the hollow root שׁוּב. According to chart 4, a 2fp imperative with no prefix and a *holem* with the first root letter is either hollow or geminate, but there is no geminate verb שׁבב. Depending on how much authority one envisions Naomi having over her daughters-in-law, the imperatives may be taken as expressing a command or advice. The first imperative ("come, go") may have the force of an introductory, attention-getting interjection when followed by another imperative. See the discussion in BDB, 234.

3. The *qere* form יַעַשׂ is a distinctly jussive form in that the final *he*, present in the imperfect 3ms (cf. יַעֲשֶׂה), has apocopated.

6. The verb is a Qal perfect 2mp from עָשָׂה. Note the distinctive 2mp ending of the perfect. When a perfect verbal form has only two root letters and there is a *yod* before the ending, the root is III-*he*. See chart 1.

1:9

1. The verb is a Qal jussive (or impf.) 3ms from נָתַן. One knows the verb is I-*nun* because of the *dagesh forte* in the *taw* indicating assimilation.

2. The verb is a Qal imperative 2fp from מָצָא. The הָ- ending is characteristic of the feminine plural in both the imperfect and the imperative. After the jussive, the imperative probably indicates purpose/result: "May the Lord give (favor) *so that* you may find."

5. The verb is a Qal wayyiqtol 3fs from נָשַׁק. One knows the verb is I-*nun* because of the *dagesh forte* in the *taw* indicating assimilation. For the verb to be Niphal the *dagesh* would have to be in the actual first root letter, in which case the root would have to be geminate שׁקק (note the *pathaq* theme vowel and see chart 10). According to *HALOT* (1647) two rare homonymic roots שׁקק appear in the Old Testament, but neither is used in the Niphal and neither meaning fits our context.

7. The verb is a Qal wayyiqtol 3fp from נָשָׂא. One knows the verb is I-*nun* because of the *dagesh forte* in the *sin* indicating assimilation. The הָ- ending is characteristic of the 3fp in the imperfect/wayyiqtol.

8. The verb is a Qal wayyiqtol 3fp from בָּכָה. The הָ- ending is characteristic of the 3fp in the imperfect/wayyiqtol. When an imperfect/wayyiqtol verbal form has only two root letters with a *hireq* prefix vowel followed by a *shewa* under a non-doubled letter, the root is III-*he* (see chart 10). The *yod* before the ending also points to this being a III-*he* root. See PVP, 177 (16.7), as well as p. 154 (14.7); Ful., 266 (37.4).

1:10

1. The verb is a Qal wayyiqtol 3fp from אָמַר. The הָ- ending is characteristic of the 3fp in the imperfect/wayyiqtol.

3. The form consists of the preposition אֵת, "with," + 2fs pronominal suffix. (Note that the *hireq* under the *aleph* and the *dagesh* in the *taw* distinguish the form from the accusative sign.)

4. The verb is a Qal imperfect 1cp from שׁוּב. The form has two root letters visible and a *qamets* prefix vowel, so the options for the stem are Qal or Hiphil. When the theme vowel is an *i/e*-class, the verb is normally Hiphil, but when the theme vowel is an *o/u*-class, the form is invariably Qal. Since the theme vowel on our form is *shureq* (long *u*) the stem is Qal and the root a hollow *u*-class. The *nun* prefix indicates the form is 1cp. In function the imperfect may be simple future (EE, 91–92), emphasizing their resolve or intention ("we *will* return"), or it may express their desire (EE, 94), "we want to return."

1:11

1. The form consists of the plural form of בַּת, "daughter," + 1cs pronominal suffix. On the irregular plural form (בָּנוֹת) of this noun, see PVP, 35 (4.8); Ful., 79–80 (13.4). The addition of the suffix causes the *qamets* to reduce to *shewa*. The noun is a vocative, identifying the addressee.

2. The imperfect may be present progressive (see EE, 91), "Why are you coming with me?" or it may indicate obligation (EE, 93), "Why should you come with me?" or desire (EE, 94), "Why do you want to come with me?"

3. The prefixed *he* indicates that the following statement is a question.

4. The form consists of the preposition -בְּ + plural form מֵעִים, "insides," + 1cs pronominal suffix. The noun is recognized as plural because the 1cs suffix is the form used with plurals, rather than י ִ-, which is the form used with singular nouns.

5. The verb is a Qal perfect 3cp from הָיָה. The *shureq* is the characteristic ending for the 3cp form of the perfect.

1:12

2. The clause is causal/explanatory (EE, 116), giving the logical reason why the girls should return to their homeland. The perfect verbal form describes Naomi's state or condition at the time she was speaking, so it can be labeled simple present (EE, 87).

3. The form is a Qal infinitive construct from הָיָה. The וֹת- ending is characteristic of the III-*he* infinitive construct (see chart 8). The preposition here has a comparative function. BDB (582) states that מִן sometimes "expresses the idea of a thing being *too much for* a person, or surpassing his powers."

1:13

2. The verb is a Piel imperfect 2fp from שָׂבַר. The prefix vowel is *shewa* followed by a *pathaq* under the first root letter, the standard pattern for the Piel. See chart 10. The נָה- ending indicates the form is 2fp. The form could be 3fp, but Naomi is speaking directly to them, not about them.

4. The verb is a Niphal imperfect 2fp from עָגַן. The *tsere* prefix vowel is followed by *qamets,* indicating a Niphal. See chart 10. The *tsere* is due to the I-guttural, which does not admit the *dagesh* and results in so-called compensatory lengthening. The נָה- ending indicates the form is 2fp.

5. The infinitive indicates result, "so as not to be/so that you would not be," or manner, "by not being."

7. The form is a Qal perfect 3ms from מָרַר. According to chart 9 (for forms with no ending), there are three basic options for a form with two root letters visible and a *pathaq.* The imperatival options do not fit this context, so this form must be from a geminate verb. The perfect describes Naomi's state at the time she was speaking; it is simple present.

8. The preposition is comparative, "more bitter."

9. The verb is a Qal perfect 3fs from יָצָא. The ה ָ- ending is characteristic of the 3fs in the perfect. The verb agrees with its subject יָד, a feminine noun. The perfect is best understood as a present perfect (EE, 88), indicating a completed action with continuing results, though simple past is a legitimate answer.

1:14

4. The clause is disjunctive, as indicated by the *waw* + non-verb (subject) + predicate pattern. The disjunctive clause contrasts Ruth's action with Orpah's (see EE, 126).

1:15

1. The verb is a Qal perfect 3fs from שׁוּב. The form has an ה ָ- ending with two root letters visible. The vowel under the first letter is *qamets* and the first syllable is accented, so the root is hollow. See chart 2. (The position of the accent distinguishes the perfect from the participle. It also indicates that this cannot be a perfect 3ms of a III-*he* verb.) In the paradigm of the perfect, the ה ָ- ending is distinctive to the 3fs.

2. The form consists of the feminine singular noun יְבָמָה/יְבִמְתּ + 2fs suffix. The *taw* before the suffix indicates the noun is feminine singular.

4. The verb is a Qal imperative 2fs from שׁוּב. The *hireq yod* is the distinctive ending of the 2fs imperative.

1:16

1. The verb is a Qal jussive 2fs from פָּגַע. The *taw* prefix in combination with the *hireq yod* ending indicates the form is 2fs.

2. The verb is a Qal infinitive construct from עָזַב with a prefixed preposition and a 2fs suffix. The form has three root letters (no verbal prefix; the preposition does not count because it is not a part of the verb) with a *qamets hatuph* (short *o*) beneath the first letter, so the stem is Qal. See chart 9. The preposition introduces a verbal complement that completes the preceding verb. The suffix indicates the object of the infinitive, "to abandon you."

3. The verb is a Qal infinitive construct from שׁוּב with a prefixed preposition. This infinitive probably explains how (i.e., the manner in which) she would abandon her mother-in-law, namely, "*by* returning." PVP (243–44) calls this use "complementary," while W-OC (608–9) calls it "gerundive, explanatory, or epexegetical."

4. The form consists of the preposition מִן + preposition אַחֲרֵי (originally derived from a noun, see W-OC, 188) + 2fs suffix: "from after you."

5. The clause is probably causal/explanatory. Ruth tells Naomi to stop urging her to go back, because she has determined that she will follow Naomi wherever her mother-in-law goes.

7. תֵּלְכִי is a Qal imperfect 2fs from הָלַךְ, while אֵלֵךְ is a Qal imperfect 1cs from הָלַךְ. Imperfect verbal forms with two root letters and a *tsere* prefix vowel followed by theme vowel *tsere* or by *shewa* are usually I-*yod*, but הָלַךְ follows the I-*yod* pattern. See chart 10.

8. תָּלִינִי is a Qal imperfect 2fs from לִין, while אָלִין is a Qal imperfect 1cs from לִין. As the workbook explains, the Qal and Hiphil imperfects of middle *i*-class hollow verbs overlap, so one must rely on context and usage to determine the stem in any given case. The basic Qal meaning fits here. (The Hiphil of לִין is very rare. See *HALOT*, 529.)

1:17

1. תָּמוּתִי is a Qal imperfect 2fs from מוּת, while אָמוּת is a Qal imperfect 1cs from מוּת. The forms have two root letters visible and a *qamets* prefix vowel, so the options for the stem are Qal or Hiphil. When the theme vowel is an *i/e*-class, the verb is normally Hiphil, but when the theme vowel is an *o/u*-class, the form is invariably Qal. Since the theme vowel on our forms is *shureq* (long *u*) the stem is Qal and the root a hollow *u*-class.

2. The verb is a Niphal imperfect 1cs from קָבַר. The *aleph* prefix is characteristic of the 1cs in the imperfect. The form has three root letters visible and a *seghol* prefix vowel. According to chart 10, there are three stem options, but the *qamets* under the first root letter indicates a Niphal. The *nun* of the stem has assimilated: *אֶנְקָבֵר > אֶקָּבֵר. The Niphal is passive here.

5. The verb is a Hiphil imperfect 3ms from פָּרַד. When an imperfect form with three root letters has a *pathaq* prefix vowel, the stem is Qal or Hiphil. See chart 10. When the theme vowel is an *i*-class (such as *hireq yod*) the stem is Hiphil. Furthermore, Qal forms take a *pathaq* prefix vowel only if they are I-guttural.

1:18

1. The verb is a Qal wayyiqtol 3fs from רָאָה.
2. This is a noun clause, functioning as the direct object of the verb "saw."
3. The form is a Hithpael participle feminine singular from אָמֵץ. See chart 7 for forms with the ending ת ֶ-. A prefixed *mem* is typical of participles in all stems except for Qal and Niphal. The participle is functioning as the predicate in the noun clause and describes continuous past action (from the narrator's perspective). The *taw* after the prefixed *mem* indicates the stem is Hithpael. The stem appears to have a reflexive sense here ("was strengthening herself"); see EE, 82. The ending ת ֶ- is one of the characteristic endings of the feminine singular participle.
4. The form is a Qal infinitive construct from הָלַךְ with a prepositional prefix. The infinitive indicates the purpose of her determination.
5. The form consists of the preposition אֵת + 3fs pronominal suffix.
6. The form is a Piel infinitive construct from דָּבַר. The form has three root letters with *pathaq* under the first letter, so it must be a Piel. See chart 9 (non-imperfect forms with no ending). Of course, the doubled second root letter is also characteristic of the Piel in verbs without a II-guttural. The preposition introduces a verbal complement that completes the preceding verb ("she stopped speaking").
7. The form consists of the preposition אֶל + 3fs pronominal suffix.

1:19a

1. The suffix appears to be 3mp, but it refers to two women (Naomi and Ruth) here. So it is probably another example of the archaic common dual.
2. The suffix is functioning here as the subject of the infinitive.

1:19b

3. The form consists of the preposition עַל, used here in a causal sense, and the 3fp pronominal suffix.
4. The prefixed *he* introduces an interrogative sentence; זֹאת is a demonstrative pronoun.

1:20

1. The form consists of the preposition אֶל + 3fp pronominal suffix.
2. The verb is a Qal jussive 2fp from קָרָא. The *taw* prefix in conjunction with the נָה- ending indicates the verb is feminine plural. Since Naomi is addressing the women, the verb must be understood as second person.
3. The verb is a Qal imperative 2fp from קָרָא. The נָה- ending indicates the form is feminine plural. The imperative can be taken as having the force of a command, since Naomi would seem to have the right to give herself whatever name she desired.
4. The clause is explanatory/causal; Naomi explains why she wants a new name.
5. The verb is a Hiphil perfect 3ms from מָרַר.

1:21

1. The adjective is feminine singular, as the ה ָ- ending makes clear. The masculine form of the adjective

is מָלֵא; with the addition of the ending the accent shifts to the end, leaving the *qamets* in an open propretonic syllable. The *qamets* reduces to *shewa* under these conditions.

4. The verb is a Qal imperfect 2fp from קָרָא. The verb is present progressive, "Why are you calling me Naomi?"

8. The verb is a Hiphil perfect 3ms from רָעַע. For help with the stem and root see chart 9. The *tsere* prefix vowel is characteristic of the Hiphil perfect of hollow verbs, but a hollow verb would have a *hireq yod* theme vowel (e.g., הֵקִים; see PVP, 361; Ful., 259). Geminate verbs also take a *tsere* prefix vowel in the Hiphil perfect, but they typically take a tone long or short theme vowel (e.g., סָבַב < הֵסֵב). When a verb is both geminate and III-guttural, a *pathaq* will appear as the theme vowel.

1:22

2. The clause is disjunctive, as the word order (*waw* + non-verb) indicates. It has a circumstantial function; Ruth accompanied Naomi on her return.

4. The form consists of the feminine singular noun כַּלָּה + 3fs pronominal suffix. Feminine singular nouns show the ending ת- before pronominal suffixes.

5. The form consists of the preposition עִם + 3fs pronominal suffix.

7. The clause is disjunctive, as the word order (*waw* + subject + verb) indicates. The clause appears to have a concluding function for the act and scene. However, it is possible that it is supplemental and introductory in relation to what follows, for it provides the setting for Ruth's request in 2:2.

8. The verb is a Qal perfect 3cp from בּוֹא. The form has no prefix, two root letters visible, a *qamets* under the first letter, and the accent on the first syllable, so it is a hollow verb. (A III-*he* verb would have the accent on the final syllable.) See chart 5. The ו- ending is characteristic of the perfect in the 3cp form.

9. The form consists of the feminine singular construct form of the noun תְּחִלָּה with a prepositional prefix. Before consonants that have a vocal *shewa*, the inseparable prepositions have a *hireq* rather than the customary *shewa*. The ת ָ- ending is characteristic of feminine singular nouns in the construct.

10. The *shewa* under the first root letter (as opposed to the *qamets* that appears in the absolute form) shows this form is construct.

2:1

1. The clause is disjunctive because of its word order: *waw* + non-verb + implied predicate. It is supplemental in function, providing background information for the scene to follow.

3. The form consists of the preposition + noun (ms) אִישׁ + 3fs pronominal suffix.

4. גִּבּוֹר is (a) a masculine singular attributive or appositional substantival adjective, or (b) a masculine singular noun (see BDB, 150; *HALOT*, 172), "mighty man, hero," that is appositional to the preceding אִישׁ and in construct with the following חַיִל. חַיִל is a masculine singular noun, "strength," that is genitival after the construct. It is attributive, describing a quality of the preceding noun (see EE, 63).

5. The ending ת ָ- is characteristic of feminine singular nouns in the construct.

6. The form consists of the conjunction + noun שֵׁם + 3ms pronominal suffix. (On the form of the conjunction here, see PVP, 44; Ful., 37 [8.3].) The clause is disjunctive because of the word order: *waw* + non-verb (subject) + predicate nominative. It has a supplementary function, identifying more specifically the man mentioned in the preceding clause.

2:2

2. The verb is a Qal cohortative 1cs from הָלַךְ. The ending is characteristic of the cohortative and the following נָא often appears after volitional forms. Ruth is making a request; Naomi later gives her permission.

3. The form is an adverbial accusative indicating the direction in which Ruth intends to go.

4. The verb is a Piel cohortative 1cs from לָקַט with a prefixed *waw* conjunctive. The prefix vowel is *shewa* (compound because of the guttural *aleph* with which it appears) followed by a *pathaq* under the first root letter, the standard pattern for the Piel. (See chart 10.) The ending is characteristic of the cohortative. When cohortatives appear in succession like this, they can be synonymous or purely sequential (EE, 109). The latter is a possibility here, but only if Naomi has the authority to grant permission to glean. It is clear that she does not (cf. v. 7). Consequently the second cohortative is better understood as indicating purpose (EE, 109): "let me go to the field in order that I may glean."

6. The verb is a Qal imperfect 1cs from מָצָא. The imperfect may be understood as indicating an anterior future action that is envisioned as occurring before another future action: "that I may glean after one in whose eyes I find favor (prior to gleaning)." For this category of the imperfect see EE, 92. Another option is that the imperfect indicates possibility: "after one in whose eyes I may find favor." See EE, 93.

7. The form consists of the preposition + 3fs pronominal suffix.

8. The verb is a Qal imperative 2fs from הָלַךְ. The form has an יִ - ending, two root letters, and a *shewa* under the first visible root letter, so one would expect it to be a 2fs imperative from either a III-*he*, I-*yod*, or I-*nun* verb. See chart 6. However הָלַךְ follows I-*yod* patterns. The יִ - ending is distinctive of the feminine singular imperative. In this case the imperative expresses permission (cf. Ruth's earlier request).

9. The form consists of the singular form of the noun בַּת, "daughter," and the 1cs pronominal suffix.

2:3

2. The verb is a Piel wayyiqtol 3fs from לָקַט. The prefix vowel is *shewa* followed by a *pathaq* under the first root letter, the standard pattern for the Piel. (See chart 10.) The *taw* is the characteristic prefix of the 3fs and 2ms in the wayyiqtol. Context indicates that Ruth is the subject, so the form is understood as 3fs.

3. The form is a Qal active participle masculine plural from קָצַר with a prefixed article. The *holem* after the first root letter is characteristic of the Qal active participle. See chart 8 and PVP, 259 (22.3); Ful., 115 (19.2). The participle is substantival here, being equivalent to a noun, "the reapers." The ים - ending is characteristic of the masculine plural in nominal, adjectival, and participial forms.

4. The verb is a Qal wayyiqtol 3ms from קָרָה. The form has two root letters visible and a *hireq* prefix vowel followed by a *seghol*, so it is a III-*he* verb. See chart 10. The final *he* apocopates in the 3ms of the wayyiqtol (just as it does in the jussive).

5. The form consists of the masculine singular noun מִקְרֶה + 3fs pronominal suffix.

6. The ending ת - is characteristic of feminine singular nouns in the construct.

7. The preposition indicates possession, "the portion of the field *belonging to* Boaz."

2:4

1. The clause is disjunctive (note the order *waw* + non-verb + subject + predicate). The use of הִנֵּה suggests that it has a dramatic function, inviting the hearer to step into the story and observe the scene as if he/she were an eyewitness. See EE, 126–27.
2. The form is either a Qal perfect 3ms from בּוֹא or a Qal participle masculine singular from בּוֹא. Note that there is no ending and the vowel under the first root letter is *qamets*. See chart 9.
3. The form consists of the preposition עִם + 2mp pronominal suffix.
4. The verb is a Piel jussive 3ms from בָּרַךְ with the 2ms pronominal suffix. The prefix vowel is *shewa* followed by a *qamets* under the first root letter, showing it to be Piel. See chart 10. The middle letter, *resh*, like guttural letters, does not admit the *dagesh forte* typical of the Piel, so the preceding vowel is long because it remains in an open syllable (compensatory lengthening). The pronominal suffix functions as the object of the verb.

2:5

1. The form consists of the preposition + noun נַעַר + 3ms pronominal suffix.
2. The form is a Niphal participle masculine singular, from נָצַב, with an article prefixed to the form. The *nun* prefix and *qamets* theme vowel mark the form as a Niphal participle. See the introduction to the parsing charts, as well as chart 9 (prefixed *nun* section). The participle can be viewed as (a) attributive or (b) substantival (being equivalent to a noun, "the appointed one/foreman") and appositional to the preceding suffixed noun, "his servant."
3. The form consists of the preposition + interrogative pronoun מִי. The preposition indicates possession.
4. The demonstrative (with prefixed article) is functioning as an attributive adjective, "this young woman."

2:6

1. The verb is a Qal wayyiqtol 3ms from עָנָה.
2. The noun is a predicate nominative, "she is a Moabite girl."
4. This independent 3fs personal pronoun is the subject of the nominal sentence (see no. 2 above).

2:7

1. The verb is a Piel cohortative 1cs from לָקַט (see 2:2, no. 4). The ־נָא ending indicates this is a volitional form (see 2:2, no. 2). The cohortative here expresses Ruth's request.
2. The verb is a Qal perfect 1cs from אָסַף with a *waw* consecutive. The ־תִי ending is characteristic of the 1cs perfect.
5. The verb is a Qal wayyiqtol 3fs from עָמַד. The *taw* prefix indicates the form is 3fs. The *pathaq* prefix vowel appears with both the Qal and Hiphil; when the theme vowel is *holem* (non-*i*-class) the form is Qal. See chart 10. The Qal typically has a *hireq* prefix vowel, but I- guttural verbs take *pathaq*.

2:8

1. The form consists of an interrogative *he* + negative particle (fully written with *holem waw*). See PVP, 145 (13.12).
2. The verb is a Qal perfect 2fs from שָׁמַע. The *taw* ending with *shewa* is characteristic of the 2fs perfect.
3. The form consists of the noun בַּת, "daughter," + 1cs pronominal suffix. It is a vocative, identifying the addressee.
4. The verb is a Qal jussive 2fs from הָלַךְ. The form has two root letters with a *tsere* prefix vowel. Consequently it appears to be I-*yod*, but הָלַךְ follows this pattern. See chart 10. The *taw* prefix in combination with the *hireq yod* ending is characteristic of the 2fs imperfect/jussive.
5. The form is a Qal infinitive construct from לָקַט, with the preposition prefixed. The form probably indicates purpose here.
6. The verb is a Qal imperfect 2fs from עָבַר. The *taw* prefix in combination with the *hireq yod* ending is characteristic of the 2fs imperfect. The *pathaq* prefix vowel, due to the guttural letter in the first position, appears with both the Qal or Hiphil; when the theme vowel is non-*i*-class (usually *holem* or *shewa*, but *shureq* here) the form is Qal.
7. The form consists of the preposition מִן + demonstrative pronoun or adjective functioning substantivally.
9. The verb is a Qal imperfect 2fs from דָּבַק. The imperfect expresses permission in this context, "so you may stay close." See EE, 93, for this use of the imperfect.
10. The form consists of the feminine plural form of the noun נַעֲרָה (note the ת - ending, characteristic of fp nouns) + 1cs pronominal suffix.

2:9

2. The verb is a Qal imperfect 3mp from קָצַר. The *yod* prefix in combination with the *shureq* ending is characteristic of the 3mp imperfect. The subject is the reapers (masculine; cf. הַקּוֹצְרִים in vv. 3–7).
3. The verb is a Qal perfect 2fs from הָלַךְ with a *waw* consecutive. The תְּ- ending is characteristic of the 2fs perfect.
4. This form consists of the preposition אַחֲרֵי + 3fp pronominal suffix. The suffix refers to Boaz's female workers (cf. נַעֲרֹתַי in v. 8).
5. The verb is a Piel perfect 1cs from צָוָה. The form has two root letters visible with a *hireq* under the first and a *dagesh forte* in the second, indicating Piel. The *yod* before the ending indicates it is a III-*he* root (see chart 1). The תִי- ending is characteristic of the perfect 1cs.
6. The form is a Qal infinitive construct from נָגַע with a 2fs pronominal suffix (see chart 9). The suffix functions as the object of the infinitive in this case ("not to touch you").
9. The verb is a Qal perfect 2fs from שָׁתָה. The form has two root letters visible with a *yod* before the ending, so it is III-*he* (see chart 1). The *taw* ending with no vowel beneath it is characteristic of the perfect 2fs with III-*he* verbs. (Normally there is a silent *shewa* beneath the *taw*, cf. קָטַלְתְּ.)
10. The verb is a Qal imperfect 3mp from שָׁאַב. The *yod* prefix in combination with the *shureq* ending is characteristic of the 3mp imperfect. The *nun* is paragogic. The imperfect is best understood as anterior future, indicating that they "will have drawn" the water prior to her drinking. Other options include present progressive ("from that which they are [presently/as we speak] drawing") or characteristic present ("from that which they [as a matter of course] draw").

2:10

1. The verb is a Qal wayyiqtol 3fs from נָפַל. One knows the verb is I-*nun* because of the *dagesh forte* in the *pe* indicating assimilation. The *taw* prefix indicates the verb is 3fs.

2. The form consists of the noun פָּנִים + 3fs pronominal suffix.

4. The unaccented *qamets he* ending indicates direction after a verb of motion.

5. The verb is a Qal perfect 1cs from מָצָא. The תִי- is typical of the 1cs form of the perfect. The perfect may be taken as present perfect, simple (recent) past, or simple present.

6. The form is a Hiphil infinitive construct from נָכַר with a prepositional prefix and a 1cs pronominal suffix. The verbal form has a prefixed *he* with a prefix vowel *pathaq*, so the stem is Hiphil. There are two root letters visible with a *dagesh forte* in the first, so the root is I-*nun*. The pronominal suffix functions as the object of the infinitive. In relation to the preceding verb, the infinitive probably indicates result, "Why have I found favor in your eyes, so that/with the result that (you) recognize me?" or manner "Why have I found favor in your eyes by your recognizing me?"

2:11

1. The *dagesh forte* in the *gimel* indicates that the initial *nun* of the root has assimilated. The infinitive absolute is used for emphasis.

2. The verb is a Hophal perfect 3ms from נָגַד. The form has two root letters with a prefixed *he* and a prefix vowel *qibbuts,* so the stem is Hophal (see chart 9). The root is I-*nun*; the *dagesh forte* in the *gimel* indicates that the initial *nun* of the root has assimilated. The Hophal indicates the passive voice.

3. כֹּל is functioning as the subject of the verb הֻגַּד, "all . . . has been told."

4. The verb is a Qal perfect 2fs from עָשָׂה. The form has no prefix, two root letters, a *qamets* under the first letter, and a *yod* before the ending, so it is III-*he*. See chart 1. The תְ- ending, with no vowel beneath it, indicates the P-G-N is 2fs.

5. The verb is a Qal wayyiqtol 2fs from עָזַב. The form has a *pathaq* prefix vowel, so it must be Qal or Hiphil. There is a *shewa* (rather than a *hireq yod* or *tsere*) in the theme vowel position, so it is Qal. See chart 10. (In other words, it has an *a* + non-*i* vowel pattern. See chart 11.) The *taw* prefix in combination with the *hireq yod* ending indicates the verb is 2fs.

6. The noun is a genitive that specifies which land is in view.

7. The relative pronoun is the object of the verb. The verb is a Qal perfect 2fs from יָדַע. The תְ- ending, with no vowel beneath it, indicates the P-G-N is 2fs.

2:12

1. The verb is a Piel jussive 3ms from שָׁלֵם. There is a *shewa* under the prefix, followed by a *pathaq* (*a*-class vowel) under the first root letter, so the stem is Piel. See chart 10. The Piel has a factitive function here. The Qal is stative (intransitive); the Piel indicates production of the state described by the Qal. (See EE, 80, no. 1.) The Qal has the basic sense, "be complete, full"; the Piel means "make complete, full." In this case, with "your labor" as object, it has the nuance "repay, reward." See BDB, 1022, Pi.5; *HALOT,* 1534–35, pi.2.b.

2. The form consists of the noun פֹּעַל + 2fs pronominal suffix. The noun is the object of the verb יְשַׁלֵּם.

3. The *taw* prefix indicates the form is either 3fs or 2ms; in this context it is 3fs since the following feminine singular noun is the subject of the verb.

4. The form consists of the feminine singular noun מַשְׂכֻּרְתֵּ + 2fs pronominal suffix. The noun is the subject of the verb תְהִי.

5. The form is a feminine singular adjective that is functioning predicatively here, "may your wage be full."

7. The verb is a Qal perfect 2fs from בּוֹא. The תְ- ending, with no vowel beneath it, indicates the P-G-N is 2fs. The subject is the addressee, Ruth.

8. The form is a Qal infinitive construct from חָסָה. It has two root letters visible with a *shewa* (compound because of the guttural) under the first root letter. The וֹת- ending indicates the verb is an infinitive construct of a III-*he* root. (See chart 8.) The infinitive indicates purpose, "you have come in order to find refuge."

2:13

1. The verb is a Qal imperfect 1cs from מָצָא. The *aleph* prefix indicates the form is 1cs. As suggested by the note in the workbook, the imperfect appears to be present progressive. (See EE, 91, no. 5.)

2. The clause is explanatory (EE, 116), explaining specifically how Boaz is showing her favor. The verb is a Piel perfect 2ms from נָחַם with a 1cs pronominal suffix. The תָּ- ending before the suffix indicates the verb is 2ms.

6. The verb is a Qal imperfect 1cs from הָיָה.

7. The form consists of the feminine plural form of the noun שִׁפְחָה + 2ms pronominal suffix. The וֹת- ending, as well as the *yod* in the suffix, indicates the noun is feminine plural.

2:14

3. The *hireq yod* ending is characteristic of the 2fs imperative.

5. The verb is a Qal perfect 2fs from אָכַל with a *waw* prefix. The תְּ- ending, with no vowel, indicates the form is 2fs. After the imperative, the *waw* on the perfect should be taken as consecutive. The form has the same force (permission) as the preceding imperative.

7. The verb is a Qal wayyiqtol 3fs from יָשַׁב. The form has two root letters visible with a *tsere* prefix vowel and a *seghol* theme vowel, so the root is I-*yod*. (See chart 10.) The *taw* prefix with no ending indicates the verb is 3fs.

9. The verb is a Qal wayyiqtol 3ms from צָבַט. The *yod* prefix with no ending indicates the verb is 3ms; Boaz is the subject.

2:15

1. The verb is a Qal wayyiqtol 3fs from קוּם. The form has two root letters with a *qamets* prefix vowel and a *qamets hatuph* (non-*i*-class) theme vowel (note that the vowel is in a closed, unaccented syllable), so the stem is Qal and the root either hollow or geminate (there is no root קמם). See chart 10. The *taw* prefix with no ending indicates the P-G-N is 3fs.

2. The form is a Piel infinitive construct from לְקֵט with a prepositional prefix. The verb form has no prefix, three root letters, and a *pathaq* under the first root letter, so the stem is Piel (note also the characteristic doubling of the second root letter). See chart 9. The infinitive indicates purpose, "she got up in order to glean."

3. The verb is a Piel wayyiqtol 3ms from צָוָה. The form has two root letters visible with a *shewa* under the prefix and a *pathaq* (*a*-class vowel) under the first root letter, so the stem is Piel. (See chart 10.) The root is III-*he*; the final *he* has apocopated in the wayyiqtol form.

4. The verb is a Piel imperfect (or jussive) 3fs from לָקַט. The form has three root letters visible with a *shewa* under the prefix and a *pathaq* (*a*-class vowel) under the first root letter, so the stem is Piel. (See chart 10.) The *taw* prefix with no ending indicates the verb is 3fs. If the form is understood as an imperfect, then it has a permissive sense, "she may [is permitted to] glean" (see EE, 93, no. 12). If it is taken as a jussive, then it has the force of a command, "let her glean" (EE, 104, no. 1).

5. The verb is a Hiphil imperfect 2mp from כָּלַם with a 3fs pronominal suffix. The form has three root letters, a *pathaq* (*a*-class vowel) under the prefix, and a *hireq yod* (*i*-class vowel) theme vowel, so the stem is Hiphil. (See chart 10.) The *taw* prefix in combination with the *shureq* ending (before the suffix) indicates the P-G-N is 2mp. The suffix is the direct object of the verb. The negated imperfect has the force of a prohibition (EE, 94, no. 14).

2:16–17a

2. The verb is a Qal imperfect 2mp from שָׁלַל. The form has two root letters with a *qamets* prefix vowel and a *holem* (non-*i*-class vowel) theme vowel, so the stem is Qal. The *dagesh forte* in the *lamed* indicates the root is geminate in this inflected form. (See chart 10.) The *taw* prefix in combination with the *shureq* ending indicates the P-G-N is 2mp. The imperfect here has the force of a command (EE, 94, no. 14).

4. The verb is a Qal perfect 2mp from עָזַב with a prefixed *waw*. The תֶּם- ending indicates the P-G-N is 2mp. After the imperfect, the *waw* should be understood as consecutive. In this context, where Boaz is giving his servants orders, the construction has the force of a command (EE, 101, no. 8).

5. The verb is a Piel perfect 3fs from לָקַט with a prefixed *waw*. The form has three root letters with a *hireq* under the first and a *dagesh forte* in the second, so the stem is Piel. (See chart 2.) The הָ- ending indicates the P-G-N is 3fs.

6. The verb is a Qal imperfect 2mp from גָּעַר. The *taw* prefix in combination with the *shureq* ending indicates the P-G-N is 2mp.

7. The verb is a Piel wayyiqtol 3fs from לָקַט. The form has three root letters visible, a *shewa* under the prefix, and a *pathaq* (*a*-class vowel) under the first root letter, so the stem is Piel. (See chart 10.) The *taw* prefix with no ending indicates the verb is 3fs.

2:17b

1. The verb is a Qal wayyiqtol 3fs from חָבַט. The form has a *pathaq* prefix vowel and a *holem* (non-*i*-class vowel) theme vowel, so the stem is Qal. (See chart 10.) The prefix is *pathaq* (*a*-class vowel) due to the I-guttural. The *taw* prefix with no ending indicates the P-G-N is 3fs.

3. The verb is a Piel perfect 3fs from לָקַט. The form has three root letters with a *hireq* under the first and a *dagesh forte* in the second, so the stem is Piel. (See chart 2.) The הָ- ending indicates the P-G-N is 3fs. The perfect is a past perfect ("had gleaned"), describing an action that occurred prior to the main verb ("she beat out"). See EE, 87, no. 2.

2:18

1. The verb is a Qal wayyiqtol 3fs from נָשָׂא. The root is I-*nun;* note the *dagesh forte* in the *sin* indicating assimilation of the first root letter, *nun.* The *qamets* theme vowel is due to the third letter being a quiescent *aleph.* The *taw* prefix with no ending indicates the P-G-N is 3fs.

2. The noun is functioning as an adverbial accusative, indicating the direction in which she went (EE, 64, no. 3).

3. The *taw* prefix and no ending indicate the P-G-N of this verb is 3fs. The subject of the Qal verb form is "her mother-in-law."

4. The perfect is functioning as a past perfect ("had gleaned"), describing an action that occurred prior to the main verb ("she saw"). See EE, 87, no. 2.

5. The verb is a Hiphil wayyiqtol 3fs from יָצָא. The form has two root letters visible and a *holem waw* prefix vowel, so the stem is Hiphil and the root I-*yod.* (See chart 10.) The *taw* prefix with no ending indicates the P-G-N is 3fs. Ruth is the subject. The Hiphil stem is functioning as a causative here, literally, "she caused to go out," that is, "she brought out."

6. The verb is a Qal wayyiqtol 3fs from נָתַן. The form has two root letters visible, a *hireq* prefix vowel followed by a doubled letter, and a *seghol,* so the stem is Qal and the root I-*nun.* (See chart 10.) The *dagesh forte* indicates assimilation of the first root letter, *nun.*

8. The verb is a Hiphil perfect 3fs from יָתַר. The form has two root letters visible, a *he* prefix, and a *holem waw* prefix vowel, so the stem is Hiphil and the root I-*yod.* (See chart 2.) The ה ָ- ending indicates the P-G-N is 3fs. The subject of the verb is Ruth. The perfect is a past perfect ("had saved"), indicating an action that occurred before the main verb ("she gave").

9. The pronominal suffix is 3fs, functioning as the subject of the verbal noun/infinitive. The antecedent of the suffix is Ruth.

2:19

1. The verb is a Piel perfect 2fs from לָקַט. The form has three root letters with a *hireq* under the first and a *dagesh forte* in the second, so the stem is Piel. (See chart 1.) The תְּ- ending with no vowel indicates the P-G-N is 2fs. Within this quotation the perfect indicates simple past action from Naomi's perspective ("Where did you glean?").

4. The verb is a Qal perfect 2fs from עָשָׂה. The form has no prefix, two root letters, a *qamets* under the first root letter, and a *yod* before the ending, so the root is III-*he.* (See chart 1.) The *taw* ending with no vowel beneath it indicates the P-G-N is 2fs.

5. The jussive is used in a prayer of blessing; Naomi requests that God reward Boaz for his kindness. See EE, 104–5, no. 3.

6. The form is a Hiphil participle masculine singular from נָכַר with a 2fs pronominal suffix. The prefixed *mem* suggests this may be a participle. The *pathaq* beneath the *mem* indicates the stem is Hiphil. (See chart 9.) The form has only two root letters with a *dagesh forte* in the *kaph* indicating assimilation of the first root letter, *nun.* The participle is substantival; it functions as the subject of יְהִי. The suffix is the object of the participle.

7. The form is a Qal passive participle masculine singular from בָּרַךְ, functioning as a predicate adjective, "be blessed."

8. The verb is a Hiphil wayyiqtol 3fs from נָגַד. The form has two root letters with a *pathaq* (*a*-class vowel)

prefix vowel and a doubled letter following the prefix, so the stem is Hiphil and the root I-*nun*. See chart 10. (Note also the characteristic *a* + *i* vowel pattern. See chart 10.) The *taw* prefix with no ending indicates the P-G-N is 3fs.

10. The verb is a Qal perfect 3fs from עָשָׂה. The form has no prefix and two root letters visible (assuming the *taw* is not a root letter), with a *qamets* under the first. The *taw* before the ending indicates the root is III-*he*. (See chart 2.) The ה ָ- ending indicates the P-G-N is 3fs. The perfect is a past perfect ("she had worked"), indicating an action that occurred prior to the main verb ("she told").

12. The verb is a Qal perfect 1cs from עָשָׂה. The form has no prefix, two root letters, a *qamets* under the first root letter, and a *yod* before the ending, so the root is III-*he*. (See chart 1.) The תִי- ending indicates the P-G-N is 1cs. Within the quotation the perfect indicates simple past action from the speaker's (Ruth's) perspective.

13. The name Boaz is a predicate nominative, "the name . . . is Boaz."

2:20

1. The pronoun is the subject of the preceding participle, "may he be blessed."
4. The noun is the object of the preceding verb.
7. The form is a predicate adjective, or perhaps substantival, functioning as a predicate nominative.
8. The form consists of the the preposition מִן + noun (mp) גֹּאֵל (actually a substantival part.) + 1cp pronominal suffix.

2:21

3. The verb is a Qal imperfect 2fs from דָּבַק. The *taw* prefix in combination with the *hireq yod* ending indicates the P-G-N is 2fs. The imperfect indicates permission ("you may stay close"). See EE, 93, no. 12.

5. The verb is a Piel perfect 3cp from כָּלָה. The form has no prefix, two root letters visible, a *hireq* under the first and a *dagesh forte* in the second, so the stem is Piel and the root III-*he*. (See chart 5.) The *shureq* ending indicates the P-G-N is 3cp. The perfect is a future perfect, indicating a future action that will be completed before the action of the main verb ("you may stay close") is completed ("until they shall have completed"). (See EE, 88–89, no. 8.) The Piel is factitive. The verb in the Qal means "be completed." The Piel indicates production of the condition, "make complete, complete."

2:22

1. The adjective is functioning predicatively.
2. The form consists of the noun בַּת + 1cs pronominal suffix. The form is a vocative.
3. The verb is a Qal imperfect 2fs from יָצָא. The form has two root letters visible with a *tsere* prefix vowel followed by a *shewa*, so the root is I-*yod*. (See chart 10.) The *taw* prefix in combination with the *hireq yod* ending indicates the P-G-N is 2fs. The imperfect probably indicates permission, "that you are allowed to go out." See EE, 93, no. 12.
4. The form consists of the feminine plural of נַעֲרָה + 3ms pronominal suffix. The form is feminine (in contrast to the masculine plural נְעָרִים), indicating that Boaz's female servants are specifically in view here.

5. The verb is a Qal imperfect 3mp from פָּגַע. The *yod* prefix in combination with the *shureq* ending indicates the P-G-N is 3mp.

2:23

2. The form is a Qal infinitive construct from כָּלָה. It has two root letters visible with a *shewa* under the first root letter. The וֹת- ending indicates the verb is an infinitive construct of a III-*he* root. (See chart 8.) The form is functioning as a noun, serving as the object of the preceding preposition (see EE, 78, no. 1).
5. The verb is a Qal wayyiqtol 3fs from יָשַׁב. The form has two root letters visible with a *tsere* prefix vowel and a *seghol* theme vowel, so the root is I-*yod*. (See chart 10.) The *taw* prefix with no ending indicates the verb is 3fs. The אֶת must be understood as the preposition "with."

3:1

1. The form is functioning as a vocative.
2. The form consists of an interrogative *he* and a negative particle.
3. The verb is a Piel imperfect 1cs from בָּקַשׁ. The form has three root letters visible, a *shewa* under the prefix, and a *pathaq* (*a*-class vowel) under the first root letter, so the stem is Piel. (See chart 10.) The *aleph* prefix indicates the verb is 1cs. The imperfect indicates obligation or propriety, "Should I not seek?" See EE, 93, no. 13.
4. This noun is the object of the verb "seek."
5. The verb is a Qal imperfect 3ms from יָטַב. The form has two root letters with a *hireq yod* prefix vowel so the root is I-*yod*. See chart 10.

3:2

1. The form consists of the noun מֹדַעַת + 1cp pronominal suffix. The noun is a predicate nominative, "Is not Boaz our relative?"
3. The verb is a Qal perfect 2fs from הָיָה. The form has two root letters visible and a *yod* before the ending, so it is III-*he* (see chart 1). The *taw* ending with no vowel beneath it is characteristic of the perfect 2fs with III-*he* verbs. (Normally there is a silent *shewa* under the *taw*, cf. קָטַלְתְּ.) The perfect is simple past here.
4. The form is a Qal active participle masculine singular from זָרָה. The *holem* after the first root letter indicates an active participle. The temporal nuance is either present ("he is winnowing") or imminent future ("he is about to winnow"). See EE, 67.

3:3

2. The verb is a Qal perfect 2fs from סוּךְ. The form has two root letters with a *pathaq* under the first, so the root is either hollow or geminate. A *dagesh* does not appear in the second letter (*kaph*), so the root is hollow (a geminate root would be סַכּוֹת). See chart 1. The *taw* ending with no vowel indicates the P-G-N is 2fs.
3. The verb is a Qal perfect 2fs from שִׂים. The form has two root letters with a *pathaq* under the first, so the root is either hollow or geminate. A *dagesh* does not appear in the second letter (*mem*), so the root is

hollow (a geminate root would be שַׁמּוֹת). See chart 1. The *taw* ending with no vowel indicates the P-G-N is 2fs.

5. The form consists of the preposition עַל + 2fs pronominal suffix.

7. The form is functioning as adverbial accusative, indicating direction. See EE, 64, no. 3.

8. The verb is a Niphal jussive 2fs from יָדַע. The form has the *i* + *dagesh* + *a* pattern with the first root letter, so the stem is Niphal. The *taw* prefix in combination with the *hireq yod* ending indicates the P-G-N is 2fs.

9. The form is a Piel infinitive construct with a 3ms pronominal suffix from כָּלָה. The form has two root letters visible with a *pathaq* under the first so the stem is Piel. (Note as well the characteristic doubling of the second root letter.) See chart 8. The ת‍ - ending indicates the root is III-*he*. The stem is factitive; the Qal means "be complete," while the Piel means "cause to be complete, complete." The suffix is functioning as the subject of the infinitive, "until he completes."

10. The two infinitives are verbal complements to כַּלֹּתוֹ, indicating what he will complete, "until he completes eating and drinking."

11. The form is a Qal infinitive construct from שָׁתָה. The תוֹ- ending is characteristic of the III-*he* infinitive construct (see chart 8).

3:4

2. The form is a Qal infinitive construct from שָׁכַב with a preposition prefixed and a 3ms pronominal suffix. The form has three root letters with a *qamets hatuph* under the first so the stem is Qal. See chart 9. The preposition has a temporal function and the suffix is the subject of the infinitive, "when he lies down."

3. The verb is a Qal perfect 2fs from יָדַע with *waw* consecutive. The *taw* ending with a *shewa* under it is characteristic of the perfect 2fs.

5. The imperfect is an anterior future. See EE, 92, no. 7. Though the action is future from the speaker's perspective, it occurs prior to the action of the main verb ("take note of").

6. The verb is a Qal perfect 2fs from בּוֹא with *waw* consecutive. The *taw* ending with no vowel beneath it is characteristic of the perfect 2fs with hollow verbs.

7. The verb is a Piel perfect 2fs from גָּלָה with *waw* consecutive. The verb has two root letters visible with a *hireq* under the first, so the stem is Piel. There is a *yod* before the ending, so it is III-*he* (see chart 1). The *taw* ending with no vowel under it is characteristic of the perfect 2fs with III-*he* verbs.

11. The verb is a Hiphil imperfect 3ms from נָגַד. The form has two root letters visible, a *pathaq* (*a*-class) prefix vowel, and a doubled letter, so it is a Hiphil imperfect of a I-*nun* root. See chart 10. (Note also the characteristic *a* + *i* vowel pattern of the Hiphil. See chart 11.)

13. The verb is a Qal imperfect 2fs from עָשָׂה. The *taw* prefix in combination with the *hireq yod* ending indicates the P-G-N is 2fs. The imperfect indicates obligation or propriety, "what you should do."

3:5

1. The form consists of the preposition אֵל + 3fs pronominal suffix.

2. כֹּל is the object of the verb, "all . . . I will do."

3. The verb is a Qal imperfect 2fs from אָמַר. The *taw* prefix in combination with the *hireq yod* ending indicates the P-G-N is 2fs. The imperfect is probably present progressive, "all which you are saying."

5. The verb is a Qal imperfect or cohortative 1cs from עָשָׂה. The *aleph* prefix indicates the P-G-N is 1cs.

3:6

1. The verb is a Qal wayyiqtol 3fs from יָרַד. The form has two root letters visible, a *tsere* prefix vowel, and a *seghol* theme vowel, so the root is I-*yod*. (See chart 10.) The *taw* prefix with no ending indicates the verb is 3fs.
2. The form is functioning as an adverbial accusative, indicating direction after the verb of motion.
3. The verb is a Qal wayyiqtol 3fs from עָשָׂה. The form has two root letters with a *pathaq* prefix vowel followed by another *pathaq*, so the root is III-*he*. See chart 10.
4. The verb is functioning as a past perfect, indicating an action that occurred before that of the main verb ("she did").
5. The form is functioning as the subject of the preceding verb.

3:7

1. The verb is a Qal wayyiqtol 3ms from שָׁתָה.
2. The verb is a Qal wayyiqtol 3ms from יָטַב. The form has two root letters with a *hireq yod* prefix vowel so the root is I-*yod*. See chart 10.
3. The form is functioning as the subject of the preceding verb.
4. The verb is a Qal wayyiqtol 3ms from בּוֹא. See chart 10. The form has two root letters visible and a *qamets* prefix vowel, so the options for the stem are Qal or Hiphil. When the theme vowel is an *i/e*-class, the verb is normally Hiphil, but when the theme vowel is an *o/u*-class, the form is invariably Qal. Since the theme vowel on this form is *holem* (long *o*) the stem is Qal. The root is either geminate or hollow, but there is no geminate root באא, so this has to be the hollow verb בּוֹא (there is no בּוֹא or בִּיא).
5. The form is a Qal infinitive construct from שָׁכַב with a prepositional prefix. The form indicates purpose, "he went in order to lie down."
7. The verb is a Qal wayyiqtol 3fs from בּוֹא. The *taw* prefix with no ending indicates the P-G-N is 3fs.
9. The verb is a Piel wayyiqtol 3fs from גָּלָה. The form has two root letters visible, a *shewa* under the prefix, and a *pathaq* (*a*-class vowel) under the first root letter, so the stem is Piel. (See chart 10.) The root is III-*he*; the final *he* has apocopated in the wayyiqtol form. The *taw* prefix with no ending indicates the P-G-N is 3fs.

3:8

3. The noun is functioning as the subject of the preceding verb. The article indicates specificity; Boaz (v. 7) is the referent.
4. The verb is a Niphal wayyiqtol 3ms from לָפַת. See chart 10. The form has three root letters visible and a *hireq* prefix vowel. There are three stem options listed, but the *qamets* under the first root letter indicates the stem is Niphal. The *nun* of the stem has assimilated: ‎*יִנְלְפֵת > יִלָּפֵת.
7. The form is a Qal active participle feminine singular from שָׁכַב. The *holem* after the first root letter indicates an active participle. The ת ֶ- ending indicates the gender/number is feminine singular. The participle is functioning predicatively in relation to the preceding noun, "a woman was lying down."
8. The form is an adverbial accusative, indicating the location where she was lying.

3:9

2. The form consists of the feminine singular noun אָמָה + 2ms pronominal suffix. The form is in apposition to the preceding proper name, "I am Ruth, your servant."
5. The clause is explanatory or causal, explaining why Boaz should provide protection for her.
6. The participle is substantival, functioning as a predicate nominative.

3:10

1. The form is a Qal passive participle feminine singular from בָּרַךְ. The הָ - ending indicates the gender/number is feminine singular. The participle is functioning predicatively.
3. The form is functioning as a vocative.
4. The verb is a Hiphil perfect 2fs from יָטַב. The form has a *he* prefix with a *tsere yod* prefix vowel, so the stem is Hiphil and the root I-*yod*. See chart 1. The *taw* ending with *shewa* indicates the P-G-N is 2fs.
5. The noun is functioning as the direct object of the preceding verb. The pronominal suffix indicates the subject or source.
10. The form is a Qal infinitive construct from הָלַךְ.

3:11

1. The verb is a Qal jussive 2fs from יָרֵא. The form has two root letters with a *hireq yod* prefix vowel, so the root is I-*yod*. The *taw* prefix in combination with the *hireq yod* ending indicates the P-G-N is 2fs. The negative particle אַל before the form indicates a jussive.
2. The form is functioning as the direct object of the verb אֶעֱשֶׂה, "I will do."
3. The verb is a Qal imperfect 2fs from אָמַר. The imperfect is probably present progressive ("all that you are requesting").
5. The clause is explanatory or causal, explaining why Boaz is willing to respond positively to her invitation.
6. The form is a Qal active participle masculine singular from יָדַע. It is functioning as the predicate in the clause and shows present action, "the entire gate of my people knows."
7. The form is the subject (nominative) of the preceding participle.
9. This is an accusative noun clause, introducing the object of "knows."
10. This is a genitive of attribute.

3:13

1. The verb is a Qal imperative feminine singular from לִין/לוּן. The form has no prefix and a *hireq yod* with the first root letter, so the root is hollow. See chart 6. The *hireq yod* ending indicates the P-G-N is 2fs.
5. The verb has a *pathaq* prefix vowel because it is I-guttural.
6. The form is a Qal infinitive construct from גָּאַל with a prepositional prefix and a 2fs pronominal suffix functioning as the object of the infinitive. The infinitive functions as a verbal complement to the preceding verb, specifying what he may not desire to do.
7. The verb is a Qal perfect 1cs from גָּאַל with a *waw* prefix and a 2fs pronominal suffix functioning as the object of the verb. The תִּי- ending indicates the P-G-N is 1cs.

10. The verb is a Qal imperative feminine singular from שְׁכַב. The *hireq yod* ending indicates the P-G-N is 2fs.

3:14

2. The verb is a Qal wayyiqtol 3fs from קוּם. See chart 10. The form has two root letters visible and a *qamets* prefix vowel, so the options for the stem are Qal or Hiphil. When the theme vowel is an *i/e*-class, the verb is normally Hiphil, but when the theme vowel is an *o/u*-class, the form is invariably Qal. Since the theme vowel here is *qamets hatuph* (short *o*) the stem is Qal. The root is either geminate or hollow, but there is no geminate root קמם, so this has to be the hollow verb קוּם (there is no קמם or קִים). The *taw* prefix with no ending indicates the P-G-N is 3fs.

4. The verb is a Hiphil imperfect 3ms from נָכַר. The form has two root letters visible with a *pathaq* (*a*-class vowel) prefix vowel and a doubled letter following the prefix, so the stem is Hiphil and the root I-*nun*. Se chart 10. (Note the characteristic *a* + *i* vowel pattern. See chart 11.)

6. The verb is a Niphal jussive 3ms from יָדַע. See chart 10. The form has three root letters visible and a *hireq* prefix vowel. There are three stem options listed, but the *qamets* under the first root letter indicates the stem is Niphal. The *nun* of the stem has assimilated: *יִנְדַע > יִוָּדַע. The stem is functioning in a passive sense.

8. The verb is a Qal perfect 3fs from בּוֹא. The form has an הָ - ending with two root letters visible. The vowel under the first letter is *qamets* and the syllable is accented, so the root is hollow. See chart 2. (The position of the accent distinguishes the perfect from the participle. It also indicates that this cannot be a perfect 3ms of a III-*he* verb.) In the paradigm of the perfect, the הָ - ending is distinctive to the 3fs.

10. The noun is functioning as an adverbial accusative of direction.

3:15

3. The antecedent of the 3fs suffix is the feminine singular noun מִטְפַּחַת, "cloak, shawl."

5. The verb is a Qal wayyiqtol 3ms from מָדַד. The form has two root letters visible and a *qamets* prefix vowel, so the options for the stem are Qal or Hiphil. When the theme vowel is an *i/e*-class, the verb is normally Hiphil, but when the theme vowel is an *o/u*-class, the form is invariably Qal. Since the theme vowel here is *qamets hatuph* (short *o*) the stem is Qal.

7. The verb is a Qal wayyiqtol 3ms from שִׁית. The form has two root letters and a *qamets* prefix vowel, so the root must be hollow or geminate. There is a rare verb שׁתת (*HALOT*, 1672), but it does not fit here, whereas the hollow root שִׁית makes good sense.

8. The verb is a Qal wayyiqtol 3ms from בּוֹא. The form has two root letters visible and a *qamets* prefix vowel, so the options for the stem are Qal or Hiphil. When the theme vowel is an *i/e*-class, the verb is normally Hiphil, but when the theme vowel is an *o/u*-class, the form is invariably Qal. Since the theme vowel here form is *holem* (long *o*) the stem is Qal. The root is either geminate or hollow, but there is no geminate root בּאא, so this has to be the hollow verb בּוֹא (there is no בּוא or בִיא).

9. The noun is an adverbial accusative indicating direction.

3:16

1. The verb is a Qal wayyiqtol 3fs from בּוֹא. The *taw* prefix with no ending indicates the P-G-N is 3fs.

3. The verb is a Hiphil wayyiqtol 3fs from נָגַד. The form has two root letters with a *pathaq* (*a*-class vowel)

prefix vowel and a doubled letter following the prefix, so the stem is Hiphil and the root I-*nun*. See chart 10. (Note also the characteristic *a + i* vowel pattern. See chart 11.) The *taw* prefix with no ending indicates the P-G-N is 3fs.

4. The form is the direct object of the verb "she told."

5. The verb is functioning as a past perfect.

6. The noun is the subject of the verb עָשָׂה.

3:17

1. The form is a demonstrative adjective modifying the preceding "six (measures) of barley."

2. This is an explanatory/causal clause, providing a statement from Boaz that explains why he gave Ruth so much barley.

4. The verb is a Qal jussive 2fs from בּוֹא. The form has two root letters visible and a *qamets* prefix vowel, so the root is either geminate or hollow. There is no geminate root בָּאא, so this has to be the hollow verb בּוֹא (there is no בּוּא or בִּיא). The *taw* prefix in combination with the *hireq yod* ending indicates the P-G-N is 2fs.

3:18

1. The verb is a Qal imperative 2fs from יָשַׁב. The form has no prefix with a *shewa* under the first visible root letter, so the root is III-*he*, I-*nun*, or I-*yod*. See chart 6. In this context the root יָשַׁב fits well. The *hireq yod* ending indicates the form is 2fs.

2. The verb is a Qal imperfect 2fs from יָדַע. The form has two root letters visible, a *tsere* prefix vowel, and a *shewa* in the theme vowel position indicating the root is I-*yod*.[2] Recall that I-*yod* verbs typically have a *tsere* prefix vowel in the Qal. The prefixed *taw* in combination with the *hireq yod* ending indicates the P-G-N is 2fs. The imperfect is functioning as an anterior future, describing an action that will occur before the action of the main verb ("sit still") is terminated.

4. The verb is a Qal imperfect 3ms from נָפַל. One knows the verb is I-*nun* because of the *dagesh forte* in the *pe* indicating assimilation. The verb is functioning as an anterior future, describing an action (the matter "falling out") that will occur before the action of the preceding clause (his "knowing").

5. The clause is explanatory/causal, explaining why Ruth should wait patiently.

7. The verb is a Piel perfect 3ms from כָּלָה. The form has two root letters visible, an accented ה-ָ ending, and a *hireq* under the first root letter, so it is a Piel perfect 3ms of a III-*he*. See chart 2. The perfect is functioning as a future perfect, describing an action (carrying out the task) that will occur before the action of the main verb (resting). The Piel is factitive—the Qal is intransitive, "be complete," while the Piel indicates causation of the state described in the Qal, "complete, make complete."

8. The noun is the direct object of the preceding verb.

---

2. A stative geminate can have a *shewa* in this position (reduced from *pathaq*) but in this case the prefix vowel would be *hireq* and there would be doubling indicating gemination; cf. וַיִּתְּמוּ >תמם in Deuteronomy 34:8. Furthermore there is no geminate verb דעע.

4:1

1. The clause is disjunctive. It interrupts the narrative main line and functions here in an introductory manner for a new scene in the story. See EE, 124, no. 1. The perfect verbal form is either simple past in function or past perfect, indicating a flashback in relation to 3:16–18 (cf. 3:15b, which says that Boaz went to the city).

2. The noun is an adverbial accusative of direction (EE, 64, no. 3); note that one must supply a preposition in translation ("went up *to* the gate").

3. The verb is a Qal wayyiqtol 3ms from יָשַׁב. The form has two root letters visible with a *tsere* prefix vowel and a *seghol* theme vowel, so the root is I-*yod*. (See chart 10.)

4. This is a disjunctive clause that interrupts the narrative main line. It has a dramatic function, drawing the reader's attention to what is being described. See EE, 126–27, no. 6.

5. The predicative participle is best taken as indicating continuous action in the past from the narrator's perspective, "was passing by." See EE, 67.

7. The verb is functioning as a past perfect ("had spoken"), describing an action (Boaz's speaking to Ruth about this individual) that occurred before this incident.

4:2

2. The form, which technically is appositional to the following noun, is functioning as the object of the preceding verb, "and he took ten, men."

4. The verb is a Qal imperative 2mp from יָשַׁב. The form has no prefix and a *shewa* under the first visible root letter, so the root is III-*he*, I-*nun*, or I-*yod*. See chart 5. In this context the root יָשַׁב fits well.

5. The verb is a Qal wayyiqtol 3mp from יָשַׁב. The form has two root letters visible, and the prefix vowel *tsere* followed by another *tsere* indicates the root is I-*yod*. See chart 10.

4:3

1. In the construct form, feminine singular nouns ending in ה ָ- (like חֶלְקָה) have the ending ת ַ-. The genitive הַשָּׂדֶה here indicates the larger entity ("the field") of which the construct noun ("portion") is a part. See EE, 64, no. 12.

3. The form consists of the preposition -לְ + noun אָח ("brother") + 1cp pronominal suffix. The phrase "to Elimelech" is appositional to the preceding phrase.

4. The verb is a Qal perfect 3fs from מָכַר. The ה ָ- ending indicates the P-G-N is 3fs.

4:4

2. The form is either an obligatory imperfect ("I should/must uncover") or a cohortative of resolve ("I will uncover").

3. The verb is a Qal imperative 2ms from קָנָה.

4. The form is a Qal active participle masculine plural from יָשַׁב. The ים ְ- ending indicates the gender/number is masculine plural. The participle is functioning substantivally, "the ones sitting."

5. The *tsere yod* ending indicates the form is construct. The genitive designates the larger group or entity of which the construct noun is a part. See EE, 64, no. 12.

7. The verb is a Qal imperative 2ms from גָּאַל.

8. The verb is a Qal imperfect 3ms from גָּאַל.
9. The verb is a Hiphil imperative 2ms from נָגַד. The form has two root letters with a *he* prefix; the prefix vowel is *pathaq*, so the stem is Hiphil. The *dagesh forte* in the *gimel* indicates assimilation of the first root letter, *nun*.
10. The verb form is from a I-*yod* root, indicated by the *tsere* prefix vowel.
11. The clause is causal/explanatory, explaining why Boaz wants the information requested.
13. The form is a Qal infinitive construct from גָּאַל with a prepositional prefix.

4:5

1. The form is a Qal infinitive construct from קָנָה with a 2ms pronominal suffix. The form has two root letters visible with an נֹ- ending, so it is from a III-*he* root. See chart 8. The suffix is functioning as the subject of the infinitive, "when you acquire."
2. The noun is the object of the infinitive, "when you acquire the field."
4. The noun is appositional to "Ruth, the Moabitess."
7. The form is a Hiphil infinitive construct from קוּם with a prepositional prefix. The form has no ending, two root letters, and a prefixed *he* with a *qamets*, so the stem is Hiphil. The *hireq yod* theme vowel indicates the form is an infinitive construct of a hollow root. See chart 9. The infinitive indicates purpose; the stem is causative.

4:6

2. The infinitive is a verbal complement to the preceding verb, indicating what he is unable to do.
3. The verb is a Hiphil imperfect 1cs from שָׁחַת. The form has a *pathaq* (*a*-class) prefix vowel and a *hireq yod* (*i*-class) theme vowel, so the stem is Hiphil. See chart 10 or chart 11.
5. The clause is causal/explanatory, explaining why he gives Boaz the right to redeem.

4:7

1. The clause is disjunctive; it interrupts the narratival sequence and parenthetically provides supplemental information.

4:9

2. The noun is a predicate nominative, "you are witnesses."
3. This is an accusative noun clause, indicating what they witnessed.
4. The verb is a Qal perfect 1cs from קָנָה. The תִי- ending indicates the P-G-N is 1cs.

4:10

2. The verb is a Niphal imperfect 3ms from כָּרַת. The form has the *i* + *dagesh* + *a* pattern, so the stem is Niphal. The Niphal has a passive function here.
4. The form consists of the noun מָקוֹם + 3ms pronominal suffix. The noun is a genitive indicating the larger entity of which the construct noun is a part.

4:11

1. The noun appears to be a compound subject of the initial verb, "and all the people who were in the gate and the elders said."
2. The verb is a Qal jussive 3ms from נָתַן. The form has a prefixed *yod,* two root letters with a *dagesh forte* in the first, and a *tsere* theme vowel. It is therefore a Qal of a I-*nun* verb. See chart 10. The form is better taken as a jussive since the people appear to be offering a prayer of blessing on behalf of Boaz and Ruth.
3. The form is a Qal participle feminine singular from בּוֹא with an article prefixed. The form has two root letters, a *qamets* under the first root letter, and the accent on the final syllable. There are two options: a feminine singular participle of a hollow root or a 3fs perfect of a III-*he* root. See chart 2. Since the form has an article, it must be a participle, not a perfect. Therefore, the root must be hollow. The *qamets he* ending indicates the gender/number is feminine singular. The participle is functioning as an attributive adjective. The time frame can be understood as future, "the one who is about to come"; present, "the one who is coming"; or past, "the one who came."
4. The verb is a Qal perfect 3cp from בָּנָה. The *shureq* ending indicates the P-G-N is 3cp.
6. The verb is a Qal imperative 2ms from עָשָׂה with a prefixed conjunction. In the volitive sequence, the imperative indicates purpose/result, "so that you may do strength."

4:12

2. The relative pronoun is the direct object of the following verb, "whom (she) bore."
3. The verb is a Qal perfect 3fs from יָלַד. The *qamets he* ending indicates the P-G-N is 3fs.
4. The proper name Tamar is the subject of the preceding verb, "whom Tamar bore."

4:13

2. The *taw* prefix indicates the P-G-N is 3fs. (Note that the *hireq yod* is part of the root, not a personal ending.)
6. The verb is a Qal wayyiqtol 3ms from נָתַן. The *dagesh forte* in the *taw* indicates the root is I-*nun.*
7. The noun is the direct object of the verb, "the LORD gave to her conception."
8. The verb is a Qal wayyiqtol 3fs from יָלַד. The form has two root letters visible with a *tsere* prefix vowel and a *seghol* theme vowel, so the root is I-*yod.* (See chart 10.)

4:14

2. The form is a Qal passive participle masculine singular, from בָּרַךְ. It is functioning as a predicate adjective, "may the LORD be blessed."
3. The divine name is the subject of the preceding participle.
5. The verb is a Hiphil perfect 3ms from שָׁבַת. The form has a *he* prefix with a *hireq* prefix vowel followed by a *shewa,* so the stem is Hiphil. See chart 9. The perfect is either simple past or present perfect in function.
6. The verb is a Niphal jussive 3ms from קָרָא with a prefixed conjunction. The form has the *i* + *dagesh* + *a* pattern with the first root letter, so the stem is Niphal. The Niphal has a passive function here.

4:15

4. The form is a Hiphil participle masculine singular from שׁוּב with a prepositional prefix. The form has a prefixed *mem* with a *tsere* prefix vowel, so it is a Hiphil participle of a hollow or geminate root. The *hireq yod* theme vowel indicates the root is hollow. See chart 9. The prefixed *mem* suggests a participle. The participle is substantival.

5. The noun is the direct object of the preceding participle.

7. The form consists of the noun שֵׂיבָה + 2fs pronominal suffix. Feminine singular nouns ending in ה ָ- have a *taw* ending before pronominal suffixes.

9. The perfect is best understood as characteristic present; it describes the subject's (Ruth's) characteristic action/attitude. See EE, 87, no. 5.

12. The adjective is functioning predicatively, "she who is good."

14. The preposition indicates a comparison, "good from" = "better than."

4:16

1. The verb is a Qal wayyiqtol 3fs from לָקַח. The *taw* prefix with no ending indicates the P-G-N is 3fs.

4. The prepositional phrase לוֹ, "to him," is possessive; it may be translated, "his."

5. The preposition -לְ, when collocated with הָיָה, indicates a transition into a new state or condition. See BDB, 512. The clause may be translated, "and she became his guardian." The *holem* with the first root letter suggests the form is a participle; the participle is substantival.

4:17

1. The verb is a Qal wayyiqtol 3fp from קָרָא. The *taw* prefix in combination with the נָה- ending indicates the P-G-N is 3fp.

3. The noun is functioning as the subject of the verb. It is feminine plural.

4:18

1. The verb is a Hiphil perfect 3ms from יָלַד. The form has two root letters, a *he* prefix, and a *holem waw* prefix vowel, so the stem is Hiphil and the root I-*yod*. See chart 9. (The *hireq yod* theme vowel appears in the perfect and the infinitive construct; in this context the form is a perfect.) The stem is causative here, "cause to be born, give birth."